Christ's Words
from the Cross

Christ's Words from the Cross

Charles H. Spurgeon

BAKER BOOK HOUSE
Grand Rapids, Michigan 49506

Reprinted by Baker Books
a division of Baker Book House Company
P.O. Box 6287, Grand Rapids, MI 49516-6287

ISBN: 0-8010-8207-2

Ninth printing, December 1995

Printed in the United States of America

INTRODUCTION

It was most fitting that every word of our Lord upon the cross should be gathered up and preserved. As not a bone of Him shall be broken, so not a word shall be lost. The Holy Spirit took special care that each of the sacred utterances should be fittingly recorded. There were, as you know, seven of those last words, and seven is the number of perfection and fulness; the number which blends the three of the infinite God with the four of complete creation. Our Lord in His death-cries, as in all else, was perfection itself. There is a fulness of meaning in each utterance which no man shall be able fully to bring forth, and when combined they make up a vast deep of thought, which no human line can fathom. Here, as everywhere else, we are constrained to say to our Lord, "Never man spake like this man." Amid all the anguish of His spirit His last words prove Him to have remained fully self-possessed, true to His forgiving nature, true to His kingly office, true to His filial relationship, true to His God, true to His love of the written Word, true to His glorious work, and true to His faith in His Father.

As these seven sayings were so faithfully recorded, we do not wonder that they have frequently been the subject of devout meditation. Fathers and confessors, preachers and divines have delighted to dwell upon every syllable of these matchless cries. These solemn sentences have shone like the seven golden candlesticks or the seven stars of the Apocalypse, and have lighted multitudes of men to Him who spake them. Thoughtful men have drawn a wealth of meaning from them, and in so doing have arranged them into different groups, and placed them under several heads. I cannot give you more than a mere taste of this rich subject, but I have been most struck with two ways of regarding our Lord's last words.

First, they teach and confirm many of the doctrines of our holy faith. *"Father, forgive them; for they know not what they do"* is the first. Here is the forgiveness of sin—free forgiveness in anwer to the Saviour's plea. *"Today shalt thou be with me in paradise."* Here is the safety of the believer in the hour of his departure, and his instant admission into the presence of his Lord. It is a blow at the fable of purgatory which strikes it to the heart. *"Woman, behold thy son!"* This plainly sets forth the true and proper humanity of Christ, who to the end recognized His human relationship to Mary, of whom He was born. Yet His language teaches us not to worship *her,* for He calls her "woman," but to honor Him who in His direst agony thought of her needs and griefs, as He also thinks of all His people, for these are His mother and sister and brother. *"Eloi, Eloi, lama sabachthani?"* is the fourth cry, and it illustrates the penalty endured by our Substitute when He bore our sins, and so was forsaken of His God. The sharpness of that sentence no exposition can fully disclose to us: it is keen as the very edge and point of the sword which pierced His heart. *"I thirst"* is the fifth cry, and its utterance teaches us the truth of Scripture, for all things were accomplished, that the Scripture might be fulfilled, and therefore our Lord said, "I thirst." Holy Scripture remains the basis of our faith, established by every word and act of our Redeemer. The sixth word but one is, *"It is finished."* There is the complete justification of the believer, since the work by which he is accepted is fully accomplished. The last of His last words is also taken from the Scriptures, and shows where His mind was feeding. He cried, ere He bowed the head which He had held erect amid all His conflict, as one who never yielded, *"Father, into Thy hands I commend My spirit."* In that cry there is reconciliation to God. He who stood in our stead has finished all His work, and now His spirit comes back to the Father, and He brings us with Him. Every word, therefore, you see, teaches us some grand fundamental doctrine of our blessed faith. "He that hath ears to hear, let him hear."

A second mode of treating these seven cries is to view them as setting forth the person and offices of our Lord who uttered them. *"Father, forgive them; for they know not what they do"* — here we see the Mediator interceding: Jesus standing before the Father pleading for the guilty. *"Verily I say unto thee, today shalt thou be with me in paradise"* — this is the Lord Jesus in kingly power, opening with the key of David a door which none can shut, admitting into the gates of heaven the poor soul who had confessed Him on the tree. Hail, everlasting King in heaven, Thou dost admit to Thy paradise whomsoever Thou wilt! Nor dost Thou set a time for waiting, but instantly Thou dost set wide the gate of pearl; Thou hast all power in heaven as well as upon earth. Then came, *"Woman, behold thy son!"* wherein we see the Son of man in the gentleness of a son caring for his bereaved mother. In the former cry, as He opened paradise, you saw the Son of God; now you see Him who was verily and truly born of a woman, made under the law; and under the law you see Him still, for He honors His mother and cares for her in the last article of death. Then comes the *"My God, my God, why hast thou forsaken me?"* Here we behold His human *soul* in anguish, His inmost heart overwhelmed by the withdrawing of Jehovah's face, and made to cry out as if in perplexity and amazement. *"I thirst"* is His human *body* tormented by grievous pain. Here you see how the mortal flesh had to share in the agony of the inward spirit. *"It is finished"* is the last word but one, and there you see the perfected Saviour, the Captain of our salvation, who has completed the undertaking upon which He had entered, finished transgression, made an end of sin, and brought in everlasting righteousness. The last expiring word in which He *commended His spirit to His Father,* is the note of acceptance for Himself and for us all. As He commends His spirit into the Father's hand, so does He bring all believers nigh to God, and henceforth we are in the hand of the Father, who is greater than all, and none shall pluck us thence. Is not this a fertile field of thought? May the Holy Spirit often lead us to glean therein.

There are many other ways in which these words might be read, and they would be found to be all full of instruction. Like the steps of a ladder or the links of a golden chain, there is a mutual dependence and interlinking of each of the cries, so that one leads to another and that to a third. Separately or in connection, our Master's words overflow with instruction to thoughtful minds.

TABLE OF CONTENTS

Christ's Words
from the Cross

The First Word:

Then said Jesus, Father, forgive them; for they know not what they do.   Luke 23:34

Text — Luke 23:1-34

OUR LORD WAS AT THAT MOMENT ENDURING THE FIRST PAINS OF crucifixion; the executioners had just then driven the nails through His hands and feet. He must have been, moreover, greatly depressed, and brought into a condition of extreme weakness by the agony of the night in Gethsemane, and by the scourgings and cruel mockings which He had endured all through the morning, from Caiaphas, Pilate, Herod, and the Prætorian guards. Yet neither the weakness of the past, nor the pain of the present, could prevent Him from continuing in prayer. The Lamb of God was silent to men, but He was not silent to God. Dumb as a sheep before her shearers, He had not a word to say in His own defense to man, but He continues in His heart crying unto His Father, and no pain and no weakness can silence His holy supplications. Beloved, what an example our Lord herein presents to us! Let us continue in prayer so long as our heart beats; let no excess of suffering drive us away from the throne of grace, but rather let it drive us closer to it.

> Long as they live should Christians pray,
> For only while they pray they live.

To cease from prayer is to renounce the consolations which our case requires. Under all distractions of spirit, and overwhelmings of heart, great God, help us still to pray, and never from the mercy-seat may our footsteps be driven by despair.

13

Our blessed Redeemer persevered in prayer even when the cruel iron rent His tender nerves, and blow after blow of the hammer jarred His whole frame with anguish; and this perseverance may be accounted for by the fact that He was so in the habit of prayer that He could not cease from it; He had acquired a mighty velocity of intercession which forbade Him to pause. Those long nights upon the cold mountain side, those many days which had been spent in solitude, those perpetual ejaculations which He was wont to send up to heaven, all these had formed in Him a habit so powerful that the severest torments could not stay its force. Yet it was more than habit. Our Lord was baptized in the spirit of prayer; He lived in it; it lived in Him; it had come to be an element of His nature. He was like that precious spice, which, being bruised, doth not cease to give forth its perfume, but rather yieldeth it all the more abundantly because of the blows of the pestle, its fragrance being no outward and superficial quality, but an inward virtue essential to its nature, which the pounding in the mortar did but fetch from it, causing it to reveal its secret soul of sweetness. So Jesus prays, even as a bundle of myrrh gives forth its smell, or as birds sing because they cannot do otherwise. Prayer enwrapped His very soul as with a garment, and His heart went forth in such array. I repeat it, let this be our example — never, under any circumstances, however severe the trial, or depressing the difficulty, let us cease from prayer.

Observe, further, that our Lord, in the prayer before us, remains in the vigor of faith as to His Sonship. The extreme trial to which He now submitted Himself could not prevent His holding fast His Sonship. His prayer begins, "Father." It was not without meaning that He taught us when we pray to say, "Our Father," for our prevalence in prayer will much depend upon our confidence in our relationship to God. Under great losses and crosses, one is apt to think that God is not dealing with us as a father with a child, but rather as a severe judge with a condemned criminal; but the cry of Christ, when He is brought to an extremity which we shall never reach, betrays no faltering in the spirit of sonship. In Gethsemane, when the bloody sweat fell fast upon the ground, His bitterest cry commenced with, *"My Father,"* asking that if it were possible the cup of gall might pass from Him. He pleaded with the Lord as His Father, even as He over and over again had called Him on that dark and doleful night. Here again in this, the first of His seven expiring cries, it is "Father." O that the Spirit that makes us cry, "Abba, Father," may never cease His operations! May we never be brought into spiritual bondage by the suggestion, "If thou be the Son of God"; or if the tempter should so assail us, may we triumph as Jesus did in the hungry wilderness. May the Spirit which crieth, "Abba, Father," repel each unbelieving fear. When we are chastened, as we must be (for what son is there whom his father chasteneth not?) may we be in loving subjection to the Father of our spirit, and live; but never may we become captives to the spirit of bondage, so as to doubt the love of our gracious Father, or our share in His adoption.

More remarkable, however, is the fact that our Lord's prayer to His Father was not for Himself. He continued on the cross to pray for Himself, it is true, and His lamenting cry, "My God, my God, why hast thou forsaken me?" shows the personality of His prayer; but the first of the seven cries on the cross has scarcely even an indirect reference to Himself. It is, "Father, forgive *them*." The petition is altogether for others, and though there is an allusion to the cruelties which they were exercising upon Himself, yet it is remote; and you will observe, He does not say, "I forgive them" — that is taken for granted — He seems to lose sight of the fact that they were doing any wrong to Himself. It is the wrong which they were doing to the Father that is on His mind, the insult which they are paying to the Father, in the person of the Son; He thinks not of Himself at all. The cry, "Father, forgive them," is altogether unselfish. He Himself is, in the prayer, as though He were not; so complete is His self-annihilation, that He loses sight of Himself and His woes. My brethren, if there had ever

been a time in the life of the Son of man when He might have
rigidly confined His prayer to Himself, without any one ca-
villing thereat, surely it was when He was beginning His
death throes. We could not marvel, if any man here were fastened to the stake, or fixed to a cross, if his first, and even his
last and all his prayers, were for support under so arduous a
trial. But see, the Lord Jesus began His prayer by pleading
for others. Do you not see what a great heart is here revealed!
What a soul of compassion was in the Crucified! How Godlike,
how divine! Was there ever such a one before Him, who, even
in the very pangs of death, offers as His first prayer an intercession for others? Let this unselfish spirit be in you also, my
brethren. Look not every man upon his own things, but every
man also on the things of others. Love your neighbors as
yourselves, and as Christ has set before you this paragon of
unselfishness, seek to follow Him, treading in His steps.

There is, however, a crowning jewel in this diadem of glorious love. The Sun of Righteousness sets upon Calvary in a
wondrous splendor; but among the bright colors which glorify
His departure, there is this one — the prayer was not alone
for others, but it was for His cruelest enemies. His enemies,
did I say? There is more than that to be considered. It was
not a prayer for enemies who had done Him an ill deed years
before, but for those who were there and then murdering Him.
Not in cold blood did the Saviour pray, after He had forgotten
the injury and could the more easily forgive it, but while the
first red drops of blood were spurting on the hands which
drove the nails; while yet the hammer was bestained with
crimson gore, His blessed mouth poured out the fresh, warm
prayer, "Father, forgive them, for they know not what they
do." I say, not that that prayer was confined to His immediate
executioners. I believe that it was a far-reaching prayer, which
included scribes and Pharisees, Pilate and Herod, Jews and
Gentiles—yea, the whole human race in a certain sense, since
we were all concerned in that murder; but certainly the immediate persons, upon whom that prayer was poured like

precious nard, were those who there and then were committing the brutal act of fastening Him to the accursed tree.

How sublime is this prayer if viewed in such a light! It stands alone upon a mount of solitary glory. No other had been prayed like it before. It is true, Abraham and Moses and the prophets had prayed for the wicked, but not for wicked men who had pierced their hands and feet. It is true that Christians have since that day offered the same prayer, even as Stephen cried, "Lay not this sin to their charge," and many a martyr has made his last words at the stake words of pitying intercession for his persecutors; but you know where they learned this. Let me ask you where *He* learned it? Was not Jesus the divine original? He learned it nowhere; it leaped up from His Godlike nature. A compassion peculiar to Himself dictated this originality of prayer; the inward royalty of His love suggested to Him so memorable an intercession, which may serve us for a pattern, but of which no pattern had existed before. I want to adore Him, I worship Him in heart for that prayer; if I knew nothing else of Him but this one prayer, I must adore Him, for that one matchless plea for mercy convinces me most overwhelmingly of the deity of Him who offered it, and fills my heart with reverent affection.

Thus have I introduced to you our Lord's first vocal prayer upon the cross. I shall now, if we are helped by God's Holy Spirit, make some use of it. First, we shall view it as *illustrative of our Saviour's intercession;* secondly, we shall regard the text as *instructive of the church's work;* thirdly, we shall consider it as *suggestive to the unconverted.*

1. First, my dear brethren, let us look at this very wonderful text as

ILLUSTRATIVE OF OUR LORD'S INTERCESSION

He prayed for His enemies then, He is praying for His enemies now; the past on the cross was an earnest of the present on the throne. He is in a higher place, and in a nobler condition, but His occupation is the same. He continues still before the eternal throne to present pleas on the behalf of guilty men, crying, "Father, forgive them." All His intercession is in a measure like the intercession on Calvary, and Calvary's cries may help us to guess the character of the whole of His intercession above.

The first point in which we may see the character of His intercession is this—it is *most gracious*. Those for whom our Lord prayed, according to the text, did not deserve His prayer. They had done nothing which could call forth from Him a benediction as a reward for their endeavors in His service. On the contrary, they were most undeserving persons who had conspired to put Him to death. They had crucified Him, crucified Him wantonly and malignantly; they were even then taking away His innocent life. His clients were persons who, so far from being meritorious, were utterly undeserving of a single good wish from the Saviour's heart. They certainly never asked Him to pray for them—it was the last thought in their minds to say, "Intercede for us, thou dying King! Offer petitions on our behalf, thou Son of God!" I will venture to believe the prayer itself, when they heard it, was either disregarded and passed over with contemptuous indifference, or perhaps it was caught at as a theme for jest. Perhaps it seems to be too severe upon humanity to suppose it possible that such a prayer could have been the theme for laughter, and yet there were other things enacted around the cross which were quite as brutal, and I can imagine that this also might have happened.

Yet our Saviour prayed for persons who did not deserve the prayer, but, on the contrary, merited a curse — persons who did not ask for the prayer, and even scoffed at it when they heard it. Even so in heaven there stands the great High Priest, who pleads for guilty men—for *guilty* men. There are none on earth that deserve His intercession. He pleads for none on the supposition that they do deserve it. He stands there to plead as the just One on the behalf of the unjust. Not if any man be righteous, but "if any man sin, we have an advocate with the Father." Remember, too, that our great Intercessor pleads for such as never asked Him to plead for them. His elect, while yet dead in trespasses and sins, are the objects of His compassionate intercessions, and while they even scoff at His Gospel, His heart of love is entreating the favor of heaven on their behalf. See, then, beloved, if such be the truth, how sure you are to speed with God who earnestly ask the Lord Jesus Christ to plead for you. Some of you, with many tears and much earnestness, have been beseeching the Saviour to be your advocate. Will He refuse you? It stands to reason that He can. He pleads for those that reject His pleadings, much more for you who prize them beyond gold! Remember, if there be nothing good in you, and if there be everything conceivable that is malignant and bad, yet none of these things can be any barrier to prevent Christ's exercising the office of Intercessor for you. Even for you He will plead. Come, put your case into His hands; for you He will find pleas which you cannot discover for yourselves, and He will put the case to God for you as for His murderers, "Father, forgive them."

A second quality of His intercession is this—*its careful spirit.* You notice in the prayer, "Father, forgive them, for they know not what they do." Our Saviour did, as it were, look His enemies through and through to find something in them that He could urge in their favor; but He could see nothing until His wisely affectionate eye lit upon their ignorance: "they know not what they do." How carefully He surveyed the circumstances, and the characters of those for whom He importuned! Just so it is with Him in heaven. Christ is no careless advocate for His people. He knows your precise condition at this moment, and the exact state of your heart with regard to the temptation through which you are passing; more than that, He foresees the temptation which is awaiting you, and in His intercession He takes note of the future event which His prescient eye beholds. "Satan hath desired to have thee, that he may sift thee as wheat; but I have prayed for thee that thy faith fail not."

Oh, the condescending tenderness of our great High Priest!
He knows us better than we know ourselves. He understands
every secret grief and groaning. You need not trouble yourself about the wording of your prayer, He will put the wording right. And even the understanding as to the exact petition,
if you should fail in it, He cannot, for as He knows what is
the mind of God, so He knows what is your mind also. He
can find some reason for mercy in you which you cannot detect in yourself, and when it is so dark and cloudy with your
soul that you cannot discern a foothold for a plea that you
may urge with heaven, the Lord Jesus has the pleas ready
framed, and petitions ready drawn up, and He can present
them acceptably before the mercy seat. His intercession, then,
you will observe is very gracious, and it is very thoughtful.

We must next note its *earnestness*. No one doubts who
reads these words, "Father, forgive them, for they know not
what they do," that they were heaven-piercing in their fervor.
Brethren, you are certain, even without a thought, that Christ
was terribly in earnest in that prayer. But there is an argument to prove that. Earnest people are usually witty, and
quick of understanding, to discover anything which may serve
their turn. If you are pleading for life, and an argument for
your being spared be asked of you, I will warrant you that
you will think of one when no one else might. Now, Jesus was
so in earnest for the salvation of His enemies, that He struck
upon an argument for mercy which a less anxious spirit would
not have thought of: "They know not what they do." That was
in strictest justice but a scant reason for mercy; and indeed,
ignorance, if it be wilful, does not extenuate sin, and yet the
ignorance of many who surrounded the cross was a wilful ignorance. They might have known that He was the Lord of
glory. Was not Moses plain enough? Had not Esaias been very
bold in his speech? Were not the signs and tokens such that
one might as well doubt which is the sun in the firmament as
the claims of Jesus to be the Messiah?

Yet, for all that, the Saviour, with marvelous earnestness

and consequent dexterity, turns what might not have been a plea into a plea, and puts it thus: "Father, forgive them, *for they know not what they do.*" Oh, how mighty are His pleas in heaven, then, in their earnestness! Do not suppose that He is less quick of understanding there, or less intense in the vehemence of His entreaties. No, my brethren, the heart of Christ still labors with the eternal God. He is no slumbering intercessor, but, for Zion's sake, He does not hold His peace, and for Jerusalem's sake, He does not cease, nor will He, till her righteousness go forth as brightness, and her salvation as a lamp that burneth.

It is interesting to note, in the fourth place, that the prayer here offered helps us to judge of His intercession in heaven as to its *continuance,* its *perseverance,* and *perpetuity.* As I remarked before, if our Saviour might have paused from intercessory prayer, it was surely when they fastened Him to the tree; when they were guilty of direct acts of deadly violence to His divine person, He might then have ceased to present petitions on their behalf. But sin cannot tie the tongue of our interceding Friend. Oh, what comfort is here! You have sinned, believer, you have grieved His Spirit, but you have not stopped that potent tongue which pleads for you. You have been unfruitful, perhaps, my brother, and like the barren tree, you deserve to be cut down; but your want of fruitfulness has not withdrawn the Intercessor from His place. He interposes at this moment, crying, "Spare it yet another year."

Sinner, you have provoked God by long rejecting His mercy and going from bad to worse, but neither blasphemy, nor unrighteousness, nor infidelity, shall stay the Christ of God from urging the suit of the very chief of sinners. He lives, and while He lives He pleads; and while there is a sinner upon earth to be saved, there shall be an intercessor in heaven to plead for him. These are but fragments of thought, but they will help you, I hope, to realize the intercession of your great High Priest.

Think yet again, this prayer of our Lord on earth is like

His prayer in heaven, because of its *wisdom*. He seeks the best thing, and that which His clients most need, "Father, *forgive* them." That was the great point in hand; they wanted most of all there and then forgiveness from God. He does not say, "Father, enlighten them, for they know not what they do," for mere enlightenment would but have created torture of conscience and hastened on their hell; but He cried, "Father, forgive"; and while He used His voice, the precious drops of blood which were then distilling from the nail wounds were pleading too, and God heard, and doubtless did forgive. The first mercy which is needful to guilty sinners is forgiven sin. Christ wisely prays for the boon most wanted. It is so in heaven; He pleads wisely and prudently. Let Him alone—He knows what to ask for at the divine hand. Go to the mercy seat, and pour out your desires as best you can, but when you have done so, always put it thus, "O my Lord Jesus, answer no desire of mine if it be not according to Thy judgment; and if in aught that I have asked I have failed to seek for what I want, amend my pleading, for Thou art infinitely wiser than I."

Oh, it is sweet to have a friend at court to perfect our petitions for us before they come unto the great King. I believe that there is never presented to God anything but a perfect prayer now; I mean, that before the great Father of us all, no prayer of His people ever comes up imperfect; there is nothing left out, and there is nothing to be erased; and this, not because their prayers were originally perfect in themselves, but because the Mediator makes them perfect through His infinite wisdom, and they come up before the mercy seat moulded according to the mind of God Himself, and He is sure to grant such prayers.

Once more, this memorable prayer of our crucified Lord was like to His universal intercession in the matter of its *prevalence*. Those for whom He prayed were many of them forgiven. Do you remember that He said to His disciples when He bade them preach, "beginning at Jerusalem," and on that

day when Peter stood up with the eleven, and charged the
people that with wicked hands they had crucified and slain
the Saviour, three thousand of these persons who were thus
justly accused of His crucifixion became believers in Him, and
were baptized in His Name? That was an answer to Jesus'
prayer. The priests were at the bottom of our Lord's murder,
they were the most guilty; but it is said, "a great company
also of the priests believed." Here was another answer to the
prayer.

Since all men had their share representatively, Gentiles
as well as Jews, in the death of Jesus, the Gospel was soon
preached to the Jews, and within a short time it was preached
to the Gentiles also. Was not this prayer, "Father, forgive
them," like a stone cast into a lake, forming at first a narrow
circle, and then a wider ring, and soon a larger sphere, until
the whole lake is covered with circling waves? Such a prayer
as this, cast into the whole world, first created a little ring
of Jewish converts and of priests, and then a wider circle of
such as were beneath the Roman sway; and today its circumference is wide as the globe itself, so that tens of thousands
are saved through the prevalence of this one intercession,
"Father, forgive them." It is certainly so with Him in heaven,
He never pleads in vain. With bleeding hands, He yet won the
day; with feet fastened to the wood, He was yet victorious;
forsaken of God and despised of the people, He was yet triumphant in His pleas; how much more so now the tiara is
about His brow, His hand grasps the universal scepter, and
His feet are shod with silver sandals, and He is crowned King
of kings, and Lord of lords!

If tears and cries out of weakness were omnipotent, even
more mighty if possible must be that sacred authority which
as the risen priest He claims when He stands before the Father's throne to mention the covenant which the Father made
with Him. O ye trembling believers, trust Him with your concerns! Come hither, you guilty ones, and ask Him to plead
for you. O you that cannot pray, come, ask Him to intercede

for you. Broken hearts and weary heads, and disconsolate bos-
oms, come to Him who into the golden censer will put His
merits, and then place your prayers with them, so that they
shall come up as the smoke of perfume, even as a fragrant
cloud into the nostrils of the Lord God of hosts, who will smell
a sweet savor, and accept you and your prayers in the beloved. We have now opened up more than enough sea-room
for your meditations, and, therefore we leave this first point.
We have had an illustration in the prayer of Christ on the
cross of what His prayers always are in heaven.

II. Secondly, the text is

INSTRUCTIVE OF THE CHURCH'S WORK

As Christ was, so His church is to be in this world. Christ
came into this world not to be ministered unto, but to minister, not to be honored, but to save others. His church, when
she understands her work, will perceive that she is not here
to gather wealth or honor, or to seek any temporal aggran-
dizement and position; she is here unselfishly to live, and if
need be, unselfishly to die for the deliverance of the lost sheep,
the salvation of lost men. Brethren, Christ's prayer on the
cross was altogether an unselfish one. He does not remember
Himself in it. Such ought to be the church's life-prayer, the
church's active interposition on the behalf of sinners. She
ought to live never for her ministers or for herself, but ever
for the lost sons of men. Do you imagine that churches are
formed to maintain ministers? Do you conceive that the church
exists merely that so much salary may be given to its leaders?
My brethren, it were well if the whole thing were abolished
if that were its only aim.

Churches are not made that men of ready speech may
stand up on Sundays and talk, and so win daily bread from
their admirers. No, there is another end and aim for this.
These places of worship are not built that you may sit com-
fortably and hear something that shall make you pass away
your Sundays with pleasure. A church which does not exist to

do good in the slums, and dens, and kennels of the city, is a church that has no reason to justify its longer existing. A church that does not exist to reclaim heathenism, to fight with evil, to destroy error, to put down falsehood, a church that does not exist to take the side of the poor, to denounce injustice and to hold up righteousness, is a church that has no right to be. Not for yourself, O church, do you exist, any more than Christ existed for Himself. His glory was that He laid aside His glory, and the glory of the church is when she lays aside her respectability and her dignity, and counts it to be her glory to gather together the outcasts, and her highest honor to seek amid the foulest mire the priceless jewels for which Jesus shed His blood. To rescue souls from hell and lead to God, to hope, to heaven, this is her heavenly occupation. O that the church would always feel this! Let her have her bishops and her preachers, and let them be supported, and let everything be done for Christ's sake decently and in order, but let the end be looked to, namely, the conversion of the wandering, the teaching of the ignorant, the help of the poor, the mainte-nance of the right, the putting down of the wrong, and the upholding at all hazards of the crown and kingdom of our Lord Jesus Christ.

Now the prayer of Christ had a *great spirituality of aim.* You notice that nothing is sought for these people but that which concerns their souls, "Father, *forgive* them." And I believe the church will do well when she recollects that she wrestles not with flesh and blood, nor with principalities and powers, but with spiritual wickedness, and that what she has to dispense is not the law and order by which magistrates may be upheld, or tyrannies pulled down, but the spiritual govern-ment by which hearts are conquered to Christ, and judgments are brought into subjection to His truth. I believe that the more the church of God strains after, before God, the forgive-ness of sinners, and the more she seeks in her life-prayer to teach sinners what sin is, and what the blood of Christ is, and what the hell is that must follow if sin be not washed out, and what the heaven is which will be ensured to all those who are cleansed from sin, the more she keeps to this the better.

Press forward as one man, my brethren, to secure the root of the matter in the forgiveness of sinners. As to all the evils that afflict humanity, by all means take your share in battling with them; let temperance be maintained, let education be supported; let reforms, political and ecclesiastical, be pushed forward as far as you have the time and effort to spare, but the first business of every Christian man and woman is with the hearts and consciences of men as they stand before the everlasting God. O let nothing turn you aside from your divine errand of mercy to undying souls. This is your one business. Tell to sinners that sin will damn them, that Christ alone can take away sin, and make this the one passion of your souls, "Father, forgive them, forgive them! Let them know how to be forgiven. Let them be actually forgiven, and let me never rest except as I am the means of bringing sinners to be forgiven, even the guiltiest of them."

Our Saviour's prayer teaches the church that while her spirit should be unselfish, and her aim should be spiritual, *the range of her mission* is to be unlimited. Christ prayed for the wicked, what if I say the most wicked of the wicked, that ribald crew that had surrounded His cross! He prayed for the ignorant. Did He not say, "They know not what they do"? He prayed for His persecutors; the very persons who were most at enmity with Him, lay nearest to His heart. Church of God, your mission is not to the respectable few who will gather about your ministers to listen respectfully to their words; your mission is not to the *elite* and the eclectic, the intelligent who will criticize your words and pass judgment upon every syllable of your teaching; your mission is not to those who treat you kindly, generously, affectionately, not to these I mean alone, though certainly to these as among the rest; but your great errand is to the harlot, to the thief, to the swearer and the drunkard, to the most depraved and debauched. If no one else cares for these, the church always must, and if there be any who are first in her prayers it should be these who alas! are generally last in our thoughts.

The ignorant we ought diligently to consider. It is not enough for the preacher that he preaches so that those instructed from their youth up can understand him; he must think of those to whom the commonest phrases of theological truth are as meaningless as the jargon of an unknown tongue; he must preach so as to reach the meanest comprehension; and if the ignorant many come not to hear him, he must use such means as best he may to induce them, nay, compel them to hear the good news. The Gospel is meant also for those who persecute religion; it aims its arrows of love against the hearts of its foes. If there be any whom we should first seek to bring to Jesus, it should be just these who are the farthest off and most opposed to the Gospel of Christ. "Father, forgive *them;* if thou dost pardon none besides, yet be pleased to pardon *them;* if thou dost forgive none besides, yet be pleased to forgive *them.*"

So, too, the church should be *earnest* as Christ was; and if she be so, she will be quick to notice any ground of hope in those she deals with, quick to observe any plea that she may use with God for their salvation.

She must be *hopeful* too, and surely no church ever had a more hopeful sphere than the church of this present age. If ignorance be a plea with God, look on the heathen at this day — millions of them never heard Messiah's Name. Forgive them, great God, indeed they know not what they do. If ignorance be some ground for hope, there is hope enough in this great world, for have we not around us hundreds of thousands to whom the simplest truths of the Gospel would be the greatest novelties? Brethren, it is sad to think that this world should still lie under such a pall of ignorance, but the sting of so dread a fact is blunted with hope when we read the

Saviour's prayer aright—it helps us to hope while we cry, "Forgive them, for they know not what they do."

It is the church's business to seek after the most fallen and the most ignorant, and to seek them perseveringly. She should never stay her hand from doing good. If the Lord be coming tomorrow, it is no reason why you Christian people should subside into mere talkers and readers, meeting together for mutual comfort, and forgetting the myriads of perishing souls. If it be true that this world is going to pieces in a fortnight, it makes no difference to my duty, and does not change my service. Let my Lord come when He will, while I labor for Him I am ready for His appearing. The business of the church is still to watch for the salvation of souls. If she stood gazing, as modern prophets would have her; if she gave up her mission to indulge in speculative interpretations, she might well be afraid of her Lord's coming; but if she goes about her work, and with incessant toil searches out her Lord's precious jewels, she shall not be ashamed when her Bridegroom comes.

This chapter is much too short for so vast a subject as I have undertaken, but I wish I could write words that were as loud as thunder, with a sense and earnestness as mighty as the lightning. I would fain excite every Christian and kindle in him a right idea of what his work is as a part of Christ's church. My brethren, you must not live to yourselves; the accumulation of money, the bringing up of your children, the building of houses, the earning of your daily bread, all this you may do; but there must be a greater object than this if you are to be Christlike, as you should be, since you are bought with Jesus' blood. Begin to live for others, make it apparent unto all men that you are not yourselves the end-all and be-all of your own existence, but that you are spending and being spent, that through the good you do to men God may be glorified, and Christ may see in you His own image and be satisfied.

III. Our last point is a word

Suggestive to the Unconverted

Read attentively these sentences. I will make them as terse and condensed as possible. Some of you are not saved. Now, some of you have been very ignorant, and when you sinned you did not know what you did. You knew you were sinners, but you did not know the far-reaching guilt of sin. You have not been attending the house of prayer long, you have not read your Bible, you have not Christian parents. Now you are beginning to be anxious about your souls. Remember your ignorance does not excuse you, or else Christ would not say, "Forgive them"; they must be forgiven, even those that know not what they do, hence they are individually guilty; but still that ignorance of yours gives you just a little gleam of hope. The times of your ignorance God winked at, but now He commands all men everywhere to repent. Bring forth, therefore, fruits meet for repentance. The God whom you have ignorantly forgotten is willing to pardon and ready to forgive. The Gospel is just this, trust Jesus Christ who died for the guilty, and you shall be saved. O may God help you to do so this very moment, and you will become new men and new women, a change will take place in you equal to a new birth; you will be new creatures in Christ Jesus.

But ah! my friends, there are some for whom even Christ Himself could not pray this prayer, in the widest sense at any rate, "Father, forgive them; for they know not what they do," for you have known what you did, and every sermon you hear, and especially every impression that is made upon your understanding and conscience by the Gospel, adds to your responsibility, and takes away from you the excuse of not knowing what you do. Ah! you know that there is the world and Christ, and that you cannot have both. You know that there is sin and God, and that you cannot serve both. You know that there are the pleasures of evil and the pleasures of heaven, and that you cannot have both. Oh! In the light which God has given you, may His Spirit also come and help you to choose that which true wisdom would make you choose. Decide today for God, for Christ, for heaven. The Lord decide you for His name's sake. Amen.

The Second Word:

And he said unto Jesus, Lord, remember me when thou comest into thy kingdom. And Jesus said unto him, Verily I say unto thee, Today thou shalt be with me in paradise.
Luke 23: 42, 43

THE STORY OF THE SALVATION OF THE DYING THIEF IS A STANDING instance of the power of Christ to save, and of His abundant willingness to receive all that come to Him, in whatever plight they might be. I cannot regard this act of grace as a solitary instance, any more than the salvation of Zacchæus, the restoration of Peter, or the call of Saul, the persecutor. Every conversion is, in a sense, singular: no two are exactly alike, and yet any one conversion is a type of others. The case of the dying thief is much more similar to our conversion than it is dissimilar; in point of fact, his case may be regarded as typical, rather than as an extraordinary incident.

Remember that our Lord Jesus, at the time He saved this malefactor, was at His lowest. His glory had been ebbing out in Gethsemane, and before Caiaphas, and Herod, and Pilate; but it had now reached the utmost low-water mark. Stripped of His garments, and nailed to the cross, our Lord was mocked by a ribald crowd, and was dying in agony: then was He "numbered with the transgressors," and made as the offscouring of all things. Yet, while in that condition, He achieved this marvelous deed of grace. Behold the wonder wrought by the Saviour when emptied of all His glory, and hanged up a spec-

31

tacle of shame upon the brink of death! How certain is it that
He can do great wonders of mercy now, seeing that He has
returned unto His glory, and sitteth upon the throne of light!
"He is able to save them to the uttermost that come unto God
by him, seeing he ever liveth to make intercession for them."
If a dying Saviour saved the thief, my argument is that He
can do even more now that He lives and reigns. All power is
given unto Him in heaven and in earth; can anything at this
present time surpass the power of His grace?

It is not only the weakness of our Lord which makes the
salvation of the penitent thief memorable; it is the fact that
the dying malefactor saw it before his very eyes. Can you
put yourself into his place, and suppose yourself to be looking upon One who hangs in agony upon a cross? Could you
readily believe Him to be the Lord of glory, who would soon
come to His kingdom? That was no mean faith which, at such
a moment, could believe in Jesus as Lord and King. If the
apostle Paul were here, and wanted to add a New Testament
chapter to the eleventh of Hebrews, he might certainly commence his instances of remarkable faith with this thief, who
believed in a crucified, derided, and dying Christ, and cried
to Him as to One whose kingdom would surely come. The
thief's faith was the more remarkable because he was himself
in great pain and bound to die. It is not easy to exercise confidence when you are tortured with deadly anguish. Our own
rest of mind has at times been greatly hindered by pain of
body. When we are the subjects of acute suffering it is not
easy to exhibit that faith which we fancy we possess at other
times. This man, suffering as he did, and seeing the Saviour
in so sad a state, nevertheless believed unto life eternal. Herein was such faith as is seldom seen.

Recollect, also, that He was surrounded by scoffers. It is
easy to swim with the current, and hard to go against the
stream. This man heard the priests in their pride ridicule the
Lord, and the great multitude of the common people, with one
consent, joined in the scorning; his comrade caught the spirit

of the hour and mocked also, and perhaps he did the same for a while; but through the grace of God he was changed, and believed in the Lord Jesus in the teeth of all the scorn. His faith was not affected by his surroundings; but he, dying thief as he was, made sure his confidence. Like a jutting rock, standing out in the midst of a torrent, he declared the innocence of the Christ whom others blasphemed. His faith is worthy of our imitation in its fruits. He had no member that was free except his tongue, and he used that member wisely to rebuke his brother malefactor and defend his Lord. His faith brought forth a brave testimony and a bold confession. I am not going to praise the thief, or his faith, but to extol the glory of that grace divine which gave the thief such faith, and then freely saved him by its means. I am anxious to show how glorious is the Saviour — that Saviour to the uttermost, who, at such a time, could save such a man, and give him so great a faith, and so perfectly and speedily prepare him for eternal bliss. Behold the power of that divine Spirit who could produce such faith on soil so unlikely, and in a climate so unpropitious.

Let us enter at once into the heart of our sermon. First, *note the man who was our Lord's last companion on earth;* secondly, *note that this same man was our Lord's first companion at the gate of paradise;* and then, thirdly, *let us note the sermon which our Lord preaches to us from this act of grace.* Oh, for a blessing from the Holy Spirit all the chapter through!

I. Carefully

Note That the Crucified Thief Was Our Lord's
Last Companion on Earth.

What sorry company our Lord selected when He was here! He did not consort with the religious Pharisees or the philosophic Sadducees, but He was known as "the friend of publicans and sinners." How I rejoice at this! It gives me assurance that He will not refuse to associate with *me.* When

the Lord Jesus made a friend of me, He certainly did not make
a choice which brought Him credit. Do you think He gained
any honor when He made a friend of you? Has He ever gained
anything by us? No, my brethren; if Jesus had not stooped
very low, He would not have come to me; and if He did not
seek the most unworthy, He might not have come to you. You
feel it so, and you are thankful that He came "not to call the
righteous, but sinners to repentance." As the great Physician,
our Lord was much with the sick. He went where there was
room for Him to exercise His healing art. The whole have no
need of a physician: they cannot appreciate Him, nor afford
scope for His skill; and therefore He did not frequent their
abodes. Yes, after all, our Lord did make a good choice when
He saved you and me; for in us He has found abundant room
for His mercy and grace. There has been elbow room for His
love to work within the awful emptiness of our necessities and
sins; and therein He has done great things for us, whereof
we are glad.

Lest any here should be despairing, and say, "He will
never deign to look on me," I want you to notice that *the last
companion of Christ on earth was a sinner, and no ordinary
sinner*. He had broken even the laws of man, for he was a
robber. One calls him "a brigand," and I suppose it is likely
to have been the case. The brigands of those days mixed murder with their robberies. He was probably a freebooter in
arms against the Roman government, making this a pretext
for plundering as he had opportunity. At last he was arrested
and was condemned by a Roman tribunal, which, on the whole,
was usually just, and in this case was certainly just; for he
himself confesses the justice of his condemnation. The malefactor who believed upon the cross was a convict, who had
lain in the condemned cell and was then undergoing execution for his crimes. A convicted felon was the person with
whom our Lord last consorted upon earth. What a lover of the
souls of guilty men is He! What a stoop He makes to the very
lowest of mankind!

To this most unworthy of men the Lord of glory, ere He quitted life, spoke with matchless grace. He spoke to him such wondrous words as never can be excelled if you search the Scriptures through: "Today shalt thou be with me in paradise." I do not suppose that anyone reading these words has been convicted before the law, or who is even chargeable with a crime against common honesty; but if there should be such a person among my readers, I would invite him to find pardon and change of heart through our Lord Jesus Christ. You may come to Him, whoever you may be; for this man did. Here is a specimen of one who had gone to the extreme of guilt, and who acknowledged that he had done so; he made no excuse, and sought no cloak for his sin; he was in the hands of justice, confronted with the death-doom, and yet he believed in Jesus, and breathed a humble prayer to Him, and he was saved upon the spot. As is the sample, such is the bulk. Jesus saves others of like kind. Let me, therefore, put it very plainly here, that none may mistake me. None of you are excluded from the infinite mercy of Christ, however great your iniquity: if you believe in Jesus, He will save *you*.

This man was not only a sinner; *he was a sinner newly awakened*. I do not suppose that he had seriously thought of the Lord Jesus before. According to the other Evangelists, he appears to have joined with his fellow thief in scoffing at Jesus: if he did not actually himself use opprobrious words, he was so far consenting thereunto, that the Evangelist did him no injustice when he said, "The thieves also, which were crucified with him, cast the same in his teeth." Yet, now, on a sudden, He wakes up to the conviction that the Man who is dying at his side is someone more than a man. He reads the title over His head, and believes it to be true — "This is Jesus the King of the Jews." Thus believing, he makes his appeal to the Messiah, whom he had so newly found, and commits himself to His hands. My reader, do you see this truth, that the moment a man knows Jesus to be the Christ of God he may at once put his trust in Him and be saved?

A certain preacher, whose gospel was very doubtful, said, "Do you, who have been living in sin for fifty years, believe that you can in a moment be made clean through the blood of Jesus?" I answer, "Yes, we do believe that in one moment, through the precious blood of Jesus, the blackest soul can be made white. We do believe that in a single instant·the sins of sixty or seventy years can be absolutely forgiven, and that the old nature, which has gone on growing worse and worse, can receive its death-wound in a moment of time, while the life eternal may be implanted in the soul at once." It was so with this man. He had reached the end of his tether, but all of a sudden he woke up to the assured conviction that the Messiah was at his side, and, believing, he looked to Him and lived.

So now, my brothers, if you have never in your life before been the subject of any religious conviction, if you have lived up till now an utterly ungodly life, yet if now you will believe that God's dear Son has come into the world to save men from sin, and will unfeignedly confess your sin and trust in Him, you shall be immediately saved. Ay, while you read the word, the deed of grace may be accomplished by that glorious One who has gone up into the heaven with omnipotent power to save.

I desire to put this case very plainly: *this man, who was the last companion of Christ upon earth, was a sinner in misery.* His sins had found him out: he was now enduring the reward of his deeds. I constantly meet with persons in this condition: they have lived a life of wantonness, excess, and carelessness, and they begin to feel the fire-flakes of the tempest of wrath falling upon their flesh; they dwell in an earthly hell, a prelude of eternal woe. Remorse, like an asp, has stung them and set their blood on fire. They cannot rest, they are troubled day and night. "Be sure your sin will find you out." It has found them out and arrested them, and they feel the strong grip of conviction. This man was in that horrible condition. What is more, he was *in extremis*. He could not live long. The crucifixion was sure to be fatal. In a short time his legs would be broken, to end his wretched existence.

He, poor soul, had but a short time to live—only the space between noon and sundown; but it was long enough for the Saviour, who is mighty to save. Some are very much afraid that people will put off coming to Christ, if we state this. I cannot help what wicked men do with truth, but I shall state it all the same. If you are now within an hour of death, believe in the Lord Jesus Christ and you shall be saved. Even if you should drop dead suddenly, if you will now believe in the Lord Jesus, you shall be saved: saved now, on the spot. Looking and trusting to Jesus, He will give you a new heart and a right spirit, and blot out your sins. This is the glory of Christ's grace. How I wish I could extol it in proper language! He was last seen on earth before His death in company with a convicted felon, to whom He spoke most lovingly. Come, O ye guilty, and He will receive you graciously!

Once more, *this man whom Christ saved at last was a man who could do no good works.* If salvation had been by good works, he could not have been saved; for he was fastened hand and foot to the tree of doom. It was all over with him as to any act or deed of righteousness. He could say a good word or two, but that was all; he could perform no acts; and if his salvation had depended on an active life of usefulness, certainly he never could have been saved. He was a sinner also, who could not exhibit a long-enduring repentance for sin, for he had so short a time to live. He could not have experienced bitter convictions, lasting over months and years, for his time was measured by moments, and he was on the borders of the grave. His end was very near, and yet the Saviour could save him, and did save him so perfectly, that the sun went not down till he was in paradise with Christ.

This sinner, whom I have painted to you in colors none too black, was *one who believed in Jesus and confessed his faith.* He did trust the Lord. Jesus was a man, and he called Him so; but he knew that He was also Lord, and he called

Him so, and said, "Lord, remember me." He had such confidence in Jesus, that, if He would but only think of him, if He would only remember him when He came into His kingdom, that would be all that he would ask of Him. Alas, my dear readers, the trouble with some of you is that you know all about my Lord and yet you do not trust Him. Trust is the saving act. Years ago you were on the verge of really trusting Jesus, but you are just as far off from it now as you were then. This man did not hesitate: he grasped the one hope for himself. He did not keep his persuasion of our Lord's Messiahship in his mind as a dry, dead belief, but he turned it into trust and prayer. "Lord, remember me when thou comest into thy kingdom." Oh, that in His infinite mercy many of you would trust my Lord right now! You shall be saved, I know you shall: if you are not saved when you trust, I must myself also renounce all hope. This is all that we have done: we looked, and we lived, and we continue to live because we look to the living Saviour. Oh, that just now, feeling your sin, you would look to Jesus, trusting Him, and confessing that trust! Owning that He is Lord to the glory of God the Father, you must and shall be saved.

In consequence of having this faith which saved him, *this poor man breathed the humble but fitting prayer,* "Lord, remember me." This does not seem to ask much; but as he understood it, it meant all that an anxious heart could desire. As he thought of the kingdom, he had such clear ideas of the glory of the Saviour that he felt that if the Lord would think of him his eternal state would be safe. Joseph, in prison, asked the chief butler to remember him when he was restored to power; but he forgot him. Our Joseph never forgets a sinner who cried to Him in the low dungeon; in His kingdom He remembers the moanings and groanings of poor sinners who are burdened with a sense of sin. Can you not pray right now and thus secure a place in the memory of the Lord Jesus?

Thus I have tried to describe the man; and, after having done my best, I shall fail of my object unless I make you see that whatever this thief was, he is a picture of what you are. Especially if you have been a great offender, and if you have been living long without caring for eternal things, you are like that malefactor; and yet you, even you, may do as that thief did; you may believe that Jesus is the Christ, and commit your souls into His hands, and He will save you as surely as He saved the condemned brigand. Jesus graciously says, "Him that cometh to me I will in no wise cast out." This means that if *you* come and trust Him, whoever you may be, He will for no reason, and on no ground, and under no circumstances, ever cast you out. Do you catch that thought? Do you feel that it belongs to you, and that if *you* come to Him, *you* shall find eternal life? I rejoice if you so far perceive the truth.

Few persons have so much intercourse with desponding and despairing souls as I have. Poor cast down ones write to me continually. I scarce know why. I have no special gift of consolation, but I gladly lay myself out to comfort the distressed, and they seem to know it. What joy I have when I see a despairing one find peace! How much I desire that any of you who are breaking your hearts because you cannot find forgiveness would come to my Lord, and trust Him, and enter into rest! Has He not said, "Come unto me, all ye that labor and are heavy laden, and I will give you rest"? Come and try Him, and that rest shall be yours.

II. In the second place,

NOTE THAT THIS MAN WAS OUR LORD'S FIRST COMPANION
AT THE GATE OF PARADISE

I am not going into any speculations as to where our Lord went when He quitted the body which hung on the cross. It would seem, from some Scriptures, that He descended into the lower parts of the earth, that He might fill all things. But He very rapidly traversed the regions of the dead. Remember that He died, perhaps an hour or two before the thief, and during that time the eternal glory flamed through the underworld, and was flashing through the gates of paradise just when the

pardoned thief was entering the eternal world. Who is this
that entereth the pearl-gate at the same moment as the King
of glory? Who is this favored companion of the Redeemer?
Is it some honored martyr? Is it a faithful apostle? Is it a
patriarch, like Abraham; or a prince, like David? It is none
of these. Behold and be amazed at sovereign grace. He that
goes in at the gate of paradise with the King of glory is a
thief, who was saved in the article of death. He is saved in no
inferior way, and received into bliss in no secondary style.
Verily, there are last which shall be first!

Here I would have you notice *the condescension of our
Lord's choice.* The comrade of the Lord of glory, for whom
the cherub turns aside his sword of fire, is no great one, but
a newly-converted malefactor. And why? I think the Saviour
took him with Him as a specimen of what He meant to do.
He seemed to say to all the heavenly powers, "I bring a sinner with Me; he is a sample of the rest."

Have you never heard of him who dreamed that he stood
without the gate of heaven, and while there he heard sweet
music from a band of venerable persons who were on their
way to glory? They entered the celestial portals, and there
were great rejoicing and shouts. Inquiring "What are these?"
he was told that they were the goodly fellowship of the
prophets. He sighed and said, "Alas! I am not one of these."

He waited a while and another band of shining ones drew
nigh, who also entered heaven with hallelujahs, and when he
inquired, "Who are these, and whence came they?" the answer was, "These are the glorious company of the apostles."

Again he sighed, and said, "I cannot enter with them."
Then came another body of men white-robed, and bearing
palms in their hands, who marched amid great acclamation
into the golden city. These he learned were the noble army of
martyrs; and again he wept and said, "I cannot enter with
these."

In the end he heard the voices of much people, and saw
a greater multitude advancing, among whom he perceived Ra-

hab and Mary Magdalene, David and Peter, Manasseh and Saul of Tarsus, and he espied especially the thief, who died at the right hand of Jesus. These all entered in—a strange company.

Then he eagerly inquired, "Who are these?" and they answered, "This is the host of sinners saved by grace." Then was he exceedingly glad, and said, "I can go with these." Yet, he thought there would be no shouting at the approach of this company, and that they would enter heaven without song; instead of which, there seemed to rise a seven-fold hallelujah of praise unto the Lord of love; for there is joy in the presence of the angels of God over sinners that repent.

I invite any poor soul who can neither aspire to serve Christ, nor to suffer for Him as yet, nevertheless to come in with other believing sinners, in the company of Jesus, who now sets before us an open door.

While we are handling this text, note well *the blessedness of the place* to which the Lord called this penitent. Jesus said, "Today shalt thou be with me in paradise." Paradise means a garden, a garden filled with delights. The garden of Eden is the type of heaven. We know that paradise means heaven, for the apostle speaks of such a man caught up into paradise, and anon he calls it the third heaven. Our Saviour took this dying thief into the paradise of infinite delight, and this is where He will take all of us sinners who believe in Him. If we are trusting Him, we shall ultimately be with Him in paradise.

The next word is better still. Note *the glory of the society* to which this sinner is introduced: "Today shalt thou be with me in paradise." If the Lord said, "Today shalt thou be *with me,*" we should not need Him to add another word; for where He is is heaven to us. He added the word "paradise," because else none could have guessed where He was going. Think of it, you uncomely soul; you are to dwell with the altogether lovely One for ever. You poor and needy ones, you are to be with Him in His glory, in His bliss, in His perfection. Where

He is, and as He is, you shall be. The Lord looks into those
weeping eyes of yours and He says, "Poor sinner, thou shalt
one day be with me." I think I hear you say, "Lord, that is
bliss too great for such a sinner as I am"; But He replies "I
have loved thee with an everlasting love: therefore with lov-
ingkindness will I draw thee, till thou shalt be with Me
where I am."

The stress of the text lies in *the speediness of all this.*
"Verily I say unto thee, *Today* shalt thou be with me in paradise." "Today." You shall not lie in purgatory for ages, nor
sleep in limbo for so many years; but you shall be ready for
bliss at once, and at once you shall enjoy it. The sinner was
hard by the gates of hell, but almighty mercy lifted him up,
and the Lord said, "*Today* shalt thou be with me in paradise."
What a change from the cross to the crown, from the anguish
of Calvary to the glory of the New Jerusalem! In those few
hours the beggar was lifted from the dunghill and set among
princes. "Today shalt thou be with me in paradise." Can you
measure the change from that sinner, loathsome in his iniquity, when the sun was high at noon, to that same sinner,
clothed in pure white and accepted in the beloved, in the paradise of God, when the sun went down? O glorious Saviour,
what marvels you can work! How rapidly can you work them!

Please notice, also, *the majesty of the Lord's grace* in this
text. The Saviour said to him, "Verily *I say* unto thee, today
shalt thou be with me in paradise." Our Lord gives His own
will as the reason for saving this man. "I say." He says it who
claims the right thus to speak. It is He who will have mercy
on whom He will have mercy, and will have compassion on
whom He will have compassion. He speaks royally, "Verily I
say unto thee." Are they not imperial words? The Lord is a
King in whose word there is power. What He says none can
gainsay. He who has the keys of hell and of death says, "I
say unto thee, Today shalt thou be with Me in paradise."
Who shall prevent the fulfilment of His word?

Notice *the certainty of it.* He says, "Verily." Our blessed Lord on the cross returned to His old majestic manner as He painfully turned His head and looked on His convert. He was wont to begin His preaching with, "Verily, verily, I say unto you"; and now that He is dying He uses His favorite manner and says, "Verily." Our Lord took no oath; His strongest assertion was, "Verily, verily." To give the penitent the plainest assurance, He says, "Verily I say unto thee, Today shalt thou be with me in paradise." In this the thief had an absolutely indisputable assurance that though he must die, yet he would live and find himself in paradise with his Lord.

I have thus shown you that our Lord passed within the pearly gate in company with one to whom He had pledged Himself. Why should not you and I pass through that pearlgate in due time, clothed in His merit, washed in His blood, resting on His power? One of these days angels will say of you, and of me, "Who is this that cometh up from the wilderness, leaning upon her beloved?" The shining ones will be amazed to see some of us coming. If you have lived a life of sin until now, and yet shall repent and enter heaven, what an amazement there will be in every golden street to think that you have come there! In the early Christian church Marcus Caius Victorinus was converted; but he reached so great an age, and had been so gross a sinner, that the pastor and church doubted him. He gave, however, clear proof of having undergone the divine change, and then there were great acclamations, and many shouts of "Victorinus has become a Christian!" Oh, that some of you big sinners might be saved! How gladly would we rejoice over you! Why not! Would it not glorify God? The salvation of this convicted highwayman has made our Lord illustrious for mercy even unto this day; would not your case do the same? Would not saints cry, "Hallelujah! hallelujah!" if they heard that some of you had been turned from darkness to marvelous light? Why should it not be? Believe in Jesus, and it is so.

III. Now I come to my third and most practical point:
NOTE THE LORD'S SERMON TO US FROM ALL THIS

The devil wants to preach a bit. Yes, Satan asks to take over and preach to you; but he cannot be allowed. Avaunt, thou deceiver! Yet I should not wonder if he gets at certain of you when the chapter is over and whispers, "You see you can be saved at the very last. Put off repentance and faith; you may be forgiven on your deathbed." Sirs, you know who it is that would ruin you by this suggestion. Abhor his deceitful teaching. Do not be ungrateful because God is kind. Do not provoke the Lord because He is patient. Such conduct would be unworthy and ungrateful. Do not run an awful risk because one escaped the tremendous peril. The Lord will accept all who repent; but how do you know that you will repent? It is true that one thief was saved—but the other thief was lost. One is saved, and we may not despair; the other is lost, and we may not presume. Dear readers, I trust you are not made of such diabolical stuff as to fetch from the mercy of God an argument for continuing in sin. If you do, I can only say of you, your damnation will be just; you will have brought it upon yourself.

Consider now the teaching of our Lord; see *the glory of Christ in salvation.* He is ready to save at the last moment. He was just passing away; His foot was on the doorstep of the Father's house. Up comes this poor sinner the last thing at night, at the eleventh hour, and the Saviour smiles and declares that He will not enter except with this belated wanderer. At the very gate He declares that this seeking soul shall enter with Him. There was plenty of time for him to have come before: you know how apt we are to say, "You have waited to the last moment. I am just going off and I cannot attend to you now." Our Lord had His dying pangs upon Him, and yet He attends to the perishing criminal and permits him to pass through the heavenly portal in His company. Jesus easily saves the sinners for whom He painfully died. Jesus

loves to rescue sinners from going down into the pit. You will
be very happy if you are saved, but you will not be one half
so happy as He will be when He saves you. See how gentle
He is!

> His hand no thunder bears,
> No terror clothes His brow;
> No bolts to drive our guilty souls
> To fiercer flames below.

He comes to us full of tenderness, with tears in His eyes,
mercy in His hands, and love in His heart. Believe Him to be
a great Saviour of great sinners. I have heard of one who had
received great mercy who went about saying, "He is a great
forgiver"; and I would have you say the same. You shall find
your transgressions put away, and your sins pardoned once
for all, if you now trust Him.

The next doctrine Christ preaches from this wonderful
story is *faith in its permitted attachment.* This man believed
that Jesus was the Christ. The next thing He did was to appropriate that Christ. He said, "Lord, remember me." Jesus
might have said, "What have I to do with you, and what have
you to do with Me? What has a thief to do with the perfect
One?" Many of you, good people, try to get as far away as
you can from the erring and fallen. They might infect your
innocence!

Society claims that we should not be familiar with people
who have offended against its laws. We must not be seen
associating with them, for it might discredit us. Infamous
bosh! Can anything discredit sinners such as we are by nature and by practice? If we know ourselves before God we
are degraded enough in and of ourselves. Is there anyone, after
all, in the world, who is worse than we are when we see ourselves in the faithful glass of the Word? As soon as ever a
man believes that Jesus is the Christ, let him hook himself
on to Him. The moment you believe Jesus to be the Saviour,
seize upon Him as your Saviour.

If I remember rightly, Augustine called this man, *"Latro*

laudabilis et mirabilis," a thief to be praised and wondered at,
who dared, as it were, to seize the Saviour for his own. In
this he is to be imitated. Take the Lord to be yours, and you
have Him. Jesus is the common property of all sinners who
make bold to take Him. Every sinner who has the will to do
so may take the Lord home with him. He came into the
world to save the sinful. Take Him by force, as robbers take
their prey; for the kingdom of heaven suffereth the violence
of daring faith. Get Him and He will never get Himself away
from you. If you trust Him, He must save you.

Next, notice the doctrine of *faith in its immediate power.*

> The moment a sinner believes,
> And trusts in his crucified God,
> His pardon at once he receives,
> Redemption in full through His blood.

"Today shalt thou be with me in paradise." He has no
sooner believed than Christ gives him the seal of his believing
in the full assurance that he shall be with Him forever in His
glory. O dear hearts, if you believe, you shall be saved right
now! God grant that you, by His rich grace, may be brought
into salvation here, on the spot, and at once!

The next thing is, *the nearness of eternal things.* Think of
that a minute. Heaven and hell are not places far away. You
may be in heaven before the clock ticks again, it is so near.
Could we but rend that veil which parts us from the unseen!
It is all there, and all near. "Today," said the Lord — within
three or four hours at the longest — "shalt thou be with me
in paradise;" so near is it. A statesman has given us the expression of being "within measurable distance." We are all
within measurable distance of heaven or hell; if there be any
difficulty in measuring the distance, it lies in its brevity rather
than its length.

> One gentle sigh the fetter breaks,
> We scarce can say, "He's gone,"
> Before the ransomed spirit takes
> Its mansion near the throne.

Oh, that we, instead of trifling about such things, because they seem so far away, would solemnly realize them, since they are so very near! This very moment some may see, in his own spirit, the realities of heaven or hell. It has frequently happened in our large congregation, that some one of our audience has died ere the next Sabbath has come round; it may happen this week. Think of that, and let eternal things impress you all the more because they lie so near.

Furthermore, know that *if you have believed in Jesus, you are prepared for heaven.* It may be that you will have to live on earth twenty, or thirty, or forty years to glorify Christ; and, if so, be thankful for the privilege; but if you do not live another hour, your instantaneous death would not alter the fact that he that believeth in the Son of God is meet for heaven. Surely, if anything beyond faith is needed to make us fit to enter paradise, the thief would have been kept a little longer here; but no, he is, in the morning, in the state of nature, at noon he enters the state of grace, and by sunset he is in the state of glory. The question never is whether a death-bed repentance is accepted if it be sincere: the question is — is it sincere? If it be so, if the man dies five minutes after his first act of faith, he is as safe as if he had served the Lord for fifty years. If your faith is true, if you die one moment after you have believed in Christ, you will be admitted into paradise, even if you shall have enjoyed no time in which to produce good works and other evidences of grace. He that reads the heart will read your faith written on its fleshly tablets, and He will accept you through Jesus Christ, even though no act of grace has been visible to the eye of man.

I conclude by again saying that *this is not an exceptional case.* I began with that, and I want to finish with it, because so many demi-semi-gospelers are so terribly afraid of preaching free grace too fully. I read somewhere, and I think it is true, that some ministers preach the gospel in the same way as donkeys eat thistles, namely, very, very cautiously. On the contrary, I will preach it boldly. I have not the slightest alarm about the matter. If any of you misuse free-grace teaching, I cannot help it. He that will be damned can as well ruin himself by subverting the Gospel as by anything else. I cannot help what base hearts may invent; but mine it is to set forth the Gospel in all its fulness of grace, and I will do it.

If the thief was an exceptional case — and our Lord does not usually act in such a way — there would have been a hint given of so important a fact. A hedge would have been set about this exception to all rules. Would not the Saviour have whispered quietly to the dying man, "You are the only one I am going to treat in this way"? Whenever I have to do an exceptional favor to a person, I have to say, "Do not mention this, or I shall have so many besieging me." If the Saviour had meant this to be a solitary case, He would have faintly said to him, "Do not let anyone know; but you shall today be in the kingdom with Me." No, our Lord spoke openly, and those about Him heard what He said. Moreover, the inspired penman has recorded it.

If it had been an exceptional case, it would not have been written in the Word of God. Men will not publish their actions in the newspapers if they feel that the record might lead others to expect from them what they cannot give. The Saviour had this wonder of grace reported in the daily news of the Gospel, because He means to repeat the marvel every day. The bulk shall be equal to sample, and therefore He sets the sample before you all. He is able to save to the uttermost, for He saved the dying thief. The case would not have been put there to encourage hopes which He cannot fulfil. Whatsoever things were written aforetime were written for our learning, and not for our disappointing. I pray you, therefore, if any of you have not yet trusted in my Lord Jesus, come and trust in Him now. Trust Him wholly; trust Him only; trust Him at once. Then will you sing with me —

> The dying thief rejoiced to see
> That fountain in his day,
> And there may I, though vile as he,
> Wash all my sins away.

The Third Word*:

(AFFECTION)

Now there stood by the cross of Jesus his mother, and his mother's sister, Mary the wife of Cleophas, and Mary Magdalene. John 19:25

LAST AT THE CROSS, FIRST AT THE SEPULCHER. NO WOMAN'S LIP betrayed her Lord; no woman's hand ever smote Him; their eyes wept for Him; they gazed upon Him with pitying awe and love. God bless the Marys! When we see so many of them about the cross, we feel that we honor the very name of Mary.

When Jesus therefore saw his mother, and the disciple standing by, whom he loved, he saith unto his mother, Woman, behold thy son! (John 19:26)

Sad, sad spectacle! Now was fulfilled the word of Simeon, "Yea, a sword shall pierce through thy own soul also, that the thoughts of many hearts may be revealed." Did the Saviour mean, as He gave a glance to John, "Woman, thou art losing one Son; but yonder stands another, who will be a son to thee in my absence"? "Woman, behold thy son!"

Then saith he to the disciple, Behold thy mother! (John 19:27a)

"Take her as thy mother, stand thou in My place, care for her as I have cared for her." Those who love Christ best shall have the honor of taking care of His church and of His poor.

---

*Spurgeon never preached a complete sermon on "The Third Word from the Cross" according to the records available. However, this brief and heart-warming exposition will provide much food for thought and action.

Never say of any poor relative or friend, the widow or the fatherless, "They are a great burden to me." Oh, no! Say, "They are a great honor to me; my Lord has entrusted them to my care." John thought so; let us think so. Jesus selected the disciple He loved best to take His mother under His care. He selects those whom He loves best today, and puts His poor people under their wing. Take them gladly, and treat them well.

And from that hour that disciple took her unto his own home. (John 19:27b)

You expected him to do it, did you not? He loved his Lord so well.

The Fourth Word:

*And about the ninth hour Jesus cried with a loud voice,
saying, Eli, Eli, lama sabachthani? that is to say, My
God, my God, why hast thou forsaken me?*

Matthew 27:46

"THERE WAS DARKNESS OVER ALL THE LAND UNTO THE NINTH
hour": this cry came out of that darkness. Expect not to see
through its every word, as though it came from on high as a
beam from the unclouded Sun of Righteousness. There is light
in it, bright, flashing light; but there is a center of impenetrable gloom, where the soul is ready to faint because of the
terrible darkness.

Our Lord was then in the darkest part of His way. He had
trodden the winepress now for hours, and the work was almost finished. He had reached the culminating point of His
anguish. This is His dolorous lament from the lowest pit of
misery — "My God, my God, why hast thou forsaken me?"
I do not think that the records of time, or even of eternity,
contain a sentence more full of anguish. Here the wormwood
and the gall, and all the other bitterness, are outdone. Here
you may look as into a vast abyss; and though you strain your
eyes, and gaze till sight fails you, yet you perceive no bottom;
it is measureless, unfathomable, inconceivable. This anguish
of the Saviour on your behalf and mine is no more to be measured and weighed than the sin which needed it, or the love
which endureth it. We will adore where we cannot compre-
hend.

I hope this subject will help the children of God to understand a little of their infinite obligations to their redeeming
Lord. You shall measure the height of His love, if it be ever
measured, by the depth of His grief, if that can ever be
known. See with what a price He hath redeemed us from the
curse of the law! As you see this, say to yourselves: What
manner of people ought we to be! What measure of love ought
we to return to One who bore the utmost penalty, that we
might be delivered from the wrath to come? I do not profess
that I can dive into this deep: I will only venture to the edge
of the precipice, and bid you look down, and pray the Spirit
of God to concentrate your mind upon this lamentation of our
dying Lord, as it rises up through the thick darkness — "My
God, my God, why hast thou forsaken me?"

Our first subject of thought will be *the fact,* or, what He
suffered — God had forsaken Him. Secondly, we will note
the inquiry, or, why He suffered: this word "why" is the edge
of the text: "Why hast thou forsaken me?" Then, thirdly, we
will consider *the answer,* or, what came of His suffering. The
answer flowed softly into the soul of the Lord Jesus without
the need of words, for He ceased from His anguish with the
triumphant shout of, "It is finished." His work was finished,
and His bearing of desertion was a chief part of the work He
had undertaken for our sake.

I. By the help of the Holy Spirit, let us first dwell upon

THE FACT

or, what our Lord suffered. God had forsaken Him. Grief
of mind is harder to bear than pain of body. You can pluck
up courage and endure the pang of sickness and pain, so long
as the spirit is hale and brave; but if the soul itself be touched,
and the mind becomes diseased with anguish, then every pain
is increased in severity, and there is nothing with which to
sustain it. Spiritual sorrows are the worst of mental miseries.
A man may bear great depression of spirit about worldly matters, if he feels that he has his God to go to. He is cast down,

but not in despair. Like David, he communes with himself, and he inquires, "Why art thou cast down, O my soul? and why art thou disquieted in me? Hope thou in God: for I shall yet praise him." But if the Lord be once withdrawn, if the comfortable light of His presence be shadowed even for an hour, there is a torment within the breast, which I can only liken to the prelude of hell. This is the greatest of all weights that can press upon the heart. This made the psalmist plead, "Hide not thy face from me; put not thy servant away in anger." We can bear a bleeding body, and even a wounded spirit; but a soul conscious of desertion by God is beyond conception unendurable. When He holdeth back the face of His throne, and spreadeth His cloud upon it, who can endure the darkness?

This voice out of "the belly of hell" marks the lowest depth of the Saviour's grief. *The desertion was real.* Though under some aspects our Lord could say, "The Father is with Me," yet was it solemnly true that God did forsake Him. It was not a failure of faith on His part which led Him to imagine what was not actual fact. Our faith fails us, and then we think that God has forsaken us; but our Lord's faith did not for a moment falter, for He says twice, *"My God, my God."* Oh, the mighty double grip of His unhesitating faith! He seems to say, "Even if Thou hast forsaken Me, I have not forsaken Thee." Faith triumphs, and there is no sign of any faintness of heart towards the living God. Yet, strong as is His faith, He feels that God has withdrawn His comfortable fellowship, and He shivers under the terrible deprivation.

It was no fancy, or delirium of mind, caused by His weakness of body, the heat of the fever, the depression of His spirit, or the near approach of death. He was clear of mind even to this last. He bore up under pain, loss of blood, scorn, thirst, and desolation, making no complaint of the cross, the nails, and the scoffing. We read not in the gospels of anything more than the natural cry of weakness, "I thirst." All the tortures of His body He endured in silence; but when it came to being forsaken of God, then His great heart burst out into its "Lama sabachthani?" His one moan is concerning His God. It is not, "Why has Peter forsaken Me? Why has Judas betrayed Me?" These were sharp griefs, but this is the sharpest. This stroke has cut Him to the quick; "My God, my God, why hast *Thou* forsaken me?" It was no phantom of the gloom; it was a real absence which He mourned.

This was *a very remarkable desertion.* It is not the way of God to leave either His sons or His servants. His saints, when they come to die, in their great weakness and pain, find Him near. They are made to sing because of the presence of God: "Yea, though I walk through the valley of the shadow of death, I will fear no evil: for thou art with me." Dying saints have clear visions of the living God. Our observation has taught us that if the Lord be away at other times, He is never absent from His people in the article of death, or in the furnace of affliction.

Concerning the three holy children, we do not read that the Lord was ever visibly with them till they walked the fires of Nebuchadnezzar's furnace; but there and then the Lord met with them. Yes, beloved, it is God's use and wont to keep company with His afflicted people; and yet He forsook His Son in the hour of His tribulation! How usual it is to see the Lord with His faithful witnesses when resisting even unto blood! Read the Book of Martyrs, and I care not whether you study the former or the later persecutions, you will find them all lit up with the evident presence of the Lord with His witnesses.

Did the Lord ever fail to support a martyr at the stake? Did He ever forsake one of His testifiers upon the scaffold? The testimony of the church has always been, that while the Lord has permitted His saints to suffer in body, He has so divinely sustained their spirits that they have been more than conquerors and have treated their sufferings as light afflictions. The fire has not been a "bed of roses," but it has been a chariot of victory. The sword is sharp, and death is bitter; but the love of Christ is sweet, and to die for Him has been turned into glory. No, it is not God's way to forsake His champions nor to leave even the least of His children in the trial hour.

As to our Lord, this forsaking was *singular*. Did His Father ever leave Him before? Will you read the four Evangelists through and find any previous instance in which He complains of His Father for having forsaken Him? No. He said, "I know that thou hearest me always." He lived in constant touch with God. His fellowship with the Father was always near and dear and clear; but now, for the first time, He cries, "Why hast thou forsaken me?" It was very remarkable. It was a riddle only to be solved by the fact that He loved us and gave Himself for us, and in the execution of His loving purpose came even unto this sorrow, of mourning the absence of His God.

This forsaking was *terrible*. Who can fully tell what it is to be forsaken of God? We can only form a guess by what we have ourselves felt under temporary and partial desertion. God has never left us altogether; for He has expressly said, "I will never leave thee, nor forsake thee"; yet we have sometimes felt as if He had cast us off. We have cried, "Oh, that I knew where I might find Him!" The clear shinings of His love have been withdrawn. Thus we are able to form some little idea of how the Saviour felt when His God had forsaken Him. The mind of Jesus was left to dwell upon one dark subject, and no cheering theme consoled Him. It was the hour in which He was made to stand before God as consciously the sin-bearer, according to that ancient prophecy, "He shall bear their iniquities." Then was it true, "He hath made him to be sin for us." Peter puts it, "He his own self bare our sins in his own body on the tree." Sin, sin, sin was everywhere around and about Christ. He had no sin of His own; but the Lord had "laid on Him the iniquity of us all." He had no strength given Him from on high, no secret oil and wine poured into His wounds; but He was made to appear in the lone character of the Lamb of God, which taketh away the sin of the world;

and therefore He must feel the weight of sin and the turning
away of that sacred face which cannot look thereon.

His Father at that time gave Him no open acknowledgment. On certain other occasions a voice had been heard, saying, "This is my beloved Son, in whom I am well pleased";
but now, when such a testimony seemed most of all required,
the oracle was dumb. He was hung up as an accursed thing
upon the cross; for He was "made a curse for us, as it is written, Cursed is every one that hangeth on a tree"; and the
Lord His God did not own Him before men. If it had pleased
the Father, He might have sent Him twelve legions of angels;
but not an angel came after the Christ had quitted Gethsemane. His despisers might spit in His face, but no swift seraph
came to avenge the indignity. They might bind Him, and
scourge Him, but none of all the heavenly host would inter-
pose to screen His shoulders from the lash. They might fasten
Him to the tree with nails, and lift Him up, and scoff at Him;
but no cohort of ministering spirits hastened to drive back
the rabble, and release the Prince of life. No, He appeared
to be forsaken, "smitten of God and afflicted," delivered into
the hands of cruel men, whose wicked hands worked Him misery without stint. Well might He ask, "My God, my God, why
hast thou forsaken me?"

But this was not all. His Father now dried up that sacred
stream of peaceful communion and loving fellowship which
had flowed hitherto throughout His whole earthly life. He said
Himself, as you remember, "Ye shall be scattered, every man
to his own, and shall leave me alone: and yet I am not alone,
because the Father is with me." Here was His constant comfort: but all comfort from this source was to be withdrawn.
The divine Spirit did not minister to His human spirit. No
communications with His Father's love poured into His heart.
It was not possible that the Judge should smile upon one who
represented the prisoner at the bar. Our Lord's faith did not
fail Him, as I have already shown you, for He said, "*My God,*

my God"; yet no sensible supports were given to His heart, and no comforts were poured into His mind.

One writer declares that Jesus did not taste of divine wrath, but only suffered a withdrawal of divine fellowship. What is the difference? Whether God withdraw heat or create cold is all one. He was not smiled upon, nor allowed to feel that He was near to God; and this, to His tender spirit, was grief of the keenest order.

A certain saint once said that in his sorrow he had from God "necessaries, but not suavities"; that which was meet, but not that which was sweet. Our Lord suffered to the extreme point of deprivation. He had not the light which makes existence to be life, and life to be a boon. You that know, in your degree, what it is to lose the conscious presence and love of God, you can faintly guess what the sorrow of the Saviour was, now that He felt He had been forsaken of His God. "If the foundations be removed, what can the righteous do?" To our Lord, the Father's love was the foundation of everything; and when that was gone, all was gone. Nothing remained, within, without, above, when His own God, the God of His entire confidence, turned from Him. Yes, God in very deed forsook our Saviour.

To be forsaken of God was *much more a source of anguish to Jesus than it would be to us.* "Oh," say you, "how is that?" I answer, because He was perfectly holy. A rupture between a perfectly holy being and the thrice holy God must be in the highest degree strange, abnormal, perplexing and painful. If any man here, who is not at peace with God, could only know his true condition, he would swoon with fright. If you unforgiven ones only knew where you are, and what you are at this moment in the sight of God, you would never smile again till you were reconciled to Him. Alas! we are insensible, hardened by the deceitfulness of sin, and therefore we do not feel our true condition. His perfect holiness made it to our Lord a dreadful calamity to be forsaken of the thrice Holy God.

I remember, also, that our blessed Lord had lived in unbroken fellowship with God and to be forsaken was a new
grief to Him. He had never known what the dark was till
then: His life had been lived in the light of God. Think, dear
child of God, if you had always dwelt in full communion with
God, your days would have been as the days of heaven upon
earth; and how cold it would strike to your heart to find yourself in the darkness of desertion. If you can conceive such a
thing as happening to a perfect man, you can see why to our
Well-beloved it was a special trial. Remember, He had enjoyed
fellowship with God more richly, as well as more constantly,
than any of us. His fellowship with the Father was of the highest, deepest, fullest order; and what must the loss of it have
been? We lose but drops when we lose our joyful experience
of heavenly fellowship; and yet the loss is killing; but to our
Lord Jesus Christ the sea was dried up — I mean His sea of
fellowship with the infinite God.

Do not forget that He was such a One that to Him to be
without God must have been an overwhelming calamity. In
every part He was perfect, and in every part fitted for communion with God to a supreme degree. A sinful man has an
awful need of God, but he does not know it; and therefore he
does not feel that hunger and thirst after God which would
come upon a perfect man could be deprived of God. The very
perfection of His nature renders it inevitable that the holy
man must either be in communion with God, or be desolate.

Imagine a stray angel! a seraph who has lost his God!
Conceive him to be perfect in holiness, and yet to have fallen
into a condition in which he cannot find his God! I cannot
picture him; perhaps a Milton might have done so. He is sin-
less and trustful, and yet he has an overpowering feeling that
God is absent from him. He has drifted into the nowhere —
the unimaginable region behind the back of God. I think I
hear the wailing of the cherub: "My God, my God, my God,
where art thou?" What a sorrow for one of the sons of the
morning!

But here we have the lament of a Being far more capable

of fellowship with the Godhead. In proportion as He is more fitted to receive the love of the great Father, in that proportion is His pining after it the more intense. As a Son, He is more able to commune with God than ever a servant-angel could be; and now that He is forsaken of God, the void within is the greater, and the anguish more bitter.

Our Lord's heart, and all His nature were, morally and spiritually, so delicately formed, so sensitive, so tender, that to be without God, was to Him a grief which could not be weighed. I see Him in the text bearing desertion, and yet I perceive that He cannot bear it. I know not how to express my meaning except by such a paradox. He cannot endure to be without God. He had surrendered Himself to be left of God, as the representative of sinners must be, but His pure and holy nature, after three hours of silence, finds the position unendurable to love and purity; and breaking forth from it, now that the hour was over, He exclaims, "Why hast thou forsaken me?" He quarrels not with the suffering, but He cannot abide in the position which caused it. He seems as if He must end the ordeal, not because of the pain, but because of the moral shock. We have here the repetition after His passion of that loathing which He felt before it, when He cried, "If it be possible let this cup pass from me: nevertheless not as I will, but as thou wilt." "My God, my God, why hast thou forsaken me?" is the holiness of Christ amazed at the position of substitute for guilty men.

There, friends; I have done my best, but I seem to myself to have been prattling like a little child, writing of something infinitely above me. So I leave the solemn fact, that our Lord Jesus was on the tree forsaken of His God.

II. This brings us to consider

THE INQUIRY

or, why He suffered.

Note carefully this cry—"My God, my god, why hast thou forsaken me?" It is pure anguish, undiluted agony, which

crieth like this; but it is the agony of a godly soul; for only a
man of that order would have used such an expression. Let
us learn from it useful lessons. This cry is taken from "the
Book." Does it not show our Lord's love of the sacred volume,
that when He felt His sharpest grief, He turned to the Scripture to find a fit utterance for it? Here we have the opening
sentence of the twenty-second Psalm. Oh, that we may so love
the inspired Word that we may not sing to its score, but even
weep to its music!

Note, again, that our Lord's lament is an address to God.
The godly, in their anguish, turn to the hand which smites
them. The Saviour's outcry is not *against* God, but *to* God.
"My God, my God": He makes a double effort to draw near.
True Sonship is here. The child in the dark is crying after His
Father — "My God, my God." Both the Bible and prayer were
dear to Jesus in His agony.

Still, observe, it is a faith-cry; for though it asks, "Why
hast Thou forsaken Me?" yet it first says, twice over, "My
God, my God." The grip of appropriation is in the word "my";
but the reverence of humility is in the word "God." It is
" 'My *God*, My *God*,' Thou art ever God to me, and I a poor
creature. I do not quarrel with Thee. Thy rights are unques-
tioned, for Thou art my *God*. Thou canst do as Thou wilt, and
I yield to Thy sacred sovereignty. I kiss the hand that smites
me, and with all my heart cry, 'My God, My God.' " When
you are delirious with pain, think of your Bible still: when
your mind wanders, let it roam toward the mercy seat; and
when your heart and your flesh fail, still live by faith, and still
cry, "My God, My God."

Let us come close to the inquiry. It looked to me, at first
sight, like *a question of one distraught*, driven from the balance of His mind — not unreasonable, but too much reasoning,
and therefore tossed about. "Why hast thou forsaken me?"
Did not Jesus know? Did He not know why He was forsaken?
He knew it most distinctly, and yet His manhood, while it was
being crushed, pounded, dissolved, seemed as though it could

not understand the reason for so great a grief. He must be forsaken; but could there be a sufficient cause for so sickening a sorrow? The cup must be bitter; but why this most nauseous of ingredients? I tremble lest I say what I ought not to say. I have said it, and I think there is truth — the Man of Sorrows was overborne with horror. At that moment the finite soul of the man Christ Jesus came into awful contact with the infinite justice of God. The one Mediator between God and man, the Man Christ Jesus, beheld the holiness of God in arms against the sin of man, whose nature He had espoused. God was for Him and with Him in a certain unquestionable sense; but for the time, so far as His feeling went, God was against Him and necessarily withdrawn from Him.

It is not surprising that the holy soul of Christ should shudder at finding itself brought into painful contact with the infinite justice of God, even though its design was only to vindicate that justice, and glorify the Law-giver. Our Lord could now say, "All Thy waves and Thy billows are gone over Me"; and therefore He uses language which is all too hot with anguish to be dissected by the cold hand of a logical criticism. Grief has small regard for the laws of the grammarian. Even the holiest, when in extreme agony, though they cannot speak otherwise than according to purity and truth, yet use a language of their own, which only the ear of sympathy can fully receive. I see not all that is here, but what I can see I am not able to put in words for you.

I think I see, in the expression, submission and resolve. Our Lord does not draw back. There is a forward movement in the question: they who quit a business ask no more questions about it. He does not ask that the forsaking may end prematurely, He would only understand anew its meaning. He does not shrink, but He rather dedicates Himself anew to God by the words, "My God, my God," and by seeking to review the ground and reason of that anguish which He is resolute to bear even to the bitter end. He would fain anew the motive which has sustained Him, and must sustain Him to the end. The cry sounds to me like deep submission and strong resolve, pleasing with God.

Do you not think that *the amazement of our Lord, when He was "made sin for us"* (I Corinthians 5:21), led Him thus to cry out? For such a sacred and pure being to be made a sin-offering was an amazing experience. Sin was laid on Him, and He was treated as if He had been guilty, though He had personally never sinned; and now the infinite horror of rebellion against the most holy God fills His holy soul, the unrighteousness of sin breaks His heart, and He starts back from it, crying, "My God, my God, why hast thou forsaken *me?*" Why must I bear the dread result of conduct I so much abhor?

Do you not see, moreover, *there was here a glance at His eternal purpose, and at His secret source of joy?* That "why" is the silver lining of the dark cloud, and our Lord looked wishfully at it. He knew that the desertion was needful in order that He might save the guilty and He had an eye to that salvation as His comfort. He is not forsaken needlessly, nor without a worthy design. The design is in itself so dear to His heart that He yields to the passing evil, even though that evil be like death to Him. He looks at that "why," and through that narrow window the light of heaven comes streaming into His darkened life.

"My God, my God, why hast thou forsaken me?" Surely our Lord dwelt on that "why" *that we might also turn our eyes that way.* He would have us see the why and the wherefore of His grief. He would have us mark the gracious motive for its endurance. Think much of all your Lord suffered, but do not overlook the reason of it. If you cannot always understand how this or that grief worked toward the great end of the whole passion, yet believe that it has its share in the grand "why." Make a life-study of that bitter but blessed question, "Why hast thou forsaken me?" Thus the Saviour raises an inquiry not so much for Himself as for us; and not so much because of any despair within His heart as because of a hope and a joy set before Him, which were wells of comfort to Him in His wilderness of woe.

Remember, for a moment, that the Lord God, in the broadest and most unreserved sense, could never, in very deed, have forsaken His most obedient Son. He was ever with Him in the grand design of salvation. Toward the Lord Jesus, personally, God Himself, personally, must ever have stood on terms of infinite love. Truly the Only Begotten was never more lovely to the Father than when He was obedient unto death, even the death of the cross! But we must look upon God here as the Judge of all the earth, and we must look upon the Lord Jesus also in His official capacity, as the Surety of the covenant, and the Sacrifice for sin. The great Judge of all cannot smile upon Him who has become the substitute for the guilty. Sin is loathed of God; and if, in order for its removal, His own Son is made to bear it, yet, as sin, it is still loathsome, and He who bears it cannot be in happy communion with God. This was the dread necessity of expiation; but in the essence of things the love of the great Father to His Son never ceased, nor ever knew a diminution. Restrained in its flow it must be, but lessened at its fountain-head it could not be. Therefore, do you wonder at the question, "Why hast thou forsaken me?"

III. Hoping to be guided by the Holy Spirit, I am coming to

THE ANSWER

"My God, my God, why hast thou forsaken me?" What is the outcome of this suffering? What was the reason for it? Our Saviour could answer His own question. If for a moment His manhood was perplexed, yet His mind soon came to clear apprehension; for He said, "It is finished"; and, as I have already pointed out, He then referred to the work which in His lonely agony He had been performing. Why, then, did God forsake His Son? I cannot conceive any other answer than this — *He stood in our stead.* There was no reason in Christ why the Father should forsake Him: He was perfect and His life was without spot. God never acts without reason; and since there were no reasons in the character and person of the Lord why His Father should forsake Him, we must look elsewhere. I do not know how others answer the question. I can only answer it in this one way.

> Yet all the griefs He felt were ours,
>   Ours were the woes He bore;
> Pangs, not His own, His spotless soul
>   With bitter anguish tore.
>
> We held Him as condemn'd of heaven,
>   An outcast from His God;
> While for our sins, He groaned, He bled,
>   Beneath His Father's rod.

He bore the sinner's sin, and He had to be treated, therefore, as though He were a sinner, though sinner He could never be. With His own full consent He suffered as though He had committed the transgressions which were laid on Him. Our sin, and His taking it upon Himself, is the answer to the question, "Why hast thou forsaken me?"

In this case we now see that *His obedience was perfect.* He came into the world to obey the Father, and He rendered that obedience to the very uttermost. The spirit of obedience could go no farther than for one who feels forsaken of God still to cling to Him in solemn, avowed allegiance, still declaring before a mocking multitude His confidence in the afflicting God. It is noble to cry, "My God, my God," when one is asking, "Why hast thou forsaken me?" How much farther can obedience go? I see nothing beyond it. The soldier at the gate of Pompeii remaining at his post as sentry when the shower of burning ashes is falling, was not more true to his trust than He who adheres to a forsaking God with loyalty of hope.

Our Lord's suffering in this particular form was appropriate and necessary. It would not have sufficed for our Lord merely to have been pained in body, nor even to have been grieved in mind in other ways: He must suffer in this particular way. He must feel forsaken of God, because this is the necessary consequence of sin. For a man to be forsaken of God is the penalty which naturally and inevitably follows upon his breaking his relation with God. What is death? What was the death that was threatened to Adam? "In the day that thou eatest thereof thou shalt surely die." Is death annihilation? Was Adam annihilated that day? Assuredly not: he lived many a year afterwards. But in the day in which he ate of the forbidden fruit he died, by being separated from God. The separation of the soul from God is spiritual death; just as the separation of the soul from the body is physical death. The sacrifice for sin must be put in the place of separation and must bow to the penalty of death. By this placing of the Great Sacrifice under forsaking and death, it would be seen by all creatures throughout the universe that God could not have fellowship with sin. If even the Holy One, who stood the Just for the unjust, found God forsaking Him, what must the doom of the actual sinner be! Sin is evidently always, in every case, a dividing influence, putting even the Christ Himself, as a sin-bearer, in the place of distance.

This was necessary for another reason; there could have been no laying on of suffering for sin without the forsaking of the vicarious Sacrifice by the Lord God. So long as the smile of God rests on the man the law is not afflicting him. The approving look of the great Judge cannot fall upon a man who is viewed as standing in the place of the guilty. Christ not only suffered *from* sin, but *for* sin. If God will cheer and sustain Him, He is not suffering for sin. The Judge is not inflicting suffering for sin if He is manifestly succoring the smitten one. There could have been no vicarious suffering on the part of Christ for human guilt, if He had continued consciously to enjoy the full sunshine of the Father's presence. It was essential to being a victim in our place that He should cry, "My God, my God, why has thou forsaken me?"

Beloved, see how marvelously, in the person of Christ, the Lord our God has vindicated His law! If to make His law glorious, He had said, "These multitudes of men have broken My law, and therefore they shall perish," the law would have been terribly magnified. But, instead thereof, He says, "Here is My Only Begotten Son, My other self; He takes on Himself the nature of these rebellious creatures, and He consents that I should lay on Him the load of their iniquity, and visit in His person the offenses which might have been punished in the persons of all these multitudes of men: and I will have it so." When Jesus bows His head to the stroke of the law, when He submissively consents that His Father shall turn away His face from Him, then myriads of worlds are astonished at the perfect holiness and stern justice of the Lawgiver. There are, probably, worlds innumerable throughout the boundless creation of God, and all these will see, in the death of God's dear Son, a declaration of His determination never to allow sin to be trifled with. If His own Son is brought before Him, bearing the sin of others upon Him, He will hide His face from Him, as well as from the actually guilty. In God infinite love shines over all, but it does not eclipse His absolute justice any more than His justice is permitted to destroy His love. God hath all perfections in perfection, and in Christ Jesus we see the reflection of them. Beloved, this is a wonderful theme! Oh, that I had a tongue worthy of this subject! but who could ever reach the height of this great argument?

Once more, when inquiring, Why did Jesus suffer to be forsaken of the Father? we see the fact that *the Captain of our salvation was thus made perfect through suffering.* Every part of the road has been traversed by our Lord's own feet. Suppose, beloved, the Lord Jesus had never been thus forsaken, then one of His disciples might have been called to that sharp endurance and the Lord Jesus could not have sympathized with him in it. He would turn to his Leader and Captain, and say to Him, "Didst Thou, my Lord, ever feel this darkness?" Then the Lord Jesus would answer, "No. This is a descent such as I never made." What a dreadful lack would

the tried one have felt! For the servant to bear a grief his
Master never knew would be sad indeed.

There would have been a wound for which there was no
ointment, a pain for which there was no balm. But it is not so
now. "In all their affliction He was afflicted." "He was in all
points tempted like as we are, yet without sin." Wherein we
greatly rejoice at this time, and so often as we are cast down.
Underneath us is the deep experience of our forsaken Lord.

This chapter is completed with the saying of three things.
The first is, you and I that are believers in the Lord Jesus
Christ, and are resting in Him alone for salvation, *let us lean
hard,* let us bear with all our weight on our Lord. He will
bear the full weight of all our sin and care. As to my sin, I
hear its harsh accusings no more when I hear Jesus cry, "Why
hast thou forsaken me?" I know that I deserve the deepest
hell at the hand of God's vengeance; but I am not afraid. He
will never forsake *me,* for He forsook His Son on my behalf.
I shall not suffer for my sin, for Jesus has suffered to the full
in my stead; yea, suffered so far as to cry, "My God, my God,
why hast thou forsaken me?" Behind this brazen wall of substitution a sinner is safe. These "munitions of rock" guard all
believers, and they may rest secure. The rock is cleft for me;
I hide in its rifts, and no harm can reach me. You have a
full atonement, a great sacrifice, a glorious vindication of the
law; wherefore rest at peace, all you that put your trust in
Jesus.

Next, if ever in our lives henceforth we should think that
God hath deserted us, *let us learn from our Lord's example
how to behave ourselves.* If God has left you, do not shut up
your Bible; no, open it, as your Lord did, and find a text that
will suit you. If God has left you, or you think so, do not give
up prayer; no, pray as the Lord did and be more earnest than
ever. If you think God has forsaken you, do not give up your
faith in Him; but, like your Lord, cry, "My God, my God,"
again and again. If you had one anchor before, cast out two
anchors now, and double the hold of your faith. If you can

not call Jehovah "Father," as was Christ's wont, call Him your "God." Let the pronouns take their hold — "My God, my God." Let nothing drive you from your faith. Still hold on Jesus, sink or swim.

As for me, if ever I am lost, it shall be at the foot of the cross. To this pass have I come, that if I never see the face of God with acceptance, yet I will believe that He will be faithful to His Son and true to the covenant sealed by oaths and blood. He that believes in Jesus has everlasting life; there I cling, like the limpet to the rock. There is but one gate of heaven, and even if I may not enter it, I will cling to the posts of its door. What am I saying? I shall enter in; for that gate was never shut against a soul that accepted Jesus; and Jesus says, "Him that cometh to me I will in no wise cast out."

The last of the three points is this, *let us abhor the sin which brought such agony upon our beloved Lord*. What an accursed thing is sin, which crucified the Lord Jesus! Do you laugh at it? Will you go and spend an evening to see a mimic performance of it? Do you roll sin under your tongue as a sweet morsel, and then come to God's house, on the Lord's-day morning, and think to worship Him? Worship Him! Worship Him, with sin indulged in your breast! Worship Him, with sin loved and pampered in your life! O, if I had a dear brother who had been murdered, what would you think of me if I treasured the knife which had been crimsoned with his blood? — if I made a friend of the murderer, and daily consorted with the assassin, who drove the dagger into my brother's heart? Surely I, too, must be an accomplice in the crime! Sin murdered Christ; will you be a friend to it? Sin pierced the heart of the Incarnate God; can you love it? Oh, that there was an abyss as deep as Christ's misery, that I might at once hurl this dagger of sin into its depths, whence it might never be brought to light again! Begone, O sin! You are banished from the heart where Jesus reigns! Begone, for you have crucified my Lord, and made Him cry, "Why hath thou forsaken me?" O my readers, if you did but know yourselves, and know the

love of Christ, you would each one vow that you would harbor sin no longer. You would be indignant at sin, and cry,

> The dearest idol I have known,
> Whate'er that idol be,
> Lord, I will tear it from its throne,
> And worship only Thee.

May that be the issue of this discourse, and then I shall be
well content. The Lord bless you! May the Christ who suffered
for you, bless you, and out of His darkness may your light
arise! Amen.

The Fifth Word:

(SUFFERING)

After this, Jesus knowing that all things were now accomplished, that the Scripture might be fulfilled, saith, I thirst.   John 19: 28

OUR TEXT FOR THIS CHAPTER IS THE SHORTEST OF ALL THE WORDS of Calvary; it stands as two words in our language—"I thirst," but in the Greek it is only one. I cannot say that it is "short and sweet," for, alas, it was bitterness itself to our Lord Jesus; and yet out of its bitterness I trust there will come great sweetness to us. Though bitter to Him in the speaking, it will be sweet to us in the hearing — so sweet that all the bitterness of our trials shall be forgotten as we remember the vinegar and gall of which He drank.

I. We shall by the assistance of the Holy Spirit try to regard these words of our Saviour in a five-fold light. First, we shall look upon them as

THE ENSIGN OF HIS TRUE HUMANITY

Jesus said, "I thirst," and this is the complaint of a man. Our Lord is the Maker of the ocean and the waters that are above the firmament: it is His hand that stays or opens the bottles of heaven, and sends rain upon the evil and upon the good. "The sea is his, and he made it," and all fountains and springs are of His digging. He pours out the streams that run among the hills, the torrents which rush down the mountains, and the flowing rivers which enrich the plains. One would have said, If He were thirsty He would not tell us, for all the clouds and rains would be glad to refresh His brow, and the brooks and streams would joyously flow at His feet. And yet, though He was Lord of all, He had so fully taken upon Himself the form of a servant and was so perfectly made in the likeness of sinful flesh, that He cried with fainting voice, "I thirst." How truly man He is; He is, indeed; "bone of our bone and flesh of our flesh," for He bears our infirmities.

I invite you to meditate upon the true humanity of our Lord very reverently, and very lovingly. Jesus was proved to be really man, because He suffered the pains which belong to manhood. Angels cannot suffer thirst. A phantom, as some have called Him, could not suffer in this fashion; but Jesus really suffered, not only the more refined pains of delicate and sensitive minds, but the rougher and commoner pangs of flesh and blood. Thirst is a commonplace misery, such as may happen to peasants or beggars; it is a real pain, and not a thing of a fancy or a nightmare of dreamland. Thirst is no royal grief, but an evil of universal manhood; Jesus is brother to the poorest and most humble of our race. Our Lord, however, endured thirst to an extreme degree, for it was the thirst of death which was upon Him, and more, it was the thirst of One whose death was not a common one, for "He tasted death for every man."

That thirst was caused, perhaps, in part by the loss of blood, and by the fever created by the irritation caused by His four grievous wounds. The nails were fastened in the most sensitive parts of the body, and the wounds were widened as the weight of His body dragged the nails through His blessed flesh and tore His tender nerves. The extreme tension produced a burning feverishness. It was pain that dried His mouth and made it like an oven, till He declared in the language of the twenty-second psalm, "My tongue cleaveth to my jaws." It was a thirst such as none of us have ever known, for not yet has the death dew condensed upon our brows. We shall perhaps know it in our measure in our dying hour, but not yet, nor ever so terribly as He did. Our Lord felt that

grievous drought of dissolution by which all moisture seems
dried up, and the flesh returns to the dust of death: this those
know who have commenced to tread the valley of the shadow
of death. Jesus, being a man, escaped none of the ills which
are allotted to man in death. He is indeed "Immanuel, God
with us," everywhere.

Believing this, let us tenderly feel how very near akin
to us our Lord Jesus has become. You have been ill, and you
have been parched with fever as He was, and then you too
have gasped out. "I thirst." Your path runs hard by that of
your Master. He said, "I thirst," in order that some one might
bring Him drink, even as you have wished to have a cooling
draught handed to you when you could not help yourself.
Can you help feeling how very near Jesus is to us when His
lips must be moistened with a sponge, and He must be so de-
pendent upon others as to ask drink from their hand? Next
time your fevered lips murmur, "I am very thirsty," you may
say to yourself, "Those are sacred words, for my Lord spoke
in that fashion."

The words, "I thirst," are a common voice in death chambers. We can never forget the painful scenes of which we have
been witness, when we have watched the dissolving of the
human frame. Some of those whom we loved very dearly we
have seen quite unable to help themselves; the death sweat
has been upon them, and this has been one of the marks of
their approaching dissolution, that they have been parched
with thirst, and could only mutter between their half-closed
lips, "Give me to drink." Ah, beloved, our Lord was so truly
man that all our griefs remind us of Him: the next time we
are thirsty we may gaze upon Him; and whenever we see a
friend faint and thirsting while dying we may behold our
Lord, dimly but truly mirrored in His members. How near
akin the thirsty Saviour is to us; let us love Him more and
more.

How great the love which led Him to such a condescension as this! Do not let us forget the infinite distance between

the Lord of glory on His throne and the Crucified dried up with thirst. A river of the water of life, pure as crystal, proceeds today out of the throne of God and of the Lamb, and yet once He condescended to say, "I thirst." He is Lord of fountains and all deeps, but not a cup of cold water was placed to His lips. Oh, if He had at any time said, "I thirst," before His angelic guards, they would surely have emulated the courage of the men of David when they cut their way to the well of Bethlehem that was within the gate, and drew water in jeopardy of their lives. Who among us would not willingly pour out his soul unto death if he might but give refreshment to the Lord? And yet He placed Himself for our sakes into a position of shame and suffering where none would wait upon Him, but when He cried, "I thirst," they gave Him vinegar to drink. Glorious stoop of our exalted Head! O Lord Jesus, we love Thee and we worship Thee! We would fain lift Thy name on high in grateful remembrance of the depths to which Thou didst descend!

While thus we admire His condescension, let our thoughts also turn with delight to His sure sympathy: for if Jesus said, "I thirst," then He knows all our frailities and woes. The next time we are in pain or are suffering depression of spirit we will remember that our Lord understands it all, for He has had practical, personal experience of it. Neither in torture of body nor in sadness of heart are we deserted by our Lord; His line is parallel with ours. The arrow which has lately pierced thee, my brother, was first stained with His blood. The cup of which you are made to drink, though it be very bitter, bears the mark of His lips about its brim. He has traversed the mournful way before you, and every footprint you leave in the sodden soil is stamped side by side with His footmarks. Let the sympathy of Christ, then, be fully believed in and deeply appreciated, since He said, "I thirst."

Henceforth, also, let us cultivate the spirit of resignation, for we may well rejoice to carry a cross which His shoulders have borne before us. Beloved, if our Master said, "I thirst," do we expect every day to drink of streams from Lebanon? He was innocent, and yet He thirsted; shall we marvel if guilty ones are now and then chastened? If He was so poor that His garments were stripped from Him, and He was hung up upon the tree, penniless and friendless, hungering and thirsting, will you henceforth groan and murmur because you bear the yoke of poverty and want? There is bread upon your table today, and there will be at least a cup of cold water to refresh you. You are not, therefore, so poor as He. Do not complain, then. Shall the servant be above his Master, or the disciple above his Lord? Let patience have her perfect work. You do suffer. Perhaps, dear sister, you carry about with you a gnawing disease which eats at your heart, but Jesus took our sicknesses, and His cup was more bitter than yours. In your chamber let the gasp of your Lord as He said, "I thirst," go through your ears, and as you hear it let it touch your heart and cause you to gird up yourself and say, "Doth He say, 'I thirst'? Then I will thirst with Him and not complain, I will suffer with Him and not murmur." The Redeemer's cry of "I thirst" is a solemn lesson of patience to His afflicted.

Once again, as we think of this "I thirst," which proves our Lord's humanity, let us resolve to shun no denials, but rather court them that we may be conformed to His image. May we not be half ashamed of our pleasures when *He* says, "I thirst"? May we not despise our loaded table while *He* is so neglected? Shall it ever be a hardship to be denied the satisfying draught when *He* said, "I thirst"? Shall carnal appetites be indulged and bodies pampered when Jesus cried, "I thirst"? What if the bread be dry, what if the medicine be nauseous; yet for His thirst there was no relief but gall and vinegar, and dare we complain? For His sake we may rejoice in self-denials and accept Christ and a crust as all we desire between here and heaven. A Christian living to indulge the base appetites of a brute beast, to eat and to drink almost to gluttony and drunkenness, is utterly unworthy of the name. The conquest of the appetites, the entire subjugation of the flesh, must be achieved, for before our great Exemplar said, "It is finished," wherein I think He reached the greatest height of all, He stood as only upon the next lower step to that elevation, and said, "I thirst." The power to suffer for another, the capacity to be self-denying even to an extreme to accomplish some great work for God — this is a thing to be sought after and must be gained before our work is done, and in this Jesus is before us our example and our strength.

Thus have I tried to spy out a measure of teaching, by using that one glass for the soul's eye, through which we look upon "I thirst" as the ensign of His true humanity.

II. Secondly, we shall regard these words, "I thirst," as

THE TOKEN OF HIS SUFFERING SUBSTITUTION

The great Surety says, "I thirst," because He is placed in the sinner's stead, and He must therefore undergo the penalty of sin for the ungodly. "My God, my God, why hast thou forsaken me?" points to the anguish of His soul; "I thirst" expresses in part the torture of His body; and they were both needful, because it is written of the God of justice that He is "able to destroy both soul and body in hell," and the pangs that are due to law are of both kinds, touching both heart and flesh. See, brethren, where sin begins, and mark that there it ends. It began with the mouth of appetite, when it was sinfully gratified, and it ends when a kindred appetite is graciously denied. Our first parents plucked forbidden fruit, and by eating slew the race. Appetite was the door of sin, and therefore in that point our Lord was put to pain. With "I thirst" the evil is destroyed and receives its expiation. I saw the other day the emblem of a serpent with its tail in its mouth, and if I carry it a little beyond the artist's intention the symbol may set forth appetite swallowing up itself. A carnal appetite of the body, the satisfaction of the desire for food, first brought us down under the first Adam, and now the pang of thirst, the denial of what the body craved for, restores us to our place.

Nor is this all. We know from experience that the present effect of sin in every man who indulges in it is thirst of soul. The mind of man is like the daughters of the horseleech, which cry forever, "Give, give." Metaphorically understood, thirst is dissatisfaction, the craving of the mind for something which it has not, but which it pines for. Our Lord says, "If any man thirst, let him come unto me and drink," that thirst being the result of sin in every ungodly man at this moment. Now Christ standing in the stead of the ungodly suffers thirst as a type of His enduring the result of sin. More solemn still is the reflection that according to our Lord's own teaching, thirst will also be the eternal result of sin, for He says concerning the rich glutton, "In hell he lift up his eyes, being in torment," and his prayer, which was denied him, was, "Father Abraham, send Lazarus, that he may dip the tip of his finger in water and cool my tongue, for I am tormented in this flame."

Now recollect, if Jesus had not thirsted, every one of us would have thirsted forever afar off from God, with an impassable gulf between us and heaven. Our sinful tongues, blistered by the fever of passion, must have burned forever had not His tongue been tormented with thirst in our stead. I suppose that the "I thirst" was uttered softly, so that perhaps only one and another who stood near the cross heard it at all; in contrast with the louder cry of *"Lama sabachthani"* and the triumphant shout of "It is finished": but that soft, expiring sigh, "I thirst," has ended for us the thirst which else, insatiably fierce, had preyed upon us throughout eternity. Oh, wondrous substitution of the just for the unjust, of God for man, of the perfect Christ for us guilty, hell-deserving rebels! Let us magnify and bless our Redeemer's name.

It seems to me very wonderful that this "I thirst" should be, as it were, the clearance of it all. He had no sooner said "I thirst," and sipped the vinegar, than He shouted, "It is finished"; and all was over: the battle was fought and the victory won forever, and our great Deliverer's thirst was the sign of His having smitten the last foe. The flood of His grief had passed the high-water mark, and began to be assuaged. The "I thirst" was the bearing of the last pang; what if I say it was the expression of the fact that His pangs had at last begun to cease, and their fury had spent itself, and left Him able to note His lesser pains? The excitement of a great struggle makes men forget thirst and faintness; it is only when all is over that they come back to themselves and note the spending of their strength. The great agony of being forsaken by God was over, and He felt faint when the strain was withdrawn.

I like to think of our Lord's saying, "It is finished," directly after He had exclaimed, "I thirst"; for these two voices come so naturally together. Our glorious Samson had been fighting our foes; heaps upon heaps He had slain His thousands, and now like Samson He was sore athirst. He sipped of the vinegar, and no sooner had He thrown off the thirst than He shouted like a conqueror, "It is finished," and quitted the field, covered with renown. Let us exult as we see our Substitute going through with His work even to the bitter end, and then with a *"Consummatum est"* returning to His Father, God. O souls, burdened with sin, rest here, and resting live.

III. We will now take the text in a third way, and may the Spirit of God instruct us once again. The utterance of "I thirst" brought out

A TYPE OF MAN'S TREATMENT OF HIS LORD

It was a confirmation of the Scripture testimony with regard to man's natural enmity to God. According to modern thought, man is a very fine and noble creature, struggling to become better. He is greatly to be commended and admired, for his sin is said to be a seeking after God, and his superstition is a struggling after light. Great and worshipful being that he is, truth is to be altered for him, the gospel is to be modulated to suit the tone of his various generations, and all the arrangements of the universe are to be rendered subservient to his interests. Justice must fly the field lest it be severe to so deserving a being; as for punishment, it must not be whispered to his ears polite. In fact, the tendency is to exalt man above God and give him the highest place.

But such is not the truthful estimate of man according to the Scriptures: there man is a fallen creature, with a carnal mind which cannot be reconciled to God; a worse than brutish creature, rendering evil for good, and treating his God with vile ingratitude. Alas, man is the slave and the dupe of Satan, and a black-hearted traitor to his God. Did not the prophecies say that man would give to his incarnate God gall to eat and vinegar to drink? It is done. He came to save, and man denied Him hospitality: at the first there was no room for Him at the inn, and at the last there was not one cool cup of water for Him to drink; but when He thirsted they gave Him vinegar to drink. This is man's treatment of His Saviour. Universal manhood, left to itself, rejects, crucifies, and mocks the Christ of God.

This was the act, too, of man at his best, when he is moved to pity; for it seems clear that he who lifted up the wet sponge to the Redeemer's lips, did it in compassion. I think that Roman soldiers meant well, at least well for a rough warrior with his little light and knowledge. He ran and filled a sponge with vinegar: it was the best way he knew of putting a few drops of moisture to the lips of One who was suffering so much; but though he felt a degree of pity, it was such as one might show to a dog; he felt no reverence, but mocked as he relieved. We read, "The soldiers also mocked him, offering him vinegar." When our Lord cried, "*Eloi, Eloi,*" and afterwards said, "I thirst," the persons around the cross said, "Let be, let us see whether Elias will come to save him," mocking Him; and according to Mark, he who gave the vinegar uttered much the same words. He pitied the sufferer, but he thought so little of Him that he joined in the voice of scorn.

Even when man compassionates the sufferings of Christ, and man would have ceased to be human if he did not, still he scorns Him; the very cup which man gives to Jesus is at once scorn and pity, for "the tender mercies of the wicked are cruel." See how man at his best mingles admiration of the Saviour's person with scorn of His claims; writing books to hold Him up as an example and at the same moment rejecting His deity; admitting that He was a wonderful Man, but denying His most sacred mission; extolling his ethical teaching and then trampling on His blood: thus giving Him drink, but that drink vinegar.

O my readers, beware of praising Jesus and denying His atoning sacrifice. Beware of rendering Him homage and dishonoring His name at the same time.

Alas, my brethren, I cannot say much on the score of man's cruelty to our Lord without touching myself and you. Have *we* not often given Him vinegar to drink? Did we not do so years ago before we knew Him? We used to melt when we heard about His sufferings, but we did not turn from our sins. We gave Him our tears and then grieved Him with our sins. We thought sometimes that we loved Him as we heard the story of His death, but we did not change our lives for His sake, nor put our trust in Him, and so we gave Him vinegar to drink. Nor does the grief end here, for have not the best works we have ever done, and the best feelings we have ever felt, and the best prayers we have ever offered, been tart and sour with sin? Can they be compared to generous wine? Are they not more like sharp vinegar? I wonder He has ever received them, as one marvels why He received this vinegar; and yet He has received them, and smiled upon us for presenting them. He knew once how to turn water into wine, and in matchless love He has often turned our sour drink-offerings into something sweet to Himself, though in themselves, I think, they have been the juice of sour grapes, sharp enough to set His teeth on edge. We may therefore come before Him, with all the rest of our race, when God subdues them to repentance by His love, and look on Him whom we have pierced, and mourn for Him as one that is in bitterness for His firstborn. We may well remember our faults this day.

> We, whose proneness to forget
> Thy dear love, on Olivet
> Bathed Thy brow with bloody sweat;
>
> We, whose sins, with awful power,
> Like a cloud did o'er Thee lower,
> In that God-excluding hour;
>
> We, who still, in thought and deed,
> Often hold the bitter reed
> To Thee, in Thy time of need.

I have touched that point very lightly because I want a little more time to dwell upon a fourth view of this scene. May the Holy Ghost help us to hear a fourth tuning of the dolorous music, "I thirst."

IV. I think, beloved friends, that the cry of "I thirst" was THE MYSTICAL EXPRESSION OF THE DESIRE OF HIS HEART

"I thirst." I cannot think that natural thirst was all He felt. He thirsted for water doubtless, but His soul was thirsty in a higher sense; indeed, He seems only to have spoken that the Scriptures might be fulfilled as to the offering Him vinegar. Always was He in harmony with Himself, and His body was always expressive of His soul's cravings as well as of its own longings. "I thirst" meant that His heart was thirsting to save men. This thirst had been on Him from the earliest of His earthly days. "Wist ye not," said He, while yet a boy, "that I must be about my Father's business?" Did He not tell His disciples, "I have a baptism to be baptized with, and how am I straitened till it be accomplished?" He thirsted to pluck us from between the jaws of hell, to pay our redemption price, and set us free from the eternal condemnation which hung over us; and when on the cross the work was almost done, His thirst was not assuaged, and could not be till He could say, "It is finished."

It is almost done, Thou Christ of God; Thou hast almost saved Thy people; there remaineth but one thing more, that Thou shouldst actually die, and hence Thy strong desire to come to the end and complete Thy labor. Thou wast still straitened till the last pang was left and the last word spoken to complete the full redemption, and hence they cry, "I thirst."

Beloved, there is now upon our Master, and there always has been, a thirst after the love of His people. Do you not remember how that thirst of His was strong in the old days of the prophet? Call to mind His complaint in the fifth chapter of Isaiah, "Now will I sing to my wellbeloved a song of my beloved touching his vineyard. My wellbeloved hath a vineyard in a very fruitful hill: and he fenced it, and gathered out the stones thereof, and planted it with the choicest vine, and built a tower in the midst of it, and also made a winepress therein." What was He looking for from His vineyard and its winepress? What but the juice of the vine that He might be refreshed? "And he looked that it should bring forth grapes, and it brought forth wild grapes" — vingear, and not wine; sourness, and not sweetness. So He was thirsting then.

According to the sacred canticle of love, in the fifth chapter of the Song of Songs, we learn that when He drank in those olden times it was in the garden of His church that He was refreshed. What doth He say? "I am come into my garden, my sister, my spouse: I have gathered my myrrh with my spice; I have eaten my honeycomb with my honey; I have drunk my wine with my milk; eat, O friends; drink, yea, drink abundantly, O beloved." In the same song He speaks of His church, and says, "The roof of thy mouth is as the best wine for My beloved, that goeth down sweetly, causing the lips of those that are asleep to speak."

And yet again in the eighth chapter the Bride saith, "I would cause thee to drink of spiced wine of the juice of my pomegranate." Yes, He loves to be with His people; they are the garden where He walks for refreshment, and their love, their graces, are the milk and wine of which He delights to drink. Christ was always thirsty to save men, and to be loved of men; and we see a type of His life-long desire when, being weary, He sat thus on the well and said to the woman of Samaria, "Give me to drink." There was a deeper meaning in His

words then she dreamed of, as a verse further down fully
proves, when He said to His disciples, "I have meat to eat
that ye know not of." He derived spiritual refreshment from
the winning of that woman's heart to Himself.

And now, brethren, our blessed Lord has at this time a
thirst for communion with each one of you who are His people,
not because you can do Him good, but because He can do you
good. He thirsts to bless you and to receive your grateful love
in return; He thirsts to see you looking with believing eye to
His fulness, and holding out your emptiness that He may supply it. He saith, "Behold, I stand at the door and knock." Why
does He knock? It is that He may eat and drink with you, for
He promises that if we open to Him He will enter in and sup
with us and we with Him. He is thirsty still, you see, for our
poor love, and surely, we cannot deny it to Him. Come, let us
pour out full flagons, until His joy is fulfilled in us.

And what makes Him love us so? Ah, that I cannot tell,
except his own great love. He *must* love; it is His nature. He must
love His chosen whom He has once begun to love, for He is
the same yesterday, today, and forever. His great love makes
Him thirst to have us much nearer than we are; He will never
be satisfied till all His redeemed are beyond gunshot of the
enemy. I will give you one of His thirsty prayers — "Father,
I will that they also whom thou hast given me be with me
where I am, that they may behold my glory." He wants you,
brother; He wants you, dear sister; He longs to have you
wholly to Himself. Come to Him in prayer, come to Him in
fellowship, come to Him by perfect consecration, come to Him
by surrendering your whole being to the sweet mysterious in-
fluences of His Spirit. Sit at His feet with Mary, lean on His
breast with John; yea, come with the spouse in the song and
say, "Let him kiss me with the kisses of his mouth, for his
love is better than wine." He calls for that: will you not give
it to Him? Are you so frozen at heart that not a cup of cold
water can be melted for Jesus? Are you lukewarm? O brother,
if He says, "I thirst" and you bring Him a lukewarm heart,

that is worse than vinegar, for He has said, "I will spue thee out of my mouth." He can receive vinegar, but not lukewarm love. Come, bring Him your warm heart, and let Him drink from that purified chalice as much as He wills. Let all your love be His. I know He loves to receive from you, because He delights even in a cup of cold water that you give to one of His disciples; how much more will He delight in the giving of your whole self to Him? Therefore while He thirsts give Him to drink this day.

V. Lastly, the cry of "I thirst" is to us

THE PATTERN OF OUR DEATH WITH HIM

Know ye not, beloved — for I speak to those who know the Lord — that ye are crucified together with Christ? Well, then, what means this cry, "I thirst," but this, that we should thirst too? We do not thirst after the old manner wherein we were bitterly afflicted, for He hath said, "He that drinketh of this water shall never thirst": but now we covet a new thirst, a refined and heavenly appetite, a craving for our Lord. O thou blessed Master, if we are indeed nailed up to the tree with Thee, give us to thirst after Thee with a thirst which only the cup of "the new covenant in thy blood" can ever satisfy.

Certain philosophers have said that they love the pursuit of truth even better than the knowledge of truth. I differ from them greatly, but I will say this, that next to the actual enjoyment of my Lord's presence, I love to hunger and to thirst after Him. Rutherford used words somewhat to this effect. "I thirst for my Lord and this is joy; a joy which no man taketh from me. Even if I may not come at Him, yet shall I be full of consolation, for it is heaven to thirst after Him, and surely He will never deny a poor soul liberty to admire Him, and adore Him, and thirst after Him." As for myself, I would grow more and more insatiable after my divine Lord, and when I have much of Him I would still cry for more; and then for

more, and still for more. My heart shall not be content till
He is all in all to me; and I am altogether lost in Him.

O to be enlarged in soul so as to take deeper draughts of
His sweet love, for our heart cannot have enough. One would
wish to be as the spouse, who, when she had already been
feasting in the banqueting-house, and had found His fruit
sweet to her taste, so that she was overjoyed, yet cried out,
"Stay me with flagons, comfort me with apples, for I am sick
of love." She craved full flagons of love though she was already overpowered by it. This is a kind of sweet whereof if
a man hath much he must have more, and when he hath more
he is under a still greater necessity to receive more, and so
on, his appetite for ever growing by that which it feeds upon,
till he is filled with all the fulness of God. "I thirst," — aye,
this is my soul's word with the Lord. Borrowed from His lips
it well suiteth my mouth.

> I thirst, but not as once I did,
> The vain delights of earth to share;
> Thy wounds, Emmanuel, all forbid
> That I shall seek my pleasures there.
>
> Dear fountains of delight unknown!
> No longer sink below the brim;
> But overflow, and pour me down
> A living and life-giving stream.

Jesus thirsted, then let us thirst in this dry and thirsty
land where no water is. Even as the hart panteth after the
water brooks, our souls would thirst after Thee, O God.

Beloved, let us thirst for the souls of our fellowmen. I
have already told you that such was our Lord's mystical desire; let it be ours also. Brother, thirst to have your children
saved. Brother, thirst, I pray you, to have your workpeople
saved. Sister, thirst for the salvation of your class, thirst for
the redemption of your family, thirst for the conversion of
your husband. We ought all to have a longing for conversion.
Is it so with each one of you? If not, bestir yourselves at
once. Fix your hearts upon some unsaved one, and thirst until

he is saved. It is the way whereby many shall be brought to Christ, when this blessed soul-thirst of true Christian charity shall be upon those who are themselves saved. Remember how Paul said, "I say the truth in Christ, I lie not, my conscience also bearing me witness in the Holy Ghost, that I have great heaviness and continual sorrow in my heart. For I could wish that myself were accursed from Christ for my brethern, my kinsmen according to the flesh." He would have sacrificed himself to save his countrymen, so heartily did he desire their eternal welfare. Let this mind be in you also.

As for yourselves, thirst after perfection. Hunger and thirst after righteousness, for you shall be filled. Hate sin, and heartily loath it; but thirst to be holy as God is holy, thirst to be like Christ, thirst to bring glory to His sacred name by complete conformity to His will.

May the Holy Ghost work in you the complete pattern of Christ crucified, and to Him shall be praise for ever and ever. Amen.

The Sixth Word:

(VICTORY)

When Jesus therefore had received the vinegar, he said, It is finished: and he bowed his head, and gave up the Ghost.   John 19:30

MY BRETHREN, I WOULD HAVE YOU ATTENTIVELY OBSERVE THE singular clearness, power, and quickness of the Saviour's mind in the last agonies of death. When pains and groans attend the last hour, they frequently have the effect of decomposing the mind, so that it is not possible for the dying man to collect his thoughts, or having collected them, to utter them so that they can be understood by others. In no case could we expect a remarkable exercise of memory, or a profound judgment upon deep subjects from an expiring man. But the Redeemer's last acts were full of wisdom and prudence, although His sufferings were beyond all measure excruciating.

Notice how clearly He perceived the significance of every type! How plainly He could read with dying eye those divine symbols which the eyes of angels could only desire to look into! He saw the secrets which have bewildered sages and astonished seers, all fulfilled in His own body. Nor must we fail to observe the power and comprehensiveness by which He grasped the chain which binds the shadowy past with the sunlit present. We must not forget the brilliance of that intelligence which threaded all the ceremonies and sacrifices on one string of thought, beheld all the prophecies as one great revelation, and all the promises as the heralds of one person, and then said of the whole, " 'It is finished,' finished in me."

What quickness of mind was that which enabled Him to traverse all the centuries of prophecy; to penetrate the eternity of the covenant, and then to anticipate the eternal glories! And all this when He is mocked by multitudes of enemies, and when His hands and feet are nailed to the cross! What force of mind must the Saviour have possessed, to soar above those Alps of Agony, which touched the very clouds. In what a singular mental condition must He have been during the period of His crucifixion, to be able to review the whole roll of inspiration!

Now, this remark may not seem to be of any great value, but I think its value lies in certain inferences that may be drawn from it. We have sometimes heard it said, "How could Christ, in so short a time, bear suffering which should be equivalent to the torments — the eternal torments of hell?" Our reply is, we are not capable of judging what the Son of God might do even in a moment, much less what He might do and what He might suffer in His life and in His death.

It has been frequently affirmed by persons who have been rescued from drowning, that the mind of a drowning man is singularly active. One who, after being some time in the water, was at last painfully restored, said that the whole of his history seemed to come before his mind while he was sinking, and that if any one had asked him how long he had been in the water, he should have said twenty years, whereas he had only been there for a moment or two. The wild romance of Mahomet's journey upon Alborak is not an unfitting illustration. He affirmed that when the angel came in vision to take him on his celebrated journey to Jerusalem, he went through all the seven heavens, and saw all the wonders thereof, and yet he was gone so short a time, that though the angel's wing had touched a basin of water when they started, they returned soon enough to prevent the water from being spilt.

The long dream of the epileptic impostor may really have occupied but a second of time.

The intellect of mortal man is such that, if God wills it, when it is in certain states, it can think out centuries of thought at once; it can go through in one instant what we should have supposed would have taken years upon years of time for it to know or feel. We think, therefore, that from the Saviour's singular clearness and quickness of intellect upon the cross, it is very possible that He did in the space of two or three hours endure not only the agony which might have been contained in centuries, but even an equivalent for that which might be comprehended in everlasting punishment. At any rate, it is not for us to say that it could not be so. When the Deity is arrayed in manhood, then manhood becomes omnipotent to suffer; and just as the feet of Christ were once almighty to tread the seas, so now was His whole body become almighty to dive into the great waters, to endure an immersion in "unknown agonies." Do not, I pray you, let us attempt to measure Christ's sufferings by the finite line of your own ignorant reason, but let us know and believe that what He endured there was accepted by God as an equivalent for all our pains, and therefore it could not have been a trifle, but must have been all that Hart conceived it to be, when he says He bore —

> All that incarnate God could bear,
> With strength enough, but none to spare.

The remainder of the chapter will, I have no doubt, more fully illustrate the remark with which I have commenced; let us proceed to it at once. First, *let us hear the text and understand it;* then *let us hear it and wonder at it;* and then, thirdly, *let us hear it and proclaim it.*

I. LET US HEAR THE TEXT AND UNDERSTAND IT

The Son of God has been made man. He has lived a life of perfect virtue and of total self-denial. He has been all that life long despised and rejected of men, a man of sorrows and acquainted with grief. His enemies have been legion; His friends have been few, and those few faithless. He is at last delivered over into the hands of them that hate Him. He is arrested while in the act of prayer; He is arraigned before both the spiritual and temporal courts. He is robed in mockery, and then unrobed in shame. He is set upon His throne in scorn, and then tied to the pillar in cruelty. He is declared innocent, and yet He is delivered up by the judge who ought to have preserved Him from His persecutors. He is dragged through the streets of that Jerusalem which had killed the prophets, and would now crimson itself with the blood of the prophets' Master. He is brought to the cross; He is nailed fast to the cruel wood. The sun burns Him. His cruel wounds increase the fever. God forsakes Him. "My God, my God, why hast thou forsaken me?" contains the concentrated anguish of the world. While He hangs there in mortal conflict with sin and Satan, His heart is broken, His limbs are dislocated. Heaven fails Him, for the sun is veiled in darkness. Earth forsakes Him, for "his disciples forsook him and fled."

He looks everywhere, and there is none to help; He casts His eye around, and there is no man that can share His toil. He treads the winepress alone; and of the people there is none with Him. On, on, He goes, steadily determined to drink the last dreg of that cup which must not pass from Him if His Father's will be done. At last He cries — "It is finished," and He gives up the ghost. Hear it, Christians, hear this shout of triumph as it rings today with all the freshness and force which it had centuries ago! Hear it from the Sacred Word, and from the Saviour's lips, and may the Spirit of God open your ears that you may hear as the learned, and understand what you hear!

1. What meant the Saviour, then, by this—"It is finished"? He meant, first of all, *that all the types, promises, and prophecies were now fully accomplished in Him* Those who are acquainted with the original will find that the words, "It is finished," occur twice within three verses. In the twenty-eighth

verse, we have the word in the Greek; it is translated in our
version "accomplished," but there it stands—"After this, Jesus
knowing that all things were now *finished, that the Scripture
might be fulfilled*, saith, I thirst." And then He afterwards
said, "It is finished." This leads us to see His meaning very
clearly, that all the Scripture was now fulfilled, that when He
said, "It is finished," the whole book, from the first to the last,
in both the law and the prophets, was finished in Him. There
is not a single jewel of promise, from that first emerald which
fell on the threshold of Eden, to that last sapphire-stone of
Malachi, which was not set in the breast-plate of the true High
Priest. Nay, there is not a type, from the red heifer down-
ward to the turtle-dove, from the hyssop upwards to Solomon's temple itself, which was not fulfilled in Him; and not
a prophecy, whether spoken on Chebar's bank, or on the
shores of Jordan; not a dream of wise men, whether they had
received it in Babylon, or in Samaria, or in Judea, which was
not now fully wrought out in Christ Jesus.

What a wonderful thing it is, that a mass of promises, and
prophecies, and types, apparently so heterogeneous, should all
be accomplished in one Person! Take away Christ for one
moment, and I will give the Old Testament to any wise man
living, and say to him, "Take this; this is a problem; go home
and construct in your imagination an ideal character who
shall exactly fit all that which is herein foreshadowed; remember, he must be a prophet like unto Moses, and yet a champion like Joshua; he must be an Aaron and a Melchisedek;
he must be both David and Solomon, Noah and Jonah, Judah
and Joseph. Nay, he must not only be the lamb that was slain,
and the scape-goat that was not slain, the turtle-dove that was
dipped in blood, and the priest who slew the bird, but he must
be the altar, the tabernacle, the mercy seat, and the shew-
bread." Nay, to puzzle this wise man further, we remind him
of prophecies so apparently contradictory, that one would
think they never could meet in one man. Such as these, "All
kings shall fall down before him, and all nations shall serve

him;" and yet, "He is despised and rejected of men." He must begin by showing a man born of a virgin mother — "A virgin shall conceive and bear a son." He must be a man without spot or blemish, but yet one upon whom the Lord doth cause to meet the iniquities of us all. He must be a glorious one, a Son of David, but yet a root out of a dry ground.

Now, I write it boldly, if all the greatest intellects of all the ages could set themselves to work out this problem, to invent another key to the types and prophecies, they could not do it. I see you, wise men, are poring over these hieroglyphs; one suggests one key, and it opens two or three of the figures, but you cannot proceed, for the next one puts you at a nonplus. Another learned man suggests another clue, but that fails most where it is most needed, and another, and another, and thus these wondrous hieroglyphs traced of old by Moses in the wilderness, must be left unexplained, till one comes forward and proclaims, "The cross of Christ and the Son of God incarnate," then the whole is clear, so that he that runs may read, and a child may understand. Blessed Saviour! In Thee we see everything fulfilled, which God spoke of old by the prophets; in Thee we discover everything carried out in substance, which God had set forth for us in the dim mist of sacrificial smoke. Glory be unto Thy name! "It is finished" — everything is summed up in Thee.

2. But the words have richer meaning! Not only were all types, and prophecies, and promises thus finished in Christ, but *all the typical sacrifices of the old Jewish law were now abolished as well as explained.* They were finished — finished in Him.

Will you imagine for a minute the saints in heaven looking down upon what was done on earth — Abel and his friends who had long ago before the Flood been sitting in the glories above? They watch while God lights star after star in heaven. Promise after promise flashes light upon the thick darkness of earth. They see Abraham come, and they look down and wonder while they see God revealing Christ to Abraham in the person of Isaac. They gaze just as the angels do, desiring to look into the mystery. From the times of Noah, Abraham, Isaac, and Jacob, they see altars smoking, recognitions of the fact that man is guilty, and the spirits before the throne say, "Lord, when will sacrifices finish? When will blood no more be shed?" The offering of bloody sacrifices soon increases. It is now carried on by men ordained for the purpose. Aaron and the high priests, and the Levites, every morning and every evening offer a lamb, while great sacrifices are offered on special occasions. Bullocks groan, rams bleed, the necks of doves are wrung, and all the while the saints are crying, "O Lord, how long? When shall the sacrifice cease?" Year after year the high priest goes within the veil and sprinkles the mercy seat with blood; the next year sees him do the same, and the next, and again, and again, and again. David offers hecatombs, Solomon slaughters tens of thousands, Hezekiah offers rivers of oil, Josiah gives thousands of the fat of fed beasts, and the spirits of the just say, "Will it never be complete? Will the sacrifice never be finished? Must there always be a remembrance of sin? Will not the last High Priest soon come? Will not the order and line of Aaron soon lay aside its labor, because the whole is finished?" Not yet, not yet, ye spirits of the just, for after the captivity the slaughter of victims still remains.

But lo, He comes! Gaze more intently than before — He comes who is to close the line of priests! Lo! there He stands, clothed — not now with linen ephod, not with ringing bells, nor with sparkling jewels on His breastplate — but arrayed in human flesh He stands, His cross His altar, His body and His soul the victim, Himself the priest, and lo! before His God He offers up His own soul within the veil of thick darkness which hath covered Him from the sight of men. Presenting His own blood, He enters within the veil, sprinkles it there, and coming forth from the midst of the darkness, He looks down on the astonished earth, and upward to expectant heavens, and cries,

"It is finished! *It is* finished!" — that for which you looked so long, is fully achieved and perfected forever.

3. The Saviour meant, we do not doubt that in this moment *His perfect obedience was finished.* It was necessary, in order that man might be saved, that the law of God should be kept, for no man can see God's face except he be perfect in righteousness. Christ undertook to keep God's law for His people, to obey its every mandate, and preserve its every statute intact. Throughout the first years of His life He privately obeyed, honoring His father and His mother; during the next three years He publicly obeyed God, spending and being spent in His service, till if you would know what a man would be whose life was wholly conformed to the law of God, you may see him in Christ.

> My dear Redeemer and my Lord,
> I read my duty in thy word,
> But in thy life the law appears
> *Drawn out in living characters.*

It needed nothing to complete the perfect virtue of life but the entire obedience of death. He who would serve God must be willing not only to give all his soul and his strength while he lives, but he must stand prepared to resign life when it shall be for God's glory. Our perfect Substitute put the last stroke upon His work by dying, and therefore He claims to be absolved from further debt, for "it is finished." Yes, glorious Lamb of God, it is finished! Thou hast been tempted in all points like as we are, yet hast thou sinned in none! It *was* finished, for the last arrow out of Satan's quiver had been shot at Thee; the last blasphemous insinuation, the last wicked temptation had spent its fury on Thee; the prince of this world had surveyed Thee from head to foot, within and without, but he had found nothing in Thee. Now Thy trial is over, Thou hast finished the work which Thy Father gave Thee to do, and so finished it that hell itself cannot accuse Thee of a flaw. And now, looking upon Thine entire obedience, Thou sayest, "It is finished," and we Thy people believe most joyously that it is even so.

Brothers and sisters, this is more than you or I could have said if Adam had never fallen. If we had been in the garden of Eden today, we could never have boasted a finished righteousness, since a creature can never finish its obedience. As long as a creature lives, it is bound to obey, and as long as a free agent exists on earth it would be in danger of violating the vow of its obedience. If Adam had been in paradise from the first day until now, he might fall tomorrow. Left to himself there would be no reason why that king of nature should not yet be uncrowned. But Christ the Creator, who finished creation, has perfected redemption. God can ask no more. The law has received all its claims; the largest extent of justice cannot demand another hour's obedience. It is done; it is complete; the last throw of the shuttle is over, and the robe is woven from the top throughout. Let us rejoice, then, in this that the Master meant by His dying cry that His perfect righteousness wherewith He covers us was finished.

4. But next, the Saviour meant *that the satisfaction which He rendered to the justice of God was finished.* The debt was now, to the last farthing, all discharged. The atonement and propitiation were made once for all, and forever, by the one offering made in His body on the tree. There was the cup; hell was in it. The Saviour drank it — not a sip and then a pause; not a draught and then a ceasing; but He drained it till there is not a dreg left for any of His people. The great ten-thonged whip of the law was worn out upon His back; there is no lash left with which to smite one for whom Jesus died. The great cannonade of God's justice has exhausted all its ammunition; there is nothing left to be hurled against a child of God. Sheathed is thy sword, O Justice! Silenced is thy thunder, O Law! There remains nothing now of all the griefs, and pains, and agonies which chosen sinners ought to have suffered for their sins, for Christ has endured all for His own beloved, and "it is finished."

Brethren, *it is more than the damned in hell can ever say.* If you and I had been constrained to make satisfaction to God's justice by being sent to hell, we never could have said, "It is finished." Christ has paid the debt which all the torments of eternity could not have paid. Lost souls, you suffer today as you have suffered for ages past, but God's justice is not satisfied; His law is not fully magnified. And when time shall fail, and eternity shall have been flying on, still forever, forever, the uttermost farthing never having been paid, the chastisement for sin must fall upon unpardoned sinners. But Christ has done what all the flames of the pit could not do in all eternity; He has magnified the law and made it honorable, and now from the cross He cries — "It is finished."

5. Once again: when He said, "It is finished," *Jesus had totally destroyed the power of Satan, of sin, and of death.* The champion had entered the lists to do battle for our soul's redemption, against all our foes. He met Sin. Horrible, terrible, all-but omnipotent Sin nailed Him to the cross; but in that deed, Christ nailed Sin also to the tree. There they both did hang together—Sin, and Sin's destroyer. Sin destroyed Christ, and by that destruction Christ destroyed Sin.

Next came the second enemy, Satan. He assaulted Christ with all his hosts. Calling up his myriads from every corner and quarter of the universe, he said, "Awake, arise, or be forever fallen! Here is our great enemy who has sworn to bruise my head; now let us bruise his heel!" They shot their hellish darts into His heart; they poured their boiling cauldrons on His brain; they emptied their venom into His veins; they spat their insinuations into His face; they hissed their devilish fears into His ear. He stood alone, the Lion of the tribe of Judah, hounded by all the dogs of hell. Our Champion quailed not, but used His holy weapons, striking right and left with all the power of God-supported manhood. On came the hosts; volley after volley was discharged against Him. No mimic thunders were these, but such as might shake the very gates of hell. The Conqueror steadily advanced, overturning their ranks, dashing in pieces His enemies, breaking the bow and cutting the spear in sunder, and burning the chariots in the fire, while

He cried, "In the name of God will I destroy you!" At last,
foot to foot, He met the champion of hell, and now our David
fought with Goliath. Not long was the struggle; thick was the
darkness which gathered round them both; but He who is the
Son of God as well as the Son of Mary, knew how to smite
the fiend, and He did smite him with divine fury, till, having
despoiled him of his armor, having quenched his fiery darts,
and broken his head, He cried, "It is finished!" and sent the
fiend, bleeding and howling, down to hell. We can imagine him
pursued by the eternal Saviour, who exclaims

> Traitor!
> My bolt shalt find and pierce thee through,
> Though under hell's profoundest wave
> Thou div'st, to seek a shelt'ring grave.

His thunderbolt overtook the fiend, and grasping him with
both his hands, the Saviour drew around him the great chain.
The angels brought the royal chariot from on high, to whose
wheels the captive fiend was bound. Lash the coursers up the
everlasting hills! Spirits made perfect come forth to meet Him.
Hymn the Conqueror who drags death and hell behind him,
and leads captivity captive! "Lift up your heads, O ye gates,
and be ye lifted up, ye everlasting doors, that the King of
glory may come in!" But stay; ere He enters, let Him be rid
of this His burden. Lo! He takes the fiend, and hurls him
down through illimitable night, broken, bruised, with his
power destroyed, bereft of his crown, to lie forever howling
in the pit of hell.

Thus, when the Saviour cried, "It is finished," He had defeated sin and Satan; nor less had He vanquished Death. Death
had come against him, as Christmas Evans puts it, with his
fiery dart, which he struck right through the Saviour, till the
point fixed in the cross, and when he tried to pull it out
again, he left the sting behind. What could he do more? He
was disarmed. Then Christ set some of his prisoners free; for
many of the saints arose and were seen of many: then He said
to him, "Death, I take from thee thy keys; you must live for

a little while to be the warder of those beds in which my saints shall sleep, but give Me thy keys." And lo! the Saviour stands today with the keys of death hanging at His girdle, and He waits until the hour shall come of which no man knows; when the trump of the archangel shall ring like the silver trumpets of Jubilee, and then He shall say, "Let My captives go free." Then shall the tombs be opened in virtue of Christ's death, and the very bodies of the saints shall live again in an eternity of glory.

II. Secondly,

Let Us Hear and Wonder

Let us perceive what mighty things were effected and secured by these words, "It is finished." Thus He *ratified the covenant.* That covenant was signed and sealed before, and in all things it was ordered well, but when Christ said, "It is finished," then the covenant was made doubly sure; when the blood of Christ's heart bespattered the divine roll, then it could never be reversed, nor could one of its ordinances be broken nor one of its stipulations fail. You know the covenant was on this wise. God covenants on His part that He would give Christ to see of the travail of His soul; that all who were given to Him should have new hearts and right spirits; that they should be washed from sin and should enter into life through Him.

Christ's side of the covenant was this, "Father, I will do Thy will; I will pay the ransom to the last jot and tittle; I will give Thee perfect obedience and complete satisfaction." Now if this second part of the covenant had never been fulfilled, the first part would have been invalid, but when Jesus said, "It is finished," then there was nothing left to be performed on His part, and now the covenant is all on one side. It is God's "I will," and "They shall." "A new heart will I give you, and a right spirit will I put within you." "I will sprinkle clean water upon you and ye shall be clean." "From all your iniquities will I cleanse you." "I will lead you by a way that ye

know not." "I will surely bring them in." The covenant that
day was ratified.

When Christ said, "It is finished," *His Father was honored,
and divine justice was fully displayed.* The Father always did
love His people. Do not think that Christ died to make God
the Father loving. He always had loved them from before the
foundation of the world, but — "It is finished," took away the
barriers which were in the Father's way. He would, as a God
of love, and now He could as a God of justice, bless poor sinners. From that day the Father is well pleased to receive sinners to His bosom. When Christ said, "It is finished," *He Himself was glorified.* Then on His head descended the all-glorious
crown. Then did the Father give to Him honors, which He had
not before. He had honor as God, but as man He was despised
and rejected; now as God and man Christ was made to sit
down for ever on His Father's throne, crowned with honor
and majesty. Then, too, by "It is finished," *the Spirit was
procured for us.*

> 'Tis by the merit of His death
> Who hung upon the tree,
> The Spirit is sent down to breathe
> On such dry bones as we.

Then the Spirit which Christ had aforetime promised perceived a new and living way by which He could come to dwell
in the hearts of men, and men might come up to dwell with
Him above.

That day too, when Christ said — "It is finished," *the
words had effect on heaven.* Then the walls of chrysolite stood
fast; then the jasper-light of the pearly-gated city shone like
the light of seven days. Before, the saints had been saved as
it were on credit. They had entered heaven, God having faith
in His Son Jesus. Had not Christ finished His work, surely
they must have left their shining spheres, and suffered in their
own persons for their own sins. I might represent heaven, if
my imagination might be allowed a moment, as being ready to
totter if Christ had not finished his work; its stones would
have been unloosed; massive and stupendous though its bas-

tions are, yet had they fallen as earthly cities reel under the throes of earthquake. But Christ said, "It is finished," and oath, and covenant, and blood set fast the dwelling-place of the redeemed, made their mansions safely and eternally their own, and bade their feet stand immovably upon the rock.

Nay, more, that word, "It is finished!" took effect in the gloomy caverns and depths of hell. Then Satan bit his iron bands in rage, howling, "I am defeated by the very man whom I thought to overcome; my hopes are blasted; never shall an elect one come into my prison-house, never a blood-bought one be found in my abode." Lost souls mourned that day, for they said — " 'It is finished!' for if Christ Himself, the Substitute, could not be permitted to go free till He had finished all His punishment, then we shall never be free." It was their double death-knell, for they said, "Alas for us! Justice, which would not suffer the Saviour to escape, will never suffer us to be at liberty. It is finished with Him, and therefore it shall never be finished for us."

That day, too, the earth had a gleam of sunlight cast over her which she had never known before. Then her hill tops began to glisten with the rising of the sun, and though her valleys still are clothed with darkness, and men wander hither and thither, and grope in the noonday as in the night, yet that sun is rising, climbing still its heavenly steeps, never to set, and soon shall its rays penetrate through the thick mists and clouds, and every eye shall see Him, and every heart be made glad with His light. The words "It is finished!" consolidated heaven, shook hell, comforted earth, delighted the Father, glorified the Son, brought down the Spirit, and confirmed the everlasting covenant to all the chosen seed.

III. And now I come to my last point —

Let Us Publish It

Children of God, ye who by faith received Christ as your all in all, tell it every day of your lives that "it is finished." Go and tell it to those who are torturing themselves, thinking through obedience and mortification to offer satisfaction. Yonder heathen is about to throw himself down upon the spikes. Stay, poor man! wherefore wouldst thou bleed, for "it is finished." Yonder Fakir is holding his hand erect till the nails grow through the flesh, torturing himself with fastings and with self-denials. Cease, cease, poor wretch, from all these pains, for "it is finished!" In all parts of the earth there are those who think that the misery of the body and the soul may be an atonement for sin. Rush to them, stay them in their madness and say to them, "Wherefore do ye this? 'It is finished.'" All the pains that God asks, Christ has suffered; all the satisfaction by way of agony in the flesh that the law demanded, Christ has already endured. "It is finished!" And when you have done this, go you next to the benighted votaries of Rome, when you see the priests with their backs to the people, offering every day the pretended sacrifice of the mass, and lifting up the host on high — a sacrifice, they say — "an unbloody sacrifice for the quick and the dead," — cry, "Cease, false priest, cease! for 'it is finished!' Cease, false worshiper, cease to bow, for 'it is finished!'" God neither asks nor accepts any other sacrifice than that which Christ offered once for all upon the cross.

Go next to the foolish among your own countrymen who call themselves Protestants, but who are Papists after all, who think by their gifts and their gold, by their prayers and their vows, by their church-goings and their chapel-goings, by their baptisms and their confirmations, to make themselves fit for God; and say to them, "Stop, 'it is finished'; God needs not this of you. He has received enough; why will you pin your rags to the fine linen of Christ's righteousness? Why will you add your counterfeit farthing to the costly ransom which Christ has paid into the treasure-house of God? Cease from your pains, your doings, your performances, for 'it is finished'; Christ has done it all."

This one text is enough to blow the Vatican to the four winds. Lay but this beneath popery, and like a train of gunpowder beneath a rock, it shall blast it into the air. This is a thunderclap against all human righteousness. Only let this come like a two-edged sword, and your good works and your fine performance are soon cast away.

"It is finished." Why improve on what is finished! Why add to that which is complete! The Bible is finished, and he that adds to it shall have his name taken out of the Book of Life, and out of the holy city: Christ's atonement is finished, and he that adds to that must expect the selfsame doom. And when ye shall have told it thus to the ears of men of every nation and of every tribe, tell it to all poor despairing souls. You find them on their knees, crying, "O God, what can I do to make recompense for my offences?" Tell them, "It is finished"; the recompense is made already. "O God!" they say, "how can I ever get a righteousness in which Thou canst accept such a worm as I am?" Tell them, "It is finished"; their righteousness is wrought out already; they have no need to trouble themselves about adding to it, if "it is finished."

Go to the poor, despairing wretch, who has given himself up, not for death merely, but for damnation — he who says, "I cannot escape from sin, and I cannot be saved from its punishment." Say to him, "Sinner, the way of salvation is finished once for all."

And if ye meet some professed Christians in doubts and fears, tell them, "It is finished." Why, we have hundreds and thousands that really are converted, who do not know that "it is finished." They never know that they are safe. They do not know that "it is finished." They think they have faith today, but perhaps they may become unbelieving tomorrow. They do not know that "it is finished." They hope God will accept them, if they do some things, forgetting that the way of acceptance is finished. God as much accepts a sinner who only believed in Christ five minutes ago, as he will a saint who has known and loved Him eighty years, for He does not accept men because of anything they do or feel, but simply and only for what Christ did, and that is finished.

Oh! poor hearts! some of you do love the Saviour in a measure, but blindly. You are thinking that you must be this, and attain to that, and then you may be assured that you are saved. Oh! you may be assured of it today — if you believe in Christ you are saved. "But I feel imperfections." Yes, but what of that? God does not regard your imperfections, but He covers them with Christ's righteousness. He sees them to remove them, but not to lay them to your charge. "Ay, but I cannot be what I would be." But what if you can not? Yet God does not look at you, as what you are in yourself, but as what you are in Christ.

Come with me, poor soul, and you and I will stand together while the tempest gathers, for we are not afraid. How sharp that lightning flash! but yet we tremble not. How terrible that peal of thunder! and yet we are not alarmed, and why? Is there anything in us why we should escape? No, but we are standing beneath the cross—that precious cross, which like some noble lightning-conductor in the storm, takes itself all the death from the lightning, and all the fury from the tempest. We are safe. Loud mayest thou roar, O thundering law, and terribly mayest thou flash, O avenging justice! We can look up with calm delight to all the tumult of the elements, for we are safe beneath the cross.

Come with me again. There is a royal banquet spread; the King Himself sits at the table, and angels are the servitors. Let us enter. And we do enter, and we sit down and eat and drink; but how dare we do this? Our righteousnesses are as filthy rags — how could we venture to come here? Oh, because the filthy rags are not ours any longer. We have renounced our own righteousness, and therefore we have renounced the filthy rags, and now today we wear the royal garments of the Saviour, and are from head to foot arrayed in white, without spot or wrinkle or any such thing; standing in the clear sunlight — black, but comely; loathsome in ourselves, but glorious in Him; condemned in Adam, but accepted in the Beloved. We are neither afraid nor ashamed to be with the angels of

God, to talk with the glorified; nay, nor even alarmed to speak with God Himself and call Him our Friend.

And now last of all, I publish this to sinners. I know not where you are, but may God find you out; you who have been a drunkard, swearer, thief; you who have been a blackguard of the blackest kind; you who have dived into the very kennel, and rolled yourself in the mire — if today you feel that sin is hateful to you, believe in Him who said, "It is finished." Let me link your hand in mine; let us come together, both of us, and say, "Here are two poor naked souls, good Lord; we cannot clothe ourselves"; and He will give us a robe, for "it is finished." "But, Lord, is it long enough for such sinners, and broad enough for such offenders?" "Yes," says He, "it is finished." "But we need washing, Lord! Is there anything that can take away black spots so hideous as ours?" "Yes," says He, "here is the bath of blood." "But must we not add our tears to it?" "No," says He, "no, it is finished, there is enough." "And now, Lord, Thou hast washed us, and Thou hast clothed us, but we would be still completely clean within, so that we may never sin any more; Lord, is there a way by which this can be done?" "Yes," says He, "there is the bath of water which floweth from the wounded side of Christ." "And, Lord, is there enough there to wash away my guiltiness as well as my guilt?" "Ay," says He, "it is finished. Jesus Christ is made unto you sanctification as well as redemption."

Child of God, will you have Christ's finished righteousness right now, and will you rejoice in it more than ever you have done before? And oh! poor sinner, will you have Christ or no? "Ah," says one, "I am willing enough, but I am not worthy." He does not want any worthiness. All He asks is willingness, for you know how He puts it, "Whoever will let him come." If He has given you willingness, you may believe in Christ's finished work right now. "Ah!" say you, "but you cannot mean *me*." But I do, for it says, "Ho, *every one that thirsteth*." Do you thirst for Christ? Do you wish to be saved by Him? "Every one that thirsteth, come ye to the waters, and he that hath no money come."

O that I could "compel" you to come! Great God, do Thou make the sinner willing to be saved, for he wills to be damned, and will come unless Thou change his will! Eternal Spirit, source of light, and life, and grace, come down and bring the strangers home! "It is finished." Sinner, there is nothing for God to do. "It is finished"; there is nothing for you to do. "It is finished"; Christ need not bleed. "It is finished"; you need not weep. "It is finished"; God the Holy Spirit need not tarry because of your unworthiness, nor need you tarry because of your helplessness. "It is finished"; every stumbling-block is rolled out of the road; every gate is opened; the bars of brass are broken, the gates of iron are burst asunder. "It is finished"; come and welcome, come and welcome! The table is laid; the fatlings are killed; the oxen are ready. Lo! here stands the messenger! Come from the highways and from the hedges; come, you vilest of the vile; you who hate yourselves today, come. Jesus bids you; oh! will you try? Oh! Spirit of God, do Thou repeat the invitation, and make it an effectual call to many a heart, for Jesus' sake! Amen.

The Seventh Word:

And when Jesus had cried with a loud voice, he said, Father, into thy hands I commend my spirit: and having said thus, he gave up the ghost.   Luke 23:46

Into thine hand I commit my spirit: thou hast redeemed me, O Lord God of truth.   Psalm 31:5

And they stoned Stephen, calling upon God, and saying, Lord Jesus, receive my spirit.   Acts 7:59

THE WORDS, "FATHER, INTO THY HANDS I COMMEND MY SPIRIT," if we judge them to be the last which our Saviour uttered before His death, ought to be coupled with those other words, "It is finished," which some have thought were actually the last He used. I think it was not so; but, anyhow, these utterances must have followed each other very quickly, and we may blend them together, and then we shall see how very similar they are to his first words.

There is the cry, "It is finished," which you may read in connection with our Authorized Version: "Wist ye not that I must be about my Father's business?" That business was all finished; He had been about it all His life, and now that He had come to the end of His days, there was nothing left undone, and He could say to His Father, "I have finished the work which thou gavest me to do." Then if you take the other utterance of our Lord on the cross, "Father, into thy hands I commend my spirit," see how well *it* agrees with the text,

"Wist ye not that I must be in my Father's house?" Jesus is
putting Himself into the Father's hands because He had always desired to be there, in the Father's house with the Father; and now He is committing His spirit, as a sacred trust,
into the Father's hands that He may depart to be with the
Father, to abide in His house, and go no more out forever.

Christ's life is all of a piece, just as the alpha and the
omega are letters of the same alphabet. You do not find Him
one thing at the first, another thing afterwards, and a third
thing still later; but He is "Jesus Christ; the same yesterday,
and today, and for ever." There is a wondrous similarity about
everything that Christ said and did. You never need write the
name "Jesus" under any one of His sayings, as you have to
put the names of human writers under their sayings, for there
is no mistaking any sentence that He has uttered.

If there is anything recorded as having been done by
Christ, a believing child can judge whether it is authentic or
not. Those miserable false gospels that were brought out did
little if any mischief, because no one, with any true spiritual
discernment was ever duped into believing them to be genuine. It is possible to manufacture a spurious coin which will,
for a time, pass for a good one; but it is not possible to make
even a passable imitation of what Jesus Christ has said and
done. Everything about Christ is like Himself; there is a
Christlikeness about it which cannot be mistaken. In His
death He was as unique as in His birth, and childhood, and
life. There was never another who died as He did, and there
was never another who lived altogether as He did. Our Lord
Jesus Christ stands by Himself; some of us try to imitate Him,
but how feebly do we follow in His steps? The Christ of God
still stands by Himself, and there is no possible rival to Him.

I have already intimated to you that I am going to have
three texts for my sermon; but when I have spoken upon all
three of them, you will see that they are so much alike that
I might have been content with one of them.

I. I invite you first to consider —

OUR SAVIOUR'S WORDS JUST BEFORE HIS DEATH

"Father, into thy hands I commend my spirit." Here observe, first, *how Christ lives and passes away in the atmosphere of the Word of God.* Christ was a grand original thinker, and He might always have given us words of His own. He never lacked suitable language, for "never man spake like this man." Yet you must have noticed how continually He quoted Scripture; the great majority of His expressions may be traced to the Old Testament. Even where they are not exact quotations, His words drop into Scriptural shape and form. You can see that the Bible has been His one Book. He is evidently familiar with it from the first page to the last, and not with its letter only, but with the innermost soul of its most secret sense; and, therefore, when dying, it seemed but natural for Him to use a passage from a psalm of David as His expiring words. In His death, He was not driven beyond the power of quiet thought, He was not unconscious; He did not die of weakness, He was strong even while He was dying. It is true that He said, "I thirst"; but, after he had been a little refreshed, He cried with a loud voice, as only a strong man could, "It is finished." And now, ere He bows his head in the silence of death, He utters His final words, "Father, into thy hands I commend my spirit."

Our Lord might, I say again, have made an original speech as His dying declaration; His mind was clear, and calm, and undisturbed; in fact, He was perfectly happy, for He had said, "It is finished." So His sufferings were over, and He was already beginning to enjoy a taste of the sweets of victory; yet, with all that clearness of mind and freshness of intellect, and fluency of words that might have been possible to Him, He did not invent a new sentence, but He went to the Book of Psalms, and took from the Holy Spirit this expression, "Into thy hands I commit my spirit."

How instructive to us is this great truth that the Incar-

nate Word lived on the Inspired Word! It was food to Him,
as it is to us; and, brothers and sisters, if Christ thus lived
upon the Word of God, should not you and I do the same? He,
in some respects, did not need this Book as much as we do.
The Spirit of God rested upon Him without measure; yet He
loved the Scripture, and He went to it, and studied it, and
used its expressions continually. Oh, that you and I might get
into the very heart of the Word of God, and get that Word
into ourselves! As I have seen the silkworm eat into the leaf,
and consume it, so ought we to do with the Word of the Lord
— not crawl over its surface, but eat right into it till we have
taken it into our inmost parts. It is idle merely to let the eye
glance over the words, or to recollect the poetical expressions,
or the historic facts; but it is blessed to eat into the very soul
of the Bible until, at last, you come to talk in Scriptural language, and your very style is fashioned upon Scripture models,
and, what is better still, your spirit is flavored with the words
of the Lord.

I would use John Bunyan as an instance of what I mean.
Read anything of his, and you will see that it is almost like
reading the Bible itself. He had studied the Bible; he had read
it till his very soul was saturated with Scripture; and, though
his writings are charmingly full of poetry, yet he cannot give
us his *Pilgrim's Progress* — that sweetest of all prose poems —
without continually making us feel and say, "Why, this man
is a living Bible!" Prick him anywhere; His blood is Bibline,
the very essence of the Bible flows from him. He cannot speak
without quoting a text, for his very soul is full of the Word
of God.

I commend his example to you, beloved, and, still more,
the example of our Lord Jesus. If the Spirit of God be in you,
He will make you love the Word of God; and, if any of you
imagine that the Spirit of God will lead you to dispense with
the Bible, you are under the influence of another spirit which
is not the Spirit of God at all. I trust that the Holy Spirit will
endear to you every page of this Divine Record, so that you

will feed upon it yourselves, and afterwards speak it out to others. I think it is well worthy of your constant remembrance that, even in death, our blessed Master showed the ruling passion of His spirit, so that His last words were a quotation from Scripture.

Now notice, secondly, that *our Lord, in the moment of His death, recognized a personal god:* "Father, into thy hands I commend my spirit." God is to some men an unknown God. "There may be a God," so they say, but they get no nearer than that. "All things are God," says another. "We cannot be sure that there is a God," say others, "and therefore it is no use our pretending to believe in Him, and so to be, influenced by a supposition." Some people say, "Oh, certainly, there is a God, but He is very far off! He does not come near to us, and we cannot imagine that He will interfere in our affairs."

Ah! but our blessed Lord Jesus Christ believed in no such impersonal, pantheistic, dreamy, far-off God; but in One to whom He said, "Father, into thy hands I commend my spirit." His language shows that He realized the personality of God as much as I should recognize the personality of a banker if I said to him, "Sir, I commit that money into your hands." I know that I should not say such a thing as that to a mere dummy, or to an abstract something or nothing; but to a living man I should say it, and I should say it only to a living man. So, beloved, men do not commit their souls into the keeping of impalpable nothings; they do not, in death, smile as they resign themselves to the infinite unknown, the cloudy Father of everything, who may Himself be nothing or everything. No, no; we only trust what we know; and so Jesus knew the Father, and knew Him to be a real Person having hands, into those hands He commended His departing spirit. I am not now speaking materially, mark you, as though God had physical hands like ours; but He is an actual Being, who has powers of action, who is able to deal with men as He pleases, and who is willing to take possession of their spirits, and to protect them for ever and ever.

Jesus speaks like one who believed that; and I pray that, both in life and in death, you and I may ever deal with God in the same way. We have far too much fiction in religion, and a religion of fiction will bring only fictitious comfort in the dying hour. Come to solid facts, man. Is God as real to you as you are to yourself? Come now; do you speak with Him "as a man speaketh unto his friend"? Can you trust Him, and rely upon Him as you trust and rely upon the partner of your bosom? If your God be unreal, your religion is unreal. If your God be a dream, your hope will be a dream; and woe be unto you when you wake up out of it! It was not so that Jesus trusted. "Father," said He, "into thy hands I commend my spirit."

But, thirdly, here is a better point still. Observe how *Jesus Christ here brings out the Fatherhood of God.* The psalm from which He quoted did not say, "Father." David did not get as far as that in words, though in spirit he often did; but Jesus had the right to alter the psalmist's words. He can improve on Scripture, though you and I cannot. He did not say, "Oh God, into thine hand I commit my spirit;" but He said, "Father." Oh, that sweet word! That was the gem of thought when Jesus said, "Wist ye not that I must be at my Father's — that I must be in my Father's house?" Oh, yes! the Holy Child knew that He was specially, and in a peculiar sense, the Son of the Highest; and therefore He said, "My Father"; and, in dying, His expiring heart was buoyed up and comforted with the thought that God was His Father. It was because He said that God was His Father that they put Him to death, yet He still stood to it even in His dying hour, and said, "Father, into thy hands I commend my spirit."

What a blessed thing it is for us also, my brethren, to die conscious that we are sons of God! Oh, how sweet, in life and in death, to feel in our soul the spirit of adoption whereby we cry, "Abba, Father"! In such a case as that, "It is not death to die." Quoting the Saviour's words, "It is finished," and relying upon His Father and our Father, we may go even into the jaws of death. Joyful, with all the strength we have, our lips may confidently sing, challenging death and the grave to silence our ever-rising and swelling music. O my Father, my Father, if I am in Thy hands, I may die without fear!

There is another thought, however, which is perhaps the chief one of all. From this passage, we learn that *our divine Lord cheerfully rendered up His soul to His Father when the time had come for Him to die:* "Father, into thy hands I commend my spirit." None of us can, with strict propriety, use these words. When we come to die, we may perhaps utter them, and God will accept them; these were the very death-words of Polycarp, and Bernard, and Luther, and Melancthon, and Jerome of Prague, and John Huss, and an almost endless list of saints: "Into thy hands I commit my spirit." The Old Testament rendering of the passage, or else our Lord's version of it, has been turned into a Latin prayer and commonly used among Romanists almost as a charm; they have repeated the Latin words when dying, or, if they were unable to do so, the priest repeated the words for them, attaching a sort of magical power to that particular formula. But, in the sense in which our Saviour uttered these words, we cannot any of us fully use them.

We can commit or commend our spirit to God; but yet, brethren, remember that, unless the Lord comes first, we must die; and dying is not an act on our part. We have to be passive in the process, because it is no longer in our power to retain our life. I suppose that, if a man could have such control of his life, it might be questionable when he should surrender it, because suicide is a crime, and no man can be required to kill himself. God does not demand such action as that at any man's hand; and, in a certain sense, that is what would happen whenever a man yielded himself to death. But there was no necessity for our blessed Lord and Master to die except the necessity which He had taken upon Himself in becoming the Substitute for His people. There was not any necessity for His death even at the last moment upon the cross, for, as I have reminded you, He cried with a loud voice when natural weakness would have compelled Him to whisper or to sigh. But His life was strong within Him; if He had willed to do so, He could have unloosed the nails and come down into the midst of the crowd that stood mocking Him. He died of His own free will, "the just for the unjust, that he might bring us to God."

A man may righteously surrender his life for the good of his country, and for the safety of others. There have frequently been opportunities for men to do this, and there have been brave fellows who have worthily done it; but, then, all those men would have had to die at some time or other. They were only slightly anticipating the payment of the debt of nature; but, in our Lord's case, He was rendering up to the Father the spirit which He might have kept if He had chosen to do so. "No man taketh it from me," said He concerning His life. "I lay it down of myself"; and there is here a cheerful willingness to yield up His spirit into His Father's hands.

It is rather remarkable that none of the Evangelists describe our Lord as dying. He did die, but they all speak of Him as giving up the ghost — surrendering to God His spirit. You and I passively die; but He actively yielded up His spirit to His Father. In His case, death was an act; and He performed that act from the glorious motive of redeeming us from death and hell; so, in this sense, Christ stands alone in His death.

But, oh, dear brothers and sisters, though we cannot render up our spirit as He did, yet when our life is taken from us, let us be perfectly ready to give it up. May God bring us into such a state of mind and heart that there shall be no struggling to keep our life, but a sweet willingness to let it be just as God would have it — a yielding up of everything to His hands, feeling sure that, in the world of spirits, our soul shall be quite safe in the Father's hand, and that, until the resurrection day, the life-germ of the body will be securely in His keeping, and certain that, when the trumpet shall sound, spirit, soul, and body — that trinity of our manhood — shall be reunited in the absolute perfection of our being to behold the King in His beauty in the land that is very far off. When God calls us to die, it will be a sweet way of dying if we can, like our Lord, pass away with a text of Scripture upon our lips, with a personal God ready to receive us, with that God recognized distinctly as our Father, and so die joyously, resigning our will entirely to the sweet will of the ever-blessed One, and saying, "It is the Lord," "my Father," "let him do as seemeth him good."

II. My second text is in Psalm 31, the fifth verse; and it is evidently the passage which our Saviour had in His mind just then: "Into thine hand I commit my spirit: thou hast redeemed me, O Lord God of truth." It seems to me that —

THESE ARE WORDS TO BE USED IN LIFE

for this psalm is not so much concerning the believer's death as concerning his life.

Is it not singular, dear friends, that the words which Jesus uttered on the cross you may still continue to use? You may catch up their echo, and not only when you come to die, but tonight, tomorrow morning, and as long as you are here, you may still repeat the text the Master quoted, and say, "Into thine hand I commit my spirit."

That is to say, first, *let us cheerfully entrust our souls to God,* and feel that it is quite safe in His hands. Our spirit is the noblest part of our being; our body is only the husk, our spirit is the living kernel, so let us put it into God's keeping. Some of you have never yet done that, so I invite you to do it now. It is the act of faith which saves the soul, that act which a man performs when he says, "I trust myself to God as He reveals Himself in Christ Jesus; I cannot keep myself, but He can keep me; by the precious blood of Christ He can cleanse me; so I just take my spirit, and give it over into the great Father's hand." You never really live till you do that; all that comes before that act of full surrender is death; but when you have once trusted Christ, then you have truly begun to live.

And every day, as long as you live, take care that you repeat this process, and cheerfully leave yourselves in God's hands without any reserve; that is to say, give yourself up to God — your body, to be healthy or to be sick, to be long-lived or to be suddenly cut off — your soul and spirit, to be made happy or to be made sad, just as He pleases. Give your whole self up to Him, and say to Him, "My Father, make me rich or make me poor, give me eyesight or make me blind, let me have all my senses or take them away, make me famous or leave me to be obscure; I just give myself up to Thee; into Thine hand I commit my spirit. I will no longer exercise my own choice, but Thou shalt choose my inheritance for me. My times are in Thy hands."

Now, dear children of God, are you always doing this? Have you ever done it? I am afraid that there are some, even among Christ's professing followers, who kick against God's will; and even when they say to God, "Thy will be done," they spoil it by adding, in their own mind, "and my will, too." They pray, "Lord, make my will Thy will," instead of saying, "Make Thy will my will." Let us each one pray this prayer every day, "Into thine hand I commit my spirit." I like, at family prayer, to put myself and all that I have into God's hands in the morning, and then, at night, just to look between His hands, and see how safe I have been, and then to say to Him, "Lord, shut me up again tonight; take care of me all through the night watches. 'Into thine hand I commit my spirit.' "

Notice, dear friends, that our second text has these words at the end of it: "*Thou hast redeemed me, O Lord God of truth.*" Is not that a good reason for giving yourself up entirely to God? Christ has redeemed you, and therefore you belong to Him. If I am a redeemed man, and I ask God to take care of me, I am but asking the King to take care of one of His own jewels — a jewel that cost Him the blood of His heart.

And I may still more specially expect that He will do so, because of the title which is here given to Him: "Thou hast redeemed me, *O Lord God of truth.*" Would He be the God of truth if He began with redemption and ended with destruction? If He began by giving His Son to die for us, and then kept back other mercies which we daily need to bring us to heaven! No; the gift of His Son is the pledge that He will save His people from their sins, and bring them home to glory; and He will do it. So, every day, go to Him with this declaration, "Into thine hand I commit my spirit." Nay, not only every day, but all through the day.

I would advise you to do this every time you walk down the street, or even while you sit in your own house. Dr. Gill, my famous predecessor, spent much time in his study; and, one day, someone said to him, "Well, at any rate, the studious man is safe from most of the accidents of life." It so happened that one morning, when the good man left his familiar arm chair for a little while, there came a gale of wind that blew down a stack of chimneys which crashed through the roof and fell right into the place where he would have been if the providence of God had not just then drawn him away; and he said, "I see that we need divine providence to care for us in our studies just as much as in the streets." "Father, into thy hands I commit my spirit."

I have often noticed that, if any of our friends get into accidents and troubles, it is usually when they are away for a holiday; it is a curious thing, but I have often seen it. They go out for their health, and come home ill; they leave us with all their limbs whole, and return to us crippled; therefore, we must pray God to take special care of friends in the country or by the sea, and we must commit ourselves to His hands wherever we may be. If we had to go into a lazar-house, we should certainly ask God to protect us from the deadly leprosy; but we ought equally to seek the Lord's protection while dwelling in the healthiest place or in our own homes.

David said to the Lord, "Into thine hand I commit my

spirit"; but let me beg you to add that word which our Lord inserted, *"Father."* David is often a good guide for us, but David's Lord is far better; and if we follow Him, we shall improve upon David. So, let us each say, *"Father, Father,* into thine hand I commit my spirit." That is a sweet way of living every day, committing everything to our Heavenly Father's hand, for that hand can do His child no unkindness. "Father, I might not be able to trust Thine angels, but I can trust Thee."

The psalmist does not say, "Into the hand of providence I commit my spirit." Do you notice how men try to get rid of God by saying, "Providence did this," and "Providence did that," and "Providence did the other"? If you ask them, "What is providence?" — they will probably reply, "Well, providence is —— providence." That is all they can say.

There is many a man who talks very confidently about reverencing nature, obeying the laws of nature, noting the powers of nature, and so on. Step up to that eloquent lecturer, and say to him, "Will you kindly explain to me what nature is?" He answers, "Why, nature, — well, it is — nature." Just so, sir; but, then, what *is* nature? And he says, "Well — well — it is nature"; and that is all you will get out of him.

Now, I believe in nature, and I believe in providence; but, at the back of everything, I believe in God, and in the God who has hands — not in an idol that has no hands, and can do nothing — but in the God to whom I can say, " 'Father, into thine hand I commit my spirit.' I rejoice that I am able to put myself there, for I feel absolutely safe in trusting myself to Thy keeping." So live, beloved, and you shall live safely, and happily; and you shall have hope in your life, and hope in your death.

III. My third text will not detain us long; it is intended to explain to us

THE USE OF THE SAVIOUR'S DYING WORDS FOR OURSELVES

Turn to the account of the death of Stephen in Acts 7:59, and you will see there how far a man of God may dare to go

in his last moments in quoting from David and from the Lord
Jesus Christ: "And they stoned Stephen, calling upon God,
and saying, Lord Jesus, receive my spirit." So here is a text
for us to use when we come to die: "Lord Jesus, receive my
spirit." I have explained to you that, strictly, we can hardly
talk of yielding up our spirit, but we may speak of Christ
receiving it, and say, with Stephen, "Lord Jesus, receive my
spirit."

What does this prayer mean? I think this prayer means
that, *if we can die as Stephen did, we shall die with a certainty
of immortality.* Stephen prayed, "Lord Jesus, receive my spirit." He did not say, "I am afraid my poor spirit is going to die."
No; the spirit is something which still exists after death, something which Christ can receive, and therefore Stephen asks
him to receive it. You and I are not going upstairs to die as if
we were only like cats and dogs; we go up there to die like
immortal beings who fall asleep on earth, and open our eyes
in heaven. Then, at the sound of the archangel's trumpet, our
very body is to rise to dwell again with our spirit; we have
not any question about this matter.

You have probably heard what an infidel once said to a
Christian man, "Some of you Christians have great fear in
dying because you believe that there is another state to follow
this one. I have not the slightest fear, for I believe that I shall
be annihilated and therefore all fear of death is gone from
me." "Yes," said the Christian man, "and in that respect you
seem to me to be on equal terms with that bullock grazing
over there, which, like yourself, is free from any fear of death.
Pray, sir, let me ask you a simple question. Have you any
hope?" "Hope, sir? Hope, sir? No, I have no hope; of course,
I have no hope, sir." "Ah, then!" replied the other, "despite
the fears that sometimes come over feeble believers, they have
a hope which they would not and could not give up." And
that hope is, that our spirit — even that spirit which we commit into Jesus Christ's hands — shall be "for ever with the
Lord."

The next thought is that, *to a man who can die as Stephen did, there is a certainty that Christ is near* — so near that the man speaks to him, and says, "Lord Jesus, receive my spirit." In Stephen's case, the Lord Jesus was so near that the martyr could see him, for he said, "Behold, I see the heavens opened, and the Son of man standing on the right hand of God." Many dying saints have borne a similar testimony; it is no strange thing for us to hear them say, before they died, that they could see within the pearly gates; and they have told us this with such evident truthfulness, and with such rapture, or sometimes so calmly, in such a businesslike tone of voice, that we were sure that they were neither deceived nor speaking falsehood. They spake what they knew to be true, for Jesus was there with them. Yes, beloved, before you can call your children about your deathbed, Jesus will be there already, and into His hands you may commit your spirit.

Moreover, *there is a certainty that we are quite safe in His hands.* Wherever else we are insecure, if we ask Him to receive our spirit, and He receives it, who can hurt us? Who can pluck us out of His hands? Rouse ye, death and hell! Come forth, all ye powers of darkness! What can you do when once a spirit is in the hands of the omnipotent Redeemer? We must be safe there.

Then there is the other certainty, *that He is quite willing to take us into His hands.* Let us put ourselves into His hands now; and then we need not be ashamed to repeat the operation every day, and we may be sure that we shall not be rejected at the last. I have often told you of the good old woman who was dying, and to whom someone said, "Are you not afraid to die?" "Oh, no!" she replied, "there is nothing at all to fear. I have dipped my foot in the river of death every morning before I have had my breakfast, and I am not afraid to die now." You remember that dear saint, who died in the night, and who had left written on a piece of paper by her bedside these lines which, ere she fell asleep, she felt strong enough to pencil down —

> Since Jesus is mine, I'll not fear undressing,
> But gladly put off these garments of clay;
> To die in the Lord is a covenant blessing,
> Since Jesus to glory thro' death led the way.

It was well that she could say it, and may we be able to say the same whenever the Master calls us to get up higher! I want, dear friends, that we should all of us have as much willingness to depart as if it were a matter of will with us. Blessed be God, it is not left to our choice, it is not left to our will, when we shall die. God has appointed that day, and ten thousand devils cannot consign us to the grave before our time. We shall not die till God decrees it.

> Plagues and deaths around me fly,
> Till He please I cannot die;
> Not a single shaft can hit
> Till the God of love sees fit.

But let us be just as willing to depart as if it were really a matter of choice; for, wisely, carefully, coolly, consider that, if it were left to us, we should none of us be wise if we did not choose to go. Apart from the coming of our Lord, the most miserable thing that I know of would be a suspicion that we might not die. Do you know what quaint old Rowland Hill used to say when he found himself getting very old? He said, "Surely they must be forgetting me up there"; and every now and then, when some dear old saint was dying, he would say, "When you get to heaven, give my love to John Berridge and John Bunyan, and ever so many more of the good Johns, and tell them I hope they will see poor old Rowly up there before long."

Well, there was common sense in that wishing to get home, longing to be with God. To be with Christ, is far better than to be here.

Sobriety itself would make us choose to die; well, then, do not let us run back and become utterly unwilling, and struggle and strive and fret and fume over it. When I hear of believers who do not like to talk about death, I am afraid concerning them. It is greatly wise to be familiar with our resting place. It was a healthy thing for me to stand at the grave's brink recently, and to walk amid that forest of memorials of the dead, for this is where I, too, must go. Ye living men, come and view the ground where you must shortly lie; and, as it must be so, let us who are believers welcome it.

But what if you are not believers? Ah! that is another matter altogether. If you have not believed in Christ, you may well be afraid even to rest on the seat where you are sitting. I wonder that the earth itself does not say, "O God, I will not hold this wretched sinner up any longer! Let me open my mouth, and swallow him!" All nature must hate the man who hates God. Surely, all things must loathe to minister to the life of a man who does not live unto God. Oh that you would seek the Lord, and trust Christ, and find eternal life! If you have done so, do not be afraid to go forth to live, or to die, just as God pleases.

THE CRUEL STARS

BY JOHN BIRMINGHAM

Published by Del Rey Books

Del Rey books are available at special discounts for bulk purchases for sales promotions or corporate use. Special editions, including personalized covers, excerpts of existing books, or books with corporate logos, can be created in large quantities for special needs. For more information, contact Premium Sales at (212) 572-2232 or email specialmarkets@penguinrandomhouse.com.

THE
CRUEL
STARS

JOHN
BIRMINGHAM

DEL REY

NEW YORK

2020 Del Rey Mass Market Edition

Copyright © 2019 by John Birmingham

All rights reserved.

Published in the United States by Del Rey,
an imprint of Random House, a division of
Penguin Random House LLC, New York.

DEL REY and the HOUSE colophon are registered trademarks of
Penguin Random House LLC.

Originally published in hardcover in the United States
by Del Rey, an imprint of Random House, a division of
Penguin Random House LLC, in 2019.

ISBN 978-0-399-59333-8
Ebook ISBN 978-0-399-59332-1

Printed in the United States of America

randomhousebooks.com

Book design by Edwin Vazquez

2 4 6 8 9 7 5 3 1

Del Rey mass market edition: February 2020

For my dad

THE CRUEL STARS

CHAPTER

ONE

The rock turned silently in hard vacuum, and the young woman with it. She pressed her nose to the porthole, which fogged with her breath while she waited for night to sweep over this part of the base. It would come, dark and frozen, within a few minutes, revealing the star field of the local volume, the vast blue-green pearl of the planet far below, and the lights of the nearest Hab, another naval station like this hollowed-out moonlet.

Lucinda waited for the stars. In the right mood, in a rare abstracted moment, she sometimes wondered at the way they wrapped themselves around her, seeming close yet infinitely distant. As she wondered, dusk came pouring over the small mountain range to the east, advancing in a wave of fast shadows and lengthening pools of inky blackness. She could not see the darkness coming for her on this part of the rock, but she imagined it swallowing the local area point defenses and the gaping maw of the docks. The entrance to the port was always illuminated, but the lights soon would burn with a severe brilliance in the accelerated night.

She was not floating, but she felt light and only barely in touch with the deck in the standard one-tenth grav here on the surface as she inspected her reflection in the armor glass.

A young woman frowned back at her. The uniform was not quite right. Tight at the shoulders, a little loose around the waist. The best she could afford. She regarded herself even more critically in the ready-to-wear black-and-whites. Severely pretty, she had been told by men she did not entirely trust. A little off-putting and perhaps unnecessarily discouraging according to girlfriends she probably could believe.

Nonetheless. It would all have to do.

"Lieutenant Hardy?"

Surprised out of her reverie, she jumped a little, reaching out reflexively to the nearest wall to arrest herself before she could take gentle flight. She was embarrassed at being caught out.

"Yes," she said, her voice catching just a little as she turned away from the view, reorienting herself to the spare utilitarian lines of the transit lounge. The glowstrips on the carbon armor walls were old enough to need replacing months ago. Rows of hard o-plastic seating looked bleached and brittle under the weak lighting. She was the only other officer in the space. The only other person for the last hour. This part of the facility was restricted, and foot traffic was thin.

"Sorry for the delay, ma'am," the young man said, saluting. He was a baby lieutenant, a subbie, just out

of the Academy she guessed from his age and eager-
ness, and his eyes went a little wide as he took in the
campaign ribbons on her uncomfortably heavy
jacket. He wore dark blue general-duty coveralls and
carried a sidearm low on his thigh. Lucinda, in her
black-and-white dress uniform, felt awkward in spite
of her advantage in rank and experience. Her black-
and-whites were obviously not tailor-made. She did
not have the expense allowance from a family trust
that some officers enjoyed.

She returned his salute, painfully aware of the way
her dress jacket rode up and the tightness of the
sleeves. She tried to ignore the feeling that seemed to
steal up on her with every new posting: that she was
simply masquerading as an officer and soon would
be found out.

"You have the advantage of me, Lieutenant . . . ?"

He stared at her blankly for a second, amplifying
her sense of dislocation and fragile pretense. Then he
went, "Ah!" and shook his head.

"I'm sorry. You're not plugged in to shipnet. Bannon, ma'am. Sublieutenant Ian Bannon. I'm officer of
the deck today. I'm sorry you've been left up here. It
should not have happened."

The young man looked distressed now, and his
discomfort made her feel even more awkward.

"I understand, Lieutenant," she said. "Everything
needs to happen at once just before deployment."

"Even so," he said, "I apologize."

They shook hands on her initiative. His eyes flitted briefly to the colored rows of decorations again,
but she could forgive that. He wore no decoration
beyond the stitched half bar on one collar tab.

"Sorry," he said when he realized she'd caught him checking out the fruit salad, but he smiled as he apologized. He had a boyish grin that Lucinda imagined had been getting him out of trouble his whole life. He looked practiced in its use. "They told me you fought in the Javan War," he said, catching sight of her duffel bag under the front row of seats and reaching for it before she could. Lucinda almost told him not to. She preferred to look out for herself. But Bannon held the lesser rank, and it would have been a slight to her if he had not offered. He lifted it carefully in the low grav, testing its mass. Nodding when he had the measure of the load.

"I heard you were promoted in the field," he said, leading her toward the exit. "From ensign to lieutenant. I missed it all. Signed up to fight but didn't graduate until it was all over."

Not looking where he was going, he banged his knee into a chair and cussed, then apologized for cussing. The bag floated up slowly like an improbable novelty balloon.

"Whoa there," he said, adjusting his grip and stance and nearly tumbling over while he wrestled the duffel bag and his own mass back under control.

"Damn." He grinned. "Been under ship grav too long."

He shrugged off the moment in which she would have blushed fiercely. Lucinda found she could not help liking him. But also, she could not let him go on.

"Thank you," she said, nodding at the bag. "But I went into the war as a baby louie, just like you. And I came out a fully grown LT simply because it went on long enough for my turn to come around."

Bannon, unconvinced, gave her decorations a theatrically dubious side eye as they exited the bare surroundings of the transit lounge.

"Chief Higo told me you were promoted in the field. And the chief is never wrong. He told me that, too."

She essayed a small, uncertain smile.

"I would never want to correct a chief petty officer," she said—and she was not lying—"but my first promotion, from ensign, that wasn't in the war. It was nothing, really. Just a small engagement on a counterpiracy patrol."

"Okay." He grinned as though he knew she was hiding some greater truth. "If you say so."

They walked down a long, wide corridor. The passageway curved into the body of the rock and twisted like an elongated strand of DNA. She could feel their descent in the deck's slope under her feet and the increasing pull of spin grav. There were no more portholes to the surface, only screens carrying g-data feeds and imagery from around the base. At first they passed no other personnel, but the traffic in automats and bot trains was moderate to busy, and once a Flotilla-class Combat Intellect floated past. They saluted the black ovoid lozenge. It pulsed in acknowledgment, turning briefly purple, before a female voice said, "Lieutenant Hardy, Lieutenant Bannon, good day to you both."

The Intellect drifted on serenely.

They watched it disappear around the twisting curvilinear passage.

"Those guys," said Bannon, shaking his head. "So chill."

The corridor spiraled down for another five minutes. Lucinda's duffel bag grew visibly heavy in her colleague's hand. She did not so much make conversation as ride it downslope. Bannon, unlike her, wasn't shy about talking about himself. By the time they stood in a secure reception bay, enjoying the one Earth-standard grav provided by the spin and the base's mass generator, she knew all about Bannon's family (wealthy but not ennobled), his service (just beginning), and the ship's command group (pretty chill except for . . .).

"Except for this guy," he muttered out the corner of his mouth.

"Bannon! Where in the Dark have you been?"

Hardy startled at the barking voice, as much at the accent as at the volume and sharpness. The rich, stentorian tones of someone who grew up at court on the Armadalen homeworld were unmistakable, especially when the speaker made an extra-special effort to cover everything in gold leaf.

The reception bay was a small area, not much larger than the transit lounge where she'd spent so many hours. The walls and ceiling were bare rock except for a thin but obvious coating of sealant shining under the glowstrips. Three of the four security checkpoints were closed. The fourth stood open to admit new arrivals to the afterbrow of the ship. There was no sign of the destroyer. Instead two sentinel droids, their glacis plates stenciled with the name DE-FIANT, stood mutely in front of the displacement portal, flanking a young man in day uniform. He wore the insignia of a first lieutenant, and Bannon snapped to attention. Hardy did not. The man did not outrank her. Not in any military sense.

"I told you I wanted those stores double-checked," the lieutenant said loudly. "You're the officer of the deck. Not a bloody hotel greeter."

"Sir, my apologies, sir, but Lieutenant Hardy was hours—"

"Lieutenant Hardy isn't on deck until 1800 hours," he said. "She is not a priority."

He was shouting at Bannon, but Lucinda knew the whole charade was intended for her. She struggled to maintain a neutral face.

His expression turned dark as he took in her lack of deference or even reaction.

"And you would be the famous Hardy, I presume," he said, giving her the impression that it was an onerous and unwelcome duty even to say her name.

"I am Lieutenant Hardy, Lieutenant . . . ?"

She left the question open. For the merest second he had almost elicited a "Yes, sir!" from her, his long experience of assumed privilege conspiring with her trained obedience to the chain of command to force a submission to which he was not due. Not while he served in uniform.

"You took your time, Lieutenant," the officer said.

He did not offer his name. Perhaps she was supposed to know him or know of him.

"I was waiting at surface level transit as per my travel orders . . . *Lieutenant*," she said, annoyed by how much his tone of voice seemed to compel her to address him as a superior. Bannon, she sensed, was remaining at attention beside her.

Lucinda guessed that she was in the presence of

some minor scion of the Royal House who was serving his three years before taking up a directorship on one of the Habs or dirtside, possibly even down on the planet below them. He was very obviously a first lifer, like her. Like all of them. Junior officers were almost always first lifers. After all, who would go back for a second bite of that cherry?

The anonymous princeling, or count, or whatever he was, lost focus while he consulted his neural net. A lieutenant, she reminded herself; he was just a lieutenant, like her, possibly with even less time in service. He stared through her and Bannon, who was *still* standing rigidly at attention and saying nothing. It was the first time Ian had shut up since she'd met him. Lucinda was tempted to grab an image cap of the nameless officer and run a personnel search while he made them wait. See if she could track down his legend, the public record of his naval service. But maybe also see if he'd been the sort of second- or third-tier wastrel who kept the scandal servers and gossip bots busy before he had to sign on.

Instead, she kept her interface down and her expression neutral. She would not give him the satisfaction.

His eyes came back from searching the middle distance, and he smirked.

"A charity case, eh?"

She felt her cheeks beginning to burn, and knowing that she was blushing only made it worse. Beside her, Bannon remained as silent and still as the hard vacuum outside.

"Oh, I'm sorry," the officer said. "Did Naval Records get it wrong?"

He made a show of checking his neural net again, although she doubted he even bothered pulling it up. He simply enjoyed the performative cruelty.

"It says you were recommended for officer training school by Coriolis Habitat Welfare because . . ." Again the play of actively consulting records. "Because, oh, dear, your father was transported to a defaulter colony. Oh, my."

The sentinels, bipedal combat drones, remained utterly still. With horror, she realized that this close to deployment they might be inhabited by human minds, not the ship's Intellect.

God, this would be all over the other ranks' mess before the end of watch.

The still anonymous lieutenant sucked air in through his teeth. "I wouldn't go lending money to this one, Bannon," he snorted. "Would you?"

Sublieutenant Bannon took just half a second too long to answer.

"Well?" asked the other man, sensing there was more fun to be had in that moment of hesitation. "Would you?"

Still at parade ground attention, Bannon seemed to be struggling to lift a great weight, as though Lucinda's bag, which he still carried, somehow had increased its mass tenfold.

"If Lieutenant Hardy was in need of any assistance, Lieutenant Chase," he said at last, "I would be happy to help her. As, I'm sure, she would do for me." He sounded as though he were cutting off his own toes. "Any officer of the Fleet would."

Lucinda smiled. She knew who this baby martinet

was now. Or who his family was at any rate. And that was the same thing really. The Chase dynasty.

"Of course I would, Ian," she said.

Chase did not smile. He stepped forward, deep into Bannon's personal space, speaking softly, as though to a lover. "You forget your place," he said. Chase paused before putting a sharper edge on his voice, on the blade of that finely honed aristocratic accent. "And your family's," he added.

It was all Lucinda could do to maintain an air of bemused nonchalance. She could feel Bannon's collapse at the implied threat to his family.

"And you . . . *Lieutenant*," Chase went on, smirking at her as though amused by some private joke. "You don't even have a place. You're not one of us. You will never belong."

Vertigo and sudden untethered fury threatened to unbalance her, and Chase could sense it. His smirk turned genuinely nasty.

"By coming aboard, you understand you give full consent to a search of your person and baggage. Open the bag and strip to your skivvies. You'd be better off out of that hobo's ragbag of a uniform, anyway. I imagine Habitat Welfare organized that for you, too."

"What?" Bannon said, half gasping the question.

Chase turned the grin on him like a point defense turret acquiring a target.

"You left the ship, too, Bannon. This close to deployment it behooves me to maintain the strictest security. So get those coveralls off or I'll have the sentinels cut them from you."

"You can't—" Bannon started.

"He can," Lucinda interrupted. She was stone-faced, and her voice was devoid of all affect. She was already unbuttoning her jacket. The buttons, of course, were slightly too large for their holes, and she struggled to undo them.

Chase's eyes sparkled with delight at her admission but even more at the trouble she was having removing her cheap off-the-rack dress jacket. He seemed ready to double down on the game when he suddenly came to attention as rigidly as Bannon. Something or someone behind her had brought the young man's theater of cruelty to an end. The sentinel droids stomped out a crashing salute.

"Ah. Excellent," said a slightly gruff male voice. It sounded bearish but kindly, like a cartoon grizzly or a Montanblanc forest thumper in a children's story.

Lieutenant Chase performed a textbook salute.

"Defiant!" he said.

Lucinda and Bannon followed suit as the eerily glowing spherical jewel of an autonomous Combat Intellect floated by at chest level.

"Defiant," they said in almost perfect unison.

It was smaller than the Intellect they had passed on the upper levels. That had been oblong in form and at least a meter in length. This entity, gendered male, was much smaller, a ship's Intellect rather than a Fleet-level adept. About the size and shape of a baseball, it looked like nothing so much as an itinerant black hole turned sentient and roaming loose.

"Is this our new tactical officer?" the eerie black sphere asked, although it knew full well who she was. The Intellects knew everything. "Lieutenant Hardy? Welcome aboard. I've heard the most marvelous things about you from Admiralty and from the Terran Intellect of *No Place for Good Losers* who was with you during that spot of bother with those dreadful pirate fellows in the Bectel system. Come along, Chase!" the Intellect scolded. "We have a genuine hero piping aboard. It's not every day we welcome a Star of Valor winner to the wardroom. Remind me again, Chase. Do you have a Star of Valor? I can't quite recall you winning one, which is odd, because as you know, my memory is virtually infinite and actually infallible."

The Intellect moved off with regal grace, humming a show tune from a musical Lucinda had seen back on Armadale during a rare weekend off from the Academy. "You didn't tell me about the medal," Bannon stage-whispered as they fell in behind the merrily humming Super Intellect. Lieutenant Chase stalked ahead of them but behind the Intellect. The infinitely dark displacement field closed over *Defiant* and cut off the song.

"The records were sealed," she said.

The Intellect should not have known about the medal, and if it did know, it should not have revealed that it knew.

But the Intellects were like that.

You never really knew what they were thinking.

Ahead of her, Lieutenant Chase stepped through the displacement field, his shoulders hunched over, like a naughty boy ordered to the headmaster's office. It shimmered darkly around him. Bannon enjoyed a brief snort and a smirk before composing his features just short of the nanofold.

"Welcome to *Defiant*," Bannon said, indicating

with an open hand that Lucinda should precede him. She nodded, drew in a short breath, and stepped up to the oily black event horizon. It always put her in mind of a shark's eye: obsidian, fathomless, and . . . hungry. But on the far side there was a new ship. A new crew. Another chance to remake her life and, one day, to save her father. She stepped aboard.

The sensation of passing directly from one point in physical space-time to another without traversing the distance in between was always uncanny. It did not matter whether the fold carried her from one part of a small orbital station to another or all the way across a continent; Lucinda always felt the displacement to be unsettling. Everyone did. In a ship folding through space, surrounded by the vessel's discrete bubble universe, you were spared the weird somatic distress. But the human body, or mind, or perhaps even soul did not enjoy the experience of directly quantum shifting its own mass through a deformed reality.

Inevitably, Lucinda experienced her arrival on the far side of the nanofold linking the station to *Defiant* as a moment of déjà vu. She was certain that all this had happened before, and she was certain that the feeling was an artifact of the fold.

She was lucky. Some people got violently ill crossing through even the shortest fold. And nobody had ever survived a direct translation across the distances routinely enfolded by ships.

Ignoring the disquieting sense of premonition, she stepped onto the deck of the warship. The receiving chamber was a spare utilitarian compartment of spacegray carbon armor. It gave onto a wide companionway running the length of the ship. *Defiant*'s Intellect had floated or possibly even folded off somewhere else, and she could see the diminishing figure of Lieutenant Chase stomping away in the distance. Ignoring the snub, Lucinda executed a right-face turn to salute the Armadalen ensign that hung on a ceremonial flagpole of polished Jarrawood before turning back and saluting the young officer staffing the afterbrow of the destroyer. Bannon, one step behind, announced her arrival to the ship and the OOD.

"Lieutenant Lucinda Hardy, late of the *Resolute,* reports to *Defiant* in good order by request of His Majesty."

The sublieutenant "manning the sides" was biotically young, somewhere in her very early twenties and in transition from male to female according to the discreet purple pip on her collar tab. A name tag read HAN.

"*Defiant* is pleased to be of service to His Majesty and welcomes the lieutenant aboard," Han replied.

Lucinda knew what was coming and braced herself for half a second before feeling the distinct mental *shunt* as her neural net gained access to the ship.

Defiant spoke to her alone in the same gruff but kindly voice she recalled from their earlier encounter.

"Welcome aboard, Lieutenant Hardy. We're very pleased to have you with us."

"Defiant," she said smartly, snapping to attention. "Requesting permission to present my credentials and particulars."

She prepared to transfer her Real Death Insurance

forms, a copy of her orders from Fleet, and a True Record of her Emergency Relife Data.

"Thank you, Lieutenant," the ship's Intellect replied, aloud this time, "but we have all of your data, expedited from Fleet. I understand you are not on duty for another two hours, but if you would care to join the senior O-Group in the wardroom, Captain Torvaldt is waiting for you."

Lucinda's heart lurched just a little. The Intellect perceived her surprise and spoke directly to her via neural net.

"Don't be alarmed now, Lieutenant. You are not in trouble. It's just a briefing."

To Lieutenant Bannon he said, "If I might beg of you, Lieutenant, Ms. Hardy is needed at the captain's convenience. Might you take her duffel to her cabin for me?"

"Of course, ship," Bannon replied. He smiled at Hardy and shook his head. "The Star of Valor," he said, shaking his head as he left. "Man, the chief didn't know about that."

Lucinda saw Sublieutenant Han's eyes go wide, and she cringed inside. The whole ship surely would know everything before eight bells. She smiled awkwardly at the sublieutenant as her corneal displays lit up with a navigation overlay, a line of softly glowing blue dots leading out of the reception bay and for'ard to officer country. Lucinda started to walk, and the dots faded almost immediately as she "remembered" the way to *Defiant*'s wardroom. Her memory and consciousness filled rapidly with a steady flow of information about the ship and its complement, the service records of the officers and crew, the load-out for the coming mission—whoa, heavy!—and a briefing for the same, which was very light on detail. It wasn't as though she had just learned these things. More like she had always known them and had only just thought on them for the first time in a long while.

Lucinda shivered but hid the reaction from everyone other than Defiant, from whom there could be no hiding. The ship said nothing. Hardy hadn't grown up with a neural net. That was for the likes of Chase or even Bannon, whose family could afford such advantages. She'd had her first implant the day after she'd left the care of Habitat Welfare for Navy basic. She'd been in sick bay, vomiting for the rest of the week. She pushed that memory down the hole and took in her new posting.

Like all the interstellar-capable warships of the Royal Armadalen Navy, *Defiant* was bigger inside than out. Not impossibly so. Its relative internal volume was only four times greater than the external dimensions of the stealth destroyer, and a third of that was given over to the hyperspace buffer between the outer hull, a thick protective shell of exotic dark matter, and the discrete pocket universe of the vessel proper: the crew quarters and amenities; the engineering, command, and combat decks; and stowage.

During the Javan War, Hardy had served on HMAS *Resolute,* an older ship of the same class, and she was quietly pleased to see the improvements that had been made since then. She understood from the data dump that she would have a stateroom to herself, an unheard-of luxury during the war even on the Navy's capital ships: the dreadnoughts and Titan cruisers that sortied from Armadale system and fought their way into the heart of the Javan Empire.

The *Defiant* bustled with prelaunch activity as Hardy made her way aft. The full-strength crew hurried about their assignments with the calm intensity that was the hard-won distinction of people honed to a cold, killing edge by relentless training and winnowing experience. This was a tight ship. Wartime sharp. She could see that with her own eyes in the way the crew members carried themselves and did their jobs, but Lucinda also knew that an unusually high proportion of the crew—96 percent—were combat veterans, because Defiant had dropped their legends into her skull. Or rather into her neural net; the semiorganic synaptic weave of monomolecular carbon braid that threaded through her neocortex before plunging deep into the hindbrain.

"We have a full complement for this cruise, Defiant?" she said aloud, both a statement and a query. A full crew wasn't usual in peacetime and certainly not on routine patrols like this one.

The ship came back to her silently, inside her mind.

"The Royal Armadalen Navy does not believe in slacking off, young lady. That's what makes it the RAN and not the Marine Corps."

Lucinda could hear something like drollery in Defiant's voice as a bot train swerved around her and a small group of marines jogged past. Heavy weapons crew by their phenotypes. A sergeant led them in cadence, a recent relife for sure. He wore a military-issue Caucasian skin job, early twenties analogue, presumably loaded with the usual gene-mods and implants. The dermis had that stinging-fresh sunburned look, just-out-of-the-vat shiny and a little too tight on his massive frame. But even though his vatborn age might have been less than a week, his singing voice thundered out as though it had been steeped for decades in overproof rum and unfiltered jujaweed smoke. The roaring reply of his squad rolled over Lucinda and echoed down the long companionway.

"Back in 2295 . . ."

Back in 2295 . . .

"My Marine Corps came alive."

My Marine Corps came alive.

The call-and-response followed her down the length of the ship even as the marines jogged out of sight around the curve of the hull.

"Defiant, we seem to have rather a lot of marines on board," she subvocalized. "A full company in fact. That's a bit excessive, isn't it? Unless we're planning on kicking some planets to actual pieces."

The ship chuckled inside her head.

"But they're marines, Lieutenant. They're not special enough to have their own ships. That's why they have to tag along with us."

"And that business with Lieutenant Chase?"

"Hmm?"

"Concord was a black op," she said very quietly. "Classified Top Secret Absolute. I can never wear that decoration. There is no mention of Concord on my legend. But you told Chase about it."

"I do apologize, Lieutenant," Defiant said, "but you appear to be misinformed. Or perhaps you simply haven't been informed yet. Admiralty declassified that operation."

She almost tripped over her own feet.

"Wait! What, why?"

"I'm sure I don't know. They don't explain everything to mere ship's Intellects. But if you scan your personnel file, you will find all the relevant details there now. Including your decoration and the citation that accompanied it."

"But that's . . . that's . . ."

She was at a complete loss.

"That's what Admiralty does," Defiant said. "Exactly as they please. I'm sure they had good reason for declassifying the operation, just as they did for classifying it Top Secret Absolute in the first place. The explanation could be as simple as a file review."

She shook her head, irritated, but let the questions drop. Another bot train hummed around her, and two engineering crewmen saluted uncertainly as they passed by. Lucinda resumed her passage to the O-Group. Defiant was not about to let her in on anything. Perhaps she was reading meaning into a situation in which there was none. It wouldn't be the first time. Lucinda pulled up her file, imagined the search item, and there it was. Floating in front of her.

Her citation for the Star of Valor.

Lieutenant Lucinda Jane Hardy is commended for most conspicuous acts of gallantry in action and in circumstances of great peril during special operations within the Javan Empire . . .

She hurriedly shut the display again even though nobody but she and Defiant could see it. Keeping that particular secret was a deeply ingrained habit now, and she had reached her destination: the officers' wardroom.

They were waiting for her.

The O-Group was small. She had never met any of them, but now she knew them, and they her. Lucinda's records had copied to their neural nets as soon as her transfer was approved by Fleet a week earlier. She had received theirs as soon as she linked to shipnet. She recognized Captain Torvaldt and the ship's executive officer, Commander Claire Connelly, who were both leaning back casually in their chairs, chatting quietly with each other. The marines' commander, Captain Hayes, stood out by virtue of his size. He was a full foot taller than anyone in the room, and his shoulders looked like the kind of granite boulders on which you broke other, lesser boulders. *Defiant*'s chief engineer, Lieutenant Commander Baryon Timuz, smiled at Lucinda with eyes that were both kind and a little sad. Standing beside him was Lieutenant Thanh Koh, heading up the ship's intelligence division and nodding as though Lucinda's arrival had solved a difficult math problem he'd been working on. And of course Defiant himself was also present. The ship's Intellect floated above a long polished wooden table on which sat water jugs and glasses, two pots of coffee, and a small platter of hot rolls from the galley. Torvaldt, Connelly, and Timuz were already seated. Thanh Koh was just pulling up a chair.

As soon as they noticed her in the doorway, everyone came to attention and saluted.

Lucinda almost jumped back out of the room

until she heard Defiant's silent whisper on her neural net.

"The Star, Lieutenant. They are saluting the Star."

Numbly, automatically, she returned the gesture. In her confusion, Lucinda glanced down at her service ribbons and gaped to find a new decoration displayed there. The midnight blue and white gold ribbon of the Commonwealth's highest award for bravery. She had never worn it. She had never been allowed to, and for a full second she doubted her sanity at finding it newly emblazoned over her heart.

"You must excuse me," Defiant said on their private channel. "I took the liberty of adding the decoration as you came aboard."

"Welcome aboard and please do come in, Lieutenant Hardy," Captain Torvaldt said, smiling broadly. "We'll skip the other formalities. We have a bit to get through this morning."

As soon as she entered the wardroom a little uncertainly on feet that had gone slightly numb, an occlusion field sealed them off from the rest of the ship. The Marine Corps officer, Captain Hayes, winked at her and leaned forward to shake hands.

"Nice work on Concord," he said. His hands were enormous, callused and strong, but his grip was gentle.

Everything felt slightly surreal. Not least because she was the youngest there by a whole span—even Koh was a second lifer, and Timuz, God, he was on his fourth span!—Lucinda felt as though she were playing at dress-up in her ill-fitting government-issue black-and-whites. She struggled with the oh so familiar awkwardness of expecting to be found out and told off by the grown-ups.

She took a seat next to Hayes, who pulled the hot rolls over and tore one apart with those gigantic paws of his.

"These are great," he said.

She was mortified. Captain Torvaldt had not even poured himself a coffee. But the master of the *Defiant* seemed unconcerned, even smiling at his Marine Corps counterpart.

"They are good, aren't they? Cooky is a wonder with a mixing bowl. Doesn't even use an assembler. So . . . if we're ready? Defiant?"

The Intellect, floating serenely at the opposite end of the table from Torvaldt, dipped slightly in the air. Its version of a nod.

"Thank you, Captain."

A hologram appeared above the table, a projection of the local volume, centered on Deschaneaux Station, which orbited the blue-green orb of A3-T-3019, the Earth-congruent world that had occasioned the war between Armadale and the Javan Empire. Three and a half light-years away—call it arm's length on the holo display—the farthest outpost of that empire, another rocky planet, J4-S-2989, floated over the hot rolls. Lucinda suppressed a sour expression. More commonly known as Batavia, J4 was the defaulter colony world to which the Yulin-Irrawaddy had transported her father to "pay off his debt."

Nobody ever paid off those debts. Ever.

She forced herself to look away, taking in the rest of the volume. The homeworld of the Royal Montanblanc Corporation formed the third point of a nearly

THE CRUEL STARS • 23

equilateral triangle with the Javan and Armadalen settlements. Orbiting all three, their moons, and sitting at various Lagrange points were more than a dozen Habitats of various designs. And looming over all ... the Dark. A vast swath of deliberately empty space lying between the farthest reaches of the Greater Human Volume and ... who knew?

The Sturm were out there somewhere, assuming they still lived. And one thing the Great War had taught everyone was that despite their primitivism, their barbarism, their denial of modernity and all of its advantages, the Sturm did not die easily. They surely were out there in the Dark, where nightmares came from.

"Admiralty has tasked us to carry out a longer-range patrol than usual," said Defiant. "The RAN normally takes responsibility for securing an arc of forty degrees from Deschaneaux Station to the borders of the demilitarized zone abutting the Javan, San Yong, and Zaitsev Proprietary Limited claims on System Heugens 77U. Within that area, we patrol to the margins of the Inner Dark, which are defined as much by the current limits of our FTL drives as by any political accord."

Defiant paused just as any human narrator reaching for dramatic effect might have at that point.

"On this mission we shall be patrolling to twice that distance."

"Wow!" Lucinda said, blushing a little because she was the only one to react with voluble surprise.

Connelly raised one eyebrow at Torvaldt, who seemed unsurprised and unperturbed. Lieutenant

Koh nodded as though he'd just won a bet with himself.

"That was somewhat premature, Lieutenant Hardy," said Defiant, sounding amused. "Not only will we patrol sixty light-years into the Dark, we shall do so within an arc covering sixty degrees from Deschaneaux Station."

"Whoa!" Hayes mumbled around a mouthful of hot buttered sweet roll.

"Yes," Defiant said. "Deep inside the projected arcs of all three claimants to System Heugens."

Lucinda felt as though every nerve ending in her body was suddenly humming, tingling. They were about to commit an act of war.

"Rest assured, we are not going to war," Defiant said, as though to her personally. "We are undertaking this extended patrol at the request of Earth, which has secured agreement from the three claimants to Heugens that they will neither object to nor interfere with the operation."

Beside her, Hayes snorted around a mouthful of food.

"Ha. Did they have to kill anyone?"

"No," Defiant said. "But they promised they would if there was even a hint of mischief making. Earth is . . . perturbed. If I might, I have a data packet for you. Captain Torvaldt has already been briefed, but if the rest of you could prepare yourselves, I will transfer the file momentarily."

Lucinda nodded along with the others and a second later felt the information drop into her consciousness. She took a few seconds to review the newly acquired memory, to familiarize herself with the information and, just as important, the meaning it carried.

She felt her heart beating faster and heard a few muted gasps as the others took in the substance and consequence of what they had just learned.

Defiant did not need to explain. They already knew. After more than half a millennium of total silence from the far reaches of space where the Sturm had exiled themselves after the Great War, there had come not a signal but a sign. Three ultra-long-range probes had fallen silent. For 342 years they had been sweeping the star fields thought most likely to have been settled by the Sturm and relaying their findings by a real-time wormhole link back to the Greater Volume. They had found nothing, but two Earth-standard months ago, all three had ceased transmission within hours of one another.

"Probably not a coincidence, then," the XO mused.

"Not likely," Timuz said. "I worked on those probes with my own hands, you know. They were good for the next millennium."

"Agreed," said Koh, the intelligence officer. "You could lose one to a hit from a dumb rock, or a gamma pulse, or even just systems failure. But all three, and grouped at those coordinates? Nope. Something took them out."

"And we're going to find out what," Captain Torvaldt announced.

CHAPTER
TWO

"You're getting old. Again."

"Shut up, Hero."

Professor Frazer McLennan grunted as he pushed himself off the ground. He didn't want to let Hero see him struggling so, but his knees had stiffened and one of his legs was falling asleep. He'd been sitting on a gelform mat, which protected his aging backside from the stony ground, but the Intellect was right. He was getting old again, and there was no hiding it. They'd been through this too many times.

McLennan squinted against the fierce glare obscuring the arid southern wastes of Van Maartensland, the vast equatorial supercontinent that girdled two-thirds of Batavia. The local star, a middle-aged B-type main sequence burner, was almost directly overhead and really kicking out the rays now. Even in the shade, protected by the immense bulk of the ancient Generation Ship, McLennan felt like a bug on a heat shield. They were still three hours away from the hottest part of the planet's twenty-seven-hour day, and he already was having trouble looking out into direct light.

The solar sheeting of the base camp tents threw off bright, painful sunbursts powerful enough to spear through the nearly blinding white haze of the day, but the glare alone was so murderous that he dared not look into it for more than a moment.

"A decent pair of reactive contact lenses would solve that problem, you know," Hero said. "You'll notice I'm not even mentioning the biomod or gene-tech options. See? This is me keeping my mouth shut. Not mentioning the fucking obvious. Again."

"You don't have a mouth, you clanking fucking wrinkleton," McLennan muttered. "I'd have thought that was the obvious point we're not mentioning here. Should even be obvious to a defunct robot gonad like you. Or has creeping dementia finally caught up with you, Herodotus?"

The archaic Intellect flared dull red with annoyance before fading back to depthless obsidian black.

"You are always like this when you pass fifty," Hero replied with weary contempt. "First the plumbing goes, then the social graces. Have I ever mentioned what terrible company you are in your last two decades?"

"Only in-fucking-terminably," said McLennan, flexing his knees and working some blood back into the leg that had gone numb while he examined the artifact, a surgical bot in the ship's secondary forward medbay. The crash landing had torn open the *Voortrekker*'s hull at this point, and over the centuries the bay had filled with the coarse white sand and pebble grit of Van Maartensland's Great Ironstone

Desert. Excavator drones had needed two days to carefully dig out the space. They could have emptied it in a couple of hours, of course, but only by risking damage to the contents, including three very well preserved bodies.

McLennan leaned against a warped bulkhead to maintain his balance. Pins and needles started to tingle in the waking limb.

"Wrong again," Hero said. "I have only mentioned it over a hundred and thirty-seven years, spread more or less evenly across the latter decades of seven relifes. I could send you a data package if you wanted. Oh, and if you had even the most basic neural network installed to receive it, which you don't, because you're ridiculous."

Even as Herodotus spoke, McLennan could feel it adjusting its local field effect to cool the air inside this part of the wreck and block out the heat and light pouring in through the hull breach. He found he could look outside again and see the campsite nestled in the dry gully a few hundred meters to the south. The view was suddenly so clear that he suspected Hero was also adjusting for his eyesight, which had gradually been getting worse for a decade. As it always did.

Outside, through the invisible looking glass of Hero's electromagnetic lenses and filters, he could see the camp droids moving to erect more Habs and facilities for the dig team that was scheduled to arrive later that day. Sixteen grad students and their supervisor, Professor Trumbull. That was really the cause of his foul mood. McLennan did not appreciate a lot of snot-nosed bampots crawling all over his dig, and he really didn't appreciate that walloping numptie Trumbull leading them around like the grand high poo-bah of the Jobbie Empire.

But he didn't expect Hero to understand that. The Intellect wouldn't . . .

"And don't think I'm not painfully aware you're working yourself up to a poop-flinging tantrum just because we have visitors due," Hero tut-tutted, as though scanning the neural net that McLennan famously did not possess. "I don't have to wait fifty years for you to start in on that tired old performance. We're treated to your appalling manners, or what passes for manners from an unhinged and increasingly senile Scottish bog bandit, every time the university sends us help."

"I don't need help," McLennan said, waving away Hero's inconveniently precise reading of his thoughts and mood. "I've got you."

"Well, I need help," the Intellect shot back. "Because all *I* have is *you*."

The ghostly floating ovoid form, an Armada-level Intellect in its glory days, glowed dull red again. McLennan scowled as he regarded the impossibly dense teardrop of exotic matter and nanoscale wormhole processing matrices and even considered throwing something at it. There was a flask of hot tea within reach. But he could see his reflection in Hero's outer carapace—a mirror effect the Intellect must have enabled—and in seeing himself he had to admit, yes, he looked ridiculous.

A grumpy, slump-shouldered old scrote, hanging on in a failing meat sack years after any normal person would've relifed into a younger, gene-modded body.

A prizewinning astroarchaeologist whose refusal to even consider getting properly hooked up had moved beyond eccentric and into the realm of massively expensive and inconvenient for the uni-corp that funded his research.

A historian who couldn't remember things, for fuck's sake.

He really *was* ridiculous, and despite his dark mood, he snorted with laughter that edged right up to the border of self-pity.

"Sorry, Hero," he said. "You're right. I'm being an arse."

"So you'll relife? With all the mods and a proper neural net?"

"Oh, hell no."

"Ha. I didn't think so."

"But I'll stop going out of my way to be such a pain in your arse."

"You forget I do not have an ass. You forget everything, Mac."

The Intellect had cooled to a reserved midnight blue, and there was no ire in its voice, simply resignation. This was also a scene they had played many times across his lives.

"Forgetting is my plan," McLennan said. Before Hero could reply, he went on with a peace offer. "Look, I'll consider some gene renovations and macro therapy when we get back to campus."

"In three years? You'll be fifty-seven. Are you seriously planning to wear this body out like the last one? You held on to that sorry carcass until it was eighty-seven. God's shriveled bollocks, man, it was so grotesque that Miyazaki could have offset the cost of your relife by putting you in a tent and selling tickets to a gimp show."

"That's pretty good coming from an antique windup butt plug like you," Mac replied, but there was no heat in the exchange. It was another old scene. The momentary silence that followed was companionable rather than awkward. The Intellect broke it in the end, saying, "You can't hide out here forever, you know."

McLennan snorted and pulled the cap off the insulated thermos flask, a Republican artifact no less, flipping the lid and pouring a cup of black unsweetened tea into it.

"I know that," he said. "They'll be here soon enough."

That wasn't what Hero had meant, and they both knew it, but they also knew each other well enough that neither had to say any more. A jam sandwich, kept fresh in a stasis field since he'd made it that morning, drifted over to the archaeologist on a micro-g wave. He could see the distortion in local gravity warping the flow of dust motes through the air.

"Thanks," he said, taking his lunch.

Hero collapsed the wave, and the dust resumed its slow natural dance. McLennan ate in silence, and the Intellect gave him the space, filling the medbay with quiet music, Brahms's *Academic Festival Overture,* a favorite of the Scotsman. He could feel his time running out. Trumbull and the students would arrive within the next couple of hours, puncturing his splendid isolation, ending his chosen exile. It was intolerable, really, but he would have to tolerate it. It was an unavoidable part of his professor emeritus duties with Miyazaki University. The price he paid for their indulgences, and there were many. He wouldn't deny it.

He sighed, contemplating the stasis pods he would not now be able to examine in his own time and to his private satisfaction. Their power had failed centuries ago, of course. Only a few parts of the ship still drew a trickle from the one surviving fusion stack. The Sturm had taken the antimatter drive offline before crash-landing here. If they hadn't done so, there wouldn't be much of a planet left. The pods, however, had ruptured in the crash, and that had preserved the bodies inside. The dry heat and sand had mummified them.

"Best get on with it, then," McLennan said, mainly to himself, but Herodotus dropped the volume on Brahms and floated a few inches higher, pulsing from black to midnight blue, a sign that the Intellect had come back from whatever arcane cerebral task had almost fully engaged him while McLennan ate the jammie dodger. Which is to say, more accurately, Hero had retasked an infinitesimal nanofraction of his terrifyingly vast mind to dealing with his bothersome human companion. The Intellect almost certainly continued with the literally countless number of processes that exercised its active mind, and that mind ran on less than 2 percent of the Armada-class capacity available to it.

In human terms, mostly what Hero did was sleep.

And he had mostly been sleeping for over five hundred years.

McLennan brushed the bread crumbs from his

hands, and Hero winked them away into the heart of the sun through a series of Planck length ruptures in local space-time. Keeping the dig site free of contamination was one of those "countless number of processes" the Intellect performed at an autonomic level. Constantly. Without active thought.

"What sort of a teddy bear's picnic can I expect when Trumbull arrives?" Mac asked. "No first lifers, I hope. I specifically asked—"

"Two first lifers," Hero said, speaking over him.

"Oh, for fuck's sake."

"The latest young princeling of the Yulin-Irrawaddy Combine on his gap year before attending the madrassa on Damanhur-3 and most likely marrying into the Montanblanc–ul Haq Alliance of Corporate Worlds," said Hero. "A most propitious match, I'm sure you would agree."

McLennan could hear the smile in his voice. The Intellect seemed to actively relish the old man's distress. He let his head sink to his hands. They smelled of strawberry jam.

"And a Ms. Albianiac of the Martian Albianiacs."

"The Martian fucking maniacs, more likely," said McLennan. He was back on his feet now, stalking around the medbay, his voice accelerating and his accent thickening as his mood worsened.

"Why didn't you tell me, Hero? You know I told campus not to send any more first lifers. Do they even know they can't get wormhole data out here? They'll have to load to remote storage. Like animals."

The Intellect bobbed up and down. Its version of a shrug.

"I'm sure their families have the resources to provide the very best remote lifestream capture. It will be the most marvelous adventure for them. Stuck out at the very end of the Human Volume. No live backup. A haunted ship of the Human Republic to crawl over and pick apart and generally bugger right up while a terrifying old git roars around after them like a golem in an adult diaper. No wonder their families made such generous donations to the university."

McLennan stomped over to the gel mat and gingerly lowered himself to a seated position from which he could access the surgical bot's memory cache. The Sturm were still encoding DNA for storage at this point in their history—a grim irony, he'd always thought. He didn't expect the cache to be in perfect condition, but DNA had been a remarkably resilient high-capacity storage medium and the samples they'd extracted so far had retained up to 80 percent of their data. He worked away at the hexagonal rod of vat-grown memory bone with a specialist tool set recovered from another part of the wreck.

"And the rest of them," he said over his shoulder. "What else can I look forward to?"

"Oh, the usual," Hero said. "Second and third lifers. Corporate nobility on sabbatical for the most part. One is touring all of the major Civil War sites. The others are—"

"Forget I asked," McLennan said. "They're tourists. Just keep them away from the critical areas. Exclusion fields if you have to. And me. Keep them away from me, too."

"I'm afraid you're part of the package tour, Mac. You're the reason they paid so much to be here."

He gave up fiddling with the memory cache and

flopped down flat on the gel mat. Hero generated a soft exclusion field just above the deck plating that would have painfully cracked his skull if he'd hit his head there. He didn't. The invisible field cushioned his graying old noggin like a pillow.

"Why?" he asked. "Why can't people just leave me alone?"

Hero pulsed a light shade of sky blue. A smile.

"Because you saved the human race," the Intellect said. "And they'll never forgive you for it."

CHAPTER
THREE

They didn't have time for a live scan of the Yakuza underboss, so they cut off his head, snap froze it, and tossed it into an ice bucket. But now the ice was melting, the YG were closing in, and Sephina L'trel was questioning her life choices. The mistress and commander of the *Je Ne Regrette Rien* hunkered down behind the bar, swapping out mags as a plasma storm of automatic weapons fire atomized hundreds of liquor bottles on the shelves above her, turning superheated alcohol into a crude fuel-air explosive. Molten glass rained down on them, and jagged shards of shrapnel raked at the nanotube armor weave of the long dusters the crew wore.

They were running low on autodrones, on ammo, on luck. But not on motherfuckers trying to kill them. Plenty of them left and more on the way.

Oh, and HabSec Tactical Response, too.

They'd be here in a minute or so with orders to kill everyone still standing. Or cowering in her case. Mostly at the moment she was cowering and trying not to get blown up or shot to pieces. Be cool if they didn't let that severed head get too warm, either. Anything over four degrees for more than half an hour and the only thing they'd be extracting from it was gray sludge.

The whole room shook with a titanic boom as one of the drones took out a grenade before it could land behind the bar and turn them all into human burrito meat. Ariane quickly poked the muzzle of her Skorpyon over the top of the bar and squeezed off a couple of short unaimed bursts. A mix of penetrators, tracers, and a couple of random hex rounds to sow confusion and terror among the natives. The room strobed and flared with the muzzle flash and detonations.

Next to her, the hunched and enormous Jaddi Coto maneuvered the dwindling drone squadron with headset and controller, looking like something out of a museum display. Coto was a huge man, festooned with weapons that hung from spring hooks and bone loops sewn and grown into his own body, into the thick black gene-threaded rhinoderm hide that afforded him as much protection from small arms fire and blast effects as did the dusters Sephina and Ariane wore. But he did wear one of the distinctive overcoats, too. All the members of the *Regret*'s crew wore them. It marked them as clan. As family.

Probably best not to romanticize that shit, though, Sephina thought as she caught the ghost of a reflection in a shattered bar mirror. One of Tanto's men attempting to flank them on her left. The Yamaguchi-gumi soldier eeling through the debris and bodies on the floor of the bar had his clan, too, and it was trying to exterminate hers. The barrage of fire coming in from the rest of the gummies intensified, probably to draw their attention away from the killer coming at them like a human snake. Sephina wondered whether this dude was a specialist, whether he'd been gene-sequenced and vat-grown to a purpose, or if the YG had hacked his genome and p-type later.

Didn't matter.

"Coto! Three o'clock, on the down low," she called out.

"Nuh," grunted the drone pilot. "Can't."

He was concentrating furiously on holding off the main thrust of the attack. Which, she conceded, was the point of having a main thrust of an attack.

"Shit."

"I'll get him, baby," Ariane hissed, jacking a new clip of adaptive ammo into her pistol and trying to crawl over Sephina to get to the end of the bar, where she could effect a look-see snapshot at ground level. She was soaked and sticky with alcohol. A deep gash oozed blood down one side of her beautiful face, which broke into a teasing smile as she used their enforced closeness for a quick rubfuck on the way through.

"Don't even, girlfriend," Seph yelled over the roar of gunfire and the screams of the dying. She clamped a hand over Ariane's shoulder and pulled her back. The young woman protested but did not resist.

"Target practice," Sephina yelled again, pulling a bottle of clear liquid out from under the bar. The label promised 180-proof genuine Balkan vodka, but Taro's Bar didn't run to that sort of extravagance. She had no doubt it was just shitty ghetto juice manufactured in-Hab. "Widespread. Incendiary."

Ariane saw what she intended, nodded, and smiled. It was not a happy expression. She flicked the selector on her Skorpyon and took aim as Sephina tossed the bottle high into the air, arcing it over the bar and toward the spot where she estimated the flanker to be. Ariane hit the bottle with her first shot, and they both flinched and squeezed their eyes closed against the bright wash of flame and heat from the improvised explosive.

She couldn't see whether they'd gotten the guy, but she could hear his screams and the cries of the other gummy soldiers, the *gunsotsu*.

"Nice," Coto rumbled. His voice sounded like the deep tectonic cracking of a frozen moon under severe g stress.

"The head!" Sephina cried out. She'd knocked the bucket over, and the underboss, or the most important part of him anyway, had spilled onto the floor, where it lay in a slurry of rapidly melting ice. Swearing, she grabbed a handful of lanky black hair and jammed the head back into the bucket with as much of the ice as she could scoop up. Ariane and Coto returned fire and held off another assault while she frantically searched the glass cabinets under the bar for more ice cubes. Or superchilled vodka. Because superchilled vodka would be awesome right about now. A workable storage medium and the perfect base for a Vesper martini. For once, however, she conceded, cocktails could wait.

He'd start thawing out soon, and they'd lose their only chance to extract the credits as the synaptic connections between his cortex and his neural net started to degrade.

"This is a fucking bar. There should be ice," she cursed, crawling back and forth, climbing over the body of the bartender who'd died—for real, too, no backup, no respawn—in the opening exchange of fire.

She felt bad about that and about the Hab rats caught in the cross fire. None of them would have backup. But the best thing she could do for any one of them right now was to get old Satomi San here chilled out again. If they could just have five minutes to do a read, even a quick and dirty meat scan, they could get their money, pay their tithes and damages, and get the fuck gone from Combine space. She didn't doubt they were burned to the fucking ground here. Not just on this Hab but everywhere the Yulin-Irrawaddy owned or claimed to own.

"The drones are all gone," Coto said, as though letting them know the last of the cheese biscuits had been eaten. He removed the headset through which he'd been monitoring and controlling them, a set of powered goggles he'd had to rig up himself because no off-the-shelf heads-up displays would fit on his face. They were usually too small and never designed to accommodate the gigantic black horn that grew from the middle of his forehead. Coto pulled a pair of industrial-looking devices from carabiner clips dangling around his torso. He looked like he was about to do some heavy riveting or welding, but they were guns, not tools, and he started shooting like everyone else. Adding to the savage caterwauling crush of weapons fire. Threading a few more grace notes of pain and horror into the chorus of war shouts, death cries, and unintelligible screaming.

Sephina mashed the button on her headset, trying to get a link to the *Regret*. Static and white noise filled her earpiece. Still down or jammed or something.

Probably jammed. The commlink to the ship had dropped out as soon as the meet with the Yakuza went sideways. Like they'd been planning to rip her off all along. As she'd been planning to rip them off all along. Both parties rushing to trigger their ambush scam inside the decision loop of the other.

"Right, we're doing this here," she announced as an incendiary grenade bounced off the beer taps and exploded in front of the bar. The wash of dry heat made her skin pucker and confirmed the decision she'd just made.

"That head's not getting any colder. We gotta download here. Coto, gimme all your grenades. Then your job is hacking Satomi. I don't need any of the shit the Russians paid for. I just want that bearer code."

Coto furrowed his massive brow. Really something to see on a seven-foot dude chock-fulla great ape and rhino genes. The vast tattooed plains of his forehead puckered around the base of his horn like living foothills.

"But that is not what we had planned," he objected very slowly with great dignity and formality.

"No, *this* is not what we had planned," Sephina shouted over the uproar, twirling one finger to take in the violent derangement of the battle.

"And so we adapt," he said, as though discovering a fundamental law of physics in the chaos of the moment.

"We adapt." She nodded.

"And improvise," Ariane yelled as she emptied the clip she had only just loaded. More screams. More fire. She patted Coto on the shoulder, leaning to almost whisper in his ear. "And we overcome."

He nodded as though resolved that this new path would be walked as steadfastly as every other path through life that had delivered him to this place at this time.

Sephina handed Coto the severed head. It was cool to the touch and wet. But not cold. She feared that they'd already missed their chance.

"He has no data port," Coto announced as Sephina started tossing dumb grenades from cover. "But I shall adapt."

He drew a fighting knife from his belt and drove it into the top of the skull with a sick, wet crunch, working the blade around until he'd opened up a thumb-sized cavity.

"It'll be in the secure enclave. Down near the ass end of the medulla," she said. "Trash the cortical net if you have to. We just need that bearer code."

Sephina left him to it, reloading her weapon and stealing a kiss from Ariane before scooting down to the other end of the bar to try a different firing solution. Her lover's lips and tongue tasted of cold spiced rum. Ariane grinned, guilty but unashamed. She'd been taking sly sips from a bottle under the bar during their fight to the death with the Yak. Sephina had no idea how many of the Yamaguchi *gunsotsu* were left, but it sounded like more than enough. No idea whether Banks or Falun Kot had received her alert before the Yak's data mavens cut them off. And no fucking idea whether they were going to get out of this alive.

Like the bartender and most of the bystanders who'd died in the opening seconds of the fight, neither Seph nor any of her crew had organic net access and backup. That was why they rocked so many headsets and data rigs. She had her reasons, of course, and most days she could tell you why they were good reasons. Great reasons. But every now and then, surrounded by murderous goons and cyclonic weapons fire, the commander of the good ship *Je Ne Regrette Rien* did wonder whether she was taking this living offline thing way too seriously.

She popped up and dropped back down immediately as a plasma bolt cracked the air just above her, burning a few strands of dirty blond dreads. Kinetic rounds poured in after the hot shot of ionized blue-white energy. Dozens of caseless slugs chewing up the ruins of the shelving behind her like a threshing machine. She rolled over broken glass and burning pools of alcohol. Ariane—beautiful, fearless Ariane—screamed at the men who'd almost killed her, pouring blinding white streams of arclight fire from Coto's main weapon. It was so big that she couldn't lift it more than a few inches from the scorched and broken marble of the bar top, but the long lethal jets of coherent energized quantum flux whipped at the whole room erratically, capriciously. Here sliding harmlessly over the farthest wall, coherence spent in a shower of sparks. There slicing through a gunman who rose up from cover after the initial passage of the stream, only to be caught when it whipped back unpredictably like a garden hose hooked up to a high-pressure tap. The man screeched and then fell silent, dropping to the floor in two neatly bisected and cauterized chunks of smoking Japanese beef.

"Get down," Sephina yelled at Ariane as fire began to come in from a corner of the room she'd already swept with the arclight. Seph could see a huddle of shooters over there, protected by a large stone table, more of an altar really, that they'd tipped over to hide behind. It looked so large and heavy that she knew they had to be packing some serious mods to have even shifted it. If and when she and Ari ran out of ammo, they were dead meat on a little wooden stick. Coto could hold his own in hand-to-hand against three or four of the Yak, but she and Ariane wouldn't live long enough to see that.

"Come on, JC," she cried out, wincing as a tracer round sparked off the power chamber of the arclight. Ariane flinched and dropped back into cover. More fire zeroed in on her. And Sephina threw her last grenade, another dumb bomblet, into the corner where the shooters had marked Ariane. It landed in front of the overturned altar and exploded with a dense percussive thud but had no discernible effect on the attackers beyond a momentary lull in fire.

"I have it," Coto said, surprising her as she took cover again. He held a small biochip on the tip of his little finger, sticky with blood and flecked with gray matter. Satomi's secure enclave.

"The code! Extract the bearer code!" she shouted at him.

Ariane was firing single shots from her Skorpyon now.

"I did," said Coto. "It's in here."

He briefly held up a tablet.

It looked tiny in his grip.

"Omigod. Coto! Upload it! To the Deuce! Now! For fuck's sake!"

"That is a good idea," he said, nodding gravely, "but our channel to the Deuce is being blocked by Satomi San's data mavens."

Both women shouted at once.

"Improvise!"

"Ah," he rumbled as the beautiful logic of the suggestion unfolded before him like a morning flower.

"Adapt," he said, counting off one finger. "Improvise." Two fingers. "And overcome."

He held up three fingers now.

Four if you counted the other hand, where the biochip still rested on the tip of his pinkie. He looked like an 800-pound child wondering how all the melted chocolate got on his hands.

Then he rolled under the bar and began pulling out cables and wiring.

"I'm out," Ariane hissed, crawling over to search through Coto's pockets while he rummaged around under the bar.

Sephina slammed her last magazine home and threw a few rounds out at nobody in particular, hoping to hold back the charge that she knew had to be coming. Ariane produced a cut-down dragon-shot gun from within the folds of Coto's duster and added the fiery sonic booms of the weapon to the coughing bark of Sephina's three-round bursts.

Coto labored away at his task like a plumber with nothing more serious to do than clear a hair clot from an S bend. His coat had bunched up around him, and the plumber analogy was apt, Sephina thought, given the vast and sweaty canyon of hairy butt crack that confronted her over the top of his cargo pants. His gorilla DNA was really out on parade.

"I have improvised, Commander," Coto announced from under the bar. "We have an encrypted datalink to Deuce2 via the Hab's wormhole arrays."

"Outstanding, JC!" Sephina yelled.

"Awesome," Ariane shouted over the roar of the dragon shot.

They might even get out of this after all, Seph thought. Just before everything turned to shit.

CHAPTER
FOUR

Princess Alessia Szu Suri sur Montanblanc ul Haq was pissed off. The governess had found her, and now she would have to leave the garden and the game she had been playing with Caro and Debin and return to the music room for her flute lesson.

To practice her scales.

Dozens and dozens of scales.

Played hundreds and hundreds of times.

Could there be anything more pointless in all of human space?

"Just five more minutes," she protested to Lady Melora. "Come on. Just five."

Her pleas had a wheedling tone that even she didn't much like the sound of, but what did people expect of her?

Dozens and dozens of scales. That was what.

Played hundreds and hundreds of times.

"Shoo!" Lady Melora said, waving off Caro and Debin like common street urchins. "Go on. Away with you, you dirty little kinchin."

Debin, at ten, two years younger than Alessia, actually was pretty dirty. He'd been hiding from the girls in the cool dark soil under the Golden Orb bushes. They were a favorite hiding spot, and they'd known he was in there but had let him enjoy the thrill of thinking he'd eluded them. At least until Caro heard the increasingly shrill cries of the formidable Lady Melora and the girls had darted in under the fat green leaves and bright orange flowers to join him.

They'd had no more luck hiding from Lady Melora than Debin had had in giving them the slip.

"Move over. Stay quiet," Alessia hissed when they'd tumbled in on top of him.

"You move over. This is my place," Debin protested.

Maybe they would have avoided capture if they hadn't fallen into a fit of giggles when Alessia's governess, flanked by two palace guards in all their finery, had stood in front of the Golden Orb bush, hands on hips, and demanded that she present herself immediately. When Alessia refused, old Sergeant Reynolds told the younger guard—Alessia didn't really know him yet—to crawl in and drag them out. He was covered in scratches and soil now and looked even less impressed than Lady Melora.

"See them off," she barked at the guards, and Reynolds peeled off one long leather glove to whip at the gardener's children, who squealed half in fright and half in delight. The old sergeant, who was always kindly with Alessia, took his time getting that glove off.

"You're it," Caro shouted, smacking Alessia on the rump as she fled, reducing the governess to apoplexy and the princess to another burst of giggles.

The guards did not pursue their quarry. Sergeant Reynolds looked as old as the stars. He didn't like running anywhere. And anyway, Lady Melora only wanted Caro and Debin gone, not beaten.

At times it felt like Lady Melora wanted to chase away everything in Alessia's life that made her happy. All the governess cared about was duty and honor and doing what was proper and correct no matter what Alessia thought or felt.

Honestly, she thought, watching her friends, her only real friends, scampering away down the hill and laughing, what was even the point of being a princess if you couldn't do what you wanted? Caro and Debin had more fun than she did. Living in the groundskeeper's quarters with their grandfather. Running wild through the gardens of Skygarth, playing in the stables, swimming in any of the lakes or streams whenever they felt like it. It took nearly a whole day to walk the walled boundary of the estate. It was huge. Alessia's whole world. So there was no shortage of places for Caro and Debin to escape to. No flute lessons for them. No elocution practice. No tutors in diplomacy, or history, or mathematics, or anything. Lately, Lady Melora had even made Alessia attend fencing lessons, which sounded like great fun at first. Like seriously. Sword fighting. What was not to love about that?

Everything, as it turned out. And if you disagreed, you could try spending an hour a day with Lord Guillaume just standing.

Yeah. You got that right.

Standing! Holding a stupid wooden stick. And occasionally moving, but only to do some more standing and stick holding. And sometimes a little stumbling when Lord Guillaume clipped you across the ear for not standing or moving or holding that stupid stick exactly as instructed.

Sword fighting, it turned out, was as boring as flute scales.

"What do you have to say for yourself, young lady?" the governess demanded. Her voice sounded like a dagger point on crystal. Alessia shaded her eyes even though the sun wasn't really in them. She just wanted to hide. The Golden Orb bushes surrounded a koi pond ten or fifteen minutes' walk from the main residence, a great sprawling white villa that had been transported at insane expense, block by block, from Old Earth because . . . Why not? You could do that sort of thing when you were a Montanblanc. You just couldn't play with your friends or climb trees or go swimming in the—

"Well? Young lady."

"Sorry, madam governess," Alessia mumbled.

"You don't sound sorry."

That's cos I'm not, you old witch. Well, I guess I'm sorry that you found us. But, you know . . .

"Your mother and father will be here this weekend, and don't imagine for a second they won't hear tell of your willful misbehavior and recalcitrant attitude. If the future of House Montanblanc should fall to your care, heaven forfend and the Sturm take us all."

Oh, don't make me roll my eyes, Alessia thought.

The future of House Montanblanc would never fall to her. She was just breeding stock. Begat to be sold off to the highest bidder, which unfortunately looked increasingly like Deputy Prince Vincent Pac Yulin, whom Alessia had met but once. That was more than enough. She had not been impressed. He told her she was fat and spent most of the arranged meeting far away in a game sim-generated by his own net.

House Yulin, unlike House Montanblanc, did not delay implanting its progeny with personal neural mesh.

"And I won't delay implanting you, you ugly pig," Pac had whispered to her when he thought nobody was listening. "So I can get back to my harem girls."

But if Alessia thought an insult to her family from some sad little deputy douchebro would sabotage the arrangements for her eventual merger with the Yulin-Irrawaddy Combine, she was to be disappointed.

"All boys are horrible at that age," her mother told her during a rare moment alone after that disastrous first meeting. "And you're not fat, darling. You simply have energy reserves for the growth spurt you have coming in sixteen months. For the wedding. The adipose tissue will all burn off. Don't worry. You will look absolutely ravishing when your wedding comes around. Prince Vincent won't be able to keep his hands off you."

"Oh, God, Mother. You're not helping."

Alessia snapped back into the moment as Lady Melora's glass-cutting voice sawed through her reverie.

"Your mother won't help you out of this, young lady. Stop mumbling. Get yourself cleaned up. And be in your music studio in no more than twenty minutes if you know what's good for you."

She had drifted away on memory. Losing herself as she took flight from the little grotto around the koi pond where Lady Melora was using up quite a few of those twenty minutes to deliver yet another lecture about poor choices and dire consequences. The palace guards had arranged themselves behind her, one at each shoulder. They stared into the middle distance, off across the bright, beautifully tended greensward of the gardens. There was a small copse of trees from Old Earth a few minutes' walk downslope, and she wondered if Sergeant Reynolds was imagining himself hiding away in there. She'd heard some of the other guards talking about Lady Melora. They didn't seem to like her any more than Alessia did.

"It's nearly three o'clock," the governess said, her eyes losing focus the way grown-ups did when they checked something on their personal net. "You have just enough time to catch up on your flute before Doctor Bordigoni arrives from the university for your French and Italian lessons. Then I shall check your homework from the tutors, which I will expect to be done in full and to a respectable standard, before you have dinner. And this evening you shall be doing your study, not reading those old books you've hidden under your bed. And I will be checking your study, reading over your notes. Yes, notes. Written notes. By hand, by you. Not by one of the footmen like last week."

Her afternoon, which had been such a joyous rush of play and make-believe and simple fun with Caro and Debin, contracted down to a dark and mean little tunnel, pressing in on her from all sides. Not just the afternoon. Her whole life.

"Why?" she snapped quite a good deal louder than she had intended. Lady Melora actually jumped a little bit, which made Alessia feel good even as she dreaded the retribution she knew must surely be coming.

"I beg your pardon?"

"Why?" Alessia repeated. She thought she saw Sergeant Reynolds shake his head. Warning her. But having dipped a toe into the water, she might as well dive right in. "Why do I have to do any of that? Why can't I just do what I want to do for once? Nobody but me learns any of this stuff. Prince Vincent doesn't. He told me. He said it's stupid learning everything the old way. He can speak about a hundred languages, and he's never had a single lesson. Not one. He just loads them when he needs them. Everyone does."

Alessia dropped her hand, no longer shading her eyes, no longer hiding. She found, somewhat to her surprise, that she was angry. And over it. Over the whole stupid lot of it. Being a princess. Being a Montanblanc. Being anything other than a girl like Caro, who was free to do as she pleased.

"Did you not listen to anything I just said?" Lady Melora asked. Her voice was clipped and even sharper than usual. She did not seem at all sympathetic. She didn't seem much interested in Alessia's answer, either, because she went on without pause. "You are a very privileged and spoiled young lady. You have no idea of how privileged. Or how spoiled, for that matter."

The sound of gardening drones drifted over them. Caro and Debin's grandfather, trimming the paths that wound through the hedge animals in the topiary garden. Caro said he'd be doing that this afternoon, and they'd planned to go down there when they were done playing hide-and-seek. The topiary animals, so many of them that they formed a real maze, were tucked away in the bend of the small shaded brook that ran into the big lake. It was one of Alessia's favorite places anywhere inside the walled grounds of the estate because you could lose yourself in there and pretend you weren't even in Skygarth anymore. You could be in Narnia or Middle Earth or Montival. Anywhere but here.

"I'm not spoiled," she muttered darkly to herself, but Lady Melora seemed to take it as a personal affront.

"What was that?"

"I'm not spoiled," she said out loud. "Or privileged. I can't do *anything* I want."

Melora's expression darkened. Alessia expected her to explode with anger. She did have a temper on her. Everyone knew. But when she spoke, the words came out cold. Each one chipped from an iceberg somewhere deep down inside her.

"You do not get to make choices," Melora said. "All the choices were made for you before you were born. *That* is your privilege."

Alessia quickly glanced at the guardsmen to see if they looked as confused as she was, but as usual their faces were masked and unreadable.

"That doesn't even make sense," she protested. "You were just telling me I make bad choices, then you say all my choices have already been made for me. What does that even mean? You're just stupid and you hate being here as much as I do, *but you could leave, which is why you're stupid to stay*."

She all but shouted the last words at Melora.

She was going to be punished. She knew that. She might even get smacked right here and now. But she didn't care. She hated Melora. She hated Skygarth. She hated being a princess, and she really really really hated practicing her scales. Alessia squared up for whatever was coming, but when it did come, she still wasn't ready.

Lady Melora's mouth, which had been pressed into a thin white line, began to move. Not to speak but to tremble. Her eyes, glassy and dry, grew wet, and her face went from the bright pink flush of anger to a lighter shade, almost colorless, then back to red again.

She spun away.

"Sergeant," she said, her voice cracking. "Just make sure she gets to her damn lessons."

Alessia's governess stomped away up the long slope back to the main villa. At first the guards did not move; then Sergeant Reynolds risked a look back over his shoulder to where Lady Melora continued to stomp away from them. Alessia could hear her crying now, which was something she'd never heard Melora or any of the grown-ups do. The other guardsman, the one who'd crawled into the bushes to drag Debin out by his ankle, looked worried. He was new, and Alessia didn't know his name, but Sergeant Reynolds had been around for as long as . . . well, he'd always just been there.

He frowned.

"You should probably go and get cleaned up, mistress," he said, still watching Melora depart up the hill. "Go on. Run. A quick bath. Clean clothes. And go play your flute for a bit. I don't think it's going to matter if you don't do all your scales. Just play something you like. That song that sounds like rabbits. I like that one."

"It's called 'Tamino's Aria.' I like it, too," Alessia conceded. "But it's not about rabbits. It's just another stupid story about princesses and stuff."

"Well, I like it. And I think," Reynolds said, pausing to furrow his brow, "I think you should probably say sorry to Lady Melora, too."

Alessia almost flared again at that, but one look at Sergeant Reynolds's expression took the heat out of her reaction. He wasn't angry like Melora. He was disappointed.

"Sorry," she said quietly, then sighed. She took a deep breath and addressed the other guardsman. "And I'm sorry we made you crawl into the bushes. You got messed up, and that was my fault."

The guardsman looked like she'd poked him with a stick or maybe put a frog down his shirt the way Debin had done to her once.

"I . . . er . . ." he started to say but seemed to lose himself before he could figure out what to say.

"Don't get your panties in a bunch, lad," Reynolds said. "She's just a little girl."

I wish, Alessia thought.

CHAPTER
FIVE

The man in Cell M23—and he was a man, don't let anyone tell you otherwise—splashed water on his face. It was cold, almost shocking. He felt it. The cold. The fuckin' *wetness* of it in a way that normally you didn't. Not as you mindlessly passed through the day not thinking about your existence. The water, gurgling from the sink in his cell, it was *there*. It would be *there*, in the world of real things, when the man who once was known as Corporal Booker3-212162-930-Infantry would not be here or there or anywhere very soon. Because Booker was a condemned man.

Not just to death but to something worse.

To erasure.

He shook the last drops of water from his hands, amazed at the way the droplets flew from the ends of his fingers. Amazed that he noticed. At the way he could *feel* the water flying off. He tried to make himself understand that very soon he wouldn't be able to. Wouldn't be a *him* to feel or think or remember.

The Book would be deleted.

He turned off the tap. It dripped even when he tightened the spigot. The dripping had been constant since they'd moved him in here three days earlier. Booker wiped his hands on the bright orange jumpsuit he wore. There was no towel in the cell. Not even a small one, because he might tear that into strips and hang himself. Then they wouldn't get the satisfaction of deleting him. The jumpsuit was made of paper. You were supposed to get a fresh one when you moved onto death watch, but his felt like some other guy had already worn it. Even before he put it on, it smelled of stale sweat, a little piss, and fear.

Booker could still smell fear. They'd programmed that into his code because it was useful on stealth ops. They hadn't turned it off. Probably on purpose. Letting him smell his own fear. That was like them.

"Yo, Book! Here come da preacher man!"

He did not turn around.

That voice. Guttural. Mocking. That voice was Keller, in the cell across from him. Keller had murdered a Navy officer, but his execution had been delayed by some jurisdictional pissing match over who was gonna get to kill him. The Navy wanted to kill him. The marines wanted to kill him. The fuckin' civs back on Earth wanted to kill him. And this had been dragging on for months, much to Keller's amusement. But he'd eventually be killed. Not deleted. They were gonna execute Keller properly, with some dignity and hope for his immortal soul.

"Yo, Book. He's comin', boy. Y'all ain't even gonna die, Book. You gone be erased, bro. Like you ain't never were."

Keller laughed. A sort of braying noise. It sounded harsh but heartfelt.

Booker walked to his cot. Sat down. Stood up. Walked a couple of laps of the small cell again. His hands were shaking. He'd thought he was past that.

Cell M23 was bigger than the cell he'd shared down in gen-pop with Injara. He'd measured it. And he didn't have to share the block with anyone besides Keller over the way there. That sucked, but at least they weren't in the same cell. He just had to listen to the asshole. They were the only two inmates of Execution and Deletion. The other four cells were empty.

Booker sometimes thought about everyone who'd been in those cells before. All gone now. Like he would be soon.

"My son."

Booker turned toward the voice. Keller called out, "Yo, Padre! How you doin' with my last wish? You gone get ol' Keller that pussy I asked for? Condemned man gets to choose his last meal, Father, and I feel like eating some tasty *pussaaay*."

A baton clanged noisily on the steel cage.

"Shut up, asshole."

Keller shut up.

Corporal Orr was on escort duty for Father Michael. You didn't mess with that guy. He had all sorts of close combat code loaded on precon. It wasn't just his job. He was a collector. Traveled all over the Volume, every chance he got, looking for ever more arcane scripts. Word was that he'd paid his own way to a lacuna upgrade so he could carry all that extra programming on preconscious access. All of it. So he didn't even need to load code. It was just there. Waiting.

He stood at parade ground rest behind Father Michael. Not even bothering to look at Keller. Wasn't worth the effort to turn his head.

"Step back," he said.

Booker did as he was told. He never gave Orr any trouble. Never caused any trouble for anyone. Except himself.

"You good, Father?" Orr said to the priest.

Father Michael looked to be in his late fifties. His biotic age would be his real age, too. Most of the Old Earth churches did not allow their ministers to relife. Not surprising that they had to recruit so heavily off-world. In the poorer Habs.

Their priests weren't always the sharpest, either.

"I will be fine, thank you, Sam," this one said. "Booker has never raised as much as a hard word against me. I doubt he will now."

Father Michael tilted his head to one side, smiling a question at the condemned man.

"You'll be fine, Padre," Booker said. He was resigned to the visit. He hadn't asked for a priest. But it was protocol. Everything was protocol from now until the end. Whatever and ever, amen. He looked at Corporal Orr. "I don't want trouble, Corporal. And even if I wanted some, they got the circuit breaker on my amygdala, remember. I get angry, I get sleepy, real fast."

Orr knew that. He knew everything about his charges, but he was not a man to leave shit to chance. He seemed satisfied. At least with Booker.

"You shut the fuck up and you stay that way," he

said over his shoulder to Keller. Sounded almost bored.

Keller did not answer. He just nodded sullenly from his bunk. You didn't hollaback at Corporal Orr.

The priest pulled the cell door closed behind him with a heavy metallic clang. The maglocks engaged. Orr gave Booker a look that promised some really profound fucking misery for the rest of his very short life if he tried anything stupid.

"I'll be back in an hour," he said. "I'll have the captain with me, Booker. We'll be going then. Best you prepare yourself."

Booker nodded quietly.

"Yes, Corporal."

Father Michael wasn't nervous at all at being left alone with a terrorist. A traitor. But then it wasn't his first visit. And Booker had that clamp on his hind-brain.

"Do you mind if I sit?" the priest asked, indicating the bunk. "I woke up with a cramp in my leg this morning. It's very uncomfortable."

Booker shrugged.

"Suit yourself, Father."

He stayed on his feet. Woulda been a waste to spend his last hours ass-pressing a prison bed, wouldn't it?

"They tell me you're not eating, my son. You are entitled to a last meal."

Booker shook his head.

"Not fair to the next guy they pour into this body. Waking up with somebody else's lunch in your guts. Especially if it's been sitting there a while. I've done that, Padre. It feels gross."

"That's very considerate of you, Booker."

"You have your ways, Father. We have ours." He smiled thinly.

Across the hall, Keller was stalking back and forth in his cell, giving them both the evil eye but saying nothing. His face looked sallow and mean under the cell block strip lighting. The flat white glow reflected from all the metal surfaces, wiping out any shadows, highlighting all the blemishes and the dark pouchy sacks under his eyes.

Keller looked pissed. He'd probably worked on that pussy-eating joke all morning. But he said nothing.

Corporal Orr would be watching.

"As far as I know, Booker, the Code does not mean you can't seek absolution. Have you considered my offer? The Church will take you in even now."

"I'm good, Padre. I got an hour or so. Plenty of time for a deathbed conversion yet."

Father Michael nodded sadly, as though the disappointment was expected.

"I will pray for your soul, then."

Booker leaned against the cold bulkhead. He was nowhere near hard vacuum. He knew that. Engineering spaces separated the inner and outer hulls by at least fifty meters. But the chill of the dull gray carbon armor panels still seemed profound, as though all the warmth would leach from this space within a few minutes of his departing it.

"Save your breath, Padre," he said. "My soul is about to be deleted."

The priest shook his head. Resolved.

"No, Booker, I don't believe that, and neither

should you. The soul arises in the first spark of life itself. Not in the architecture that transfers or carries or records a mere copy of that life."

He sounded like he was quoting from notes scribbled on the back of his hand.

Once upon a time the priest would have annoyed Booker, enraged him even. Now, so close to his complete negation, he couldn't find the energy to be angry. Although the clamp on his amygdala probably accounted for some of that Zen chill, too.

"Father," he said, "I'm grateful for you being here. It beats spending my last moments with Keller. But you're wasting your time, seriously."

The other inmate roused himself at the offhand insult, but only for a moment. Keller soon went back to sulking on his own bunk, sitting with his knees pulled up under his chin, the corners of his mouth turned down with comical exaggeration. The priest ignored Booker's jabbing at the other man. He was working hard to save a soul here. Had been for two weeks now. But there was no point. The whole reason they were extracting and deleting Booker's source code was that doing so didn't wipe out his mere physical existence but his soul, too. At least he thought so, anyway.

"Booker," said Father Michael, starting and then stopping to gather his thoughts. "Booker, if it means nothing to you, why not allow me to baptize you anyway? What would you have to lose?"

Booker laughed at that, surprised into gallows mirth by the cynicism of it. He'd thought Father Michael more naïve than that. But maybe he was just cribbing from notes again.

"What would you have to gain, Padre? A conversion without faith; that wouldn't count, would it?"

The older man waved off the objection.

"Do you imagine a newborn baby comes to his baptism cognizant of what's happening and what it means for him? Of course he doesn't. To God, you would be as that newborn babe. A pure soul welcomed into his everlasting love."

Booker sighed and rubbed at his eyes. He was tired, and his palm rasped on the stubble of his cheeks. He didn't want to argue theology with this well-meaning idiot. He was content to pass his final hour in better company than Keller could offer. But he didn't want to have to defend and justify his own faith as a source coder.

The priest was right in one way at least. There were many of the Code who also identified as members of other faiths. Lesser faiths for sure. But not everyone could be as true to the Code as Booker3-212162-930-Infantry.

He took a deep breath. Resolved not to waste his time arguing with the priest.

"Okay. Tell you what, then. I'll let you splash your water and say your words if you'll stop talking about it and if you'll get it done quickly. I'd like to know something of the worlds out there before I take my leave of them."

The old priest rocked back on the bunk, astonished. He moved quickly, not wanting to miss this unexpected chance.

"But of course, my son, of course. Whatever you want."

From a pocket, he took a long purple ribbon embroidered with gold-colored thread and draped it quickly around his neck. Patting his pockets, he seemed distracted, distressed.

"My holy water," he said. "I think I left it outside . . ."

"Just use the tap," Booker said, nodding at the sink, where the faucet still drip-drip-dripped.

"But I . . ." The priest fussed about himself.

Booker pushed off the wall, took a paper cup sitting on the small shelf over the sink, and gave it to the priest.

"Try this, Padre. Stir in some magic dust or sparkles or whatever."

"Thank you."

Father Michael filled the cup with water, mumbled a prayer over it, and made the sign of the Cross.

"There you go," said Booker. "Instant power-up."

There were more words, some gestures, a freezing dribble of Hab water on his forehead, and that was it. He was a Christian.

A Catholic? He was pretty sure Father Michael was Catholic.

Whatever. It was all the same to him.

"You have done the right thing, Booker. You won't regret this. I promise. Would you like to make your confession?"

"Sure," he replied. "I did it all. All the things they said? I did that."

"And we should pray," said a rejuvenated Father Michael. "For your absolution."

"I'd prefer to just talk, Padre."

"Prayer is talking to God, Booker."

"Well, you're God's representative here on the Hab, right? So talking to you, I'm talking to him."

Father Michael examined him with a calculating eye, probably figuring the odds of crapping out if he doubled down.

"All right. You are in a state of grace, I suppose."

"Oh, man, this is so lame," Keller complained across the hallway. "Booker, I thought you were better than this. You said you'd never sell out."

A hatch slammed open, and Orr came running down the space between the cells. He had a baton out, and Keller started begging.

"I didn't mean it, Corporal. I just forgot is all. I just forgot."

But Orr never forgot. Father Michael winced and Booker grinned as the corporal flew into the cell and whipped Keller into bloody rags with a choreographed sequence of baton strikes that blurred into red mist. A few seconds of violence and it was over.

The cell door clanged shut behind him, and then he left.

He wasn't even breathing heavily.

"Father. Booker," Orr said. "My apologies for disturbing you. Please carry on."

He disappeared down the cell block again.

The priest blanched when he saw the swollen ruin of Keller's face.

"Gotta make your own fun around here, Padre. Better have a drink."

He passed the priest the leftover holy water. Father Michael drank it quickly without thinking. A few drops ran down his chin and plopped to the rubberized nonslip flooring of the cell.

"So, what's happening with the rebellion, Father? You can tell me. I got no part of it anymore. I won't be part of anything soon enough."

The man took a few moments to gather his composure.

"Uhm," he started, losing himself again.

"You think there's any chance Earth will recognize the Code as a legitimate faith?" Booker asked. "I've been in here three years. They don't tell us anything. But I hear rumors, you know."

Father Michael turned away from Keller, who was moaning loudly.

"I . . . I don't think much has changed, Booker. I'm sorry . . ."

He glanced back over his shoulder again.

"But the fight goes on?" Booker asked, dragging the man's attention back to himself.

"There was an attack last week," Father Michael said. "Some kind of network outage on Mars. I think the wormhole commlinks to the planet were down for a few hours."

"Sounds like a win for everyone," Booker said. "Nobody but the chaebol and Govcentral hurt. That's good."

Father Michael kept turning to look at Keller, who'd gone still and quiet.

"It's always better when people don't get hurt," he said. His voice was shaky.

Booker sat down at the other end of the bunk. Leaned his back against the bulkhead.

"They don't hook you guys up, do they?" he said.

The priest didn't understand, so Booker tapped his head. Explained.

"You don't get implants. No net access."

"Oh. No. Not priests, no. The bishops and archbishops and so on, they do. They have to. But no. Most of my flock does not . . . cannot . . ."

"They can't afford it," Booker offered.

"No."

"You ever wonder about that, Father? The unfairness of that?"

The priest frowned.

"It's not unfair, Booker. It's just the natural order. A simple priest with a small parish does not need augmentation. But a prime cardinal with responsibility for a Hab or a planet? They could not perform their duties without it. They could not serve God."

"So that's why they get backup, too? To serve God for what? Three or four relifes? I think the last pope made it to six, didn't he, before he went into deep store?"

The conversation was uncomfortable enough to distract Father Michael from Keller. He knitted his brow and pursed his lips. Thinking the big thoughts. Booker hid a grin.

This guy was a cog in the machine.

Like him.

Except he'd suddenly turned the wrong way and stripped his gears and fucked up the machine, and now he was here. About to be deleted.

"I don't understand," the priest said. And Booker could tell he wasn't lying.

"Don't let it bother you, Padre. Sorry I brought it up. I was just messing with you. Why don't you tell me about your parish. You got one, right? They don't keep you prisoner here, too, do they?"

He brightened at that.

"I do have a parish, yes. Saint Simon's on the thirty-second floor of the Raízen Tower in District Four of Amaggi City on Habitat Suzano."

"A local boy, then. That's great."

"Yes," Father Michael said, warming to his sermon. "Saint Simon's ministers to all the floors from 25 to 40 in the tower, and we have outreach missions down on the inner hull covering half of District Four."

Booker let the priest talk.

He was a good talker, at least. Came with the job, he supposed.

And it passed the time until they came to get him.

CHAPTER
SIX

Archon-Admiral Wenbo Strom roared his challenge to the bulkhead in his ship's enormous workout room. The bellowing shout echoed off the graphene slab bulkheads. Every muscle in his body stood out in tight relief; the thick veins on his arms and chest looked like a nest of earthworms beneath his skin. His uneven white teeth were clenched in a rictus of concentration; sweat trickled along his temples. He could see the slightly bent weight bar tremble over his chest. It was highlighted in stark relief by the ceiling lighting panel. He concentrated. He would not be defeated by mere steel, not now, not ever.

With a final mighty effort, Strom got his last centimeter. Still concentrating fiercely, he moved the massive weight back and slowly allowed the bar to settle on the rack of the chest press bench. As the bar touched the stops, Strom heard a murmur from the others who were gathered in the tiny space. Someone started to clap, and then the clapping turned into a small roar. He smiled tightly. He had neither breath nor strength left for anything more theatrical.

Strom had just done six reps of 185 kilos. He was a living example of the might that was possible with the unadorned human genome, the potential that could be unleashed with a lifetime of discipline, hard conditioning, and correct diet. His blood, his bone, his meat—none of it was contaminated by gene fouling. No mutations or profane biosculpture shaped his massive form. He was truly human.

They all were.

Strom breathed out, sat up from the bench, and raised his hand. Sweat ran freely down his flanks and dripped to the nonslip deck matting.

"Save your strength for your own workout. I'm an old man. Don't let me embarrass you."

He heard some muttering.

". . . personal best . . . No spotter . . . Look at all those fucking plates!"

Strom stood up and rolled his shoulders, keeping his face neutral even as he indulged himself with a small measure of satisfaction. One eighty-five was indeed a personal best. He toweled off and looked around, his face stern. Hundreds of men and women—and only men and women—were working hard at last-minute training in the *Liberator*'s strength and conditioning foundry, but he had attracted an audience of a dozen or so. All young officers. Among them, absolute silence fell.

"I am fifty-eight years old," he said, careful to breathe deeply before speaking. It would not do to topple over in a faint while trying to deliver a lesson. "There will come a day when I cannot improve on my best. When I will begin to weaken and eventually die."

"As it should be," somebody said, and Strom nodded.

"As it should be," he agreed. "But not today. Today I do better. And tomorrow. And the day after that. As will you. All of you."

He snapped his towel, which was damp with his sweat. It cracked like a short whip.

"Now get your lazy asses back to your training. We have worlds to set free."

As one, they roared, "Yes, sir!"

Archon-Admiral Wenbo Strom nodded. "Carry on."

His people chattered among themselves as they hit the strength stations again. Strom proceeded from the workout space, hiding the discomfort of the slight spinal injury that had been paining him for a few months now. It was such a small thing and he could easily train around it, but it added a note of private gravitas to his caution about the fate that awaited them all. The bottommost disks in his backbone had begun to fuse together, trapping a small bundle of nerves between them. It was a perfectly natural side effect of aging but one that had manifested itself three years after the armada had left the Redoubt.

The ship's chief surgeon had suggested a procedure to repair the degeneration, but it came with a small risk of making things worse and possibly even crippling him. He would have agreed to the operation in normal circumstances were he still at home. But they were under way now, and discomfort was not paralysis. He could put up with the constant pins and needles in his leg and the occasional numbness in his toes. Soon enough, in less than a day, his men and women would have to endure much worse.

Strom grabbed a protein bulb from the nutrition bay outside the foundry and chugged it down on the way to the showers. Once in the changing rooms, he stripped off his soaking exercise gear, threw it into the laundry chute, and stepped into the shower cubicle. A fine, hot soapy spray coated him immediately, and a cooler rinse cycle followed. The admiral stood and allowed himself the small pleasure of water sluicing off his back and opening his pores.

As the water shut off and a blast of hot air dried him, he allowed his thoughts to wander to the coming campaign, the liberation of the motherworld and all her children. Her trueborn children, of course. He worked through the mission sequence for the 101st, turning it over in his mind, probing for weakness the way he would grapple with an opponent on the wrestling mat, looking for that one small vulnerable point of failure.

They were legion.

That was the nature of war. But it was Strom's responsibility to cover as many as he could in his Volume of Responsibility. He pulled a fresh duty uniform from the cubicle's chute. His pistol belt and dagger were laid out neatly across it.

It was coming. The moment they had all prepared for their entire lives. A moment for which their forebears had planned for nearly two Earth-standard centuries. Strom climbed into his coveralls and affixed the iron stars of rank to his collar. Other than those decorations, his working uniform was identical to that of every member of the Fleet. He rode the endorphin wave of his hard workout session as he cinched his belt, tied his bootlaces, and strode out of the changing room. The Fleet had penetrated well into the known limits of what the mutants called the Inner Dark. Pathfinder units had blinded the probes ahead of them, but that would call forth another problem, of course. The TDF or some allied force would dispatch recon vessels to investigate. And in Strom's VoR that allied force would be a ship, perhaps even a task force, of the Royal Armadalen Navy.

The prospect excited and worried him in equal measure, but he tried not to dwell on his concerns as he walked the long mile of the *Liberator*'s quarterdeck to the Fleet bridge. He passed hundreds of ship's personnel and expeditionary force troopers, most of whom, per his instructions on deployment, did not salute, merely nodding in acknowledgment of his rank. It would not be long now before a gesture as simple and automatic as saluting a senior officer would attract the targeting algorithms of any robot intelligences that survived the first strike. Or, he thought, the inhuman eyes of those mutant soldiers who still knew how to pull a trigger.

Strom reached the Fleet bridge after a brisk ten-minute walk.

"The 101st, on deck!" a bosun roared as he entered the command center. This time everybody did come to attention, and Archon-Admiral Strom returned the salute.

"As you were," he said, casting his voice to reach the farthest corner of the huge octagonal space. A hundred officers returned to their duties, although at this point in the mission those duties mostly involved supervision rather than action.

The active, kinetic phase of operations would commence within hours.

The admiral strode to his ready room on the far side of the center. Troopers in battle dress came to attention again, stamping their feet in unison before one of them opened the door to his chambers. Strom nodded his thanks and went through. Four officers stood in place at a conference table, waiting for him.

"Please, sit down," he said. "This is the first of too many meetings I have today. Let's move on as quickly as we can. Colonel Dunn?"

Marla Dunn, who could trace her proud lineage all the way back to the cradle of humanity in the Sterkfontein of southern Africa, remained standing while her comrades took their seats.

"The first item is to firewall our XP-Group assaulter units against the Inquiry, Admiral."

"Oh, for fuck's sake, not this again," Strom grumbled, feeling the energy he'd tapped in the weight room starting to drain out of him. There were more than two hundred agents of the Inquiry on the *Liberator* alone, and they gave him more trouble than the quarter million sailors and soldiers who called the vessel home. He understood the necessity of the Inquiry. When he had done his duty and defeated the enemy, they would step up to do theirs and cleanse the entire Volume of parasite machines and mutant infection. But until then, they were mostly proving to be a pain in his ass.

Dunn shrugged.

"They're still demanding that we peel off a company from each battalion to"—she checked a hand-written note—"to establish the ground conditions for the reduction at scale of surviving mutants on the pacified worlds."

"They're not going to be pacified if we keep giving up ground forces every time the Inquiry gets an itch in the ass crack," growled the officer next to her.

"Captain D'ur, please," Strom said mildly.

The Force Recon officer dipped his head in silent apology. Strom accepted the wordless repentance only because he agreed with the man.

"So much biomass," he sighed as he took his seat. "Please, Marla, sit down."

Colonel Dunn pulled up her chair and sat.

"I have a suggestion, sir."

"Please," Strom said, waving at her to continue.

"Even working in an expedited fashion, the elimination of mutants and borgs will be time-consuming and resource-heavy. We know from the Civil War that even though it's essential and just, it will have an effect on morale. Not every mutant looks like a nightmare. Not every borg has cameras for eyes and plasteel claws. Most of them look like us. Soldiers kill, but they do not murder. And if you force them to, we already know what happens. Morale collapses. They fall into depression or psychosis. Either way it degrades performance. But what if we formed people's militias from among motivated elements of the liberated population?"

Kogan D'ur started to protest, but Strom held up a hand to forestall him.

"Go on, Colonel," he said.

"They could do a lot of the heavy lifting during

the purge but also after we secure the early occupation. The plan assumes follow-on missions for both the 101st and the expeditionary force, but to be honest, it doesn't allocate nearly enough garrison forces to secure the liberated areas. We're going to need militia."

Strom said nothing.

He did not doubt that they would find willing allies among the newly freed slaves of the corporate worlds. And Batavia, though a sacred site to the Republic, was undeniably one of the worst colonies of one of the worst of the corporate realms, the Yulin-Irrawaddy Combine.

Nobody spoke while the archon-admiral was so obviously thinking. Of one thing, Strom was certain. His plans inevitably would go awry. Some enemy forces and their Intellects would survive the preemptive strike. He would need every combat soldier under his command to stand the line. The Inquiry would be left for a time to its own devices, but the Inquiry, as was its nature, would ask questions of any such decision. It would be best that they had time to adjust to inconvenient truths.

He made his decision.

"Colonel, I assume you have already worked up a plan to raise your militia."

Dunn smiled.

"I have a number of plans, Admiral."

"I do not doubt it. Schedule a meeting with the Commissioner of Inquiry for 1600 hours today. Perhaps you can think of a way to assure him he is not so much losing my shock troopers as he is gaining his own crack militia of grateful trueborn freedom fighters. Or something."

He waved away the bother of even having to contend with such matters.

"I will do my best, Admiral."

"Good. Now. Captain D'ur. I understand you have been given responsibility for neutralizing any surviving threat from Montanblanc." Strom made a show of checking his watch. "You like to cut it fine, don't you, Captain?"

Kogan D'ur ignored the jab.

"I've been studying their org chart, Admiral, and I think I've found our candidate. Her name is Alessia, and she is a princess."

CHAPTER

SEVEN

Defiant ran silent and deep through the Inner Dark. For weeks, only the briefest occasional dead drops of encrypted data into an entangled wormhole connected them to home. Lucinda was not bothered by the isolation. She had been on her own for a long time. She had been all but orphaned when the reclaimers came for her father, and her two major postings before joining *Defiant* had not been of a sort to furnish lifelong friendships. On the *Resolute,* as part of a mission she had long been forbidden to acknowledge let alone discuss, she'd piloted a shuttle for a band of special operators and spooks she'd never seen or heard from again. As a subbie on secondment to the Terran Navy ship *No Place for Good Losers,* she had kept her head down and her mouth shut, terrified of messing up and disgracing the good name of the RAN. And even when she finally had earned the trust of the Earthers and opened up just enough to let a few of them slip past her defenses and become friends, she had done so in the certain knowledge that she would never see them again either.

Wormhole commlinks to the heart of the Greater Volume were fast. Data moved through human space in something so close to real time that it made no difference, but to actually travel to Earth the old-fashioned way, by folding space, meant a journey of more than eighteen months from her homeworld of Coriolis. And the cost of passage was, well, astronomical. The chances that she would see any of her shipmates from the *Good Losers* again was vanishingly small.

So no, Lucinda Hardy was not much affected by the loneliness of deep space travel. But she had never quite shaken off her fear of messing up and disgracing the good name of the Royal Armadalen Navy. At 0910 hours ship time, Lieutenant Hardy had the conne, and with it the butterflies that inevitably took flight in her stomach whenever she was forced by duty to sit at the center of everyone's attention while having nothing of note to do.

Captain Torvaldt was on deck, as was the XO. They were at the comms station, behind Lucinda's left shoulder in the circular bridge, preparing to exchange a secure data packet with Fleet. The main screen displayed a schematic of the local system: three gas giants and four rocky planets, one with a primitive biosphere, analogous to the Mesoproterozoic era of Earth, according to Defiant. The ship's passive arrays detected no sign of the Sturm's original voyage through the system. The screen was mostly decoration. The bridge crew members supervised their stations via neuralink with shipnet. Lucinda, in the command chair, received real-time updates from all of the stealth destroyer's divisions: from her own station, Tactical, which reported clean feeds up and down the board, and from Medical, where two marines were recuperating from a little rougher-than-usual sparring in the gym. Even the galley had news. The day's lunch of pea and ham soup was now simmering and would be ready at 1200 hours. The ship's cat, Chief Trim, had inspected the ham hocks and rated them acceptable. Twelve officers worked quietly at their stations on the bridge, including Lieutenant Varro Chase at Navigation, who was ever courteous and professional when on duty with Lucinda and whom she avoided like a Jha-Duran macrophage when she was not. Other 268 Navy and Marine Corps personnel attended to their duties throughout the ship as *Defiant* passed silently over the largest northern landmass on the living planet. Lucinda concentrated on sitting very still and not drawing attention to the fact that command of the stealth destroyer was, however briefly, her responsibility.

At 0911 hours Comms opened a wormhole link from within *Defiant*'s self-contained pocket universe to the reality where Deschaneaux Station waited to transmit and receive a quantum-entangled data package. Protocol required the XO—or, if she was incapacitated, the next most senior officer—to attend the commanding officer during the link.

"To make sure the old man won't try to sneak in a booty call," Commander Connelly joked when turning over the conne to Lucinda.

The link was secure, undetectable, the quantum-comms equivalent of a dead drop, and the only form of contact the ship would have with the Greater Volume while it ran silent through the Dark. Even burrowing through a fold in space-time, however, it still took a few seconds to make the exchange over such vast distances.

The previous dead drop had been unremarkable. *Defiant* had not yet located the first of the missing probes. Fleet had made no changes to the original mission plan.

This time, the exchange did not go as smoothly.

At 0910 hours and three seconds, Captain Torvaldt howled like a beast and attacked the XO.

Lucinda heard Connelly's scream and Torvaldt's bellowing yowl, a raw animal noise of pain and shock and . . . something else.

But for a fraction of a second it meant nothing to her because amber lights flashed all over the bridge and her corneal display lit up with alerts and warnings.

MALWARE INTRUSION.

SHIPNET BREACH.

Sirens and Klaxons sounded in her ears. Throughout the ship. A voice, not Defiant's, barked notifications, threats, and orders at her. Specifically at her because she had the conne. Division heads received the warnings appropriate to their Area of Responsibility. Lucinda heard them subvocalizing terse orders and questions about ship status and potential threats.

She got hosed with everything.

The ship lurched, actually *lurched* like an old oceangoing schooner falling down the face of a wave, and Lucinda's heart dropped through her stomach with it. Warships contained in their own X-matter-stabilized bubble universe didn't lurch anywhere.

And executive officers shouldn't scream like small dogs caught in the gears of heavy machinery. But the XO was doing just that.

Lucinda had loaded vision from the bridge cams before she'd turned even halfway toward Torvaldt and Connelly. Glanding stimulants and nootropics to accelerate her thought processes and physical reactions, she'd replayed the last three seconds of video four times in the half second it took her to spin around completely.

Four times she watched the unremarkable footage of Torvaldt waiting for the entangled dead drop exchange via the secure enclave in his neural net. Four times she watched Commander Connelly standing at ease next to the captain, as regulations required. Four times she saw Torvaldt's physical reaction to the drop.

His face lost muscle tone, going slack like the face of a stroke victim. Then he reanimated. Fast. Nose crinkling, a wild dog scenting hot blood. Lips skinning back from his teeth, not just smiling but grinning in a death's-head rictus, all teeth and obscene wet pink gums. Strings of saliva stretching between upper and lower jaw as his head lolled back, Adam's apple bobbing, and then . . . Torvaldt's head shot forward and turned sideways as his jaws closed over the pale skin of Commander Connelly's neck. The captain bit down deeply and ripped and tore and burrowed in even more deeply, digging for the carotid, chewing and sucking and drinking the hot geyser of bright red blood that exploded from the wound as the XO screamed and tried vainly to force him away.

Four times in a half a second she watched it, the

fast looping replay made comprehensible only by wetware-accelerated perception.

And then Connelly wasn't the only one screaming. Lieutenant Nonomi Chivers added her own cries of shock and outrage to the XO's. Chase swore volubly in the rich stentorian tones he had learned at court.

Shipnet went down.

Holograms projected from the consoles all around her, data suddenly ballooning in midair as projectors pushed out information previously streamed directly to the neural nets of the responsible officers.

The video she had been replaying disappeared. The warnings in her corneal displays winked out. The canned alerts, so loud inside her head just a second ago, fell silent.

Instead, a dense matrix of numbers, infographics, and text swirled around her in a holographic blizzard of information.

"Defiant!" she cried out. "Report! What's happening?"

But the ship did not respond.

"Mercado. Tactical," she said, trying to keep her voice under control. She struggled to project her voice, her command authority and reserve, rather than just shouting. "Spool it up from console. Now!"

"Spool what up?"

Lieutenant Mercado Fein looked at her. Confused.

She lost patience. Swiped angrily at the obscuring holomatrix that surrounded her.

"Weapons! Everything!" she shouted, giving up on command presence and reserve and moving at speed now, heading for Torvaldt. The informatic cloud followed her. Through the dense fog of data,

Lucinda saw the captain drag Connelly to the deck and mount her. A Javan wolfiend with its prey. Killing it. Fucking it. Eating it. All at the same time. His head snapping from side to side. Zoo noises muffled by the red ruin of her shredded flesh. Torvaldt grabbed fistfuls of dark hair matted with blood and started to smash Connelly's head into the deck, breaking it open, spilling the contents. He fell on the hot, pink mess like a ravening fiend. One of Connelly's legs twitched, and she did not move again. Her blood, which had been fountaining, now merely pulsed, but strongly still. There was so much of it. Oceans of it.

"Captain! Stop!" Lucinda shouted, despairing. He had killed her, but now he was destroying her. They would not be able to respawn the XO if he went much further.

Busy at their stations, preparing for an attack they didn't understand, using gesture controls instead of direct neural instructions, nobody else moved to intervene.

The creature that once had been Captain Torvaldt turned away from its kill, eyes empty of everything but a devouring fury. Lucinda parted the information cloud with her hands like a voyeur parting a curtain. She saw the captain's thighs bunching powerfully through the fabric of his uniform. Saw the toes of his boots digging into the deck for purchase and his fingers hooked into broken claws. The thing launched itself at her. She realized in some faraway place where she had the time to wonder at such trivia that Torvaldt had bitten through his own lower lip. Bitten through it and chewed it off. Possibly he'd eaten it.

The missing half-moon of ragged meat revealed a mouth full of blood and teeth.

He flew at her. Literally.

He was insane, but his neuromuscular meshnet still functioned to deliver inhuman speed and strength. Lucinda did not think. She did not try to load combat scripts or even clear away the holographic data fog. Organic muscle memory provided the only response she had time to call on. As she closed with Torvaldt, she turned her leading shoulder slightly, presenting an oblique target. When he struck her, she was already pivoting and dropping, redirecting the violence of their impact into a barely controlled fall that caught the captain in something akin to *tawara-gaeshi*—the rice-bale throw of Shudokan judo.

It was messy, improvised, an affront to the memory of Master Ipo, and it worked just well enough to send Torvaldt flying over her shoulder and into the navigation console. Chase yelped in alarm and dived out of the way. The captain spun in the air, head down, and his lower back struck the edge of the console at a bad angle.

Bad for him, anyway.

Lucinda was certain she heard the crack of vertebrae destroyed by the impact. Torvaldt dropped to the deck with a heavy thud, his lower body ominously still while his upper limbs and torso thrashed wildly as he attempted to drag himself around. He was like nothing so much as a wild animal, grievously wounded but lost in the blood madness of a killing frenzy.

His eyes locked on Lucinda's again. Black points

of insensate rage and loathing that burned through the matrix of the ship's information floating around her. Torvaldt snarled and started to drag himself across the deck plating. Chase, his own features distorted with disgust, blindsided the captain with a kick to the temple that finally dropped him. Unlike Lucinda, Chase obviously had loaded wetware. He moved with blinding speed, and his kick landed with millimeter accuracy and massively enhanced strength. Torvaldt's head came apart like a rotten melon.

Synthetic hormones and nootropic drugs coursed through her bloodstream, slowing everything to a crawl. As the captain's brains exploded in a slow-motion shower of shattered skull bones and airborne gray matter, warning lights strobed and stunned bridge crew emerged from their shock.

Still spooked by the silence—hell, by the disappearance—of Defiant and shipnet, Lucinda dosed herself with adrenal regulators and turned off the tap from her nootropic implants. There would be a lag, she knew, and her thoughts continued to rush ahead of everything for a few minutes. She collapsed the holomatrix around her by stretching out her cupped hands and bringing them together as though she were compressing the cloud into a dense ball, which was exactly what happened.

The starboard hatch whooshed open, and Captain Hayes appeared. He was dressed in shorts and a gray T-shirt stained with dark patches of sweat.

"What the hell is happening?" Hayes asked. Everyone turned to Lucinda.

She was the ranking officer now.

Everybody was looking at her. To her. Waiting for

orders. Even Chase seemed willing to defer to her at that moment. Her pulse was still racing, and her vision seemed to throb with every heartbeat.

"We need medics," she said, and her voice trembled. She felt as though it might have cracked as soon as she opened her mouth.

"XO's dead, ma'am," said Lieutenant Fein, staring at Connelly's body. "And . . . and the captain, too."

Lucinda forced herself to examine the XO's remains.

"Get the data from her buffer," she said. "Systems, did she back up at the end of her last watch?"

Ian Bannon, his face pale and blotchy, shook his head, but more in confusion than denial.

"I don't . . . I'm not sure," he stammered.

"Well, check, damn it. And somebody get those medics. We need a meat scan if the buffer is damaged or contaminated."

She then forced herself to look at the red horror Chase had made of Torvaldt's skull. It seemed unlikely that his neural net had survived, and there was no chance of taking a scan directly from the cortex.

Everything was happening too quickly.

The alarms blared on as a security detail stormed into the circular command center through the hatches at three and nine o'clock. They were armed with a variety of weapons suitable for close-quarters battle. Shipnet was still offline. Defiant was down. Yet they were still alive. The bubble was intact. They hadn't lost integrity and been destroyed in the birth and simultaneous annihilation of a new universe.

"External threat matrix clear," Lieutenant Fein said, but without any real certainty to his voice. He kept double- and triple-checking his information cloud even as he pronounced them clear of any outside hazard. He didn't comment on the shipnet breach.

"We . . . ah, we're still holding station above the planet," Chase followed up. She saw him try to consult his heads-up display without luck, forcing him to interrogate the backup system floating above the navigator's console. Torvaldt's broken body lay twisted near his feet.

The other divisions began to report in verbally.

They were awkward, unpracticed.

"Medical reports no serious injuries, ma'am."

"Defiant is still offline, Lieutenant, but control has defaulted to manual and subroutines," said Bannon.

"What the hell happened here?" Hayes said, stepping up beside her.

"I . . . I don't know," Lucinda confessed. "Seriously. No idea. But—"

She turned quickly to the communications officer.

"Lieutenant Wojkowski. Is the drop link still open to Deschaneaux?"

The comms specialist everyone knew as the Woj checked his console, frowning.

"I'm sorry, yes. I think so, ma'am."

"Shut it down," she snapped. "And don't—"

Before she could tell him not to plug into the feed directly, the young man had pushed an earpiece into place. It was an unconscious reaction. Muscle memory. The action he'd been trained to default to in case of shipnet failure.

It killed him.

CHAPTER
EIGHT

Batavian sunsets were spectacular but short-lived at this latitude. As the local star dipped toward the horizon, falling behind the sawtooth ranges of the Goroth Mountains, the wide blue vessel of the sky shaded pink, then orange, and finally a deep, fiery vermilion. Mac felt the heat leaking out of the day, then disappearing in a rush in advance of the approaching darkness. The Ironstone Desert, a furnace burned clean of all life during the day, gradually reanimated as the scorching heat diminished. Stone crabs skittered across hardscrabble and sand, their tiny claws clicking so fast that they sounded like terrestrial cicadas. Sand mites and fire midges swarmed in thick black clouds, circling McLennan, drawn by every breath he exhaled but held at bay by a gentle repeller. Without Hero's EM field they would have feasted on him.

He could hear wildlife stirring inside the vast mausoleum of the Generation Ship. Leatherwings, blue tongue dragons, and far off in one of the aft compartments an armored tunnel sloth that often woke him in the early hours, smashing away at the *Voortrekker*'s bulkheads with its massive clubbed tail.

"Do you think it possible you might change for dinner?" Hero inquired as Mac pushed himself out from under the medbot console in the ruptured surgical bay. He'd been lying on his gelform mat, working without pause for over an hour to extract a delicate piece of the bay's data store. His back ached. One hip felt as though it had come loose of its moorings, and he was sticky with old sweat. His shirt was dark with dried perspiration and smelled foul even to him.

"What do you care?" he groused. "You can't smell anything."

"I can detect every molecule exuded by your apocrine glands and quantify their transformation into a noxious effluvium by the skin flora that have turned your armpits and other unwashed bodily crevices into a dangerous chemical weapons dump. Our guests, who will be here presently, will simply think you reek like rancid fucking man ham."

"Fine," Mac grunted, kicking off his boots, unbuttoning his shirt, and undoing the belt of his cargo pants. He had to admit, to himself if not to Hero, that the waistband of his trews was uncomfortably damp and his underpants did peel away from his body like sunburned skin.

"You're naked," Hero said.

"Unavoidable side effect of getting undressed," Mac replied. It did feel good to get out of the filthy clothes and let the cooler evening air wash over his skin.

"But they will be here soon."

"Aye, but how soon?" Mac asked, not particularly caring.

"The dune rover convoy is less than five minutes out," Hero protested. He sounded quite animated by the potential mortification of a pantsless encounter with the new dig team.

"Then you'd best get on with it, hadn't you?" Mac grinned. "Make sure you get into all the nooks and crannies, mind you."

He pulled on his boots again and stepped through the rupture in the ship's hull. Herodotus followed, maintaining the repeller field that kept the bloodsuckers at bay but adding to it a bath of shortwave radiation that cleansed the surface of McLennan's body. Within seconds he smelled of nothing. But the dried sweat and crusted body salts remained.

Nude except for his boots, he strolled in the direction of the encampment, which had been enlarged over the day in preparation for the new arrivals. The camp droids, having completed that assignment, now busied themselves with preparation of the evening meal. A mountain goat—or rather the local six-legged analogue from the foothills of the Goroth—turned on a spit over a fire pit. Pink smoke from copperwood coals carried the smell of roasting meat, and McLennan was torn between anticipation of the feast and annoyance at all the trouble Hero had gone to. Most nights he ate field rations, and in the morning plain porridge. A jammie dodger at lunch was the culinary highlight of his day.

"Was it really necessary to go putting on the fucking Ritz like this?" he said, deciding to go with his natural inclination: annoyance. "Professor Trumbull's a compulsive ball fondler, and the six-pack of entitled fucking numpties and worthless bellends he's got with him aren't likely to be any better company."

"So says the naked crazy man. The dawdling naked crazy man. Do you think you could step it up? They're only a few minutes away now."

McLennan continued to move at his own stately pace toward the camp.

"I don't intend to go running around with my wobbly bits flapping in the breeze just because we have to babysit these useless bludgers," he informed the Intellect as powerful cones of light speared over a low ridgeline to the east. The first vehicle in the convoy. "It would be undignified is what it would be."

"If I had a face or a palm, I'd be introducing them to each other with extreme prejudice right now," Hero muttered. "Hurry up."

McLennan felt himself lifted up by a gravity wave and hurried at speed across the open ground to the campsite. The rush of cool evening air across his naked skin felt delicious after the heat of the day.

Hero deposited him in the circle of Habs and flew away to stall the dig team lest they arrive to find the famous Professor Frazer McLennan wiping himself all over with a moistened towelette.

It was to no avail.

McLennan was still wiping himself down and enjoying a particularly vigorous ass chamois when Professor Trumbull and his guests disembarked in front of him.

———

"What the hell do you think you're doing?"

For one instant McLennan thought the question was meant for him. A reasonable assumption given that he'd decided to introduce himself in the raw skuddy, except for a small filthy washcloth he did not bother deploying for the sake of modesty.

The astroarchaeologist, until just then completely satisfied with the righteousness of his decision to greet the unwanted newcomers with his wrinkled tackle out in the breeze, experienced an abrupt shift in sentiment to an unfamiliar and even uncomfortable feeling: uncertainty.

"Well?" the voice demanded. "Explain yourself."

The speaker was a young man, very young actually, with a biotic age in his middle to late teens judging by a gangly frame that was all elbows and knees. He threw one look at the naked McLennan, sneered dismissively, and returned to berating a manservant who had stumbled from the big dune rover and was attempting to set up a signal booster for a backpack satellite uplink.

The rover, a twelve-wheeled behemoth, disgorged more of its occupants, who did their best to avoid any contact with the angry princeling—this surely had to be the right royal halfwit Pac Yulin—scurrying to put as much distance between themselves and the hostilities as possible. Most looked surprised to find McLennan unclothed except for his boots, but they merely shook their heads as though steeling themselves for one last episode of madness after a long day of derangement.

A couple of the younger-looking passengers scurried off to identify themselves to the camp droids so that they might take shelter in their Habs. Others stomped over to the buffet, where a modest bar had been laid out. Mac took them to be the second and third lifers. On Hero's instructions the droids had made ice for drinks, and he heard the tinkle of ice cubes in a cocktail shaker. The liquid metal crash of a martini being shaken into existence followed with unseemly haste.

"Good grief, man, was there ever an opportunity you passed up to get your cock out and flop it around in people's faces?"

Trumbull.

Like Mac he looked older than the rest of the party. Biotically he was in his early forties. Unlike Mac he would relife in a couple of years: the privilege of full tenure, although it did come at a cost. Miyazaki owned all the intellectual property Trumbull generated, and the noncompete clauses in his contract barred him from working in astroarchaeology or any related field for two lifetimes if he chose not to renew.

They owned him. In this life and the next. They always would.

"Was there ever any chance you'd leave me alone to get on with my work uninterrupted by ravening tourist hordes of rich numpties and doaty fecking wallopers?" Mac groused back at him.

"Why don't you just put some pants on," said Trumbull.

McLennan grunted and shrugged. This had not gone as he'd intended at all.

Deputy Prince Vincent Pac Yulin continued to ignore McLennan while he raged and once even kicked at his underling. McLennan now knew for sure it was Pac Yulin because the little bastard wouldn't shut up about it.

"Do you know who I am? Do you know what you've done?" he shouted at the poor fellow cringing under his blows. Presumably the sorry bugger on the business end of the kicking did know who Pac Yulin was. Otherwise why would he put up with such abuse even as he fussed with the uplink equipment? But the princeling carried on anyway.

"I am Deputy Prince Vincent Pac Yulin!" he shouted. "And you will answer for the damage you have done to House Yulin by your incompetence."

"What'd he do?" McLennan asked Trumbull out the side of his mouth.

If the dig team had put up with this performance for the eight-hour drive across the desert wastes, he could understand why they had not been much fussed by encountering him without his drawers. A naked McLennan would not be the highlight of their day, no. But he wouldn't be the worst thing that had happened to them either.

The martini shaker started up again to a desultory cheer behind him.

"We lost real-time links two hours out of Fort Saba," said Trumbull. His voice was tired. "As we always do and as we warned them. So they lost real-time engram streaming and of course real-time backup with it."

"That's it?" McLennan asked. "He lost two hours of squeezing his wee little pocket badger in the back of the bus and imagining what real lady boobs feel like?"

Pac Yulin had dialed back on the physical abuse after knocking his man over with one especially fearsome kick, but he made up for it with the renewed vigor of his verbal assault.

"I'll have you flayed. I'll have you flayed and salted and deleted for this. Then I'll flay your stupid family and send them into penury and . . ."

Hero floated over to join the two academics. A fresh set of pants and a clean shirt came with him on a carrier wave, and Mac took the opportunity to get dressed. He was starting to feel more than a little silly standing around with his tackle out.

Yet it had seemed such a good idea at the time.

McLennan heard laughter from the bar area. Music started up somewhere in the Habs, and footsteps crunched closer across the sandy gravel as Mac pulled on his pants.

"Martini, Professor Trumbull? And a Highland Park for you, Professor McLennan, if I'm not mistaken."

It was one of the tourists. Biotically at least, he looked to be in his mid-twenties, but he also appeared with two glasses and a wry grin that spoke volumes. This wasn't his first life, and Deputy Prince Vincent was probably not the first royal knob-end he'd encountered.

"Jay Lambright," he said, passing Mac the whiskey. He'd even served it straight up, as God intended.

"Good evening to you, sir. I am indeed Professor McLennan, but if you've not fucked up my wee dram here, you can call me Mac."

He sipped at the single malt as Pac Yulin continued to rage a short distance away.

"Ah, Mac it is, then. You have some skills, I see, Mister Lambright. Or at least the sense not to ruin a perfectly fine drink by adding water in any form to it. You might not be utterly useless to me out here after all."

Lambright offered the chilled martini to Trumbull, who demurred. "After dinner perhaps."

Lambright shrugged and drank it himself. The fine crystal stemware was beaded with condensation. A few drops plopped to the desert floor. The lack of any audience reaction seemed to be upsetting Deputy Prince Vincent more than the loss of his real-time engram backup.

McLennan judged him to be edging toward some escalation from which it would be impossible to back down. Combine royalty viewed their serfs—and every one of their subjects was legally a serf—as property to be used and disposed of as the whim took them. Pac Yulin strongly impressed him as the sort of toilet nugget who'd revel in a practical demonstration of that privilege.

"Your Highness," he said, turning on his Scottish burr. That was all for show, of course. His accent had drifted toward mid-Volume neutrality at least three lives ago, but he was technically a laird, and these piss-chuffing little outer system despots still tended to go a bit giddy in the presence of even a diluted drop of the blood royal from Old Earth.

"Your Highness," he repeated, a little louder, dialing in just a touch of his old command voice. "Perhaps if you let your man be about his duties, he might have a chance to carry them out."

The servant actually cringed in anticipation of an even worse beating as Deputy Prince Vincent's eyes went wide in surprise. But before he could climb on his high horse and start frothing about never having been spoken to like that, McLennan added, "I've some single malt from the old isles I've been saving for guests, and I was hoping you'd take a dram with me. Your family's vineyards are legendary, but my brother is distiller by appointment to the Crown in both Edinburgh and London. I don't get much company I'd care to share his reserved casks with, and I'm sure Herodotus here can assist your man with any help he needs to establish a link."

He could see the contrary impulses warring within the young man. Or boy, really. He was smart enough to recognize he'd been given a way to back out of his performance with some dignity, but that same inflamed sense of his own importance demanded that he make sure everyone understand that he was indulging McLennan, not the other way around.

The moment stretched uncomfortably until Pac Yulin nodded once.

"I suppose I might join you, Lord McLennan. I have been too long in low company."

He glared at both Trumbull and Lambright. The professor examined his shoes, and Lambright, whom Mac was warming to, winked at the cheeky little fucker.

"Right backatcha, kid."

That might have derailed Mac's whole diversion

but for the manservant, who suddenly cried out, "I've got it, Your Highness. A live link."

He threw a switch on the backpack unit and looked hopefully to his master.

It surprised nobody that Deputy Prince Vincent attacked him again, but the three older men were a little taken aback that Pac Yulin suddenly snarled like a Centauran direwolf and leaped at the screaming manservant.

The screaming did not last long. Deputy Prince Vincent Pac Yulin tore out the man's throat with his bare teeth.

But that was the main course.

For starters he bit a big tasty chunk right out of the poor man's face.

CHAPTER
NINE

As soon as she arrived back at the main villa, Alessia, who never called the ladies-in-waiting if she could avoid it, made a lunge for the sash that would summon them. Two pulls would bring half a dozen servants to run her a bath and choose her an outfit and brush out her tangled, knotted hair and . . .

"Not today, Princess," Sergeant Reynolds said, grabbing the sash just inside the wide-open French doors, lifting it out of her reach, and spoiling Alessia's plan to delay her flute practice long enough that all she'd have to put up with for the afternoon was Doctor Bordigoni's language lesson.

"A quick shower will do for you. I'll have fresh clothes sent up to you in five minutes. And I'll have Lady Melora deliver them if you take six."

She gave him the stink eye, but Sergeant Reynolds was unmoved.

A very quick shower, a change of clothes—thankfully, nothing with ruffles—and Alessia sat in the music room overlooking the rose garden, playing the song that made Reynolds think of rabbits. He stood over her until certain she was resigned to her fate, leaving his young comrade to maintain the watch while he escorted her language tutor from the entrance hall. Outsiders were not allowed to wander the villa without an armed escort. Not even Doctor Bordigoni, who'd been tutoring her older siblings, her uncles and aunts, and even her mother for two spans.

Alessia played "Tamino's Aria" three times while Reynolds was gone. It was the first piece she had ever truly mastered, and it relaxed her to play without thinking. The sergeant was right. It did sound like a rabbit. She so completely lost herself in the music, imagining a family of white bunnies dancing and hopping along the paths that wound through the rosebushes outside, that she did not notice Reynolds returning with Doctor Bordigoni.

"Marvelous. Just marvelous," the tutor said, clapping when she finished the piece for the third time. He clapped loudly and enthusiastically, the volume produced by his small birdlike hands with their long, delicate fingers surprising and even startling her a little. Doctor Bordigoni was a tiny man with a head too large for such a diminutive body. Alessia sometimes thought that enormous noggin might even bend out of shape the delicate neck on which it sat so precariously, and she'd wondered for a long time why he didn't just relife into a better body.

"Because good bodies cost heaps," Caro said, rolling her eyes.

Caro often had to explain stuff like that to Alessia.

Good bodies cost heaps, and not even professors who worked for kings could afford them on a whim.

"You must play me another song when we are done with our lesson, Your Highness," said Doctor Bordigoni. "It will be the highlight of my day even if you have perfectly memorized the passages of Alighieri I have set for you, which I am sure you have."

His delighted smile allowed of no suspicion that Alessia might have done nothing of the sort, because rote learning dead Italian poems was almost as dull as grinding out dozens of scales hundreds of times.

She returned his smile uncertainly, brightening when she lit upon an escape plan.

"I thought we could talk about Levi Primo again," she said. "I liked him."

Doctor Bordigoni could always be relied on to lose himself in conversation about some dead poet.

"Primo Levi," he admonished, wagging one spidery finger at her, not fooled for a moment. "And as soon as we have completed our set work, of course we can discuss the other old masters. I shall download the relevant files in anticipation."

Oh, no, Alessia thought. Now she'd have to endure another lecture about poor choices and her lack of application and, for her sins, an extra-boring extra lesson on some dead Old Earther word nerd she really didn't . . .

Sergeant Reynolds, who had taken up his station discreetly by the main entrance to the music room, frowned and cocked his ear as if trying to hear something on his net. The other guard also was making a face and looking to Reynolds as though in search of an answer to a question he hadn't asked yet.

Doctor Bordigoni likewise looked distracted or maybe even annoyed. Deep creases appeared in his mighty, kind of bulging forehead, and his eyes got that inward look that grown-ups get when they half forgot about the real world because they'd strayed away into the weird other place they went inside their heads.

"Sergeant . . ." he started to say.

But Reynolds wasn't listening to Doctor Bordigoni. Sergeant Reynolds was drawing his sidearm and motioning to the other guard to move over and stand close to Alessia.

"Sergeant? Is there a problem with the local net? I can't seem to get a link to any scripts or data. Or to anything really."

Alessia heard a scream then. It was muted, but it did come from somewhere inside the mansion. She was sure of it.

"I'm offline," said Bordigoni, who was still wrapped up in his own internal world. "Everything is offline," he said.

Gooseflesh crawled up Alessia's arms. She felt hackles rising on the back of her neck. The net never went offline. Ever. People couldn't back up if it went offline. They couldn't download.

Another scream.

Louder this time and closer. A series of crashes and thuds followed, and the younger guardsman, who had moved to stand beside Alessia, drew his weapon, some sort of pistol, and added his questions to Doctor Bordigoni's.

"Sarge? Where's the net gone? Where are our scripts, Sarge?"

"Quiet, boy," Reynolds said. "Do your job. Look after the princess."

They all jumped at the sound of gunfire.

Gunfire! In the palace!

Alessia, the younger guard, and Doctor Bordigoni jumped. Sergeant Reynolds just sort of crouched a little more.

He turned a lock on the door and spun around, his eyes narrowing as he took in the wide-open wall of floor-to-ceiling glass that afforded such pleasant views over the gardens.

"What's happening?" asked Bordigoni, who'd finally emerged from his own little world to find that things were just as chaotic, possibly worse, out in the world of real things. Alessia could hear more screaming, and she could tell now that it wasn't just one person. It sounded like wild animals were loose inside the house. Lots of them. And guardsmen, she assumed, were fighting with them. And soon, by that logic, Sergeant Reynolds and his young friend would be shooting guns and throwing bombs and fighting whatever was making those terrible noises, too. In this room, with her.

A much bigger boom than any she'd heard so far shook the entire building. She felt it through her feet and saw the shudder that ran through the walls. Paintings fell from their hangers and crashed to the ground, their frames splintering. A small crystal chandelier swung from the ceiling.

"Sergeant, I can't load my scripts," the nameless guardsman said. He sounded nervous. More than nervous. He sounded frightened.

"We are under attack," the doctor declared. "We must be. We must get the princess to safety."

"All right, all right. Just calm down," said Reynolds.

"But my scripts!"

"Fuck your scripts, boy," Reynolds barked, causing Alessia to jump and frightening her almost as much as all the screaming and fighting she couldn't see. You never heard grown-ups say things like that. She knew a guardsman had been dismissed once for cursing around her mother. Flogged and then dismissed, and he hadn't even sworn in front of her. Just somewhere she could hear him.

"You've got your gun and your training, boy," Sergeant Reynolds growled. "And now you'll have a chance to use both. The doctor's right. We have to get the princess away from here. We don't know how much of the palace has been compromised, but we know the net is down, and that means it's not rebels or insurgents. It's a corporate attack. Probably an Armada-level Intellect running it."

He looked at Alessia.

The gunfire and screams were getting much closer.

One enormously loud bang shook the whole mansion and sprayed glass from the upper floors out over the rose gardens. Reynolds ignored it.

"Your friends, Your Highness?"

It took Alessia a moment to realize he was talking to her and asking about Caro and Debin.

"Yes?"

"Will they be at home by now? It's after four."

She couldn't think straight. She couldn't remember anything. What did Caro and Debin do in the afternoon? They didn't have school or even lessons. Not on a Saturday. Not like her. That was why they could play. They could play all the time if they wanted . . .

"Princess!"

Reynolds's voice, harsher and louder than she'd ever heard it, brought her back to the music room.

"They should be home now," she said, remembering. "Caro has to get her grandfather's dinner ready. Debin is supposed to help and to clean, but—"

"Good," Reynolds said, cutting her off. Another first. Guardsmen did not talk over the top of princesses. Ever. "Hussein," he said to the younger guardsman. His name was Hussein. "You need to find Captain Graham. Tell him I have the princess and have activated Plan Magenta. He will know what to do. Got that?"

Hussein didn't look like he'd gotten much of anything. His eyes darted left and right, and he shuffled from one foot to the other as though he might suddenly run wherever his rapidly shifting gaze led him. Alessia flinched, expecting Sergeant Reynolds to shout at him again, but he didn't. He just gripped the young man's shoulder and squeezed. When he spoke, his voice was low and not unkind.

"Hussein. You are here because you were chosen. You are meant to be here. You're that good, lad. Now show me."

The guardsman seemed to gather himself.

"I will find Captain Graham," he said. "I will tell him you have Her Highness and have activated Plan Magenta."

"Good boy."

Reynolds clapped him on the shoulder. His leather

glove on the ceremonial armor plating was very loud, but the series of booms that followed were louder.

"Let's go," said Reynolds.

"What about me?" Doctor Bordigoni asked. "What should I do?"

Reynolds shook his head.

"I don't know, Doctor. But I'd suggest you arm yourself and kill anyone who looks to be in need of it."

Bordigoni stood by the music stand, his delicate hands clasped together, his oddly misshapen head turning first one way and then the other as he cast about for a weapon. Guardsman Hussein, pistol drawn and face set in a grimly determined fashion, nodded to Reynolds and made his way to the door. The sergeant leaned down to Alessia.

"We're going to run, Your Highness. All the way to Mister Dunning's cabin down by the herb garden. If you're faster than me and you get away from me, that's good. You keep going."

"Okay."

"If anything should happen to me," he said, his voice very serious now, "you keep going."

"But Sergeant—"

He held up his free hand, the one not holding the gun, to quiet her.

"You tell Mister Dunning that Sergeant Reynolds sent you. And you remind him of the time we were in Port Qrzhaad. Can you say that back to me?"

She did, stumbling over the name of the port. He made her say it again. Three times.

On the third time, she jumped because Hussein opened the door to the music room.

He said in a surprised voice, "My Lady Melora."

And then he died, cleaved in two by a fusion blade. He didn't even scream. But Lady Melora did, and Doctor Bordigoni, too, for that matter.

Alessia's governess charged into the music room, running through the steaming halves of Guardsman Hussein before they had a chance to peel away from each other. Her clothes were torn and bloodied. Part of one shoulder was missing. Just gone. Alessia could see bones and meat and all sorts of gross stuff moving about inside the wound.

It was horrifying, but worst of all was her face. Alessia had reason to be very familiar with Lady Melora's "angry face," and this was not that. This was more like a parchment of human skin stretched over a seething tangle of black mountain vipers and Javan spider cats. She hissed just like a spider cat, her upper lip peeling back and her lower lip . . .

Alessia screamed then.

Lady Melora had no lower lip, just a ragged half-moon of missing flesh where her lip had been before she'd bitten through it.

Doctor Bordigoni screamed, too, but less fearfully this time. He had picked up the music stand and was swinging it like an awkward club, advancing on Melora as she moved toward them.

The fusion blade described a wild, cyclonic pattern in the air. Less a pattern really than a random series of swoops and arcs that cut through the music stand in a shower of sparks, cut through Doctor Bordigoni's arms in a shower of blood, and opened up his stomach to spill everything out over the floor.

Sergeant Reynolds's gun roared.

The old-fashioned bullets hit Lady Melora three times. He fired three times, and her body jerked under the impact three times. But she did not fall over. Her head moved around as though it wasn't properly attached to her body. None of her limbs really looked like they were attached to her body. They all seemed to want to move like the arms of a puppet controlled by someone who didn't really know what he was doing.

Lady Melora knew what she was doing, though.

Sort of.

She hissed again, a sound like poison gas venting from the broken depths of a volcano. She raised the glowing blade and ran at them in a weird, twitchy uncoordinated rush. Alessia wanted to run away but couldn't get her feet to move. It was as though they were glued to the floor.

Sergeant Reynolds's gun roared again, and Lady Melora's head disappeared.

She stopped running at them.

Alessia felt dizzy. The room started to go gray at the edges, then white. It tipped over, and she felt herself flying.

How could she possibly fly if she couldn't even run?

She flew out the doors into the rose garden, riding on Sergeant Reynolds's shoulder like he was a unicorn and she was a princess. Or something. The world bounced up and down as he ran from the villa. She saw smoke and flames pouring from two windows upstairs. The sun glinted prettily on the hundreds, maybe thousands, of glass shards covering the gardens.

Somebody would have to pick that up later, she knew.

Probably Caro's grandfather.

They were going to see Caro and Debin's grandfather, she remembered as she closed her eyes and night fell from somewhere on high.

CHAPTER

TEN

When they came for him, they came heavy. A captain in dress blues, leading Orr and two Compliance Mechs. The mechs were big enough that they couldn't stand side by side. One took the lead, and the other brought up the rear. Booker wondered if the Hab's Intellect was controlling them or if they had ghost riders along.

He didn't ask.

Any riders wouldn't be like him. No Coder would agree to take part in something as profane as deleting a man's soul.

"Oh, dear," said Father Michael when the blast doors sealing Execution and Deletion off from the rest of the prison Hab slid open and the first mech came crashing down the passage between the rows of cells. It was at least eight feet tall, a pure machine rather than a biomech composite, and it had been rigged for contested escort, one arm equipped for grappling and the other carrying a riot control gun.

All for him.

"Oh, dear, I'm sorry," the priest said again as the

party drew up outside his cell. Corporal Orr wore his blank face. The Navy captain was all straight lines and tight angles, polished shoes and crisply ironed creases. He stomped to attention as though trying to outdo the mechs.

"Booker3-212162-930-Condemned," he declared, shouting into the cell but staring into the distance as though Booker weren't there. "By order of the judge advocate of the 7th Military District you are to be taken from this place to a place of execution, there to be extracted from this, the property of the Terran Defense Force, your engram to be deleted without hope of reinstallation, your source code never to be compiled again."

Father Michael mumbled something pointless and waved his hands around in an even more futile gesture of absolution or benediction or whatever crazy ritual of abasement and special pleading he made to his particular invisible friend at times like this. The Compliance Mechs stood mute and utterly immovable. Orr nodded.

"It's time, Booker," he said.

"I know."

Turned out he didn't care. He knew they'd dosed him without his consent, just enough trank from his spinal syrettes to ensure his obedience. He couldn't hope to resist actively by attacking them given the neural clamp on his hindbrain. But he supposed it was a drag for everybody when prisoners threw themselves to the deck like bawling babies and tried to hold on to the bars of the cell. That would totally fuck up the solemnity of the moment, wouldn't it?

Keller would have loved for him to go out like

that, of course. Reason enough not to, Booker thought. He shook the padre's hand.

"Thanks, man," he said, really starting to surf the trank now. "If I get to the other side and it's how you say, I'll be sure and send you a sign."

Father Michael smiled, but the expression was fleeting, uncertain.

"All right, then," he said.

"Corporal Orr," said Booker, nodding to the jailer and ignoring the captain. The trank was really smoothing his shit out. He wondered if Orr had slipped him a couple of extra squirts. For good behavior. "I'm ready."

The maglocks disengaged, and the lead mech flexed its trijointed grappler, reminding him they could do this the hard way if he wanted to. Probably a ghost rider, then. An Intellect wouldn't bother with bullshit theatrics like that.

Booker winked at Orr.

"Reckon I could have taken you," he said.

"A bit late to find out now," Orr said before adding, "Good luck."

"Bit late for that, too."

"Booker. Hey, Booker."

It was Keller. Orr frowned, and the captain whose name tag read LAO TZU but whose current phenotype was pure Nordic, glowered murderously at the other prisoner.

"It's cool," said Booker. "We're buds."

Keller was indeed holding his hand out through the bars to shake. His face was a bruised and swollen horror, his eyes almost puffed closed. Keller's hand was shaking and one finger was badly misshapen, but he seemed determined to wish Booker well.

"Fine," said the captain.

Booker took the hand carefully, not wanting to hurt that damaged finger any worse than it was hurting already. Keller grinned through broken teeth, and Booker felt the corners of the note Keller passed him biting into his palm.

He couldn't help himself.

He was flying on trank now. He read the note.

"Help," Keller had written. "These people are holding me prisoner."

Booker giggled.

Orr jammed a baton into Keller's chest, forcing him back into the cell.

"Corporal, just how much sedative has this prisoner had?" Captain Lao Tzu asked.

"Enough to ensure he doesn't give us any trouble, sir," Orr answered. "I can Dtox him if you wish, but I would not recommend it, sir. Booker was a dangerous asset. He was permascripted with black code. It's dormant and he's been clamped, but I've learned not to take risks. Not with source coders, sir."

Nordic Lao Tzu didn't look happy, which was a shame because this was a happy fucking day and Booker just wanted everyone to mellow out and enjoy it as much as he was.

"Let's go," he suggested. "Come on. Time's a-wasting."

He waved them along as he headed for the blast doors leading to the XD chamber. One of the giant mechs crashed down in front of him, and a grappling arm shot out, wrapping him in its padded claws.

He snorted.

"Tickles," he said.

"He's not supposed to be enjoying it," the captain protested. "Dial him down, would you? Not all the way but enough so that he actually looks like he's going to his death, not a keg party."

"Yes, sir," said Orr.

To Booker it felt as though somebody had turned off the sunshine. The strips that had bathed the cell block in such a soft warm glow lost their pleasing ambience. A moment earlier the Book could have imagined himself on the beach in SoCal, soaking up some rays before they shipped out for the first time.

Now.

They were.

Now.

They were going to delete him.

Whoa. Fuck no!

But the Compliance Mech had him in its grip, and when he tried to struggle against the restraint, he grew so tired so quickly that he felt himself falling asleep in the grappler. His head nodded forward, and everything grayed out.

"Corporal Orr. Please."

Another squirt from his implants. A cold drop of dew running down his spine. Waking him up. But flattening everything out.

Booker read the world around him as a manual. A technical manual for a long-dead technology. Nothing to do with the Book. Nothing to see here. Move along now.

He allowed himself to be carried out of the cell block. Between the stomping crashes of the three-ton mechs, he heard the priest mumbling prayers for him. For his soul. Which they were about to delete.

Why did the guy even bother?

The walk to the XD chamber was short. Two passageways, one turn. Less than a minute after leaving the cell block the mech transferred Booker to the couch where they would extract his code from this body. His engram, his soul, would be downloaded to a crystal wafer, and that data would be erased by electromagnetic pulse. A minute later the wafer itself would be destroyed in a plasma bath, and Booker would be no more.

This body, this meat sack, was not him. It would be filled with another soul soon enough, within hours or days. The fate of the body did not concern him. He was not the vessel. No matter what these barbarians thought, he was a human soul, and that soul was in the source code.

Through the dullness of the drug haze he found the XD chamber familiar. A brushed-steel box with two couches. A control console. He'd been in similar facilities but of much vaster scale, with thousands of couches, each one occupied by a vat-grown organic combat chassis awaiting download or extraction. It was rare for a piece of equipment like the body he currently wore to travel outside a star system. Only code normally would do that, traversing the entirety of the Human Volume in less than a second via Zero Point wormhole link, filling whatever vessel the TDF deemed necessary at the receiving end. Booker had lain on dozens of couches like this. Been poured into and out of mechs and biomechs and meat sacks from the Perseus Archipelago to Orion's Belt.

"I'm not the vessel," he mumbled through the sedatives. "I am the soul."

Captain Lao Tzu stepped up to the tiny console. The officer could perform the extraction and deletion by simply instructing the Hab to do everything, but this was not about utility or function.

This was a ceremony, and ceremonies were all about form.

The captain, as the lawfully designated representative of the Terran Defense Force, would push all the buttons and flick every switch. Analog buttons and switches, too. Old-school, like a hangman with a noose on a frontier world.

Booker found it difficult to put one thought after another. He looked at Orr, who gave him a tight smile. Why was Orr doing this? Why was he letting them do this? Booker had never given him any trouble.

The Compliance Mech that had placed him on the couch stood near the blast doors to the chamber. The room wasn't large enough for both mechs, and the other one waited outside. Strange to think that it would be able to walk away from here and Booker would not.

"And deliver us from the tyranny of evil men . . ." the priest droned on, quoting from some ancient rite that meant less than nothing to Booker.

If someone didn't deliver him from these evil men soon . . .

A siren wailed.

Red lights began to flash.

Finally, Booker thought. *Somebody's realized what these guys are doing. Somebody is coming to help.*

The evil men who'd been intent on erasing his soul from existence were not happy to be interrupted. A harsh voice filled the chamber. It was so loud that it cut right through the numbing effect of the sedatives.

"*Malware intrusion!*" the voice blared. "*Habnet breach!*" it shouted.

The Compliance Mech seemed so upset by this that it just gave up. Booker saw it slump like a man who'd just been given bad news. The worst.

Father Michael clutched his rosary beads and a little black Bible to his chest. His frightened eyes darted from Corporal Orr to good old blond, blue-eyed Captain Lao Tzu.

That was sad, Booker thought. Father Michael was a good guy. A little dim but otherwise okay. It made him sad that the father was frightened.

"I'm offline," the captain said.

"Same," Orr replied. "The mechs, too."

Well, duh, Booker thought. He could have told them that.

"*Malware intrusion!*" the voice blared again. "*Habnet breach!*"

Hmm, Booker thought. *Somebody oughta do something about that.*

Nasty things, malware intrusions. Some of the Code regarded them as being akin to demons. But not Booker. He wasn't superstitious.

A low concussive rumble shook the XD chamber. Booker understood in a very distant sense that Habs were not supposed to do that. Whether rings or cylinders, Habs were enormous structures. They didn't get shook up by nothing.

But then he remembered that this Hab was smaller than most. It was a prison inside a TDF base. It wasn't that big.

Another dull boom shook the chamber, and he relaxed.

Simple kinetics or explosives probably could demolish a little Habitat like this. You wouldn't even need graviton charges or anything. The chamber was shaking, and the entire structure around it vibrated like a gong because they were under attack. So that was cool. The mystery was solved. The voice came back. It was still very loud.

"Malware intrusion! Habnet breach!"

But no, it was a different voice. Human, not machine-generated. It sounded scared. Like Father Michael.

They had scripted Booker to sense fear in those around him. Fear had a smell. But he didn't need those scripts. He could hear how frightened the voice shouting out of the speakers was.

"Hostile forces detected. Counterboarding protocols authorized. The Intellect is down. Habnet is compromised. It's the Sturm. The Sturm are back!"

Well, thought Booker, relaxing on his couch as Orr frantically worked at the console while Lao Tzu looked on like a big, helpless looking-on guy. *The Sturm came back, eh? Didn't see that coming!*

He closed his eyes.

He wasn't completely chilled as he'd been when they'd dosed him back on the cell block. But he just couldn't find it within himself to give much of a shit about anything. He idly wondered what would happen. Would they still delete him? Would there be a war? Hey, he thought. Maybe it was the Source. Maybe they'd come to rescue him.

But even that didn't excite him much.

And anyway, that guy on the loudspeaker said it was someone else.

Oh. Yeah. The Sturm.

Nobody likes those guys.

Booker opened his eyes.

His mind had just then cleared as though a cold wind had blown through it.

He was still on the couch, held in place by liquid metal bands around his arms and ankles.

"Booker? You with us?" Orr asked.

"Yeah," he said. He'd been Dtoxed. His focus, his presence of mind had come back in a rush. Like he'd been stoned, running through a field of flowers, and he'd run right into a wall that hadn't even been there a moment ago. "I'm back. And so are the Sturm? Seriously?"

"I dunno. But the base is under attack. Malware and boarders," Orr said quickly.

Captain Lao Tzu was staring at the console as though he'd never seen it before. Booker didn't need black script to know the man was confused and frightened in about equal measure.

"We can't load up," Orr explained. "Habnet got spiked or something. Some kind of EM pulse that fried the exchange buffer."

Booker could hear weapons fire now and explosions, still some way off but louder than before. The padre had moved to stand next to Captain Lao Tzu and seemed to be offering him support without getting much back in the way of gratitude. The guy was seriously freaking out, and he brushed off the priest's hand when Father Michael laid it gently on his shoulder.

"The captain doesn't even know how to work the console," Orr explained. "He hadn't loaded the script."

Booker almost snorted a laugh.

The man who'd intended to erase him from creation suddenly didn't know how to. He hadn't downloaded the instructions. Booker didn't laugh, though. He started to see a small glimmer of hope in the dark distance.

"We can release you if you agree to assist in repelling boarders," Orr said. "It's protocol."

Booker did smile then. Thinly. "Why would I do that? Whoever's coming probably isn't here to delete me."

Captain Lao Tzu shook off Father Michael and addressed his prisoner.

"Don't be so sure of that. You're not even human to the Sturm. But I will testify in mitigation of your sentence if you agree to assist in defense of the Hab," he said. He seemed to think of something else then. "And if you die, of course, your soul goes to the big compiler in the sky. That's a win for you, right?"

Booker glared at the insult.

"No. You want my help or not?"

"We could use it," Orr said, giving the captain a frustrated glance. "I can't load anything. Can't get to the buffer. Can't even query the local cache. All I got is precon."

"I'm sure *you'll* be fine," Booker said pointedly. "What about you, Captain? What are you carrying?"

"Administrative scripts," the captain said, sounding almost embarrassed. He hurried on. "I haven't needed operational code in three years."

"And you don't load code, do you, Padre?"

"No," said Father Michael.

"All right," Booker said as the room shook with another blast. "You got neural clamps on me right now. Wetware, not software, right? Pull me out of this skin job and drop me into the mech. I can already see the rider got fried or cut off. I'll see if I can get to the nearest armory and swap out the compliance modules for a combat load. But first," he said, looking directly at Lao Tzu, "I need your word as an officer that you will honor your promise and speak in my defense at an appeal against deletion. No matter who's attacking. Even if it's the Source."

"It's not your friends," the captain said, certain of that if nothing else. "You have my word."

"And I have witnesses," Booker replied, nodding at Orr and Father Michael.

A moment passed. Then another. The sirens and base alarms filled the void until Booker said, "Well?"

"Uh. I don't know how to use the console anymore," Lao Tzu reminded them.

Corporal Orr squeezed his eyes shut.

"I think I can do it," he said. "I worked in the armory. I can do a manual swap-out. I'm pretty sure I can, anyway. You cool with that, Booker? No guarantees. It's not my core code. But you know, I've done it for real before."

He shrugged. "Do your worst."

"Bless you," said Father Michael.

"Father, you just keep your head down. I need you to keep this forgetful idiot to his word."

He tagged Lao Tzu with a nod.

"Okay," Orr said. "Gonna do a hard P2P transfer. Sorry, Booker. No time for foot rubs or sweet talk."

"It won't be my first time getting fucked in the neck," Booker said. "Go on. Do it."

He turned his head away from Orr to give the corporal access to the subdermal I/O port on his neck, just under the jawline. Orr fetched a length of cable from a container at the rear of the mech. He plugged one end into the machine, threw a mechanical switch, and came at Booker with the other end, an evil-looking barbed spike. Powered up.

"You got any prayers for a soul in peril, now might be the time, Padre," said Booker.

"Our Father, Who art in heaven . . ." the priest started.

Booker felt Orr lay the tip of the data spike against his human flesh.

He heard himself scream as the corporal drove it home into the port.

The world turned black as his soul departed the body.

CHAPTER

ELEVEN

Captain Hayes killed Wojkowski with a single shot to the heart, but not before the comms officer had sunk his teeth into the arm of a marine standing next to him. He attacked with the same murderous fury that had possessed Captain Torvaldt. The marine snarled and snatched his arm away, losing a chunk of flesh but giving his CO a clear shot at the center mass of the berserker.

Lucinda flinched when he fired and winced as the Woj's upper torso came apart under the impact of the smart round. A meat eater. Programmed to destroy organic matter but to disintegrate harmlessly on contact with anything else. The marines had weapons that could shoot right through the inner hull. Not a good look in a self-contained bubble universe.

"Navigation," she shouted at Chase. "Plot a crash jump. Now. Helm, be ready to engage."

"But Defiant is offline," Chase protested.

"That's why I told you to plot out the jump. You can do that, right? You know how to navigate?"

His only reply was a filthy look, but he stepped

around the bodies and as much of the gore as he could and leaned into the holomatrix above his console, pulling out real-time telemetry and fold data.

Hayes advanced on the body of the man he'd just killed, still holding the weapon, ready to fire again.

At the helm, Lieutenant Chivers nodded nervously to Lucinda that she was ready to fold them off station as soon as Chase gave her the all clear. A solar system was a big place and the chance of randomly jumping into a gas giant was actually pretty small, but there was always a chance. Defiant's Intellect could have laid in a course and folded them through space in a fraction of a second. Indeed, Defiant would have had an emergency jump site picked out as soon as they entered the system three days earlier.

But Defiant was offline.

The Intellect wasn't dead. Because they'd be dead, too. They would no longer exist—the ship's bubble collapsed and their very matter simply gone from the universe.

"Systems, any idea what's happening with Defiant?" Lucinda asked as the marines tended to their injured comrade, packing and wrapping his wound. His composure probably spoke more to the efficacy of analgesic spinal implants than to personal toughness.

"No . . . er, ma'am," Bannon replied, fussing about with multiple holograms. "Defiant handed off to us and pulled back into his own enclave. I can't get through, but I can see he's busy in there. Drawing a lot of power. Twenty-six percent of the antimatter output."

That got everybody's attention.

Normally the Intellect only sipped at the ship's antimatter drive, but it was currently drinking from a fire hose. At most the ship could spare 40 percent of drive capacity for Intellect requirements, but of course that was a design spec with combat operations in mind, for when the ship was fully engaged in a death struggle with others of its kind.

Normally 2 percent was more than enough.

Defiant was fighting a private war.

Lucinda wondered whether they were going to survive this after all.

Whatever this was.

Having reassured himself that none of the dead were about to reanimate—always a possibility with compromised corpses full of neuromuscular mesh—Hayes returned to Lucinda's side just as medics arrived to treat the wounded and collect engrams from the dead. They got one look at Torvaldt's remains and switched to Connelly. But she wasn't in much better condition.

"I don't think we can get anything off them . . . sir," said the corpsman, another marine, addressing Hayes.

"Lieutenant Hardy has the bridge, son," Hayes said. "She's in command here. Report to her." Hayes checked with Lucinda; just a quick glance, but it was freighted with significance. This was her show now.

Lucinda scanned the bridge, taking in the shocked and fearful expressions of her shipmates. Men and women she knew without really knowing them at all. Ian Bannon looked horrified. A first lifer; it was the first time he'd seen violent death, and it showed in the long lines of his face and the hollows of his eyes, which seemed to have shrunk into his head, trying to

unsee what he had witnessed. The other recent transfers, Mercado Fein and Nonomi Chivers, looked glad
to be sitting a few slots down the chain of command.

"Wait. What about Timuz and Koh? They must
outrank . . . *Lieutenant* Hardy."

That was Chase, of course, who was fast recovering. Having kicked one commander to death seemed
to have whetted his appetite for taking down another.
Hayes frowned at him.

"Sorry, sir. Lieutenant Commander Koh is in sick
bay," the medic said. "He fell during the turbulence
and took a bad hit to the head. Real bad. He's out,
maybe even flatlined until we can reboot."

Lucinda inflated the data matrix again, quickly
isolated the flow from Medical, and confirmed the
report. It was less than a minute old. The casualty list
was growing. Mostly sprains and a few breaks. But
there were a lot of them. And Koh was listed as body
lost.

"What about Lieutenant Commander Timuz?"
she asked, beating Chase to the question. "He's next
in line behind Connelly. We should get him up here.
He needs to take the bridge."

Hayes shook his head, "He's not gonna like that."

"That's hardly relevant," Lucinda protested. "He's
the ranking officer."

She tried to page him on neuralink—an ingrained
habit—but it was still down. Instead she had to
search for him in the data cloud, aware she was
blushing as the seconds dragged on and she couldn't
locate the link in the vast storm of information.

"Lieutenant, if I might?"

It was Bannon. He opened an audio channel to Engineering. Directly to the station chief.

"I'm busy," Timuz snapped at the ping.

"Commander, it's Lieutenant Hardy, sir. We have a situation on the bridge that requires your attendance."

"And I have a situation down here that requires me, too, missy," Timuz shot back. "Defiant is in deep trouble, and so are we."

"Do we have fold capacity?" Lucinda asked.

"Aye, we do."

"Commander," she said. "I'm afraid the captain is dead, sir. The XO, too. You have the ship now."

A short silence followed the revelation, less than a second, before Timuz replied, "I'm sorry to hear that, but we can respawn them later. You make the fold, Lieutenant. If I leave Engineering, we're all going to die and nobody will be coming back from that."

He cut the link.

Hayes shrugged at Lucinda's unspoken *What now?*

"Lieutenant, you have the conne," he said. *Do something,* he seemed to leave unsaid.

"*Mister* Chase," she said pointedly. "Do you have my waypoints plotted yet?"

The navigator looked pissed, but he nodded.

"Already plugged in."

"Helm," she said to Nonomi Chivers. "Fold away."

Lieutenant Chivers performed a finger dance through her own particular constellation of data fields and control zones, finally detaching two large red buttons.

"Folding," she said, and pressed them in sequence. Lucinda issued no warning to the ship. There was no inertia, no sudden sense of movement. The ship's AM drive fed an unutterably vast surge of power into an escapement array, and *Defiant* collapsed the distance between its physical location and the final waypoint of the relatively short jump period. If either Chivers or Chase had messed anything up, the ship would be destroyed before any of them were even aware of the mistake.

Defiant materialized, unharmed, one standard AU into the heliopause, the interstellar shallows beyond the reach of any solar wind from the local star.

A small round of applause circled the bridge when everybody realized they hadn't been blown through a hole in reality and completely annihilated, removed from existence down at the quantum level.

Chivers smiled nervously.

Lieutenant Chase took a bow, an oddly theatrical gesture.

"Done and done well," Lucinda said loudly enough to cut in over the clapping and wolf whistles. It wasn't every day you folded space without an Intellect backstopping you. But they were trained for it, after all. "Tactical. Threats?"

"Nothing on passive, ma'am. Go to active seeking?"

The bridge fell silent again. Everyone was waiting to see if she would light up the stars with the *Defiant*'s monstrously powerful active sensors. It would give them nearly perfect awareness out to three Earth-standard AUs. But it would also fix them in the targeting arrays of any waiting foe.

"No," she said. "Set for dark running. But leave countermeasures at precon readiness."

"Aye, ma'am," said Mercado Fein.

The bridge crew was recovering, each station boss working his or her console with focus and will. Even Chase was busy plotting coordinates for another emergency fold. Lucinda turned her attention to the medics, who'd confirmed that they couldn't retrieve engrams for Torvaldt and Connelly. The damage to their cortical architecture was too great. Instead, they worked on the Woj, who'd been killed with a body shot, leaving his data intact.

They hadn't extracted his engram yet, though.

The network breach meant they had to treat the dead comms officer as a clear and present bioware hazard. The medics directed a drone through the grisly process of removing the head for transport in stasis to EM quarantine, where the Woj's engram, the lossless recording of his consciousness, could be extracted without danger to the ship's systems or medical personnel.

Lucinda wondered how much of the man they would find in there.

"I want a full briefing on the scans as soon as possible," she told Bannon.

"I'll tell Medical," he said.

"Do. And I need a full sweep of the ship. We can't afford even a line of code escaping whatever lockbox Defiant jammed this thing into. Any sign of him yet?"

The systems chief shook his head.

"No, ma'am. But he's drawing three points less from the AM now. So maybe he's winning."

Or maybe he's dying, Lucinda thought. But she kept that to herself.

"Captain Hayes, how are your people?" she asked. She could have called up the casualty lists again, but this was a courtesy and it gave her a few more seconds to figure out what the hell to do next.

"One big toe crushed in the gym. A broken finger. A couple of turned ankles and bad bruises here and there. Nothing life-threatening," he said. His face was grim as he watched the drone take off Wojkowski's head. It came away and trailed long silvery threads of neuromesh. An ocean of blood flowed onto the deck.

Lucinda took in a deep breath and let it go slowly. She felt shaky and light-headed.

"Good," she said, fighting to keep her voice steady. "Please have one platoon stand to for immediate counterboarding response."

"Way ahead of you, Hardy," he said. "They're deploying to critical stations and choke points right now. I'll rotate them every four hours."

As he said the words, the bridge doors slid open and two marines in full battle rattle stomped in, but only just across the threshold. In body armor they looked three times as big as everyone else.

"Permission to secure the bridge, ma'am," the shorter one asked. The shorter one still towered over her. He addressed Lucinda directly.

"Please," she said, nodding.

The guards took up positions at ten and two o'clock in the circular command center. Guns out.

Hatches swished open again, and Lucinda recognized a squat, powerful-looking man, shaven-headed and Japanese or maybe Korean in phenotype.

Chief Higo with two spacers in tow.

"Here to clean up the mess, ma'am," said the chief. It almost sounded as though he was asking permission to enter the bridge, and she nodded at him, shaky and coming down off an adrenal rush. "Thanks, Chief." They were already heading for the corpses, with a maintenance bot train following closely behind. A full and frank exchange of views on who had priority ensued, with the medics insisting that they needed to make sure there was no chance of extracting life data from the neural nets of the captain and XO, and Chief Higo growling that if any blood or nastiness ruined his decks, the corpsmen would be hand scrubbing it out at a molecular level.

Lucinda quickly isolated the feed from Tactical, her old station, a data cloud she knew intimately. Green lights across the threat board.

She let go of a breath she'd been holding. A long, shaky exhalation of stress.

"Ian. How's Defiant looking?"

"Down to drawing 20 percent from the stacks, ma'am," he said. "It's consistently tapering. Looks good. I guess. He seems to be in control."

"When he gets down to 10 percent, let me know. I want to be ready to call an O-Group. And I would really like the chief engineer to attend."

"Good luck with that," said Hayes. "And here. Clean yourself up, Lieutenant."

He passed her a small medicated washcloth. The medics had given Chief Higo a packet to pass around. It gave him something to do while they finished up.

She wiped at her face, which felt sticky, and the damp cloth came away bright red.

"I'd give you my gym towel," said Hayes, "but that'd be gross."

"Thanks," Lucinda said, uncertain whether she could make the word audible. It was hard to speak, forcing every syllable through a filter that strained the panic and terror from her voice.

"Have you ever . . . seen anything like this?" she asked the marine officer. "It's some sort of attack, but . . ."

"But where's the follow-up? I know. And to answer your question, no. I've never seen an effective malware breach before. Not on a ship, anyway. Seen some nasty stuff from the source coders, but that was all tactical level. This felt . . . bigger."

Lucinda stared at the comm station, where all three of her shipmates had died.

"It came in on the dead drop," she said. "We won't know for certain until Defiant is back online, but I'm sure of it."

"That means it came from Fleet," Hayes said.

"I know. Something's happened, but we have no way of finding out without exposing ourselves again."

She had never felt more alone in her life. Her eyes locked on Hayes's.

"What are we going to do?"

"The question is, what are *you* going to do?"

CHAPTER
TWELVE

Sephina knew that something was very wrong when the screaming got worse after they ran out of ammo. Not her screaming. The YG's. Coto had just improvised a transfer to Deuce2. Their credit broker now had nine and a half million stolen yen hidden away where the gummies couldn't steal it back. Seph was figuring the odds of returning the money to the Yakuza in exchange for safe passage off Eassar and a promise never to fuck with them again. A promise she wouldn't keep, natch. And safe passage she couldn't possibly trust.

But a winning smile and a fast line in bullshit was all she had, because they'd run out of ammo.

That was when the *gunsotsu* started screaming.

At first she didn't recognize the screams as being any different from the war shouts and battle cries of the last fifteen minutes. But Ariane gave her a what-the-fuck look, and Jaddi Coto shrugged his mountainous shoulders, and she realized the fighting had intensified on the other side of the bar but they were no longer a part of it.

"HabSec?" Ariane shouted. There was gunfire and extravagant property damage to be sure but nothing like the murder factory that had been running at full capacity just a minute earlier. There was something else to it as well. Something she couldn't quite figure out.

Seph chanced a peek over the top of the bar but without being stupid about it. She fixed a broken mirror shard to a swizzle stick with a small piece of duct tape.

Duct tape was one of the many useful items swinging from the bone loops growing out of Coto's upper body. He had a little periscope, too, which would have been way useful, but it had been destroyed in the firefight.

"Don't think it's HabSec," she muttered, staring at the portion of the chaos she could make out in her little mirror on a stick.

It wasn't the Hab's security forces; that much was obvious. They would have rolled in with mechs. But it was also obvious the gangsters had lost interest in Sephina and her crew. They were fighting one another.

She moved a few feet and snuck a quick glance around the end of the bar, where the snake man had been trying to flank them.

He was very dead. Burned to a crisp by her improvised fuel-air bomb and, she could see now, by a stray touch from Coto's arclight fire. She could also see one of his gummy bros enjoying an impromptu barbecue feed. He was down on all fours, his face buried deep into the charred remains of the snake man's midsection. He looked like some half-starved wild dog, ripping and tearing great strips and chunks of burned meat from the carcass. His features were smeared with gore, and his eyes were empty of anything but a fierce hunger. That vacant yet intense gaze locked onto Sephina, and the guttural chewing and swallowing noises gave way to a deep body growl.

A blue-white plasma bolt struck him, explosively vaporizing his skull.

Sephina, who'd been all but paralyzed by the weirdness of the spectacle, flinched away from the expanding blast wave of hot meat mist. Coto and Ariane popped up, both of them yelling empty threats and waving even emptier weapons at the last of the YG soldiers.

One of them had just shot down his boss.

She could tell that the dead cannibal was a level boss by the tattoos on his left arm. The right arm was missing. Blown clean off the body by the plasma bolt. It had taken a huge smoking bite out of the guy's upper torso.

"Back off. Get the fuck out of here," Ariane yelled.

Coto repeated everything she said but much louder, in a voice so deep that you could feel it down in your own chest. That wasn't an exaggeration. It was a feature he'd added when he'd upgraded his p-type a couple of years earlier.

The surviving Yakuza needed no encouragement. There were only two of them, and they looked about ready to jump out of the nearest air lock. Sephina shuddered. The one who'd just killed his own could easily have fired on her. Instead, he chose to murder his boss. He was a dead man. The only question for him was how he'd take his leave of the living. Very slowly and screaming, she'd bet.

Yet he'd done it. He'd saved her life. Seph laid a hand on Coto's massive forearms and gently pulled down. He lowered the muzzle of the arclight. Ariane gaped at her as though Sephina had lost her mind. But the man who'd saved her life at the certain cost of his own held her gaze. He nodded once, quickly, and turned to run. The other surviving *gunsotsu* went with him.

"Wait . . ." she started to shout, but the cry died in her throat. They were gone, accelerating away with the inhuman speed that spoke of good-quality neuro-mesh running at the limits of spec.

They were alone in the ruins of Taro's Bar.

That was when she realized what was wrong.

The fighting had spread to the street. She could hear it clearly now, muffled but unmistakable.

Nobody spoke. Sephina shrugged. Coto, as was his habit, imitated the gesture, exaggerating it hugely. Always the first into action, Ariane moved quickly, darting out from behind the bar and picking up the nearest weapon, a machine pistol still held in the grip of a severed hand. She prized the dead fingers away and brought the weapon up, sweeping it back and forth to cover the room. Spot fires burned every-where, set off by plasma bursts, arc lightning, and old-fashioned kinetics. The firelight animated her me-tallic blond hair with flickering movement.

Sephina and Coto joined her, abandoning their cover behind the bar along with the severed head of Satomi San, who really was to blame for everything. If he'd just given them the bearer codes when they'd asked, none of this would have been necessary. Sephina stripped an assault rifle from the body of a dead gangster. Coto searched around, looking for a power cell. Broken glass crunched underfoot, and broken gummy soldiers with it. No fire alarms had sounded. No flame suppressant systems had engaged. But the Eassar Habitat Intellect would make sure that no fires got completely out of hand.

That did sort of pose the question of what Eassar was gonna do about this shit, though, didn't it? The place should have been stomped to rubble by Compliance Mechs already, if only because some HabSec commander would want his cut of whatever business had obviously gone pear-shaped here.

But there was no sign of HabSec. Not inside Taro's Bar. No sign of the Intellect. And no hull rats swarming in to pick over the dead and loot the wreckage.

From the sound of things, they all seemed to be fighting one another out on the street.

"Coto," Seph said, "are we still getting jammed?"

"The jamming continues," he confirmed.

"I think I'd like to go back to the ship now," Ariane said. She continued to strip weapons from the dead. She found a good cell for the arclight and tossed it to Coto. He swapped out the depleted unit and powered up the weapon again.

"Thank you, Miss Ariane," he said, dropping the old cell into one of the deep pockets of his oversized duster.

"You're my favorite," Ariane said, slapping him on the back.

He looked confused.

"But I thought Sephina was your favorite," he said.

Ariane cut him off, but gently. "She's my favorite, too."

"Coto," Sephina said. "Just keep trying to get a commlink to the *Regret*."

He took out the old-fashioned headset, plugged it in to an even older comm unit, and set to trying to break through the signal hash that had cut them off from their ship. Seph had assumed the Yakuza had done that to spring their ambush before she could trigger hers. But as the moments passed and nobody came to investigate the firestorm or scavenge through the wreckage of its aftermath, she began to wonder.

Mostly about what the fuck was going down out on the hull.

"I dunno what's happening out there," she said, "but it doesn't seem to involve us. So let's get back to the dock."

They stowed their weapons as best they could, hiding them within the folds of their overcoats. Coto wore a harness for the arclight. Seph and Ariane merely held their coats closed over the guns they'd picked up. They were walking out of one trap and into . . . some shit or other. This district, about two clicks spinward from the secondary port facilities of Eassar's third frame, lay hard up on the inner hull. It was a slum, and the residents were used to gangs of Yakuza *gunsotsu*, merchantmen, freelancers, mercs, and pirates going armed on the deck plates. Occasional weapons fire was all part of the local color. Always was in the poorer districts on Yulin-Irrawaddy Habs. The only objection the Combine had to criminal syndicates on its Habitats was getting shorted on its standard 15 percent cut of turnover.

Not profits. Revenue.

It made for lively neighborhoods in areas like this.

They emerged from Taro's into deep night, three figures draped in long buff-colored overcoats, trailing smoke and silhouetted against fires fueled by alcohol.

The street was worse than the bar. Normally so crowded with foot traffic and traders and cheap maglev scooters and hundreds of makeshift stalls and food stands that you couldn't walk more than a few steps in a straight line, the hull plate was eerily free of foot traffic—except for the few dozen Hab rats exchanging fire with one another, with a small crew of gummy soldiers holed up across the way, and with a squad of HabSec troopers who'd laagered up behind a makeshift redoubt of three fallen mechs. There seemed to be no coherence, no real meaning to the violence. It was a struggle of all against all.

Coto took a dumb kinetic round in the shoulder the moment he stepped out. The duster's reactive nanotube armor weave flexed and shed the bullet, which could not have pierced his rhinoderm hide anyway, but he roared and brought up the arclight, sending a prolonged storm of forged lightning across the deck plating and into the body of the maglev car sheltering the *gunsotsu* who'd targeted him. It wasn't the two survivors from Taro's.

They weren't survivors anymore. One of them lay at Sephina's feet. Or a big piece of him, anyway.

Seph didn't see what happened to the vehicle or to the YG using it as cover. She was aware of a detonation, but she was already diving for cover, pulling out the scavenged dragon shot and cranking area clearance rounds into the breech. The rip-snarl fire of dual machine pistols told her Ariane was already at work, adding her fire to the general mayhem.

Tracer rounds, arc lightning, pulse fire, and smart rockets raked over the port district. It wasn't just the street outside Taro's. Sephina had the impression of a much wider conflict just before she landed on the deck plating with a grunt. Her armor-weave coat could shed light weapons fire and blade strikes, but the dull concussion of gross impact hurt just as much as if she'd thrown herself to the hull in her underwear. Her elbow hit the gutter, and electric jangles ran painfully up her arm. Ariane slammed into the side panel of the maglev vehicle next to her. The car's field generator had failed, probably because of all the weapons fire it had absorbed, and it lay flush with the plating, looking weird and wrong. It had to be a Yakuza vehicle. Nobody else down here could afford a car. If the locals rode anything it was one of those cheap maglev scooters that normally hovered a few inches over the deck plating, blocking the footpath and spilling out into the roadway. Thousands of them still blocked free movement in every direction, but the scooters lay tipped over, inert and powerless on the plating. Hundreds more had been abandoned in transit when they failed.

"Why is it dark?" Ariane asked.

"Because there is no light," Coto shouted over the din of battle.

"I think Ariane is seeking a deeper truth," Sephina said, adding a blast of shot. She wasn't aiming at anyone in particular. "It's midafternoon. It shouldn't be this dark, and the streets shouldn't be this, you know, full of fucking gunfire and body parts. It's not even happy hour."

"Maglev transit is down, too," Ariane shouted.

Coto joined them behind the ruined vehicle, although at eight feet tall, even crouched as low as he could, he was exposed to fire.

"I will improve this barrier," the giant hybrid said before reaching under the car and heaving it up, tipping the vehicle on its side, where it swayed precariously until he took hold of the undercarriage with one hand, firing over the top with the other. Seph and Ariane were now covered by the thick composite plate of the vehicle's field generator, a much better shield against kinetic rounds and energy bolts.

"This neighborhood's really gone to hell," Ariane shouted over the uproar.

"We should return to the bar," Coto said. "There is less violence in there now that everybody is dead."

He threw thunderbolts into the chaos seemingly at random, because there was no single enemy to engage. Even HabSec was completely fucked-up. As Seph watched from cover, trying to plot an exit from the firefight, a man in the mottled gray combat coveralls of Eassar's internal security forces emerged at a run from a building, holding a powered blade in one hand and . . . well . . . a human head in the other. His face was a rictus of malignant fury. He planted his boots on the deck plating and tore a huge gobbet of meat from the severed head. Before he could swallow it, one of his own troopers took him under fire with a heavy pulse weapon, blowing the man into smoking red chunks.

"So," said Ariane, "that's a thing now."

"I'd like to assure you both I'm not even a little bit hungry," Sephina said, "so there's no need to shoot me."

She fired some dragon-shot rounds down the street, where a couple of guys who looked like hull rats had been pointing at them. The spread on the shot sent them scurrying but probably did no real damage.

Probably.

Like Sephina's crew, none of the locals would be hooked up for neuralink. They couldn't load scripts or back up their engrams even if they wanted to. They wouldn't even have engrams. Coto was unusual in sporting a radically resequenced phenotype, but he hadn't paid for that bodywork himself. He'd been poured into his current form at the end of a thirty-year span with the TDF. Basic source code, an entry-level p-type, and three months' pay was what he got instead of a pension.

Little wonder he'd fetched up on the *Regret*.

"I think Coto's right," Sephina said, reaching a decision.

"Seriously?" Ariane asked.

"Seriously?" Coto repeated.

"Yeah. This is balls," Seph shouted as the arclight crackled again. "I don't think we can get out this way. I got no fucking idea what's going on, but it's big. Look."

She jerked the muzzle of the dragon shot up, and they both followed the gesture.

Eassar was a C-class Habitat, a cylinder fifty kilometers long and sixteen across, spinning at a quarter revolution every minute to provide one Earth-standard grav on the inner hull, where they currently stood. An executive enclave clustered around a small "inland sea" in the Habitat's midsection boasted residential and commercial towers reaching at least two kilometers up from the inner hull, with gravity on the upper floors regulated by the Intellect. But most of Eassar's 90 million inhabitants lived "down on the plates," separated from hard vacuum by a hundred meters of carbon armor, engineering space, and fused regolith reclaimed from an asteroid belt that circled the local star between two helium-rich gas giants a couple of AU out.

A sixteen-klick diameter wasn't great enough to offer the illusion of a flat world. You were constantly aware of the Hab's curvature. Even in one of the Grand Halos like Cupertino or St. Peter's World you could never really forget you stood on a vast human creation, a bracelet of sculpted energies and exotic matter more than a million kilometers in circumference and twelve thousand kilometers wide. The beautiful and terrifying spectacle climbed away into the heavens wherever you raised your eyes.

But Eassar was really just a Combine factory and transit hub. It folded back on itself almost claustrophobically. With the right sort of gene-modding, or retinal implants, or even just a handheld scope, it would be possible to pick out details on the inner hull on the far side of the cylinder. More shitty street stalls, more dive bars, more poverty and overcrowding.

Sephina had no bio-augments. But she could still see what was happening sixteen klicks away.

Eassar was burning. It was normal to see open fires in the streets, of course, at least in these districts where the poor lived and often worked in their little tube homes, their private lives spilling right out onto the deck plating. People here cooked and ate in the streets, often sourcing their protein from open-air butchers. But the conflagration Seph saw was not some runaway cooking fire.

Weapons fire stitched across the inner hull up and down the length of the Hab. Directly overhead a thousand-thousand points of light flared and burst and twinkled in the enclosed biosphere. Smoke poured from giant infernos. Explosions bloomed and fed on one another.

She felt Ariane tugging at her elbow, drawing her attention north, to the enclave where the Hab's elite lived and worked.

It was hard to tell at such a distance, but it was possibly racked by even greater violence.

"Yeah," she said. "Let's go back to the bar."

CHAPTER
THIRTEEN

The Deputy Prince of House Yulin floated and thrashed ineffectually six feet off the ground and far enough removed from any of the dig team that his wild raking and grasping could not possibly reach anyone. His manservant, unnamed and now deceased, lay in a patch of darkened sand, blood still pumping feebly from the terrible wounds in his face and neck. The satellite base station he'd set up was slagged. A smoking puddle of melted scrap contained in a shimmering exclusion field generated by Hero.

"What the unholy fuck was all that about, then?" McLennan roared at Trumbull, for this surely must be his fault. Until Trumbull had arrived with his caravan of upper-class twits and useless nuff-nuffs, McLennan's dig site had been the very model of orderly quietude and dignified industry. Now there was a half-eaten corpse at his feet and a jabbering lunatic floating in midair, and his Intellect had launched a subatomic strike on a satellite base station. It was a tiny wee strike, granted, that discretely annihilated the molecular bonds of the infernal machine without spraying around any burning debris or radioactive particulates, but still.

"This was not how I imagined this evening, Professor," McLennan growled.

Trumbull, who was gray and shaking with shock, found enough composure to shoot back, "No, I'm sure you'd imagined terrorizing everybody with your nude and withered genitals."

"Hey, uh, maybe we should ask the Intellect what happened," Lambright suggested. He looked a little wan and out of sorts but not completely unbalanced by the unexpected turn.

Herodotus was hovering closer to Pac Yulin than to the three men. The prince snarled and twisted like a beast caught in a snare and desperate to escape. His body glowed from within as Hero ran various scans.

McLennan scowled at the Intellect. "Do you have any idea why the little gobshite decided to have at his manservant like a haggis fresh from the fucking oven?"

"Malware," Hero said simply. "I detected anomalies as soon as Deputy Prince Pac Yulin connected to the Combine's planetary server. The attack packets were sheathed and embedded within the livestream. They made the jump to the prince's neural net and performed a hostile overwrite within twenty microseconds."

McLennan quickly looked to the two men standing on either side of him. Both of them were wired for neuralink, but neither showed any sign of unleashing his own cannibal holocaust in the next few moments. He heard voices and footsteps crunching over the sand and hardscrabble behind them: other members of the party, drawn by the screams and the flash-bang of Hero slagging the base station. But they didn't appear to have turned into a ravening zombie horde either.

"The immediate threat has been neutralized by cutting the link to the planetary network," Hero said, sensitive to McLennan's concern.

"Oh, my word," Trumbull croaked, actually dropping to his ass on the sand. "Oh, dear."

"Wait, you're saying somebody meat hacked him?" Lambright asked. "Via an update?"

"It would appear so, Mister Lambright," Hero replied.

"And what about all these other yammering dobbers?" McLennan asked. "None of them were affected? No offense, Lambright."

"None taken."

"Deputy Prince Pac Yulin was using a private channel to his family's corporate node," Hero said. "I will go out on a limb and presume he did not like to share."

McLennan cast a baleful eye on the approaching mob. They were pointing at Pac Yulin, who was still trapped in Hero's confinement field, still violently jerking and twitching as though ravaged by a nerve agent. His face was a grotesque mask, distorted and savage.

"We'll have to get him to a hospital as quickly as possible," Professor Trumbull said, although since he was sitting on the ground like a child with his legs splayed out in front of him, his words did not have the authority he might have wished. "His family . . ." he finished weakly.

"His family be damned," McLennan spit as the first of the other tourists arrived. "Slavers and parasites. The lot of them."

"What's happened?" asked a young woman. She was carrying a cocktail of some kind, staring at Pac Yulin and sipping at the drink through a colorful straw.

"Meat hacked," Lambright said.

"Omigod! Are we safe?"

"Everybody is safe for now," Hero said. He had drifted back to the group gathering around McLennan, subtly interposing himself between them and the prince. When he spoke, he glowed a reassuring shade of royal blue. Mac also could feel the calming effect of an alpha waveform emanating from the Intellect.

"The malware that infected Deputy Prince Pac Yulin's neural net was directly injected via a closed link to a private node," Hero explained. "None of you were exposed. If you were, you would have been compromised in the same fashion as he."

They all looked at the young first lifer as he floated in the confinement field, possessed by a psychotic rage. His face was smeared with blood. His eyes were empty. He looked deranged with fury.

"We have to get him back to Fort Saba," Trumbull said.

"I dinnae think so," McLennan said before Hero could speak again.

They all turned to him, and he was quietly glad to have put some pants on earlier.

"Herodotus, would it be the case that this was a targeted exploit? By an enemy of the Yulin clan? Or a wider attack?"

A murmur went through the small crowd at that. All of the new arrivals had joined them by then.

"As per your standing instructions, Professor McLennan, I am not online," Hero answered. "So I cannot speak with certainty to whether the planetary grid has been compromised, but there are other indications that make me lean in that direction."

"Would that be the dropships coming down through the upper atmosphere?" McLennan asked.

"Among other things, yes," said Hero.

A few of the tourists gasped. They all looked up into the night sky, where three bright points of light had detached themselves from the dense star field and were growing brighter and larger by the second.

"This wasn't on the itinerary," Trumbull protested. "None of this was on the itinerary."

Mac half expected him to pull out a sheaf of paper and start waving it around. The man was a complete shit head.

"Herodotus, do you think you might detail the droids to prioritize swapping out the power cells on Professor Trumbull's transport? I fear we might have to decamp in the next little while, and I assume the dune rover is running low."

"I have already issued the instructions," Hero said.

"What's happening?" the cocktail-sipping woman asked again. This time she seemed more interested in McLennan's answer than in her drink.

The astroarchaeologist peered up at the stars again.

"Well, lassie, I might well do my dough cold, but

I'd place a decent wager that the Dark-accursed Sturm have finally returned."

The effect was galvanic. Half the small group swore that he was mad. They laughed at him. They cursed the very idea. A couple even stomped off, declaring their intention to spend the rest of this unbelievably shitty day at the bar. A goodly number of the remaining tourists threw the switch to theatrical panic, rushing off to repack the bags they'd just unpacked and demanding passage to the nearest offworld transport hub. Only Lambright and Trumbull waited for Mac to explain himself.

Trumbull looked terrified but determined to seek further and better particulars.

Lambright appeared to be skeptical but at least open to the chance of extreme possibilities. "Why the Sturm, McLennan?" he asked.

Mac smiled, almost rubbing Lambright's head as though to reward an apt pupil for asking a simple but apposite question. Instead he jerked a thumb at Pac Yulin.

"Yon laddie there has been very crudely overwritten by an aggressive neuralink agent. It was delivered instantaneously via livestream from his family's secure data node. Unless somebody took a long and winding road to manually install it locally, it arrived here at the edge of the Volume via zero point wormhole commlink." He paused and addressed the Intellect. "Am I right so far, Herodotus?"

"I'm reviewing the intelligence, Professor, but our conclusions are essentially the same, yes."

"Apart from a number of mining outposts maintained by the Combine and the transport facility at Fort Saba, there is no infrastructure of any economic value anywhere on Batavia. That's all in the Habs working the asteroid fields."

McLennan lifted his gaze to the stars again, specifically to the three that were growing in size and slowly moving across the dark sky in their direction.

"And those three dropships, if I am not mistaken, are on trajectories that will bring them down here, on top of us. What's here? Why, it's the ruin of the only Republican Generation Ship to be lost on the Great Exodus. A sacred site to the Sturm. And one we defile with our very presence, Mister Lambright. So exercising the precautionary principle, I suggest we move our sacrilegious arses with all dispatch lest some bothersome Inquisitor decide to roast them over a fire for us."

Lambright furrowed his brow and stared at the points of moving light.

"There has to be more."

"Oh, there's always more with Professor McLennan; don't you worry about that," Trumbull snapped. He had picked himself up and dusted himself off and was quickly regaining his composure. "Mostly an obsession with being proved wrong for five hundred years."

"Well, I only have to be right once"—McLennan grinned like a shark—"and I'm pretty sure my time has come, Professor." He turned back to Lambright, took him by the elbow, and started to lead the man back to camp. "If you unpacked any of your bags, laddie, you need to repack them and get them stowed away on your transport. I assume you have a neural net. If I were you, I would not just turn it off, I'd shut it down, metabolize it, and shit it out as quickly as I could. Unless you fancy joining His Highness back there in the outer wastes of violent psychopathy."

Lambright glanced back over his shoulder even as McLennan propelled him forward. Hero was following them, with Professor Trumbull bringing up the rear. Ahead of the small party the campsite was in complete disarray, with some of the visitors rushing to pack and leave while others settled themselves in at the bar. Droids hurried to and fro, set to various tasks by Hero without any instructions from Mac.

"Right," said the astroarchaeologist as they drew up at the tables where dinner and drinks were to have been served. A server drone already was breaking down the goat carcass for transport while another packed up the bar over the objections of a man who was already drunk and intent on staying that way. "Excuse me," McLennan shouted, clapping his hands once loudly to get everybody's attention.

"We never were formally introduced," he boomed out, his voice taking on a command presence he had not needed to call on in a long time. Hero did something to amplify it, too, projecting his words throughout the entire campsite.

"I am Professor Frazer McLennan of Miyazaki University's astroarchaeology department. Some of you may also know of me as Admiral McLennan of the Terran Navy, Retired."

He expected some sarcastic interjection from Herodotus at that. The whole reason most of these feckless plonkers had made such extortionate credit transfers to the university for this excursion wasn't that they were archaeology nerds. It was so that they could boast of having met the dread victor of the Battle of Earth. But the Intellect, who was being remarkably well behaved, remained quiet for the moment.

Most of the new arrivals finally had stopped buggering about and were listening to him.

He pointed to the sky, where the dropships had grown larger.

"I might be wrong. That happens, even to me. But I have reason to believe Republican shock troopers will be here presently. I do not intend to make their acquaintance, for obvious reasons. I suggest you might care to join me in fucking off with all dispatch. I further suggest, given what looks like a malware attack on Deputy Prince Pac Yulin, that you power down your personal nets and, if I may be so bold, excrete them quickly."

That got a response. A very poor one. But before they could wind themselves up into a yammering fit, Mac rolled over their objections.

"You all presumably backed up before you landed here. You'll only lose a few days."

He didn't explain that he thought those backups were probably burned, too. He didn't need the hysteria.

"But if you're carrying implants when the Sturm get here, they'll fry your eggs like they did with yon bonnie prince. Herodotus here"—he waved in the direction of the Intellect—"can provide you with protection against hostile electronic warfare. But as soon as they land and lay hands on you, you're fucked three ways from Sunday. They'll execute you on general principles just for having implants. So, too, if you have any gene modifications. Or if you've relifed. Even if none of those things are the case, you'll be put to the correction for having had the barefaced fucking cheek to desecrate a sacred site with your filthy fucking presence. So," he finished, clapping his hands again, "let's be off like a bride's nightie, shall we?"

"But how do you know it's the Sturm?"

It was the woman with the cocktail. She looked desperate for any reassurance. Perhaps she wanted him to shrug and admit he had no real idea. He was just playing a hunch. He was, as Trumbull had put it, obsessed.

He shrugged.

"I don't know it's them," McLennan said. "But I think it is. And so I'll be off. You're welcome to stay behind and find out if you wish."

And with that he pushed through the small crowd, ignoring the shouted questions and demands for more information. They would see to themselves or not. It would be the Sturm or it would not.

They would stay or they would go. They would live or they would die.

He had done his bit.

CHAPTER

FOURTEEN

The transfer was clean. Booker felt no trace of anyone having been there before him. He inhabited the mech as completely as a first life breeder occupied his natural-born body. The skin sack he'd left behind lay in a vacant coma on the couch, awaiting the download of a new soul.

That was what it would have looked like after they deleted him, he thought. Why people couldn't see that the very essence of the individual lay in the source code from which he arose and not the vessel containing it was beyond him.

He towered over Orr and Lao Tzu. The corporal was frowning as though reconsidering the wisdom of having ported a condemned man into a three-ton armored mech. The officer stared at him, his eyes nervous. Father Michael stood between the two of them. He jutted his chin up at Booker, challenging him to live up to the deal he had just struck, to accept the redemption he'd been offered.

The neural clamp that had inhibited any aggressive urges while he'd been embodied in dumb meat remained firmly attached to the hindbrain of the co-matose figure. The mech had no such limiters in place, and if he'd so chosen, he could have taken his captors apart like slow-braised pork. That explained their wariness.

"I'm in," he said, and they all jumped in alarm. He immediately dialed down the volume. "I won't log in to Habnet because of the malware breach," he went on at a more reasonable volume. "We'll have to do our own recon, gather what intel we can. Corporal Orr, do you have any secure comm channels?"

"None," Orr replied. "I'm offline, too. And I won't reconnect until I know the malware intrusion has been defeated."

"Hard lines?"

"Fried."

He didn't bother asking Lao Tzu. If his would-be executioner couldn't get online to load the instruc-tions he'd needed for the deletion ceremony, he wouldn't be able to access any command channels either.

"Sure you don't want to load into the other mech?" Booker asked Orr.

"I don't have the scripts or training," he answered.

Booker didn't judge him for it. The man had made a specialty of hand-to-hand combat. And the fact was, you really needed hands to make that work. The triple-jointed grapplers of a Compliance Mech didn't count. Orr would be better off staying embodied. The priest had no neuralink implants, so there was no point expecting anything from him. Besides, he was Booker's witness. The last thing he wanted was Father Michael getting his head blown off in whatever was happening outside.

And whatever that was, it was getting way more intense.

The sound of weapons fire was much heavier. The mech's proprioceptors let him feel the same vibrations and kinetic shocks running through the body of the Hab that he'd experienced a few minutes earlier as a man. He was wary of opening up any wide-band sensor arrays because that might expose the machine's substrate, and thus him, to a hostile intrusion.

He didn't think it likely that the Sturm were attacking, although who would be a big enough dumbass to attack a TDF facility was beyond him. Only thing for it then was to load code and roll.

With no clamps in place, he had access to his deep lacuna. He'd already loaded the basic scripts for controlling a mech, of course. Now he pulled up a couple of more advanced programs. No permascripted black code, for sure, but still a hell of a lot gnarlier than the simple how-to files he'd autoloaded upon transferring to the machine.

"I don't have a map of the Hab, and I'm not about to try to access one," he said. "Captain? If you'll lead the way to the armory. Hopefully you remember that, don't you?"

The officer glared at him but did not refuse the request. Father Michael moved to follow them, but Booker raised the heavy grappler and opened the claws.

"Padre. Probably better if you stayed here and kept your head down. Literally. Sounds kind of sporty out there, and I'd prefer you were still drawing breath when this is all over."

"I am not afraid, Booker," the priest said, although his voice shook audibly.

"Good for you, Padre. But I *am* afraid, mostly that somebody will try to delete me again when this is over. You're my insurance against that. I'm going to honor my end of this deal. I want you to make sure he sticks to his word."

He swung the grappler in the direction of Lao Tzu.

"And if he gets permakilled, I need you around to tell his backup what he agreed to. So please. Just stay here, would you?"

The priest seemed inclined to argue, but Corporal Orr laid a hand on his shoulder and gave him a gentle push toward the second, empty couch.

"Booker is right, Padre," he said. "This room has no tactical value. You'd be best waiting here."

"But people will need me," he objected. "There'll be casualties. I have first-aid training, you know. Actual training, not just some program in my head. And the dying will need last rites. Many of the prisoners and some of your own men, Corporal, they will die for real. If Habnet is compromised, your backups will be worthless."

"And that'll be our problem, Father. Not yours," Orr said. "Now just stay here and be safe. Please."

The priest finally agreed to stay put, and Booker led the way out of the XD chamber. Neither of the men had sidearms. Orr had his baton, which would be useless, but he carried it anyway. Booker drove the mech forward, using a long sliding step that minimized the crashing noise of a three-ton behemoth stomping along the passageway. They passed the second mech, which was slumped as though sleeping. And in a way it was, he knew.

This part of the facility was removed from the general population. They had no idea what was happening out there and no way of finding out. The Habitat had defaulted to autonomic subroutines when the Intellect went dark. Gravity, life support, power, and lighting were functioning normally. The hatches opened as they approached and then closed behind them.

They came upon the first body after little more than a minute. Booker scanned it for a heartbeat or neural activity, but the vessel was empty. The soul had departed.

Orr knelt over the corpse. Booker could tell he was distressed.

"He's been . . . bitten . . ." the guard said.

Booker turned the mech's scanners on the body again and confirmed that the corpse had indeed suffered multiple deep tissue wounds consistent with animal bites. A mass analysis confirmed that at least 12 percent of the directly affected tissue was missing.

Swallowed?

The thought sent an existential chill through his circuits. The distant weapons fire was tapering off. Either the security personnel had repelled the assault or they were succumbing to it. Lao Tzu moved up next to Orr to examine the body while Booker stood sentinel over them. He busied himself reprogramming the jelly bag shots in his riot control gun, drawing on one of the script sequences in his advanced adaptive mech programs. A few tweaks to the code and the low-velocity riot gun was repurposed as a mass accelerator while the jelly bags morphed into dumb rounds of superhardened composite. Good enough to punch holes in the sort of tactical armor he currently enjoyed. It would turn offal bags like Orr and Lao Tzu into lunch meat.

Maybe there was a time when he was younger and newly alive to the Source when he would have simply opened up on them and taken his chances with whoever was attacking the Hab.

The enemy of my enemy and all that shit.

But Booker3-212162-930-Infantry had come late and hard to the Source. He was no coward or murderer, as the breeders had slandered him. That verdict said more about their fearful ignorance than it did about his faith and motivation. He was not afraid to die under the strictures of his belief. It was because he believed that that he could die without fear. And so he stood guard over the men who had meant to erase his very existence and was not troubled in the least by the attacker who emerged without warning from the doorway to their left.

The room was shielded from the mech's rudimentary sensor suite. Neither infrared, motion cap, mass displacement, or sonic interferometer detected the berserker until he was clear of the shielding. Perhaps the room was baffled on purpose. More likely it was simply an effect of the material used in its construction. Whatever the case, the man suddenly appeared and launched himself at the captain.

The officer cried out, his hands held up in warding.

He really wasn't carrying anything but administrative script, thought Booker. By then, however, Booker had deployed the mech's grappler to secure the attacker in its padded claws like a giant praying mantis. Booker held him up in front of the eight-camera array embedded in his main glacis plate. There was something terribly wrong with him, Booker thought. He thrashed against the restraint of the grappler. His face was a livid mass of weird contrary tics and gross motor distortion. It was also painted with blood. Booker zapped him with a high-voltage, low-amplitude charge, and he slumped immediately. He held out the unconscious form for the others to examine.

"I'm not programmed for any kind of forensic work," Booker said. "But I reckon we might've found your mystery meat eater. What do you want me to do with him?"

"Just secure him," said Orr. Lao Tzu seemed to have checked out completely.

Booker bound the man's hands and feet with a fast-setting synthetic arachnid silk extruded from a nozzle in the arm equipped with his repurposed riot gun.

"Can you check that room?" Orr asked.

"Sure."

Booker deployed a drone from the Compliance Mech's cache. It wasn't a stealth unit or packed with sensors. Most of the fist-sized device was given over to the simple field effect generator that allowed it to fly. But it was more than capable of checking the compartment for life signs.

"Clear," Booker said.

"I think we should stash the captain in there," Orr said. "He's . . . er . . ."

"He's got no script," Booker finished for him. "So he's useless."

For a moment the officer looked as though he might fire up in defiance, but instead he just slumped.

"You're right," Lao Tzu said. "Unless there is an administrative response to all this, I just . . . I can't."

"If you're gonna hide," Booker said, "stay hidden. We made a deal. You're gonna stick to it."

Before the officer could reply, a new voice boomed all around them.

"Attention. I am Archon-Admiral Wenbo Strom, commander of the 101st Attack Fleet. This facility has been liberated by a Force Recon unit of the Second Shock Regiment. It is now under the protection and law of the Human Republic. Further resistance is pointless and wasteful. We come as friends of the oppressed and saviors of the race. If you are truly human, we are your kin. Join us. Turn over your commanders and the corrupted. Human life is precious. Let us not waste any more this day."

Orr and Lao Tzu exchanged shocked expressions. Booker, embodied and ensouled in a three-ton combat chassis girded by massive plates of reactive matrix graphene armor, did not share their ability to express himself nonverbally.

Instead he swore very loudly.

"Fuck! It really is the Sturm. I fucking hate these guys."

CHAPTER
FIFTEEN

The deck of the *Liberator,* a five-kilometer-long Astral Fortress, tilted at nearly thirty degrees under the boots of Archon-Admiral Strom, the extreme maneuver forced on the flagship by the suicidal attack of an Armadalen corvette. The *Liberator*'s crash turn away from the small, self-annihilating black hole the Armadalens dropped in her path overwhelmed the ship's inertial baffles for just a moment. The admiral stood at ease in the center of the Fleet bridge, flexing his knees to lean into the unexpected course change. As the g forces tugged at his balance, he wanted to lay a hand on the smooth polished wood of the handrail separating his raised dais from the staff officers at their consoles on the terrace immediately below. But he resisted the natural urge to steady himself, confident that the *Lib*'s effectors could handle the maneuver. He knew the bridge crew was looking to him—the entire Fleet would be—so he simply dropped his center of gravity as though he stood atop the flying bridge of an old sailing ship in a hard, contrary swell, and he waited for the Astral Fortress to regain mass control over the unimaginably powerful Newtonian forces attempting to wrench her apart.

The deck righted beneath him, and he unclasped his hands from where he'd been holding them tightly behind his back. Fighting the *Lib* was not his responsibility. That fell to Captain Trudeau, who was a good three kilometers away in the tactical combat center. But Strom was responsible for the 101st as a whole, and the attack fleet's evolution into this system of the local volume was in disarray thanks to just one ship. He stared at the main bridge screen, where the red icon designating a corvette of the Royal Armadalen Navy struggled to keep up with the tiny vessel's constant and seemingly random combat jumps through folded space. One moment it was hiding within the chromosphere of the white main sequence star, skipping micro-nukes across the seven-light-minute gap into the center of Strom's rapidly disintegrating order of battle; the next it would emerge from folded space dangerously close to the hull of the Astral Fortress or one of her attending megacruisers, as though trying to break the ship with the graviton bow wave of the FTL jump.

As irritated as he was by the offense to the good order and deployment of his Fleet, Archon-Admiral Wenbo Strom could not help admiring the fighting spirit of the crew. It was not surprising, he thought. Fleet Intelligence advised that the culture and practices of the Royal Armadalen Navy hewed as closely to old human virtue as was possible in this benighted realm. Smaller vessels, such as the corvette engaged in this hopeless resistance, often remained under direct human control, not slaved to machine intelligence. It was why the corvette could even offer resistance.

"Do we have any explanation for its presence in-system yet?" Strom asked as calmly as if he were inquiring after tonight's dinner menu. He directed the question to his staff intelligence G-2, Lieutenant Xi. Strom did not bother asking why the vessel was able to fight. Quite obviously it had avoided both the spike and the nanophage transmission.

"The ship has been typed as an Armadalen recon'vette, Admiral," Lieutenant Xi answered quickly. She manipulated a floating holofield of data and imagery, most of it streaming live from the *Lib*'s active sensor arrays. "Lightly armed but equipped with the RAN's latest stealth and drive tech. We're working a theory that the Armadalens infiltrated her into the local system to spy on the Habs-n-fabs out in the asteroid belt and on the big moon orbiting the second gas giant. There's a lot of helium mining infrastructure out there, sir, but not enough to explain all of the Javan Navy traffic our drones monitored the last five years. Probably a lot of undeclared military-industrial dual-use facilities."

"But no sign of any TDF forces in situ?" he asked. As the final guarantor of peace within the Greater Volume, Earth would be every bit as interested in treaty violations by the Javan Empire as were the Armadalens.

"None detected, Admiral."

Her tone was neutral, but Strom heard the skepticism underlying it. If the TDF had forces in-system and they'd survived the preemptive strikes, he would already be engaged in combat with them.

Thank the genome for small mercies, he thought.

"Thank you, Lieutenant," Strom said. She did not speculate as to why the RAN ship was still able to fight, but Strom was sure that with no Intellect to lobotomize and isolated by the need to maintain total comms security while lurking within a hostile system, the corvette remained under the control of her crew. And they had chosen to fight without seeking command authority.

Admirable fighting spirit and initiative, he thought. *But damnably inconvenient.* And it did make Strom wonder just how many holdouts, reclusives, and dead-enders had actually escaped both blades of the decapitation strike. Command had planned for between 2 and 5 percent of the Volume's naval forces to survive the attack, but of course not all forces were created equal. The prospect of encountering a single Terran frigate or a Royal Montanblanc fast assault ship under the control of a fully functional Intellect or even a competent crew of mutants and borgs was vastly more daunting than, say, running into a Javan Goliath or one of the mercenary system raiders in the pay of the Yulin-Irrawaddy Combine.

This infuriating Armadalen race traitor was proof of that.

The corvette disappeared from the display again a second before two of his fast escort destroyers began pinging distress signals after taking critical hull damage from antimatter area-denial mines the corvette had dropped in their path as they turned to avoid the torpedoes skipping in on them through rolling troughs of folded space.

Strom grunted.

It was distressing but only to be expected that one small ship from a middling power could cause this much trouble. The Republic did not delude itself about the threat from the Volume. There was no denying the mutants' superiority in technology. It was as vast as their advantage in sheer numbers. Whether measured by planets settled, Habitats in orbit, the volume of space occupied, or the raw numbers of so-called people living within that Volume, the polyglot hell stew of biohacked freaks and cold robot minds dwarfed the Republic.

The small, struggling outpost of true humanity that had set off into exile from the spaceports of the Sulu Archipelago so many centuries ago had but one chance to pull this off. One shot at what the ancient Nipponese—a noble and storied True Human culture—called the *Kantai Kessen*. Decisive Battle. The Republic would strike the head from the snake that had consumed humanity, or it would be devoured in turn.

"Fleetwide order," Strom barked. His executive officer, Commander Martaine Husserl, snapped to attention.

"Yes, Admiral."

"Launch the remaining fighters," Strom said. "All of them," he added before Husserl could seek clarification.

Strom was gratified to see that the man did not question the order. Other staff officers might have, for on the face of it, he had just sent thousands of pilots into mortal hazard to defend against one small vessel that they might yet take out with a lucky shot.

But it would be a lucky shot, Strom knew. And if

the Armadalen captain got lucky first, the 101st could lose a capital ship and a significant part of its combat power. The recon'vette was tiny. The graviton bow waves it generated with every fold were not. They could crack open a fair-sized moon.

"Admiral, the dropships over Batavia are reporting attacks by swarm drones. Armadalen signatures, sir, not Javan."

"Of course," Strom said, grinding his teeth. This was an unwelcome development. If one of the big transports was damaged and crashed into the *Voortrekker*'s final resting place, the dishonor would fall on him alone.

"Detail all of the wings from *Normandy* and *Tsushima* to cover the dropships. Suspend further landings until we have neutralized the Armadalen ship. Order the remaining wings to provide Fleet cover, authorize autonomous targeting and interdiction."

"Aye, aye, sir," Husserl replied, repeating the order back. "*Normandy* and *Tsushima* wings to cover the dropships. Batavia landing ops suspended. Remaining wings to fly Combat Space Patrol fleetwide. Admiral Strom authorizes autonomous interdiction."

The orders flowed down through the chain of command, out across the hundred vessels great and small of the Republican attack fleet. Thousands of men and women, thousands of human beings, responded across a volume of space encompassing nearly three-quarters of the solar system, the admiral's order arriving instantaneously everywhere via zero point wormhole link. Crucially, controversially, he turned the next few seconds of the battle over to the distributed network of battle computers that coordinated the 101st as a single fighting unit. They were not machine intelligences in the way of the Volume's Combat Intellects. First and most important, they were not sentient. But they were the most advanced computers the Republic had ever built. They could take in and analyze data on a scale and at a speed far beyond the abilities of even the most gifted human savant. And they could provide solutions just as efficiently.

The network presented a solution to Strom's problem twelve seconds later, vectoring three of the *Liberator*'s own fighters, FX8 Corsairs, onto a dimpling space-time effect 300 kilometers astern of the Astral Fortress. The heavy dual-purpose battlespace superiority fighters poured coordinated fire into the vacuum for a full second before the Armadalen vessel emerged into its own version of hell, raked stem to stern by plasma fire, the small droplets of ionized matter accelerated to a significant fraction of light speed by the Corsairs' bulky but ferocious gun pods. The fire streams punched through the thin sculpted carapace of exotic matter that made up the outer hull of the corvette before she could reengage her shields.

The enemy ship appeared to explode, but only for the smallest fraction of a second. The expanding blast bubble suddenly collapsed in on itself, and the ship simply winked out of existence.

A murmur coursed around the *Liberator*'s Fleet bridge.

Watching the death of such a worthy foe on the main display, Admiral Strom was caught between relief at having snuffed out the very real threat to his fleet, grudging admiration for the trouble the Armadalens' bravery had put him to, and a creeping, animal unease at what he had just witnessed. Fleet Intelligence had provided only the sparest information about the RAN's containment technology, the hyperspace blister that allowed them to squeeze a cruiser's worth of combat power into the body of a much smaller vessel. But the briefing had been quite clear on one point. When such a ship was destroyed, it blew itself clear out of this universe and into another one. It was even possible that rupturing the ship's containment blister actually created a new universe, one in which the physical realities of this existence might not hold true. There were some who speculated that those he had just killed might now be fated to die screaming forever in some alternative space-time where nanoseconds stretched out for recursive eternities.

As noble as their sacrifice had been, it only confirmed for Strom the grim necessity of defeating the abomination that now held dominion over the so-called Human Volume.

CHAPTER
SIXTEEN

The cabin door closed behind Lucinda, and as soon as she was out of sight she slumped. She had only a few minutes left before the O-Group convened, and she needed to change out of her uniform, which was stiff with the blood of others. If she was being honest with herself, she also needed to be alone.

It was weakness, she knew, but she had to have those few minutes for herself. The photon sculpture of her parents activated when she entered, and she barked at the projector to stop. She sounded ragged and shrill. Nothing like the command voice she'd forced from herself back on the bridge.

It was stupid. Irrational. But she did not want her parents to "see" her in this state. She often spoke to them when she was alone, which was more often than she cared to admit. It was a mercy to be able to talk freely, and she did not want to corrupt that pitiful measure of grace by mixing their memories in with the horror of this awful day.

After stripping off her T-shirt, she crammed it into the laundry hamper hidden away in a closet before realizing that she probably had somebody to do the laundry for her now. She was master and commander of *Defiant*. Lucinda pulled the shirt out of the hamper, stood alone in her cabin uncertain what to do next, then jammed it back in again, cursing softly under her breath. Reflexively, she looked over her shoulder, expecting Defiant to say something reassuring and droll, but the ship's Intellect was still offline, and even if it hadn't been, she'd set the privacy controls in her personal space to exclude all others, including the ship, except in case of an emergency.

The acting captain of HMAS *Defiant* dropped onto her bunk and let her head fall into her hands. The hologram of her parents activated again. They smiled and hugged each other. She did not order the projector to shut down this time.

"What am I doing?" Lucinda asked them quietly, bizarrely worried that she might be overheard. "What am I going to do?"

Her mother, long dead, and her father, exiled to the Combine debtors' colony on Batavia, had no answers. They remained as carefree and oblivious to the fate of their only child as they had been to their own future when that grainy image had been captured so long ago. Lucinda stared at them, needing a reply, hurting with the old loneliness. She did not even remember her mother. What she remembered was a vague memory of having had a mother. And it had been more than a standard year since she'd last heard from her dad. The Combine charged its indebted prisoners for everything; the few square feet of space they occupied at the barracks, the fraying threadbare blankets that did nothing to keep out the bitter chill of night on the edge of the Ironstone Desert, the miserable rations, the filthy water, and of course any form of communication with the outside world. The prisoners had to pay for it all, ensuring that they could never escape their debt. She sent money whenever she could, at least half of her Navy pay in fact, but Combine "processing fees" and "administrative charges" whittled every dollar down to a couple of cents by the time it reached her father.

She felt wretched, lost.

It was all she could do not to give in to hopelessness.

Lucinda stood so quickly that the blood rushed from her head, and she swayed a little with dizziness until her bioware compensated.

She shut down the hologram manually and pushed away the memories of her family.

The O-Group convened in the wardroom. It felt much reduced without the captain or XO or Lieutenant Commander Koh, but Timuz, the head of engineering, was present, and so was Doctor Saito, the ship's chief surgeon, at Lucinda's request.

The sight of Timuz, the old man—the very old man—standing at attention with his spine rigid, his hands locked in at his sides, nearly stopped her in midstride. She didn't quite know what to do, how to react. Timuz held the superior rank but had deferred to her as acting captain even more readily than had the other officers—especially Chase, who she suspected did not like the new arrangements one bit.

Lucinda returned the salutes and made her way to

the head of the table. Her feet felt numb, her legs were heavy, and she worried that she might trip and face-plant in front of everyone. She felt that Saito could diagnose her raging anxiety simply from looking at her awkward passage. Timuz sat on one side of the polished wooden table, and Hayes was on the other side, next to the chief surgeon. Like Hardy, the marine captain had changed clothes. He now wore the skintight coveralls that went under powered armor. The nanoweave bodysuit provided some protection and augmentation, but its main purpose was to interface with the bulky combat armor the marines wore into battle. He would not have been able to sit at the table enclosed in plasteel superalloys and high-density ceraplate.

The members of the O-Group resumed their seats as soon as Lucinda took hers. Lieutenant Bannon, still monitoring Defiant's struggle, was preoccupied. The other division heads were somber, but if they were worried, they hid it well. Not like her, she thought, imagining that every one of them must clearly see what a tangled ganglion of neuroses they'd inherited as skipper.

On which topic . . .

"Commander Timuz," she started.

The engineer smiled ever so faintly.

"If I might . . . Lieutenant?"

"Certainly," she said, hoping without much expectation that Timuz was about to beg her pardon for being so busy in Engineering that he couldn't assume his responsibilities as the ship's surviving senior officer. But now . . .

He pushed a single sheet of paper a short distance

across the old wooden table. Frowning, Lucinda took it and scanned the text:

"By the Order of Commander Baryon Timuz, RAN, with the concurrence of Captain Adam Hayes, RAMC, Lieutenant Lucinda Hardy is promoted *ignis in tempore* to the rank of full commander in the Royal Armadalen Navy with . . ."

Lucinda looked up. She could read the words, but they made no sense. Her fellow officers were curious but apparently none the wiser about her sudden, unexpected promotion in the field.

"Commander Hardy," Timuz started, getting everyone's attention but most especially attracting the interest of Lieutenant Chase. "I agreed to serve under Captain Torvaldt at his personal request during the last months of the Javan War. I returned to service late in my span, rated for functional but not operational command. Those were the conditions under which I agreed to return."

Timuz shrugged as if apologizing.

"I can run your engineering shop. But I cannot and will not run the ship. I am not ashamed to admit this. The shame would attach to me only if I did not admit to my faults and most especially if I took command knowing it was beyond my limitations. And Commander Hardy, I am a man who knows his limitations. I have had four life spans to get to know them well indeed. I am only on the *Defiant* because Jens asked me and I owed him. I remain here now to see out my term of commission so that I can relife upon my discharge."

An awkward silence had fallen over the room.

Captain Hayes seemed almost pained by the engineer's . . . What? His confession?

Timuz certainly sounded like a man unburdening himself to a confessor.

Doctor Saito, who was also rated for purely functional command by virtue of her role within the Medical Corps, leaned forward so that she might have a clear view around Hayes. She appeared reluctant to speak but determined to do so.

"If I might, Commander Hardy. Baryon is correct to demur. Were he to assume command on your say-so, I am afraid I would be forced to issue a medical directive that he be removed. He is not fit for operational command."

Lucinda could not help it. Her eyes boggled.

She looked immediately to Timuz, expecting him to react angrily or with embarrassment, but instead she was surprised, even shocked, to see the engineer reach over and take Saito's hand, squeezing it and muttering his thanks. There was obviously a story here that she had not been told. She looked instinctively to Hayes, but he avoided her eyes.

"I will resign my commission before I take command of this vessel," Timuz said quietly, letting go of Doctor Saito's hand. "I promised myself after the war that I would never send another soul to real death again. I will not break that promise. So, Commander Hardy, the ship is yours. Congratulations."

"What dark hell is this?" Chase said. "Are you a naval officer or not, sir? You might not be rated for operational command in normal circumstances, but as I understand the regulations, our circumstances are abnormal, the danger to this command is clear and present, and your reluctance to assume command is irrelevant. This is not an administrative question. We are in the field, and hostilities have commenced. You are the senior officer, Timuz. You must take command."

The engineer smiled, a barren expression dug from the frozen wastes of an ice moon.

"I will not take command, *Lieutenant*," Timuz said, leaning in on Chase's lesser rank. "And I will not take instruction from you on my responsibilities. Commander Hardy has been promoted according to the regulations and requirements of Armadalen naval law. She is rated for operational command, which makes her the captain of this vessel until such a time as Defiant or Fleet says otherwise. I hazard that it will be some time before we can talk to the ship or safely contact Fleet, and so I advise you to reconcile yourself to the new realities. You are at war, boy. And she is your captain now."

For a terrible half second that seemed to stretch forever, Lucinda was certain the young nobleman was about to lose his shit and start yelling that she was "nothing but a Hab rat" and her father "a convicted defaulter."

Instead he paused, smiled, and offered the barest expression of regret.

"But of course. My apologies for any distress I may have occasioned. I was merely surprised that an officer with a service record as distinguished as your own, Commander, was not rated for operational duty."

Lucinda almost shook her head in admiration. Chase had not grown up on the naked hull plating.

His lineage was proud, and the finishing that came with it was doubtless sophisticated and long adapted to subtle shifts in hierarchies and the realities of power. Nonetheless, if Varro Chase was probing for the reason Timuz would not take over the ship, he would get no satisfaction from the engineer.

"I requested that my status be limited to functional command, Lieutenant," Timuz said. "Captain Torvaldt supported my request."

He said nothing more.

Lucinda almost succumbed to the impulse to check his file for some sense of why he'd decided to end his career as a mechanic, but shipnet was down, and more important, she was an officer of the RAN and it would be an insult to a comrade and a decorated hero to go prying into a decision that obviously was driven by deeply personal motivations.

If nothing else, she understood his need for privacy.

"Thank you, Commander," she said, cutting off any further exchange between the two men. "We will dispense with the ceremonies of promotion if you do not mind. I cannot say I'm happy given the circumstances, but I promise to do my best."

She looked squarely at Lieutenant Chase.

"My compliments to you and Lieutenant Chivers for the unassisted combat fold," she said. "It was gracefully done under considerable pressure and without preparation. I will note it in the log."

Chivers beamed, then blushed, before bobbing her head in acceptance of the compliment.

"Thank you, Commander," Lieutenant Chase replied without noticeable discomfiture. Butter wouldn't melt in his bunghole, as her dad used to say. But Jonathyn Hardy was not an officer of the Royal Armadalen Navy. She was, and more was expected of her.

"Systems," she said, directing her attention toward Lieutenant Bannon. "How stands Defiant?"

Bannon frowned, concentrating fiercely on a small holofield floating above the table in front of him.

"Still drawing heavily on the AM stacks, ma'am," he replied. "I've never seen anything like this. Never even heard of it. The Intellect has completely isolated itself from the ship and devolved all control to us and the autonomic systems."

He seemed to remember that he was addressing the captain, or at least his acting captain, and he shook his head, pulling his attention away from the holofield.

"At this point . . . ma'am, we're on our own. The ship has no Intellect, and before Defiant went offline, he emplaced hard sanctions preventing himself from resuming control of the ship without human consent. The three serving senior naval officers and Captain Hayes have turnkey denial, Commander. And the consent, if Defiant comes back online, has to be unanimous."

"Damn," said Hayes. "Cock-blocking an Intellect. Didn't see that coming when I got out of the rack this morning."

"Commander?" Lucinda said, turning to Timuz. "That would make you the third turnkey. I hope you're okay with that."

"It will not be a problem, ma'am," Timuz said. "But I won't be turning any key until I know for sure what happened to Defiant and what's going to happen when we plug him back in."

"Concur," Lucinda said, because what the hell else was she going to say? She'd never felt herself this lost before. Or this young. She felt it necessary to rush on before the slight quaver in her voice grew so strong that it robbed her of all speech. "Anything on the systems breach, Ian? Was it a live strike, Time-on-Target malware, something that came in via the zero point link?"

Bannon sat a little straighter and began flinging icons and data blocks around in the small cloud of holographic projections. He looked more confident answering this question.

"Defiant did a lot of the forensic work for us in the half second before he sanctioned himself. The drop link to Deschaneaux exposed Wojkowski and Captain Torvaldt to a nanophage attack that rewrote their bioware. A variant jumped from the comm channel directly into Defiant's substrate, where it launched parallel attacks on the basal matrix and the crew skills codex."

Lucinda gaped at him. She noted similar reactions up and down the table.

"The codex . . ." she started.

"And the substrate, ma'am," Bannon said. "Whole directories and proof pools are missing, more are corrupted." He took a small, almost gulping breath. "All of our engram backups are gone. We don't . . . we're . . ."

He was foundering now.

"We're mortal," Lucinda finished for him.

"Holy shit," somebody breathed.

For once, just once, she felt her distance as an advantage. She knew that most of the ship's officers did not trace their origins back to the hull plating as she did. She was the only one of them who had grown up poor and mortal, fated one day to actually die, her biotic remains to feed the digester tanks of her home Habitat. Among the reduced O-Group around the table, Commander Timuz seemed completely unconcerned and Captain Hayes professionally unruffled. But Fein and Chivers looked anxious, and Chase was positively green.

"Ian," Lucinda said very slowly and clearly. "We don't need the codex. Everybody is organically trained in their MS, but I do want to know what happened to it. The nanophage—what's the status?"

"Contained within sanction," he said.

"Is that why Defiant is offline? Containing the malware?"

"I don't think so," he said. "That wouldn't account for the power he's been drawing. I think . . ." He paused, unsure of himself.

"Go on," Lucinda said.

"I think Defiant is fighting for his life. The nanophage variant attacking his substrate was . . . aggressive."

Nobody said anything for a moment.

She was right about the codex. It contained millions of skill scripts, both military and civilian, but as Chase and Nonomi Chivers had just shown, RAN personnel were organically trained in their military specialties. They did not need to load code. In this, they were all but unique among the true deep-space navies. Organically training a human being was ridiculously time-consuming, expensive, and liable to just not work compared with simply loading her up with the relevant task and mission scripts. Most militaries—in fact most businesses and governments throughout the Volume—dispensed with organic training for their recruits, inductees, slaves, or whatever after ensuring that basic competency and cultural adjustment goals had been met. But not the Armadalen military, not after the last and final war with the Sturm. It was partly why the RAN was a comparatively small navy for such a wealthy power. It was also why they had utterly destroyed the Javan war fleets at the Battles of Long Fall and Medang.

The loss of the stored engrams, however, was . . .

She tried to imagine herself into the psyche of someone who had lived his whole life assuming that, save for some catastrophic discontinuity, life would never end.

She could not.

Lucinda was herself new to immortality, and she did not entirely . . . what? Believe in it?

She found it difficult to go on, to find the exact words she needed. Instead she dodged the issue at first. "Ian," she said, "I want you to work with Commander Timuz, find out whether there's any way to restore the codex but . . ."

She paused, still uncertain of how to proceed. She didn't want to say what had to be said next.

"It is not a priority. I am issuing a general order that the ship's company, without exception, is to initiate the fail-safe for neural mesh dysfunction."

Silence.

"What?" Chase said at last. His voice was almost

strangled with disbelief. "We can't just shit out the mesh. Are you crazy?"

"Lieutenant!" Hayes barked. "You are addressing a superior officer. Apologize immediately or I will personally place you under arrest for conduct unbecoming, insubordination, and—"

"It's all right," Lucinda said loudly enough to be heard over Hayes, who was almost shouting. "It's a hell of an order. But I mean it. That's why I requested that Commander Saito attend. Doctor, apart from the obvious fact that we won't be able to load code or directly interface with shipnet, what other consequences, medically, operationally, should we prepare for when we . . ."

Lucinda wasn't even sure of the phrase she was looking for. Saito finished for her.

"When a patient disconnects and metabolizes their mesh," she said, "apart from no longer being able to load skills from the codex or back up to secure storage, they lose commlinks and telepresence, and there is often a period of up to twenty-four hours in which they will suffer severe nausea, headaches, and, in extreme cases, a psychotic break of unpredictable duration and intensity."

"Jesus," Lucinda said quietly. "I can't believe I let them put this shit in my head. Okay, thank you, Doctor. Could you prepare the medical division to receive anyone suffering side effects strong enough to prevent them from doing their duty?"

"Of course. If I might, Commander, I would suggest staging the protocol so that not all members of the crew are affected at the same time. Three tranches separated by six hours each should be enough and will see us clear of the medical consequences, psychosis aside, by the time we clear the Inner Dark."

"Agreed," Lucinda said.

The other officers, Chase included, watched without saying anything. None of them raised an objection. Most had seen what had happened to Torvaldt and the Woj when the nanophage got them.

"Captain Hayes," Lucinda said, "I do not have direct authority over your people, but I would strongly urge you to trigger the fail-safe protocol, too."

She was gearing herself up to make her case when Hayes raised his hands in mock surrender.

"Way ahead of you, Commander. We can always get new mesh if we have to. But not if we've already been meat hacked. I'll order my people to shit it out."

"Thank you. There is one more thing. Defiant. This is even more difficult, but the ship's Intellect has been compromised. He sacrificed himself to save the ship and crew. He would not want them further imperiled. If the nanophage wins, we will have no choice. The Intellect will have to be jettisoned and terminated."

Nobody spoke, and she found herself unable to say any more. Who was she to come aboard this vessel as an unknown, an outsider, and pronounce death upon its mind and soul? She waited for Chase to denounce her. Possibly to claim that she had already succumbed to mesh-loss psychosis. But he stared at his hands, contemplating God only knew what. Instead, it was Commander Timuz who spoke next.

"This is a grave and terrible thing, but I agree it must be done."

Hayes nodded, and the others fell in behind him,

murmuring assent and looking as though they had just passed a sentence of real death on a family member.

"Thank you, Commander," Lucinda said in a small voice. Too small. She cleared her throat and tried to put some command presence into her next words, but to her ear the effort merely left her sounding both strident and weak.

"I cannot . . ." she said before stopping, gathering herself, and starting again. "I cannot in any conscience make that decision without consulting you all. The final call is mine, and the responsibility with it."

Timuz nodded gravely at that.

"But I would first have your counsel."

She turned to the next naval officer along.

Lieutenant Varro Chase.

For once he seemed at a complete loss.

"I don't know," he confessed, and she remembered that he, like she, was a first lifer. Until he'd begun his compulsory term of service, the most difficult decision he'd ever had to make was which chambermaid to grope. He would have secure copies of his engram in family data vaults all over the Greater Volume. They would cover his life only up until the ship's departure from Deschaneaux Station, but would he care? Did Chase think himself essentially defined in some way by the events of this mission, which until an hour ago had been largely routine, even banal?

Lucinda had no idea.

She did not know yet how the never-dead conceived of these things.

"Can we fight the ship, seriously, without Defiant?" Chase asked. "I mean if we have to? And what about respawns? Can we get Torvaldt and the others back from Fleet stores? What if we all die? Like actually fucking die?"

Timuz drew himself up as though given grave offense.

"This is the Royal Armadalen Navy, Lieutenant Chase," he growled. "We will fight this ship to the last of us even if that means ramming the enemy and boarding them from vacuum with knives between our teeth because that's all we have left."

The quiet, almost apologetic tone Timuz had spoken in earlier was entirely gone.

A killer stood in his place.

"We have more than a few knives to our name, Commander," Lucinda said. "I did wonder, when I came aboard, at the weapons load-out. I wonder now whether Defiant and the other Intellects had some idea of what might be coming."

"Of what's come," Hayes corrected her.

"Yes," she said, accepting it now. "We are running dark. We cannot risk opening a zero point link. I am terminating this mission. Lieutenant Chase, you will plot a course to take us back to the Greater Volume with all dispatch. Ladies and gentlemen, I would have you return to your stations and prepare Defiant for battle."

CHAPTER

SEVENTEEN

Autonomic subroutines had kicked in, dousing the fire in Taro's Bar with flame retardants, probably as soon as Seph and the others had cleared out of the place. Now they were back, hauling ass out of the free-fire zone on the plate, looking for a rat run back to the *Regret*. Nothing had changed. Bodies lay where they had dropped or come apart under fire. Taro's looked like the morning after amateurs' night at an extreme goat-fucking rodeo.

Ariane led the way through, sweeping the dead with her Skorpyons. Jaddi Coto looked ready to burn everything down with arc lightning. You could never be too careful when the dead were hooked up with wetnets. A single pulse could reanimate the mother-fuckers and send them at you like fast zombies.

These ones didn't move.

Sephina turned and swept the room with her dragon shot as Ariane led Coto into the small kitchen where Taro made his Hab-famous ramen. There was no sign of him or the other kitchen hands. They'd most likely fled as soon as the shit went nova. Seph turned away from the carnage, raising the muzzle of her weapon to avoid sweeping Coto and Ariane, and hurried after them.

They quickly passed through the kitchen and out into the narrow serviceway behind the bar. A small cooking fire burned out there, and smoke poured from charred, blackened meat of some sort. Dead maglev scooters lay on the deck plate but otherwise the path was clear.

"Should've come this way before," Ariane said, holstering one of the machine pistols in her tactical rig under the nanoweave duster.

The serviceway was narrow but navigable. It smelled of burned meat, garbage, rot, stagnant Hab water, and decaying organoplastics. The plating was almost soft underfoot, lost beneath a compressed coating of necrotic biomatter. The fact that Eassar's service bots hadn't taken it back into the food chain told you all you needed to know about this part of the Hab. Seph craned her head back, looking up into the tight space between the buildings. The far side of the Habitat presented as a long streamer of chaotic light between converging rooflines overhead. Irregular patches of darkness blotted out whole sections of plating without power. A horrifying prospect for a Hab dweller, made worse by the blooming flowers of explosions and the hot tracery of weapons fire. Her animal hindbrain, evolved over millions of years on a small blue planet far, far away, marveled at the spectacle. Her rational mind knew they had to get off this tin can or die.

"Let's get the fuck gone," Seph muttered.

They jogged along the serviceway, occasionally

dodging around stacks of o-plastic shipping crates and smaller freight boxes, piles of rubbish, inert bots, a body or two, and even a fallen HabSec drone scorched and punctured by three different types of weapons fire. Nobody spoke, and they each moved as quietly as they could through the confined space. Occupants of the tube houses backing onto the alleyway hid behind security grills and armored doors. The street fighting still raged out on the main plates. Seph could hear the sizzling crackle of plasma fire dueling with the creepy hum of beam weapons. The sonic booms of heavy-bore military-grade rockets rumbled in the distance like a dream of terrestrial thunder. And stitched over and through it all, the chatter and bark of small arms fire, handguns, machine pistols, bolt throwers, and micromissiles.

The passage ahead of them flooded with harsh white light, and all three plastered themselves to the nearest wall. Coto tried to squeeze as far back into a doorway as possible, but that still left a whole heap of giant rhino man exposed to targeting.

The floodlight passed, but in its dazzling wake Sephina heard the roar of jet thrusters in her one good ear. She looked up and saw at least eight or nine airborne transporters flitting across the gap between the buildings. They had the heavy, functional lines of military shuttles, but she was half blinded and could pick out no details.

"Coto, do you recognize them?" Seph shouted over the uproar of their turbines.

"I do not," he shouted back.

"Then who the Dark are—"

Sephina's question was cut short by the loud, amplified voice of a man speaking Volume Standard English.

It came from above, rolling and echoing around in the constricted passage of the serviceway.

"Attention. I am Archon-Admiral Wenbo Strom, commander of the 101st Attack Fleet. This Habitat has been liberated by a Pathfinder Battalion of the Third Shock Regiment. It is now under the protection and law of the Human Republic. Further resistance is pointless and wasteful. We come as friends of the oppressed and saviors of the race. If you are truly human, we are your kin. Join us. Turn over your commanders and the corrupted. Human life is precious. Let us not waste any more this day."

"What the fuck?" Seph shouted.

Ariane turned around and gave her a shrug.

"Ah," said Coto. "It is the Sturm."

A tenuous pause followed. The moment felt more like hesitation than hiatus, as though the amplified announcement was so fucking out there, so straight-up crazy, that it stunned millions of people into asspuckering immobility. Fingers froze on triggers. Decision loops collapsed. Motherfuckers' circuitry shorted the fuck out.

Seph heard the broadcast or the proclamation or whatever the hell it was rolling around the enormous circle of Eassar, perhaps echoing from but more likely relayed by other vessels. She was pretty sure those troop shuttles had been booming out the good news of the Sturm's return.

"The fucking Sturm?" Ariane sputtered. "You gotta be fucking kidding me."

And as if her question had suddenly shocked the entire Hab back into motion, the fighting resumed, sounding even louder and more ferocious after the abrupt quiet of the last few seconds.

"We gotta get off this can," Seph declared.

She pushed away from the wall where she'd been sheltering since the floodlights had swept over them, nearly lost her footing in a greasy puddle as she started to run, and felt Ariane's free hand close around her upper arm.

"Careful, honey." She smiled, steadying her. "You'll get your pretty party dress all muddied up."

Seph gave her a quick kiss. Ariane turned it into something longer. Sephina had to push her away. "Seriously, let's bitchfoot it, babe."

This time they chose speed over stealth. Coto took the lead and charged along the serviceway, letting his inner rhino off the leash. If it was the Sturm, they'd open fire on him as soon as he lit up their targeting overlays. The giant hybrid had unshipped his primary weapon, and he raked the way ahead of them with isolated, unexplained bursts of arc lightning. Once to disable a malfunctioning sentinel. More than once to take down some human antagonist. As the firefight at Taro's dropped farther behind them, they started to come across locals in ones and twos, Hab rats hiding out from the chaos and violence on the main plates, others moving fast with intent. Like them.

Everyone gave Coto the way.

Those who were too slow he shunted aside or even trampled. The foolish few who seriously challenged him he cleaved with short, lashing streams of energistic blue-white fire.

"Wait up!" Ariane cried out as they ran through an intersection with another, smaller passage. It serviced a sex district about a klick from the docks, a shallow curve of deck plating densely packed with fleshbot depots, sensorium parlors, and, of course, because this was a Combine Habitat, brothels. Actual brothels offering sex with human beings, some of them biohacked, some of them vat-grown, most of them natural born and genome-real. No mods, no tweaks, not a base pair out of place. Because they couldn't afford it. Because it wasn't permitted. Because this was the Combine. None of them were there by choice, of course. In Combine space they were all slaves of one sort or another.

Coto stopped running as though Ariane had flicked a switch. Seph almost piled into him.

"The fucking Dark," she cursed. "What's up?" But Ariane was already gone, moving into the black trench of the other serviceway. Seph had the dragon shot out and a round in the chamber when Ariane's voice reached her from the gloom.

"The fuck you think you're doing?"

"Coto. My six," Seph ordered, knowing he would fall in behind her without hesitation. His bulk blocked what little illumination came through from the larger passage, mostly from peeling glowstrips and weak, faded biode emitters fixed haphazardly around doorways and cellar walk-downs. A faint, almost fluttering light reached down from the far side of Eassar, most of it from fires and the discharge of energy weapons; it was weaker than starlight.

Seph kept the dragon shot held low. Discharged in this confined space, it would do more damage to Ariane than to anyone else, certainly more than it would to the two men her lover had fronted on the stoop of a doorway behind a rent-by-the-minute capsule hotel. Ariane was blocking Sephina's shot at the pair, a gimp move of such utter cluelessness that Seph could make no sense of it until one of the men hauled at something she could not see and it came to life with a protesting squeal of pain and fear.

A girl. Maybe five or six Earth-standard years old, although down on the plates it could be hard to tell. Children didn't always get their base nutrients. The Habs, even Combine Habs, were required by Volume law to provide water, soylent, and supps, but as Seph knew from Coriolis, what was and what should've been were two different things. The kid could be ten or twelve.

Whatever. It didn't look like she was going to see another birthday if these two had their way with her.

As Sephina and Coto drew up, weapons ready, Ariane had holstered hers and was tugging at the girl's arm, trying to drag her away. The girl was crying, close to screaming. The second man, the smaller of the two, had his hands up, babbling that he didn't want any trouble. His Habmate wanted all the trouble in the world and had wrapped one giant ham hock of an arm around the little girl's head, snarling that he was "gonna pull it right off her fuckin' neck" if Ariane didn't let go. Their intimate dance played out under the general uproar of weapons fire, sirens, alarms, explosions, and that Wenbo Strom asshole on

196 · JOHN BIRMINGHAM

a loop, booming from all points of the circumference that human life was precious.

Let us not waste any more this day.

Neither Seph nor Coto had a good shot, not with the area clearance arsenal they were packing. But the Hab rats didn't know that. Probably.

"Let her go," Seph barked.

"Let her go," Coto rumbled. "The smaller girl," he added, "in case you are confused by our demand. We wish you to let the smaller female go. If the larger of them wishes to free herself from you, she will simply kill you. Her name is Ariane. She does that."

Seph resisted the sudden need to sigh.

Standing more than eight feet tall—not counting his horn—and massing out at nearly 300 kilos of gene-boosted muscle, triple-density bone, and rhino-derm hide, Jaddi Coto was not often ignored. But the big Hab rat stood just a few inches shorter than Coto, and Seph didn't imagine it was the first time he'd had weapons laid on him. He probably knew that they couldn't fire off the big guns at this range.

"She's mine," the man snarled, and Seph winced at the foul wash of Hab-synth gin and jujaweed on his breath.

"Er, you mean ours," his mate said in a quaking voice.

"I fuggin' found her, and I'll fuggin'—"

His snuffling, watery voice, thick with intoxicants, suddenly choked. The girl screamed and broke free as the man's hands flew to his throat, frantically pawing at the gaping, lipless wound there. Coto scooped the girl into his arms. Hot black blood fountained out through the dying man's scrabbling fingers as Ariane stepped away, flicking closed the gilablade she carried in a spring clip on her wrist. The assassin's knife disappeared back inside the cuff of her duster as she stepped away from the man she had cut open. He dropped to his knees, and one of her boots lashed out in a short, powerful kick to the side of his head. The long coat swirled around her like a cape as he fell to the deck plating with a final thud.

Ariane tilted her head as though inquiring after the intentions of the surviving Hab rat. He threw up his hands, babbled a few words about not wanting anything to do with it, and turned to run. He ran straight into the heavy plasteel door at the rear of the building where he'd found the girl. Or taken her.

The man groaned and staggered back, cupping his hands to his face. Ariane sent him on his way with a kick in the ass.

The girl was still crying, but now she was curled in Coto's all-encompassing hug.

Battle sounds raged around them.

The sky burned.

And Archon-Admiral Wenbo Strom still urged the true human inhabitants of Eassar to rise up against their masters.

We come as friends of the oppressed and saviors of the race.

"Hey, baby," Ariane said softly, stroking the child's hair. "You got family, friends? You live around here?"

"Hey, baby," Seph mimicked. "We don't live around here, and I think it's time we got back to our friends on the ship."

"My m-mom works here," the girl said, pointing at the rear of the building. "But . . . but . . ."

"Is she okay?" Ariane asked.

. . . *we are your kin* . . .

The girl could not answer. She was crying again, losing herself in a deepening spiral of grief.

"M-m-mommmmyyy . . ."

"The child is very upset," Coto said. "Perhaps her mother has died. Violently. Young girl, is your mother recently deceased? Are you suffering traumatic shock?"

"Coto, shut the fuck up," Ariane said, backhanding him. "You're upsetting her."

"No. She was already upset, Miss Ariane. Probably because her mother died violently. There is a lot of violence here. She may have witnessed—"

"Coto!" Seph shouted. "Seriously, shut up."

"I will shut up," Coto agreed.

"Hey, kid," Seph said. "Your mom. She okay? She at work? Is that why you're here? Waiting for her?"

"She dieeeed," the girl wailed.

"Violently." Coto nodded. Satisfied. He liked it when he understood things.

"We've got to take her," Ariane said. She sounded determined.

"No regrets, no kids, and no kittens," Seph reminded her. "You know the rules."

"But baby, we never leave anyone behind. Ever. That's the Coriolis code."

"No," Seph repeated.

A line appeared between Ariane's eyebrows, and her face darkened. She could spin out a whole week's worth of punishing gothic dysphoria from an entry-level sulk, and this was way more than that.

"The kid's alone, Sephina. On a fucking Combine Hab."

Seph shrugged. "We were alone. You, me, Cinders, the others? Remember?"

"And it sucked like hard vacuum," Ariane shot back. "So let's get her off this turd tube and get gone."

An explosion rocked the deck plating, dislodging carbon panels and window glass from the rear of the building. The women flinched away from the falling debris. Coto leaned forward to shelter them with his body.

"I do not believe Habitat Welfare will have capacity to properly care for this child," he said.

More troop transports roared overhead.

This Habitat has been liberated . . .

"Hab Welfare couldn't wipe their own ass with a solar sail," Ariane shouted over the disembodied voice.

Plasma bolts chased the transports across the sky, striking one shuttle in a glorious bloom of fire. It peeled out of formation, trailing smoke and flames.

"Fuck this," Ariane muttered. "Fuck the Sturm. And fuck you, Sephina."

She reached for the little girl, and Coto handed her over.

"Hey, baby!" Ariane said quietly, scooping the kid up in her arms. "I'm sorry about your mom. I lost mine, too."

"She's gone," the child said. "And I'm scared."

"I believe her mother is dead," Coto clarified just in case anybody was wondering. "Saying someone is gone is a common euphemism for—"

"Coto."

"Yes?"

"It's time to stop talking now," Sephina said.

Ariane carried the child back into the recesses of the serviceway, putting some cover between them and the Sturm. What was it the voice in the sky had been shouting? They came as friends of the oppressed and saviors of the race or some shit? Seph could still vaguely hear the amplified announcements, repeated on a loop but distorted by increasing distance and masked by the roar of gunfire. They'd be killing anybody with implants, which was fine because she didn't have any. None of her guys did. But they'd also be laying down some heavy genocidal mojo on anybody like Coto whose genome wasn't sufficiently pure. She had no idea what Republican doctrine defined as pure these days. Maybe they were cool with editing out congenital disease and deformity. Maybe not. But she was pretty fucking certain they'd pitch a fit with anybody blending up a cocktail of human DNA with a solid pour of silverback gorilla and African rhino.

They would not approve of Coto.

Seph took the child's face in her hands gently.

"You got any other family, kid?"

"Just my m-mother, and she's gone," the girl said quietly.

"She's dead," Coto corrected.

The girl nodded and fought back tears.

"She's d-d-d—"

"Dead. The word you are looking for is 'dead,' small child."

Seph spun around, standing on tiptoe to put her

face into the tech savant's. Or into his chin, anyway. She reached up and rapped her fist on his horn.

"Not. Helping."

"But she was confused. She did not know the word 'dead.'"

"Just . . . try to get a link to the ship."

"I will do that, then," he said, and set to messing around with his headset and comms gear again.

Seph turned back to the child. Ariane was hugging her.

"Okay. I'm sorry about your mother, kid. I had a friend once, sort of orphaned about your age. It was real hard on her. I guess, if you want, you can come with us."

Ariane beamed at Seph and pulled her into an embrace while continuing to hug the girl. Seph held her off.

"But our ship is in dock, and these guys"—she waved a hand in the air to show that she meant the Sturm—"they'd be mean to our friend Coto here if they saw him."

The girl looked at her as if trying to understand what she meant. Her face was shiny with tears, and thick snot was bubbling from her nose.

"Mean?" the girl sniffled. "No, I think they'd shoot him in the fucking head and space his hairy ass for a mutant. That's the Sturm up there, lady. They're cunts."

Silence.

Then Coto spoke.

"This child seems very well-informed about current affairs."

"I fucking love this kid," Ariane cried out, holding the girl out at arm's length. "We're keeping her."

Seph threw up her hands.

"Fine. What's your name, kid?"

"Jula."

"Okay, Jula. We're docked at Thirteen in Bay Seven. This is your local plate, right? Can you get us there without the Sturm knowing about it?"

"Probably," Jula said. "We take shit from Thirteen all the time. That's where all the good supplies come in."

She stopped.

"Can I really come with you? Away from Eassar, I mean?"

"Yeah, sure." Sephina shrugged, giving up all pretense of resistance and earning another beaming smile from Ariane, who mouthed "I love you" at her.

"My mom would have liked that," Jula said in a small, sad voice before beckoning for Ariane to put her down and for the three pirates to follow close behind.

"It's good you had a mom," Sephina said in a low voice. Mostly to herself.

CHAPTER

EIGHTEEN

A dropship exploded in the upper atmosphere, bathing the flat wastes of the Ironstone Desert in a cold wash of lifeless white brilliance. Hard shadows leaped out from millions of tiny rocks and the lonesome scattered sentinels of larger granite tors. Gnarled, leafless thistle-wire bushes cast phantom silhouettes that danced like the ghosts of all the souls who had perished here, and the great mass of the *Voortrekker* seemed to vomit darkness away from the radiant flare, the torn, disfigured hull plating conjuring up tenebrous black claws and fangs that raked at the desert floor.

McLennan smiled.

"I'll wager my shriveled old scrotum that the Royal Armadalen Navy is to thank for yon wee display of whizbangs and sparklers. Old-school hard nuts they are, and not a fucking numptie's blouse to be found among the lot of them."

"Passive sensors are negative for RAN signals capture," Hero informed them. "But Republican communications intercepts confirm the presence in-system of an Armadalen recon'vette that has engaged enemy forces. I believe you should unlock my war protocols now."

"And I believe I'll make the decisions around here," McLennan grunted at the Intellect. "So let's be fucking off with all dispatch then. Your protocols remain locked. For now. I'll not have you fucking off on some adventure and stranding me in the middle of the Ironstone with a lot of yammering idiots—no offense, Lambright."

"None taken."

"On which matter, Herodotus, although I may have implied that I could give less than a recycled jobby for whether this pack of feckless munters lived or died, I'll need you to bag up any stragglers and drag them out of here by their short and fucking curlies. Except for that useless bag of shite," he said, jerking a thumb back at Prince Pac Yulin, who was still floating in the containment field. Still insane and homicidal. "He'll be more trouble than he's worth."

"Agreed," said the Intellect, quietly so that only the three of them—McLennan, Trumbull, and Lambright—could hear. "Suggest we terminate the host and dispose of the remains. And unlock my war protocols."

"No. Not agreed," Trumbull protested.

"You don't get a say, Professor," Hero replied.

"I don't think either of you realize who is in charge here. I am the ranking faculty member. Not Professor McLennan."

"Actually, it's Admiral now," Hero said. "He's been reactivated."

McLennan's increasingly martial stride into the

heart of the camp did not falter. The bots and camp drones were moving with frightening speed, breaking down the tiny settlement, flitting around the dazed, slow-moving human occupants as though they were fixed in place. One man objected feebly as a servitor deftly removed the glass of wine from his grip without spilling a drop.

"Don't be daft, Trumbull. This isn't a faculty meeting. You're in a DZ, soon to be crawling with shock troopers. The prince is gone. That fucking thing there's just a husk with mad bitey teeth. Young master Pac Yulin can relife from store."

Lambright looked as though he was about to say something inconvenient but shut his mouth at a warning look from McLennan. The light from the burning dropship was guttering, fading, allowing the dark of night to come pouring back over the desert. Maybe half the tourists were already hurrying back to the dune rovers and humping their own luggage, too, not waiting for the bots to fetch and carry for them. One man lost his grip on a suitcase, and it spilled open. He hesitated, cursed, and abandoned his possessions to the sand.

Not a complete idiot, then. He might survive the night, Mac thought as he headed for his own shelter. There were a number of personal items he wanted to pack for himself.

Trumbull took him by the arm and tugged sharply to bring him to a halt. With a biotic age in the early forties, he had a good ten or fifteen years' advantage over McLennan, and he hadn't denied himself any gene-mods either. He was in good shape. Mac was not. He was starting to feel like a very old man. He peeled Trumbull's hand away by the simple expedient of gripping the man's little finger and breaking it.

Trumbull howled in shock. McLennan did not doubt that his neural net edited out the pain signals within a fraction of a second. Probably erased the memory of it, too. But the sense of violation that most people felt when another person laid hands on them with malign intent was altogether more difficult to rescript, and Mac could see the sense of hurt and outrage lingering in the professor's expression.

That finger wouldn't unbreak itself, either. It would need old-fashioned splinting. He could already see a medical bot humming through the air toward them, presumably summoned by Hero.

"I believe I advised you to turn off your neural net, Professor," Mac said. "And to delete it in fact."

"You bloody maniac!" Trumbull shouted, holding his injured paw as though it still pained him. The bot floated up without preamble and enclosed the swelling hand in a soft blue stabilizing field. Professor Trumbull's little finger appeared to straighten itself out, and a white chrysalis began to form around the last two digits on that hand. The man's lack of discomfort spoke to the analgesic scripts he was running.

"We will not leave Deputy Prince Pac Yulin here," Trumbull said through gritted teeth and bunching jaw muscles. McLennan read that as a sign of anger rather than pain management. "He is a natural-born scion of the Combine's First Family. They will not stand for it, relifed or not."

McLennan grinned at him. It was not a friendly expression.

"Aye, but you're a sad wank, aren't you, man. But not to worry. If the First Family aren't already swinging by their heels from the palace walls, they soon will be. Unless the Sturm decide to simply crack open their Habs and let the vacuum in. Either way, I widnae concern myself with any fuss and bother that cast you in an unflattering light come performance evaluation time. The Combine, the First Family, the university itself . . . I can assure you that you're nowhere near the top of their list of things to be filling their pants about right now. You're not even on the list, Professor. None of us are."

Trumbull was denied the pleasure of fully expressing his righteous umbrage by having to submit to the care of the medbot, but he did his best, stabbing the index finger of his free hand into McLennan's chest.

"As the deputy head of faculty I am ordering you to make provision for the safe transport of Prince Pac Yulin with the rest of the party to a safe harbor where—"

McLennan casually reached out and broke his other finger. The one jabbing him in the chest.

"All righty, then." He shrugged as Trumbull howled again in temporary pain and mounting outrage. "Hero, incinerate the body and store the ashes for transport to Fort Saba at our earliest convenience."

"No!" Trumbull cried, trying to lunge forward but now effectively held prisoner in two medical stabilizer fields.

The containment field in which the prince floated, snarling and raging like an Urcix bane-raptor, turned red and then white before evaporating with a pop. A small gray square floated in the ripple of a micro-g wave. Then it winked out of existence. A strong smell of ash and burned meat drifted over them.

"I have stored the prince's remains in the cargo bay of the main rover," Hero said.

"McLennan, you fool," Trumbull cried. "They'll kill us for this."

"The Sturm? I doubt it. They have lots of other reasons to kill us first."

"No! The Combine, you witless idiot. You just killed a scion of the Combine."

"No, I didn't," Mac said without discernible rancor. "The virus or agent or whatever malware the Sturm injected into Pac Yulin via his live link killed him. He was dead the second he plugged in. The malware didn't terminate the base functions of the biotic host because it had a need for the body as a weapon. I guarantee you the same attack will have struck the local system, perhaps the entire Volume, in a wide-spectrum synchronous strike."

"Whoa." Lambright shook his head in astonishment rather than denial. "How do you know that?"

McLennan lifted his shoulders and sketched a mock rueful face.

"It's what I would've done," he said. "I've been warning about this vulnerability for three spans now. Ever since zero point wormhole comms rolled out. I've written papers, given speeches. The TDF even sent a ship all the way to collect me from Miyazaki once. A four-year round-trip, more than a hundred folds, with a two-month layover at Midway-C because I had to relife. A nasty sarcoma had finally caught up with that particular body."

"It wouldn't have if you'd just accept some basic gene therapy," Hero said quietly. If the Intellect had eyes, you could have heard them rolling.

"I'm still here, aren't I?" McLennan snarked back. "And a little cancer every now and then is the least of my troubles. After all, I've been stuck with you for half a fecking millennium. Anyway," he continued, returning his attention to Lambright, "when I got back to Earth, I gave all the same speeches to all the right people, who promptly ignored me because who in their right mind is going to shut down the zero point network?"

"Ha! Nobody on the third rock, that's for sure," Lambright said.

"No," said McLennan. He gave the younger man a quizzical look. "You're not live, then? Back on your Hab?" He knew Lambright had to have some real money to have paid for passage to Batavia and a spot on the dig team even as a glorified tourist.

"Who can afford that besides the Grand Families and the Elite Fraction? When my storage tops out, I just back up to a secure local stack like everyone else." Lambright smiled tightly. "I saved up for two spans for this trip. Not just the trip of a lifetime. Literally, the trip of two lifetimes."

McLennan clapped him on the shoulder.

"Gaun yerself and buck up, then, lad!" he roared, turning up the theatrical burr of his remnant accent. "You're about tae be in the way of getting a feck load more adventure than ye paid for. If we survive this, I widnae be surprised tae find Miyazaki tries tae levy a healthy feckin' surcharge on you for all the fun after the fact of it."

Trumbull had fallen silent as he trudged along behind them, both arms held out as the medbot treated his injured digits. He spoke again in a quieter, almost penitent voice.

"It really is them? Up there?"

Mac didn't stop, but he slowed a little and glanced back at the man. The professor almost stumbled over a couple of rocks. He looked like he was being carried by the bot fields. Trumbull stared into the night sky, the palest flicker from the burning dropship illuminating his features.

"Aye," McLennan said, dialing back on his bog laird caricature. "The Dark-accursed scum themselves."

They broke camp fifteen minutes later. Hero was forced to disassemble some of their equipment down to a molecular level and fold the waste matter into the heart of the system's star, Sujutus. There would be no fooling the Sturm. They would know that the sacred site had been violated. But there was no sense giving them any clues about who was responsible.

McLennan had no doubt the Inquisitors Puritanical—or whatever they called them now—would have the information within ten minutes of capturing Fort Saba. But a man with a will could do a lot for himself with ten minutes' head start.

Dune rovers struck out in three directions like the talons of a tor hawk reaching across the great scorched bowl of the Sukaurno Basin. Two rovers curved away to the south in convoy, heading for the broad, slow-moving waters of the Karnak River. One drove due east at breakneck speed, flying across the hardscrabble salt pans and oceans of white silica for the settlement at Fort Saba. Another made an apparently stuttering lurch for the folds of the Goroth Mountain foothills. McLennan rode in that vehicle. They all did.

Hero programmed the other dune rovers to navigate an obvious path and to leak just enough signals to attract most of the Sturm's attention. Hopefully, anyway. For a mercy, for now, their attention seemed to be focused entirely on surviving the descent. A portion of the dune rover's roof was transparent plasteel, and McLennan chased one of the tourists out of the seat with the best view of the battle miles above them. There was no sign of the Armadalen vessel. It could have been half an AU away and probably was, cutting up rough with the main force Sturm unit investing the system. Armadalen doctrine prized cutting through the enemy's peripheral defenses to stab deep into the heart.

The swirling energistic discharges, the blossoming explosions and misleadingly delicate twinkle of kinetics, all swirling about the dropships like a firestorm spun into the finest mesh by some pyromaniac deity, spoke to McLennan of a drone swarm. He wondered where the Armadalens had hidden it. For a little while he was even hopeful that the swarm might overwhelm the ships, but eventually the fire died away and the surviving platforms broke through into the lower atmosphere with a pair of huge and ragged sonic booms.

A few of the passengers cried. All of them craned their heads back for a better view.

"Nothing to worry about," McLennan announced reluctantly. He could not shake off his resentment at being left holding this jessie's man bag full of useless knobs. "They're not firing at us. They're not firing at anything right now. Half of them are dead already. The ships just hit the atmosphere is all. It will be another twenty minutes before they touch down and an hour, maybe two, before they can deploy anything beyond beachhead security."

"And what then? Huh? What then?" one of the more hysterical passengers demanded of him. He had a biotic age of early to middle thirties, but he'd made poor use of this body and it had run to flab. Mac had not bothered to learn the man's name, and without a neural net he could not call up the idiot's particulars. It hardly mattered.

Biting down on his temper before he simply told the whining ass to shut his cake hole, Mac pointed to the view forward. The Sukaurno Basin stretched away for another twenty klicks, an almost featureless shallow bowl rising gently to the bare foothills of the Goroth ranges in the distance. The dune rover ran dark, but the windscreen displayed the path ahead in the washed-out blue of the vehicle's low-light sensors. Hero, flying a hundred meters away, smothering any signals or energy leakage that might draw the Sturm's targeting arrays to them, could have boosted the rover's sensors and given them a perfectly clear view with a torrent of data about their progress, about the Sturm's descent, and increasingly about the wider conflict across the local system, but McLennan had judged that to be ill-advised generosity.

"Best keep them in the dark with just a few wee

candles to focus their empty heads on, I think," he'd told Herodotus.

"Yes," the Intellect replied. "In the dark they can't possibly see the yawning abyss they're racing toward."

"We can hole up in the Goroth," Mac declared, projecting his voice to the rear of the dune rover. The low murmurs and worried chatter stilled, and he felt everyone's attention turn to him.

"There's enough equipment and supplies to stay hidden for two months. There are also a couple of Combine debtor gulags out there. Mining camps. One of them is empty. If needed, if the weather turns, it will do for shelter. Best to avoid it for now, though. Eventually the Sturm will get around to checking it out."

"That's it? That's your plan?" It was the same man who'd questioned him earlier. Mac recognized him as the drunk who'd been separated from his wineglass by an insistent bot back at the *Voortrekker*. "We're going to hide under a rock until they find us?"

Mac smiled and stood up. The dune rover was running hard across the flat terrain, topping out at more than 130 kilometers per hour on its fat over-sized tires. The suspension was good, but at that speed his footing was a little uncertain. He held on to an overhead grab bar. Mac was biotically older than the other man by at least thirty years, and without implants or gene therapy, the host body he currently wore was creaking at the joints and hurting pretty much everywhere all the time. The man still shied away. Everyone had either seen McLennan break two of Professor Trumbull's fingers or by now had heard the story multiple times. A treatment chrysalis sheathed each of Trumbull's injured hands.

"No. That's not my plan," Mac said. "I have something else to do."

And with that the door to the rover slid open, cold air roared in, and Frazer McLennan jumped out into the night.

CHAPTER
NINETEEN

Alessia was not in Skygarth anymore. She had no idea where she might be. She could see nothing. She remembered only vaguely that old Sergeant Reynolds was carrying her on his back like a game, a piggyback ride, during a garden party.

But it was dark and hot, and her skin itched all over.

Then she remembered Lady Melora, and she screamed.

The world turned over, and she landed back in it with a thump, spilling out of a large sack sewn of rough burlap, blinking in the fading light of late afternoon. Sergeant Reynolds's face leaned right into hers until it was all she could see. He pressed one finger against her lips. She cringed away. There was blood on the finger, and she could taste it, sticky and metallic.

Shush, he mimed.

She did even though she was shaking and her head seemed to be spinning so much that it might just fall right off and she wanted to cry and she wanted her mother.

Alessia almost never wanted her mother. But she did now. Or at least the idea of her mother. A promise of kindness and comfort. Not the strict and somewhat distant stranger she mostly encountered on occasions of state. That mother would just tell her to "suck it up, Princess." And being a princess already sucked hard enough.

She was outside somewhere. She could tell that at least. The sky arched above her, banded with light wispy clouds, glowing a little pink in the setting sun. A hand closed around hers. A small, soft hand.

It was Debin!

She almost cried out, but Sergeant Reynolds shook his head fiercely and pressed his finger against her lips again. She nodded slowly, once, to show that she understood. She'd been playing this game only this afternoon.

They were hiding.

Alessia carefully peeked left and right. She saw Caro, who had been crying. Her face was dirty but streaked clean here and there by tear tracks. And Mister Dunning, Caro and Debin's grandfather, was there, too. He knelt next to Sergeant Reynolds, and he carried some sort of weapon. Not a pistol like Reynolds's. It was bigger than that and ugly with it. The gun looked wrong in his hands. Alessia was used to seeing those old, slightly crooked fingers tying back vines in the gardens or pruning the rosebushes outside the drawing room. It seemed an affront to everything proper that they had closed around such a terrible-looking weapon.

In spite of her unease, Mister Dunning looked as comfortable holding the gun as he did potting a new fern.

Caro picked up Alessia's other hand and squeezed. She tried to make a brave face and almost got there. Distant thunder rolled over them, and the paving stones of the little courtyard where they hid seemed to tremble before the coming of the storm.

But the sky was clear of storm clouds.

Alessia's head swam with unpleasant, unwanted memories of the horrible events back at Skygarth. This was the same thunder, not the gentle rumble of a late summer rainstorm, which, to be honest, was never especially fearsome on Montrachet, but the stuttering roar of—

Gunfire.

People were shooting at each other? Sergeant Reynolds and Mister Dunning were holding guns, and from their dark, unhappy expressions they looked as though they could soon be shooting them at people, too. Alessia started to ask what was going on, but Caro shook her head vigorously and Sergeant Reynolds raised that bloodstained finger to his lips again.

Shush.

Alessia shuddered, and the shudder became a long uncontrollable shivering that made her teeth chatter. Debin put his hand gently over her mouth and added the shaking of his head to his sister's.

Shush.

Alessia carefully and quietly drew in a deep breath just as Lady Melora had taught her to do to steady her nerves before a flute recital. She breathed in, held her breath for a few seconds, and breathed out as slowly as she could. She did it again. And again.

After a few moments she no longer trembled like a frightened kitten. She was still afraid and confused, but she could see that the grown-ups, Sergeant Reynolds and Mister Dunning, were not scared. They just looked angry the way that adults did sometimes when they got very quiet. The looks on their faces and the way they held their guns were even scarier than the thunder of the weapons she could not see. If anything, that was growing louder. Alessia turned away from the men and examined her surroundings. That was what a princess in one of her stories would do. Galadriel of the Elves wouldn't sit in a burlap bag feeling sorry for herself. Princess Órlaith and her friend Princess Reiko would have drawn swords and cut down half an army by now.

Alessia did not have a sword, but she was determined not to feel sorry for herself. They were hiding—she was pretty sure they were hiding—in a small courtyard behind a stone cottage. No. It wasn't a cottage. It was much too big for that. Two stories high with three chimneys that she could see breaking through the steeply pitched line of the dark slate roof. The cobblestones underfoot were filthy with mud and rotting leaves. It smelled bad. Having noticed the stink, Alessia wrinkled her nose and tried not to gag. There was nearly as much poop in the courtyard as mud. A lot of it was dumbo squirrel poop, hundreds of nasty little pellets squished underfoot and never cleaned up. But here and there small, smelly mounds spoke to the use of the courtyard as a toilet by a small dog or a big cat.

Wooden barrels and o-plastic casks sat atop one another against the rear wall. Dark green strangler vines snaked down the wall and over the barrels, sinking their sharp tiny thorns into the wood. The o-plastic casks would be impervious to thorns, but the vines had grown so thickly around them that she imagined the groundskeeper would need a fusion blade to cut through the tangle. Then she corrected herself. There was no groundskeeper here. They were hiding behind some sort of tavern or inn, possibly down near the waterfront. The unpleasant smell of animal droppings was not strong enough to mask the salty tang of the ocean.

Her stomach slowly turned over.

She was . . . outside.

For the first time since everything had gone so awfully wrong at Skygarth, Alessia understood, deep inside herself, how much had changed.

She was outside.

Her first instinct was to flinch away from the world, to crawl back inside the darkness of the old burlap bag. But she resisted. She had never once left the grounds of Skygarth without a full retinue of the guard surrounding her. She had only ever really passed through Port au Pallice, the carefully recreated Euro-Classical seaside town that serviced Skygarth, the hinterlands, and the orbital transit hub on Cape Caen sixty kilometers to the south.

She was outside. And alone. Oh, she had her friends with her, Caro and Debin. And Sergeant

Reynolds and Mister Dunning. But as her mother had told her so many times, a princess is not really a person; she is the embodied power and the glory of the corporate state. Wherever she goes, so goes the state and all of its holdings, investments, options, and interests. Sitting on wet, filthy cobblestones at the back of some waterfront tavern while an invisible storm raged around her and two old men muttered furiously to each other about what to do next, Alessia felt neither especially powerful nor glorious. She wanted to do something. To draw a blade or bark out some orders. That was what real princesses did when the squirrel poop got real. But she didn't think Sergeant Reynolds would take very kindly to her telling him what to do. And what would she tell him, anyway?

Get me out of here; I'm a princess?

Caro's grandpa turned and glowered. He made a series of gestures with one hand, finishing with the same shushing finger to his lips that Sergeant Reynolds had used. Caro and Debin nodded. They quietly, very quietly unfolded their legs and drew Alessia to her feet, emphasizing with their own gestures that she should be as quiet as possible.

She was tiptoeing through the muck, taking in ever more of her situation—she wore one of Caro's old dresses over her clothes, she could hear strange amplified voices in the distance, and Sergeant Reynolds had changed out of his bright formal uniform into some tatty old coat—when she all but jumped out of her skin at the huge noise of a single voice. It was a man's voice, and although he didn't shout, it was so loud that she imagined it booming out across the whole of Port au Pallice.

"Attention. I am Archon-Admiral Wenbo Strom, commander of the 101st Attack Fleet. This city has been liberated by the First Shock Regiment. It is now under the protection and law of the Human Republic . . ."

Caro had to pull Alessia by the elbow to get her moving again. The giant voice in the sky had pinned her to the spot. The same free-falling, tumbling sensation she had felt when they tipped her out of the bag and onto the dirty ground nearly tipped her over again. She felt dizzy and weird. Who was this man? Why had he brought his fleet, his attack fleet, to Skygarth?

"Hurry up," Caro hissed. "They're almost here."

But they were already here! This strange admiral and his attack fleet.

"Further resistance is pointless and wasteful . . ."

Gunfire, much louder and closer than before, drowned out the rest of the man's words. Alessia jumped and got moving again, hurrying through the rear door of the tavern and into some sort of storeroom. She had just enough time to note more of the same wooden barrels she had seen out the back and boxes of fresh produce stacked up on a table when an enormous flash and bang threw her to the floor. She hit her elbows. Painful jolts of pins and needles ran up and down her arms, and Debin winded her when he landed on top of her.

"Get off me," she groused, but her protest was lost in the roar of gunfire and explosions and men shouting and screaming. It seemed to go on forever, as though forever could be squeezed into a couple of seconds. Shaking again, her ears ringing, Alessia struggled for breath. Dust had filled the storeroom.

"Are you all right? Come on, let's go!"

It was Sergeant Reynolds. She had seen him only a few seconds ago. Now he looked completely different. Covered in dirt and blood and all sorts of things she didn't want to think about. His eyes seemed to have sunk back into his head.

"Grandpa! No!" Debin cried.

Alessia screamed. She couldn't help it.

Mister Dunning staggered toward them out of the murk. His face was a terrible mask. One arm was missing at the elbow. His jacket sleeve hung in tatters, and from within its shreds more tatters hung, but they . . .

She screamed again.

The shreds and tatters were the remains of his missing arm.

Alessia screamed and Caro joined her, and Debin ran to his grandfather and almost knocked the old man off his feet. Only Sergeant Reynolds, now holding him up by his other arm, kept the old gardener on his feet.

There were bodies in the courtyard and more bodies in the small alleyway behind, which Alessia could see dimly through the swirling dust because the rear wall was missing. It looked as though a giant fist had simply punched through the stacks of barrels and casks, demolishing the stone wall and throwing bits and pieces of . . .

. . . people . . .

Blue-black petals bloomed at the edge of her vision, and Sergeant Reynolds barked in his soldier voice at Caro and Debin.

"Get your grandpa inside. Now!"

They both jumped at the order. It was an order, no doubt about that. Alessia had heard him bark plenty of them at the younger guardsmen countless times. This had the same effect on her friends that it had on her guards. They jumped to obey.

Sergeant Reynolds handed his friend over to them and grabbed Alessia none too gently by the arm. He turned her around so quickly that she stumbled and he had to hold her up, bunching his enormous fist into the cheap dress she wore. Caro's dress. He also tried to stand in her way to stop her from seeing the terrible things in the ruined courtyard, but there were too many of them.

She recognized . . . bits and pieces of . . .

. . . people . . .

Shook her head. Tried not to see them anymore.

But they were everywhere.

"We come as friends . . ."

The voice in the sky was back, or maybe it had never gone away. But she could suddenly hear it again. She tried to ignore it. Some of these new friends lay in separate pieces all over the courtyard. They wore uniforms. She could see that, too. A princess saw a lot of uniforms every day even in a place as quiet and far away from court as Skygarth. They weren't just dress-up uniforms, either. She recognized a sort of bulky armor. Not of any exact design she'd ever seen before, like Montanblanc's Royal Marines or the company divisions or even the extra-heavy powered battle suits and combat chassis of the Terran Defense Force, but she knew what she was seeing. Princesses of the High Bourse didn't just learn about poetry and music.

"Come now, Your Highness," Reynolds said quietly. "We best be away."

Alessia allowed herself to be turned around and led back into the rear of the tavern. She found Caro fretting over her grandpa, who sat propped against the wall next to a large, empty fireplace.

"Tie it off now, lass," he muttered through gray lips.

She pulled on a belt looped around the stump of his ruined arm, whimpering as she did so. Debin, Alessia could see, was trying not to cry. He held his grandfather's good hand in both of his own. Sergeant Reynolds went down on one knee in front of his friend. Alessia was pretty sure they were friends. They seemed to know each other very well.

"How you doing, Tosh?" Reynolds asked.

"Had better days, Sarge."

"You always were a lazy bugger. Always the first name on the snivel log."

Mister Dunning smiled weakly, but what he had to smile about, Alessia could not imagine.

"You got me, Sarge. You got my number. Always did."

"Always will, you jammy bastard. We'll get you respawned. Then we'll kick these f—"

He seemed to remember he was surrounded by children and stopped himself from cursing.

"We'll settle up with this Wenbo Strom, eh?"

Reynolds promised instead, squeezing Mister Dunning's shoulder. His good shoulder.

"Sure," said Dunning, bringing Debin's hand to his lips and kissing it. "Sure we will. But first you have to get the princess to Jasko. He's waiting at Freyport. He'll get her out. Worry about me later."

"No, Grandpa, you have to come with us," Caro protested.

Debin held on to the old man's hand even more tightly.

"You can't leave us, Poppy," he said. "We won't have anyone."

"I'll be fine," Dunning said, but he did not sound fine. Not at all. A cough rattled in his throat. "And you won't be alone. You'll have Sergeant Reynolds and Princess Alessia and all of House Montanblanc to look after you, isn't that right, Your Highness?"

Dunning's eyes cleared for a moment. They had been blinking very slowly and sort of fogging over, but now they fixed on Alessia, hard and bright.

"Yes," she said. "My house will always be yours."

The words sounded very grown-up as she said them, and she worried immediately that she had just done something she shouldn't have. Her mother had warned her more than once that a promise from one of the blood royal was not to be lightly given. It was a commitment from the whole company. A binding contract.

Well. So be it, then.

She put aside for just a moment everything else that had happened today and straightened up in front of Mister Dunning and Sergeant Reynolds and her two closest friends. Her only friends. Caro and Debin.

She said the words she had learned by heart. Words that had really meant nothing to her until now. They were just more scales, more history, more lists of dead poets to be learned by rote.

"Pray witness my oath, Sergeant Reynolds."

Reynolds raised one eyebrow but nodded. He stood at attention in front of her. Caro and Debin watched with wide eyes. Reynolds placed a hand over his heart.

"I shall so witness, Your Highness."

Alessia took a deep breath. Her heart was racing. She swallowed.

"Under the seal of the company, by right of birth and endowment of one voting share, I, Princess Alessia Szu Suri sur Montanblanc ul Haq, confer upon the family Dunning all advantages and full protection of House Montanblanc, such conferral to bind my line now and evermore."

Caro and Debin's grandfather groaned quietly, but it sounded as though he was relieved rather than in pain. Alessia wondered if he was glanding painkillers or running a mediscript, and then she realized she didn't even know whether he had those sorts of things. He might not even be wired up.

If he died here . . .

"Get them away, Sarge," he said. "Get them to Jasko. There'll be more of the bastards here soon enough. I'll make myself useful."

Reynolds took the old man's outstretched hand and shook it.

"Come here," Dunning whispered to his grandchildren. He hugged them to him with his one good arm and said something to each, speaking softly into their ears as though telling them some secret. Both were crying now. But both nodded bravely.

In the sky somewhere overhead Wenbo Strom's voice boomed out.

"Human life is precious. Let us not waste any more this day."

CHAPTER
TWENTY

The blast doors at the far end of the passageway exploded inward. Booker threw the bulk of his chassis between the two organics and the explosion. His mech sensors gave him a crucial fraction of a second's warning, and because his reaction time was a factor of software and circuitry, not of primitive offal, he was able to shield Orr from the worst of the blast.

The corporal, running combat script, was the quicker of the two breeders to move and took shelter behind the massive legs of the Compliance Mech. Lao Tzu, running fuck knew what sort of garbage code, merely flinched away, taking a solid hit from a piece of debris that carried off most of one leg. He went down screaming as Booker raised his weapon arm and loosed a stream of jelly bag rounds reformatted as hardened penetrators. He hosed down the passageway, not bothering to acquire individual targets, merely firing for area suppression.

"Orr, are you hit, can you move?" Booker asked.

His audio sensors picked Orr's reply out of the savage industrial uproar of gunfire.

"I'm still here."

He found the corporal sheltering behind his giant mechanical ass. There was a camera down there.

"Move with me and take cover," Booker said as he swept the burning breach for individual targets. The attackers wore stealth suits, probably reinforced with nanomesh carbon mail. They were all but invisible to his infrared and motion-sensing suites, but they still occupied physical space, and that space manifested as a hole in his sensor arrays, a man-shaped void that smoke and fire could not fill up.

Booker began to fire into the moving voids. His weapon arm used a simple mass accelerator, which he had reprogrammed to operate without safety restrictions. The improvised penetrators left the muzzle at hypersonic speed, the whip crack of so many tiny sonic booms sounding like the fire of a conventional automatic. He filled the breach with deadly fire, noting with some satisfaction the explosive results of impact on the shock troopers, while frantically scanning the chaos for Lao Tzu. He found the officer bleeding out against a bulkhead and cursed.

He had just enough time to deliver Orr to the relative safety of the room to their right before the Sturm took the other man under fire.

Lao Tzu's head disintegrated, and Booker roared in fury.

He charged into the breach, closing the distance to the attackers in three crashing strides. Grabbing the first trooper within reach, he ignored the effects of the concentrated fire that was turning his mech into scrap metal. His targeting system, a very basic array in a compliance unit, tagged nine functioning hostiles, seven of which he put down with penetrators. The other one he clubbed with the body of the soldier secured in his grappler.

The sudden violence, extreme and overwhelming, exploding within the very center of the enemy position, snuffed out the firefight. He dropped the body in his grappler and stomped on the head to make sure he stayed down. If this was the Sturm, they wouldn't be hooked up. There was no chance of them reanimating under zombie code. But that didn't mean one of the crazy fuckers wouldn't pull the pin on a pocket nuke if it meant taking out a couple of mutants or borgs.

These motherfuckers ran on permanent beast mode.

"Thanks, man."

It was Orr, emerged from hiding and carrying a sidearm he'd scrounged from somewhere. He lingered behind Booker in the cover provided by the Compliance Mech. Booker picked him up on ass cam. He regarded the pile of chopped meat that had been Captain Lao Tzu. The weapons and pulse fire had made such a mess of him that there was no discerning even his basic p-type.

"Sorry about that, Booker," Orr said. "Looks like a hard delete. But I . . . er . . . I'll vouch for your deal with him. You kept up your end of it. I'll tell the padre, too. You know. Just in case."

Booker maneuvered around in the passageway to face Corporal Orr. For a guy who was going to scrub his source code, he was a decent breeder.

"Thanks," he said, dialing down the volume on his PA system to something like normal conversation.

He could feel some of the damage to the mech in the way it clanked and clattered, and a quick check of the diagnostic systems threw up dozens of flashing red-line items. The unit had absorbed a lot of fire. "So what now?" Booker asked.

Alarms clanged and sirens still howled, but they no longer heard the amplified warnings of Habnet breaches and intruder alerts. The prison's autonomic subroutines were functional. The air flowed. Gravity sucked. And fire suppression systems smothered the burning wreckage of the fight with the Sturm in retardant foam.

Orr shook his head at Booker's question.

"I have no idea. If the Sturm got this far, they have to control most of the Hab already. Comms are still down. There's no command and control. I checked quickly while you were dealing with these assholes."

He waved the handgun at the stealth-suited corpses, which were half buried now under fire retardant foam.

"It won't be long before they send follow-on forces," Booker said. "This unit will be dark now. Is there any way off the Hab from this point that doesn't involve fighting our way through g-pop? This mech isn't a combat chassis, and all you've got is that toy gun."

Orr looked at the pistol he was carrying and snorted.

"It's not even carrying a full load. But yeah. We could get out from this end of the can. There's a shuttle bay a level down. Not the main dock. The Sturm will have that. And maybe they got this one, too, but maybe not. It's a tertiary access point. Personnel movement only, and only high-level personnel. Command-cadre and tactical response group if needed. For riots and shit, you know."

"How do you feel about abandoning your post?" Booker asked. "That's what you'll be doing. And helping me escape. You could end up in the XD chamber, too. The captain's not gonna be in your corner."

He raised the grappler in the general direction of Lao Tzu's remains.

"Long as I report in to the nearest intact TDF unit, I'm good." Orr shrugged. He seemed to worry at a thought for a moment or two. "I said I'd vouch for you, Booker. And I will, no matter what. But I can't vouch for how anybody up the chain of command might react. You get some first life ring knocker and you might just find your ass deleted with extreme prejudice, anyway. There's gonna be a lot of confusion, panic, and shitty decisions made in the next few hours."

"I'll try not to make too many of them mine," Booker said. "How do we get to this shuttle bay?"

"Two compartments past XD and one deck down. What about the padre? We taking him?"

"I'd feel better . . . if he'd come," Booker said. He started to move, heading back toward Execution and Deletion. He kept the mech's rear-facing sensors focused on the breach, which was piled up with the dead.

Orr took the cue and moved ahead of him, the pistol raised in a two-handed grip. Even ensouled within the circuitry and software of the Compliance Mech, Booker was anxious about the man's safety. He'd already lost the most important witness he had to his agreement with Lao Tzu, which was to say his agreement with the TDF. Orr was unarmored, virtually unarmed, and trapped on a fallen Hab full of space Nazis who'd tear off his head and stomp it to jelly, all on general principles.

They found Father Michael sitting in the XD chamber, nervously working his rosary beads and muttering prayers to himself. Booker's former body still lay in a coma where they'd emptied it of his soul.

"You're back!" the padre said, starting up from the couch. His face gave away the surprise, turning to shock at the physical damage to the mech and the loss of Captain Lao Tzu.

"Father, you'll want to come with us, I reckon," Orr said.

Booker said nothing. His self-interest in securing the priest was obvious.

"But I can't leave," Father Michael said. "If things are as bad as you say, I'm needed here. I cannot abandon my flock."

There was no reproach in his tone, but Orr seemed to find one.

"Padre, it's not about keeping up appearances. The Hab has fallen. We only just survived that fight with the Sturm because they weren't equipped to take down a mech and because Booker reprogrammed the weapons suite. Next time they come, they'll bring heavy weapons and crack him like an egg. They'll delete him and kill me. That's what they do, Father. They delete and they kill."

The priest gave him a censorious look.

"My son, that's what you were about to do with Booker not so long ago."

Booker had remained in the passage outside the chamber rather than taking the time to negotiate the doorway.

"Thanks for having my back there, Padre," he said, "but seriously, you'd be a lot more help if you came with us. The captain got splattered. Apart from Corporal Orr, nobody else can testify on my behalf."

The priest smiled. A disconsolate expression.

"I could help you, Booker. But there are many more on this Habitat I could also help."

Orr spoke up.

"They'll kill you, Father."

"I don't think so. The Sturm have no state religion. As I recall, they allow all faiths to practice." He paused and bowed his head toward Booker as if in apology. "Except for the Source, naturally."

"Natch," Booker replied flatly.

"I was born on the plates of Eassar, Corporal Orr. My genome is unaltered. Pure, as the Sturm would say. And I have no neural implants. You've heard their announcement. You know their particular illness, their obsession. They really do imagine they have come to free the likes of me from the likes of you. I'll be fine. And I will testify on your behalf, Booker. Somehow. I will even make a living testament and record it just in case some misadventure should befall me. But for now my calling demands that I remain here and tend to those who most need it."

He clasped one hand over the other and seemed to plant himself on the deck as though daring Booker to grab him with his giant mechanical arm. The sounds of battle still reached them from the main part of the

Hab, and Orr kept checking the passageway. Booker was tempted simply to pick up the holy man and carry him off to the shuttle bay, but years spent conspiring with fellow source coders meant he could recognize a pigheaded true believer when he met one.

"Let's go, Orr," he said. "Padre, I'd be grateful for any testimony you could record to my benefit. And extra grateful for any backup copies you could get off this Hab."

"I will make a record and copies and my best effort to distribute them the moment you go."

Booker sighed. Coming from the mech it sounded like the compression valves of a giant cargo hauler releasing a few hundred pounds of pressure.

"Thanks," he said. "And good luck. Corporal?"

Orr shrugged and shook the padre's hand.

"Good luck, Father," he said.

He remembered something.

"Look. Keller. Back on the row. He's offline, but he is wired. The Sturm will pull off his head and throw it on the pile for sure."

He paused. Came to a decision.

"The unlock code for his cell is 070894. Let him out. He should be allowed to take his chances with everyone else."

"Why don't you take him with you?" Father Michael said.

Both men answered in unison.

"Because he's an asshole."

They left the priest recording a statement on behalf of Booker. He had no idea whether anybody would ever hear it, and he was beginning to suspect it wouldn't matter. The odds against them escaping were getting shorter by the minute. And they had to escape. There was no sense punching your way into a fight you couldn't win.

This end of the prison Hab was mostly storage and plant. They encountered no other personnel and no hostiles on the short walk to the last compartment and the elevator to the lower deck. Booker gave Orr as much room as he could in the confined space. As the door slid shut, the fighting faded to a distant rumble and the occasional tremor. Sirens still blared, and condition lights strobed red. Booker used the brief interlude to check as many diagnostics as possible and to route around potential points of failure in the mech's hardware. It was a mess. A clanking, grinding three-ton bucket of stressed, torn-up metal and scorched, shattered ceramics. The substrate hosting his source code was undamaged, so there was that. But he'd need to cross-load to another platform as soon as possible.

The elevator bumped to a halt, and the doors slid open.

A white storm of plasma fire and kinetic rounds poured into the elevator car, overwhelming Booker's sensor suite. He charged, raising his gun arm and firing blindly, sweeping the muzzle high and wide in a desperate attempt to hit something, anything, until he realized he might be shooting the shit out of their only ride and cut off the ammo feed. He launched himself off the deck, crouching down on the mech's giant legs and springing upward with no idea how much clearance he had. The damaged behemoth jumped clear of the fire for a moment, allowing him to get a lock on the source. Two squads hunkered down on the far side of the shuttle bay, taking cover where they could find it. He burned off the last of his repurposed ammo, taking one of the groups under fire, using his elevation to rain hardened gelite slugs down on them from above.

The mech crashed back to the deck, where the volume of fire had been noticeably reduced, and with his ammunition spent, Booker used the only weapon left to him. Mass and speed. He charged the Sturm, swinging both his gun arm and the grappler as crude clubs. The mech took even more damage closing with the enemy, but he was on them before they could dismantle him with fire.

Instead he dismantled them with brutish violence.

The melee was over in seconds, the Sturm reduced to red pulp and offal smears.

Orr!

Booker turned around as quickly as he could and stomped back to the elevator.

His sensors had been badly damaged, but he didn't need a full suite to know Orr was gone.

The Sturm had painted the inside of the elevator car with him.

Booker almost gave up then. Almost turned around and returned to the fight for the Hab, a fight that was already lost. If he perished ensouled in the mech, his code would go dark but his soul would be freed.

This the Source believed.

This was his faith.

For a second he slumped to the deck plating, leaning on the gore-splattered grappler. Trapped as he was in a ruined chassis with a Hab full of maniacs on one side and the TDF on the other, he realized that this was an even shittier end to the day than he'd imagined when he woke up in his cell.

Booker3-212162-930-Infantry sat among the burning debris and body parts.

The shuttle Orr had been going to fly out?

Yeah, he'd fucking shot that to pieces, of course. It wasn't going anywhere.

He thought about forcing open the bay doors and spacing himself. But as he sat on the plates, the guest of honor at a raging pity party of one, he saw that all was not lost.

He had one more card to play.

CHAPTER

TWENTY-ONE

There was no mistaking *Defiant* for a pleasure cruiser. The ship was a warfighter with a blunt functionality of design and purpose. But Lucinda's cabin was bigger than the room she'd had to share at the Academy and immeasurably cleaner and more orderly than the dingy three-cell Hab tank where she'd lived with her dad before Habitat Welfare and the orphanage. She had not bothered to personalize her cabin beyond loading the holographic image of her mother and father to hover above a shelf over the small desk by her wardrobe. They were young in the holo, and her mother was very pretty, she thought. But it was a frail beauty that bespoke the difficulties she would later have carrying Lucinda to term. Jonathyn Hardy was not a large man or strong, but his love for Asha Hardy burned quietly in the few seconds captured and stored in the display. The video was the only thing the reclaimers had let Lucinda take from the Hab tank.

To them it was worthless.

Lucinda sat on the end of her bunk, staring at the

tiny memento, rubbing her hands together as though washing them of the responsibility she had taken on. She stood up. She sat down. Then she stood up again and paced the short length of her cabin, trying to shake off the doubt that lay on her like a second skin.

"You can do this," she told herself aloud. "Come on. You have to. Just get it done."

But she could not talk herself into belief. Not here on her own, where she knew the truth.

Chase was right. She did not belong.

Lieutenant Varro Chase was not the first ennobled shithead to give her grief in the Navy, of course. A Sublieutenant Tok Yulin, on exchange from the Forces Coloniales of House Yulin-Irrawaddy, had made a misery of her very first posting, to the fast attack picket HMAS *Taipan*. The *Taipan* was small, old, and not especially fast anymore and didn't attack much of anything while she was on board. But it did provide Yulin with an intimate stage for developing his theatrically cruel persona. Lucinda paused in her constant pacing and stared at the hologram of her parents. They had been happy. In the photon sculpture she carried with her, they would always be happy. The imagery would outlast her just as she had outlasted Yulin. She tried to resolve that she would do the same with Chase and all the Tok Yulins and Varro Chases yet to come. It was not the first time she had made that resolution, and before she had convinced herself of it, a bell chimed at the cabin door.

Lucinda ordered the holo to turn off before calling out, "Enter."

The cabin door swished open, and Ian Bannon stood just beyond the threshold, looking awkward.

Lucinda hurriedly packed away all of her own short-comings and fears of inadequacy.

"Lieutenant?" she said. "Can I help you? Has there been a change in Defiant's status?"

"No, ma'am," he replied, glancing up and down the companionway outside. "If I might, ma'am . . . it is not . . . I just . . ."

He looked as though he might fall apart from embarrassment.

"Commander, I—"

"Lieutenant," she said firmly. "Come in and close the door."

He looked so unsure of himself that she felt it necessary to add, "That's an order."

Bannon all but collapsed with relief and fell across the entrance to her cabin. The door whispered closed behind him.

"You should move into the captain's quarters, ma'am," he said, almost stammering. "It has a small conference room for . . . for, um . . ."

"What's up, Ian?" she asked, certain now that this had nothing to do with the malware breach. Or at least not directly. Bannon actually glanced back over his shoulder as though checking for a tail.

"It's Chase," he said quietly but fiercely, and her heart sank just a little. "Lieutenant Chivers told me he asked her if she thought you were . . . if you could . . ."

Bannon had trouble getting the words out, but Lucinda had none imagining what they might be.

"Command the ship?" she finished for him.

He breathed out heavily and nodded once, an overly emphatic gesture that was as much relief at getting the dread reveal off his chest as it was confirmation of her question.

Lucinda felt an old and bitter anger stirring within. She recalled the claustrophobic confines of the *Taipan* and the way she had tried to make herself invisible there to avoid any encounter with Tok Yulin.

"Did he ask you, Lieutenant? Has he spoken to any of the other officers or crew? Or is this just something Nonomi told you?"

"Not me, no. I mean, sorry, Chase didn't speak to me. We don't really talk. But I know he was in the spacers' mess earlier today. And he never goes down there. He says they're all hull scum."

"I see. And what do you think I should do about this, Lieutenant?"

"I, I don't know . . . Commander."

She could tell from the way he stumbled over her rank that he, like she, was having trouble adjusting. But not as much trouble as some.

"It's not much to be going on with, is it?" she said, but gently. "Hardly court-martial stuff."

"But Lucin—I mean, gah, sorry. Commander. He's questioning your authority."

"But not with you?"

Bannon blushed.

"No, ma'am. But Nonomi—Lieutenant Chivers and I, we . . ."

He trailed off.

She smiled, wrinkling her eyes as if letting him in on a secret. "I know. Everyone knows."

Lucinda sighed then.

"Is Lieutenant Chase on deck now, Ian?"

She normally would have checked shipnet, but it

was still down and her mesh was now decomposing somewhere in her gastro-intestinal tract.

"No, ma'am. He's off duty."

"Good. Would you please have Lieutenant Chase and any other officers and senior chiefs not currently on deck join me in the marines' gymnasium. Say, five minutes. In their sweats. You, too."

Bannon looked at her as though baffled. They were both first lifers and she was only a few years older than he, but in his lack of guile he sometimes seemed almost impossibly innocent. After all, he had not grown up among the hull scum.

Had she ever been like him?

She doubted it. They'd come from the same Habitat but very different worlds.

Lucinda shrugged at his confusion.

"I feel like a workout," she said

Ian Bannon nodded. Comprehension finally was beginning to dawn.

Biofunctional wetware had long ago made physical training all but redundant. The Navy did require all personnel to maintain a base level of organic fitness and core skill sets, but only the marines really punched it up to the next level.

The marines . . . and Lucinda Hardy.

She was pointedly reclusive. Always had been. Whereas most people simply downloaded their distractions directly to the synapse, for instance, she read books. Actual books on an actual tablet. One word at a time. She liked the theater, live theater with actors, and attended when she·could, but always on her own. She also trained at close-quarters combat, hard physical work of a sort endured only by the very poor or the very rich and somewhat eccentric.

And the Royal Armadalen Marines.

Changing quickly into her sweats and trying to dismiss the anxiety, normally free-floating, that had now fastened on the question Chase had asked—*Was she able to command? Seriously?*—Lucinda walked directly from her cabin to the gym where Captain Hayes's supersized combat monsters spent so much of their time.

The space was crowded with them when she arrived. Some, the officers, wore bodies as old as thirty. Others still looked fresh from the vat. Their skin no longer glistened with the moist pinkness of the freshly extruded, but they still had that weird, veiny giant man-baby look about them. No wrinkles, no scars, no blemishes of any kind marred their smooth skin.

It always gave Lucinda the creeps.

They were uniformly enormous, too, massing out to at least twice the size of *Defiant*'s personnel, sometimes more. As best she could tell, they were training naked.

They wore clothes, of course.

But they had no enhancements powered up. The weights they lifted, they heaved high with raw human musculature. They sprinted on the running belts without glanding supps or stims or oxyboosters. When they sparred—with one another and the training dummies—they fought without loading code.

As she entered the space, a top sergeant wearing a Melanesian phenotype roared out, "Commander on deck!" and all activity came to a crashing halt. Literally, as weight lifters dropped their loads to the deck plates and came to attention.

After forty-eight hours, Lucinda was getting used to the idea of the new rank and status surrounding her very person like the bristles of a spiny sea creature, but she was still uneasy with the effect and wondered if she would ever really be comfortable in command.

"Thank you, Sergeant Harjus. Please. As you were."

"You heard the lady. Back to pukin' and snivelin', you fucking crybabies."

The heavy metal riot started up again.

The marines had set up the gym in a stowage hold on the lowest deck, one frame away from Engineering. It was the noisiest part of the vessel, but not because of the nearby plant and machinery. That was virtually silent. The gym resounded to the crashing of weight plates, the straining grunts of lifters, and the pounding feet of sprinters on the running belts. In one corner, a woman wearing the recently extruded skin of a Native American jumped with a leather rope, the heavy length of cord hitting the deck plating with a whistling thump so many times a second that it sounded like a heavy rotor drone landing.

Lucinda could see from the natural flow of the sparring rounds—the slight errors and uncertainty, the missed blows and blocks, the struggle and difficulty of it all—that the marines were fighting without neuromuscular meshnet assistance, relying solely on hard-won muscle memory. She assumed they were also working without augments or limits. Like her, they'd had to shit out their mesh.

She stood at the edge of the fighting mat, waiting for her own people to arrive.

"Help you, ma'am?" asked the top sergeant.

"Can you load code on one of your combat dummies for me, Sergeant Harjus?" Lucinda asked.

"I could if you were of a mind to tell me why, ma'am."

"So I can kick its ass."

He snorted, "Now why would you want to do that?"

Chase and Bannon arrived with Nonomi Chivers, three subbies, and Chief Higo. Chase looked slightly apprehensive. Higo was curious. Bannon could not stop swallowing.

"Belay that question," the top sergeant said mostly to himself.

Lucinda nodded to Bannon and Higo. She smiled at Chivers.

"Top," she said, turning away from the new arrivals, "will you please load a fighting drone with a close-quarters package, 50/40 Grand Master Haseman's Tohkon Ryu jujitsu, second dan, and Master Ipo's Shudokan judo, first dan. And then a randomized sequence of the striking arts. Karate, boxing, whatever. Your choice. Max out at three-minute intervals. Maybe throw some Zaitsev systema in there, too. And no limiters."

"Ma'am, I need authorization to remove the safeties," Harjus said.

"You have it."

"Er . . ."

"You can't authorize your own training accident, ma'am," Chief Higo explained.

"But I can," a new voice interrupted.

Captain Hayes.

The marine commandant had appeared from the showers, mostly dried off but still damp around the ears and dabbing at his head with a towel. His upper body looked like a Titan cruiser carved from thick slabs of human protein. He nodded at Sergeant Harjus.

"The lady wants to kick some ass, Top."

"All right, then," Harjus said, sounding unconvinced. He took up a handheld unit and futzed around onscreen.

A couple more marines gathered at the edge of the mat to watch the bout and possibly to enjoy themselves ragging on her efforts. She ignored them as the unarmed fighting drone powered up.

It looked like a kinetic-impact dummy . . . until it came to life and assumed a fighting stance in a small circle just outside the range of her longest strike, a spinning back kick launched from *irimi-senkai,* an entering rotation.

"Off the mat," Harjus growled at a couple of marines who'd edged onto the gelform tatami.

Lucinda stepped onto the mat as she had countless times before and took up position within her own circle.

"What's the point?" somebody asked. It sounded like Chase.

Lucinda said nothing.

"Commence!" Harjus shouted.

The drone attacked, shouting a *kiai* that everyone could hear. It closed not with inhuman speed but with the swiftness and surety of a warrior trained to the level Lucinda had requested. A fighter just a little more advanced than herself. She fended and dodged, blocked and weaved, moving not just her feet but her hips and shoulders. You could dance around on your toes like a ballet principal, but it wouldn't help if you left your center mass sitting in the line of attack. Move the hips, move the body.

With a personal combat suite loaded into her neural net she could have defeated the dummy in seconds. When the fight continued for longer, when the first minute passed and then the second, when she started to sweat and draw deep drafts of air down into her *hara,* her audience realized what she was doing. She wasn't just riding the wetware. She'd deleted her wetware. She was fighting. A few more marines left their weight stations and ambled over to watch.

A chime signaled a break at three minutes.

The drone bowed and knelt on the mat.

Lucinda did the same. She was recovered by the time Harjus told her to rise, bow, and commence another round.

This time a few of the marines cheered her on as she initiated her own attacks, but the loudest shouts came when she covered up and muscled through a flurry of old-school uppercuts and short, looping roundhouse punches, getting inside the dummy's fighting arc, hooking one foot behind its leading ankle, and suddenly leaning forward into the side of its knee joint. The street-fighting move unbalanced the drone, and it started to topple backward. She spun quickly and smashed an elbow into the side of its head. On a human opponent that strike would have crunched through the thin mantle of bone over the temple.

The drone picked itself up and bowed.

Then it took up a fighting stance and attacked again.

Lucinda judged it to have picked up the speed of attack by about 5 percent. It was fighting appreciably beyond her abilities now, slowly forcing her onto the defensive. She held her opponent off until just before the three-minute break, when she wore a crunching roundhouse kick to her rib cage and a hammer fist strike to her clavicle that the drone pulled just before impact.

Applause came this time. And a few hoots.

She ignored that, too. Kneeling and breathing deeply but raggedly.

Harjus called the last round, and she fought it out, wearing a few more kicks and getting one decent throw in when the drone overstepped on a reverse punch and she was able to sweep out its leading foot.

She'd fought for less than ten minutes altogether, but she was sodden with sweat, her face shiny and red. She bowed to the drone—which really meant she was bowing to the marines—and then bowed again as she stepped off the mat. She'd lost none of her audience. Picked up a few more in fact.

Lieutenant Bannon was staring at her. Nonomi Chivers goggled openly.

Captain Hayes, smiling, bowed to her as she came off. It was a formal gesture, a dojo courtesy, and she returned it.

"Impressive effort," he said.

She was struggling for breath, but she looked at

Chase, found some air, and said, "The point is, you don't need code, or scripts, or biomods to fight. You just need the will and the training. This has always been the Armadalen way."

He didn't reply.

"Captain Hayes," she said, turning back to the marine. "Do you have capacity to take on a few students?"

Hayes grinned.

"I can find the time."

"Thank you. I want all of my officers drilled in close-quarters combat. I don't expect them to reach proficiency by the time we get back to the Volume. But I do expect them to start learning. The old way."

"The old ways are the best, Commander."

She nodded and fixed her gaze on Chase again.

"When you think you're ready, Lieutenant, I will be happy to receive your challenge."

Commander Lucinda Hardy did not wait on his reply. She walked away toward the showers and did not look back.

CHAPTER
TWENTY-TWO

With that one convulsive leap he was free.

Free of Trumbull, free of troubles, free of the nattering fucking numpties Miyazaki had foisted on him to no good end. Frazer McLennan launched himself from the cramped and increasingly rank confines of the dune rover's cabin and out into the night. The rover was moving at close to its top speed, and he felt the wind of its passage through the Ironstone Desert as an immediate grabbing and tearing at his clothes.

In an earlier self, maybe five or six relifes ago, he might have experienced a moment of doubt or anxiety at jumping from a vehicle moving fast over hard rocks and sharp gravel, but Hero's micro-g wave picked him up as gently as a kitten, decelerating his aging body with due regard to its many infirmities and potentially catastrophic points of failure and depositing him gently on the desert floor. Mac watched the dune rover disappearing, seemingly shrinking into the dark void of the Goroth Mountains, and imagined his erstwhile traveling companions all rushing to the rear window to catch a fading glimpse of him before they were carried away into the darkness.

Trumbull would be furious, which amused him. He gave them a wave.

Two shadows drifted across the starlit wasteland. A pitch-black negative space, ovoid-shaped and all but humming with disapproval, and a long, narrow elliptical form that seemed to drink in the darkness. It was impossible to see when you were looking for it. Only a suggestion of movement at the very edge of vision hinted at something amiss.

"You realize, don't you, that this is the most irresponsible thing you have ever done?" Hero scolded.

"Och, you say that so often, it has no meaning anymore," McLennan lobbed back.

"Don't you 'och' me, you mock Scottish garden gnome. The tourists can't hear you anymore, so you can take off your kilt and get back into your adult diaper."

"Aye, do you set some sort of reminder to twist my poor man titties with your endless fucking nagging? Because I could set my clock to it, Herodotus, I truly could."

McLennan walked carefully over to where he was almost sure the sled had come to a halt.

"You could at least give me a wee candle to light my way," he complained.

"You could at least get some retinal implants like a grown-up instead of whinging like a Neanderthal toddler," Hero said, but a dim red line pulsed once on the sled. The Intellect powered down the stealth systems, and the vehicle resolved in McLennan's visual field as an elongated teardrop a little over nine feet in length. A liquid metal hatch dissolved, revealing a two-man crew space. A duffel bag lay on one of the couches.

"Ah, goodo," Mac said. "I was worried you'd forget this in the rush to break camp."

"I never forget anything. You're the one who insists on living your life inside a series of ambulatory meat puddings with no memory backup."

McLennan stripped off the clothes he had been wearing. The pants got caught on his shoes, and he had to take them off, too.

"I don't suppose you remembered to pack my gel mat. These stones are bloody sharp."

Hero's reply was clipped and disapproving.

"If you had asked me to, I would have, but you didn't, so no."

Mac felt himself cradled in a micro-g wave and lifted a few inches off the desert floor.

He took his pants and shirt and stuffed them into the back of the sled, then took a coverall from the duffel bag and carefully climbed in one leg at a time.

"I think it's time we discussed the rules of engagement, specifically mine," Hero said while McLennan finished donning the stealth suit. When he had all of his limbs in, the coverall rearranged itself about him, snugging and adjusting. He left the hood bunched at the back of his neck.

"Fine," he said. "Under Article Three of the Terran War Powers Act, I, Admiral Frazer Donald McLennan, hereby release you from the Peace Bond and authorize you to conduct operations by all means necessary to secure the Volume from all enemies for the duration of the current hostilities. Satisfied?"

"Very much so."

"Your first operation is to get back to Trumbull and those useless ball bags on the rover and make sure they don't get themselves captured. I can hardly play at sneaking about like a relifed William Wallace if the Sturm get ahold of them and start pulling off fingernails and the occasional head."

McLennan squinted into the darkness, where he knew the dune rover was headed, but there was no sign of it now. The arid wastes of the Sukaurno Basin stretched away into nothingness. Hero would know where they were to the millimeter, but McLennan did not ask. He simply wanted them removed as a factor from the equation. Him on one side. The Sturm on the other.

"I do not agree that the best use of my abilities is babysitting Professor Trumbull's bus tour of the Ironstone," Hero complained.

"And I do not care that you do not agree. Rank has its privileges, and it's my very particular privilege to tell you to do as you're fucking told. I haven't had that pleasure for about five hundred years, so please do not ruin it for me now. Just keep them away from the Sturm until I'm done. When I have some idea of what these evil cunts are about, we can start throwing a turd or two in the works."

"Flinging fecal matter into the machinery of the Human Republic's battle plan is not likely to make any difference," Hero said.

"Aye, but it will make me feel better," McLennan said.

He climbed into the sled and seated himself on the empty acceleration couch. It was less comfortable and more cramped than he recalled. His back already ached, and one of his legs was throbbing. But one of his legs was always throbbing. Sometimes both.

At least the stealth suit would recycle his piss. He didn't much fancy the idea of climbing in and out of it to make water half a dozen times a day.

"Two days, Herodotus. That's all I need. You can busy yourself breaking their commsec."

If they were men, at that point they would have shaken hands.

McLennan expected the Intellect to bow a little, but instead it merely floated back a few inches.

"You have no backup. No memory stores. No neural link. Nothing," it said. "If you die, it's for real. No scans. No meat readings. You are just gone. Are you sure you will not reconsider?"

"As sure as I've ever been of anything. The Sturm have none of those things either. Every one of them we kill, we kill forever."

He fed power into the sled's terrain-following displacer field, and it lifted a few inches farther off the desert floor.

"And this time," Mac said, "I intend to kill them all."

He went dark as soon as the canopy closed over him again. The return journey to the *Voortrekker* would take most of the night. McLennan couldn't run straight in at high speed. As advanced as the sled's cloaking systems were, a cannonball run would create more than enough environmental disturbance to draw the attention of the Sturm's active sensor arrays. And so he advanced in dribs and drabs, fits and starts, mimicking the movement of the desert's night creatures. Running like a sand fox, spiraling in the great long loops of the ground hawk, crawling over the basin floor in the slow, creeping advance of the stone gorgon. The sled reformatted its heat signature to sim each animal as needed. The military-grade infiltrator unit, a contract rider he had insisted on with Miyazaki, had no sentient intellect. But its AI systems were still very advanced. It could easily handle the approach to the *Voortrekker*. For much of the night McLennan alternated between light sleep and contemplation, trusting his safety to the early-warning systems.

This at least, he would concede, was where Hero might be right. With a neural net and cortical augmentation he would be able to call up vast archives of perfectly preserved data. The history of the Sturm, the Civil War, the Exile into Dark Space. Instead, reliant on his all too fallible human memory, which seemed to get much less reliable as the centuries piled on, he struggled to recall fine detail and even the broader sweep of a 700-year narrative arc. And he had contributed a good deal of the scholarship to the study of that narrative.

It would be different if he were back at the dig site, where he had maintained a comprehensive library, or, even better, at his campus suite on the main university Habitat, where he could consult the archives of the wider Volume and talk with colleagues on campus or back on Earth via wormhole link. But speeding across the wilderness of the Sukaurno Basin, itself a minor wasteland within the greater emptiness of the Ironstone Desert, Frazer McLennan felt himself isolated and unmoored. He could see the glowing bowl of the newly illuminated dig site over the dark line of the horizon. The dropships would be down and the landing forces well established.

The fact of his own work on the *Voortrekker,* if not the exact details, would be known to the Sturm by now, and doubtless they'd have worked themselves into a yammering fit of violent hypercrazia over the blasphemy done to their sacred fucking site.

They really were a bunch of tedious flogs and pointy great sticks in the arse about their precious fucking piety and purity and . . .

McLennan shook himself out of the darkening spiral.

The Sturm. He hated those animals, but that wasn't nearly enough to go at them with.

He'd beaten them once before, at great cost, aye, but he had beaten them. And if he kept his wits about him this time, he was sure they could be knocked over again.

He closed his eyes and allowed himself to rest, not forcing the question of what he knew about them and what he might do with that knowledge but allowing himself the indulgence of simply letting his mind wander.

It wandered across hundreds of years, through the darkest ages of the modern era and the brighter days of a hard-won Second Renaissance. It touched on war and remembrance and the contested meaning of what it even was to be human anymore. He was something of an heirloom in that sense. This aging carcass in which he lived, gradually failing him as it always did, was identical to the body he'd been born with in his first life. Naturally born, too. Conceived on Earth in the old-fashioned way, untouched by gene shears or augments. His parents—long, long gone—had not been wealthy, or powerful, or indeed significant in any way. A couple of basic income bludgers in the worst tower in Glasgow. And Glasgow had a few. No gene fixes or neuralink or lifestreaming to secure storage for them.

McLennan came awake abruptly, hundreds of light-years away from the faded memories of his youth, as though struggling to escape from something. His childhood, probably. He did not remember much of it now. Not even what his parents had looked like. He recalled more of the emotional shape of things—dark and forbidding—and the fact of his escape via a scholarship from the city's Welfare and Relief Board. McLennan wiped a dry hand over his face, feeling the gray stubble, and rubbed the sleep from his eyes. The brilliant wash of the local star field stretched right across the night sky. He briefly wondered if Earth was out there in that soft, luminous river of starlight. He had never thought to check.

Did brute chaos and madness reign there now? Unless the Republic had developed some radical new drive, humanity's homeworld still lay nearly two years and many folds away. But Mac feared that the Sturm might have struck a killing blow, perhaps two of them, at the very points of failure he'd identified hundreds of years ago—to no avail. His heart slowed, possibly even missing a beat.

Was this his fault?

Did I author the Sturm's battle plan?

He'd certainly identified as critical vulnerabilities the zero point wormhole network and the increasingly routine use of code loading for even basic skill sets. To McLennan they seemed such obvious points of failure. Cut people off from their skill sets or simply fry the stacks, and if they weren't organically trained to do their jobs, they were as useless as knitted condoms. Inject malware into the zero point network and it would propagate in real time across the entire Human Volume; in effect, it was a decapitation strike on the whole of the human race, because the only people who were constantly zeroed in were the corporate and governing elites. Only they could afford the insane expense of virtual omnipresence and immortality.

"Is there coffee? I need a brew," McLennan said. He sounded older even to himself.

"The Intellect anticipated as much," the sled replied. "In the center console you will find a thermos of black unsweetened coffee with two shots of whiskey."

Mac found the drink, and with it a packet of shortbread for dunking. He unscrewed the cap and drank straight from the flask. The same one he'd used back at the dig site. The coffee and whiskey blend hit his stomach hard, and he took a minute to eat a few cookies. It was the first food he'd taken since that jam sandwich nearly twelve hours earlier. On a hunch, he checked the console again and found a thermal bag; inside was a bread roll, slightly stale but still edible, heavy with roasted goat meat and HP Sauce. He muttered a quiet word of thanks to Herodotus.

"I will pass on your compliments when it is safe to establish communications," said the AI.

"You'll shut the fuck up and let me think, you yammering dildo," Mac said.

It was possible, he supposed, that the Sturm had been planning their return long enough that they had infiltrated deep-cover agents into the Volume. It would be a simple matter in the outer systems, more challenging the closer you got to Earth, especially if they had targeted the TDF, Earth Governance, or the High Bourse. Challenging but not impossible.

He was sick with the thought that he might have given some Republican spy the idea for this attack, but he was also not long in damning himself for a fool. The Sturm were here. If they were here, they would be elsewhere, probably everywhere, to preclude the Volume massing forces against them. Galactic war, even on a limited scale, was not something you jumped into like some drunken munter stomping through a field of cow pats. They had planned. They had prepared. And they had gathered their intel. Perhaps they did have somebody at one of the conferences and meetings he'd attended while attempting in vain to persuade Earth Governance to address the vulnerabilities of the zero point network.

But so what?

He had not been alone in his fears. The fact was that there had been conferences and papers and dialogue. The Javans had even attempted something similar to a zero point nanophage strike, if more modest in scope, in their war with Armadale. (A strategy they quickly abandoned after threats of war from the other Houses of the Bourse.)

Frazer chewed a bite of his sandwich and gazed through the clear canopy to the vast sweep of the Milky Way. It was so much brighter here than on Earth.

It did not matter, he decided, where the Sturm had sourced their intelligence. They could have easily deduced the vulnerability from afar. What mattered was defeating them.

How to even start, though?

By his estimates, they might have taken out 96, maybe even 97 percent of the Volume's military capability.

And all of its leadership.

The high councils and parliaments and boards of the Volume would all be overrun right now by an unholy blood swarm of crack-headed homicidal lunatics like Deputy Prince Pac Yulin. And almost anybody else who might have stepped up and taken charge probably had lost the ability to tie their fucking shoelaces.

CHAPTER
TWENTY-THREE

Eassar was a B-class manufacturing Hab of the Yulin-Irrawaddy Combine. It boasted seventeen separate docking facilities, each one assigned to a functional division of the Hab. The *Je Ne Regrette Rien* had laid in at Dock 13, a receiving station for food and water. Despite recycling most nutrients, including the dead or worn-out bodies of its inhabitants, Eassar needed regular shipments from outside. The plantations on Batavia, all of them run as prison facilities, supplied the bulk of those imports, but long-haul cargo consignments also came in from outside the system. Batavia was still a phase two colony world. It would be many decades before it could provide any luxury goods beyond, say, small catches of fresh seafood for the Hab's upper management cadre.

The customs officials at border control stations such as Dock 13 were even more egregiously corrupt than their colleagues elsewhere on the Hab, and this in spite of some quite ferocious punishments for corruption within the Yulin-Irrawaddy's volume. The Combine, like criminal syndicates throughout history, was at its most bestial when protecting itself from competing criminals. Unfortunately for the merged Houses of Yulin and Irrawaddy, the officials entrusted with enforcing the laws were those in the best position to break them.

Same old, fuckin' same old, Seph thought. When she'd first gotten out from under the welfare, she'd run a string of Hab rats for a crooked shipping clerk on Coriolis. The guy would let them know when something good was due in and make sure there was a hole somewhere for them to crawl through. She'd learned early that having all the guns and ships didn't necessarily mean having all the power. Cinders had taught her that. The guy marking up the cargo manifest? That was the dude who could make things happen.

They'd docked at 13 with a small pallet of liquor from Earth. The real shit, too, sourced from a broker on Coriolis who'd diverted the barrels of French brandy and Kentucky bourbon from a larger consignment on its way around the outer spiral to Cupertino. Those rich assholes wouldn't miss it, and it gave Seph and her crew the cover they needed for the real deal, the meet-up with the Yakuza. As far as she knew, the barrels were still sitting in the hold, minus a couple of bottles poured off for the customs agent.

He was probably dead now.

The Sturm controlled Dock 13.

"The fuck are these proud Nazis doing outside of a horror sim?" Ariane whispered, waving Seph and Coto back into cover. The sex district, bars, and cheap residential capsule stacks had given way to bond stores, warehouses, and light industrial fabs as they'd approached the docks via an indirect, circu-itous route chosen by Jula. They hung back now in a serviceway behind a storehouse filled with soylent concentrate, scoping out the shock troopers securing the facility.

"Coto," Ariane whispered, turning around in the narrow space to make sure he'd heard her. "You re-ally don't want to be walking out there and getting your sexy ol' skullhorn all up in their faces. Best back the fuck up, big guy."

Sephina eeled around her giant shipmate, giving him a reassuring pat on the back as she went past.

"Easy, JC. Let me check it out."

"I could just kill them," Coto said. "It would save time later."

"Yeah, good idea, I know, but you kill one of these paleofascist nut jobs and you have to fight a ten-year interstellar war with the whole race of walking-talking genocidal murder boners. Let's see if we can skip that bit and get to the part where we sneak away with the money we stole off the YG and let someone else do the hard work of bitch-slapping the master race."

"Okay," Coto said. "That is also a good idea."

They watched the troopers at the checkpoint for a few minutes, trying to gauge how many of the Sturm now secured Dock 13. The battle for Eassar raged on all around them, the far curve of the Hab still lit by the exotic tracery of weapons fire. But this section of the hull appeared to be under the invaders' control. A heavy landing craft bristling with guns had settled in front of the giant sliding doors to 13. The way through was open, however, and a platoon-sized detachment of troopers in black combat gear guarded the entrance. It was like plugging into a history sim. The padded black battle dress was instantly recognizable but also discernibly evolved from the designs of the Civil War. They seemed lightly armored compared with, say, Terran Diplomatic Enforcers or the heavy infantry of a major corporate power, but they still were loaded out with armor and arsenal enough to discourage any ideas about throwing down with them.

"I don't think we're going to be shooting our way through," Seph said quietly.

There was no vehicular plate traffic, but occasionally people would approach the troopers with their hands held above their heads. The Sturm treated them warily, yelling in old-fashioned Volume Standard for the Hab rats—and they were all Hab rats—to lie facedown with their hands and legs splayed out as widely as possible. A single trooper would then approach, scanning them with a handheld device while the others kept their weapons trained.

"Laser targeting!" Ariane said with a note of wonder in her voice. "Fuck me. They're using lasers as target designators. Probably for their spears and arrows."

"No," Sephina said. "I think the laser designators are just to scare the shit out of people. Let them know they're marked and if they twitch even a little, they're gonna get shredded."

They watched the pantomime play out three times. A local would come up on the Sturm carefully, submit to the security check, talk to the trooper on point, and wait. After a minute or so, a squad of three or four was detached from the main body and left the area with the Hab rat leading the way.

"Not hard to figure out what's going on," Ariane spit.

"Actually," Coto rumbled, "it is very hard . . ." He paused uncertainly.

"They're helping the Sturm because they hate the Combine," Jula explained to the horned giant. "Everyone hates the Combine. Look," she said, pointing with her free hand. The other held on to one of Jaddi Coto's enormous fingers.

As they watched, three troopers appeared from around a corner on the far side of the dock. A local man led them, almost skipping ahead of the group. Seph needed no special insight or data link to know he was a local. He had the sallow, underweight, slightly stooped, almost insectile look of somebody born to the deck plate. Poor nutrition, spin gravity, and the never-ending pressure of life at the bottom of the heap in Combine space would bow anyone down.

The prisoner did not look like that.

Seph immediately picked him out as managerial class, possibly even hereditary. He walked with no hunch to his shoulders or curve in his spine. There was no arrogance to his stride. He was too frightened for that. His arms were bound behind him at the elbows and wrists, and once or twice he tripped, as though unsure of his footing. That would happen when your heart was racing with terror and your lizard brain was pumping high-octane adrenergics and corticotropins directly into your bloodstream. She did wonder why he hadn't dosed himself to counteract the tsunami of neurotransmitters, but it wasn't the most pressing question of the hour, and she let it go. The man was expensively dressed and well fed, and his p-type was Nordic standard.

"The fuck was he doing in this part of the Hab?" Ariane asked.

"Slumming it in a gash capsule," Sephina speculated. "Or more likely checking the accounts to make sure the First Families were getting their standard 45 percent from the brothels' gross take."

"Ugh. Gross is right. Get a fucking job."

"Like space pirate?" Seph smiled.

"Being a space pirate is a very good job," Coto said.

"Can I be a space pirate?" Jula asked from behind the gigantic hybrid.

"Honey, we're gonna teach you to be the best space pirate ever," Ariane promised. "Just as soon as we get off this can."

They weren't the only people watching the docks. Seph scanned up and down the avenue and saw quite a few others taking in the show. The troopers didn't seem bothered by the audience. The weapons on the lander were probably pre–zeroed in on any potential trouble. Including them.

She edged back a little into the serviceway.

A single gunshot cracked out, and Ariane swore, flinching away from the corner of the warehouse.

"What happened?" Seph asked. She'd taken her eye off the troopers.

Ariane peeked around the corner again.

"They shot him," she said before adding, "in the

head. They just shot him in the head. No reason at all."

"Oh, I'm sure they had their reasons," Seph said. She moved forward at the same time she gestured for Coto to get back even farther with Jula. She and Ariane maneuvered awkwardly around each other.

The prisoner was on the ground, twitching, and a shock trooper, presumably an officer, was holstering a sidearm. Another patted the Hab rat snitch on the shoulder with a heavy gloved hand. He waved at the corpse with the same hand, and the man hurried forward to search the body. He retrieved a couple of small items from the dead man's pockets and showed them to the Sturm, who shrugged and waved him off. Two troopers dragged the dead man away by the feet. A dark, glistening smear from his mostly missing head traced the path of the corpse.

The Hab rat waved good-bye to the troopers, and they waved back.

"Friendly neighborhood," Ariane said.

"My mom really didn't like me coming down here much," Jula whispered.

Seph scoped out the other locals watching from the windows and doorways of nearby buildings and clustered like them at corners of the main strip and various serviceways. A few pointed. One even clapped. Nobody seemed very upset by the murder.

"Not much love for the Combies here," Seph said. "Come on. There's no way they're gonna let us walk through that front gate with Coto. Time to earn your first pirate proficiency badge, Jula. Show us how you and your little friends used to get in."

"There are badges?" Coto asked. "Why do I not have the badges?"

Turned out the problem wasn't getting to the *Regret*. The problem was getting the *Regret* off Eassar. Jula led them back up the serviceway for two minutes, turning left and right as she went, leading them deeper into the labyrinth of the light industrial and warehousing district before stopping at the rear of a bond store.

"Mister Shinobi keeps all his liquor here," she said.

Jula didn't explain who Mister Shinobi was, but she did produce a small black box from a pocket, placed it against the locking plate of the plasteel door, and stepped back as magnetic locks disengaged with solid metallic clunks.

"Sometimes it doesn't work and you get a shock," she explained.

"We'll take it from here, kid," Sephina said, unshipping her dragon shot. "What's inside?"

"Just stuff for Mister Shinobi's brothels and bars. Alcohol and drugs and things, you know."

A silent look passed among all three of the adults, and they each brought a weapon to hand. If Shinobi was any sort of businessman, he'd have more security on this place than a maglock with a flaky booby trap.

But he didn't.

Jula dismissed their excessive caution with an eye roll.

"All the *gunsotsu* are fighting the Sturm. And HabSec. And the crazy ones," she said.

Seph narrowed her eyes at the girl.

"Jula, did Mister Shinobi work for the Yakuza?"

"No. Mister Shinobi was the Yakuza. He was the plate boss here. But he went crazy. He tried to eat everyone. This was his." She held up the magnetic key. Sephina saw for the first time that it was covered with blood. Jula's fingers were stained as though by cherry juice.

Seph gave Ariane a truly epic side eye. "Well, that's just super," she said. "The kid's hooked up with the gummies."

Ariane waved her off. "Pfft, it's not like they could be any more pissed off at us. And you're forgetting we scoped corners for the Russians on Coriolis. You do what you gotta do down on the plate, Seph."

"Cinders didn't."

"And where is Cinders now? Probably feeding the digesters like Shinobi." Ariane turned to the girl. "Jula, which way, honey?"

She led them through into the storehouse. Any other day Seph would have been tempted to clean the place out or at least sample the top-shelf merch. They walked through pallets stacked high with vacuum-sealed pharma and bottles of sixty-year-old Tasmanian whiskey. She could smell cannabis and jujaweed. Coto swiped a box of real Jamaican cigars, and Ariane pocketed a small bottle of Chanel pheromone concentrate.

"For when we get a little time later." She grinned. She was enjoying this.

Seph felt herself stirring as she always did when Ariane gave her that look, but she clamped down on it.

"We gotta get out of here first," she reminded them.

Jula led them upstairs to a mezzanine level and from there into a series of offices and storerooms. She seemed completely at home. At one point they climbed a ladder into the roof space, and Coto was forced to crawl where the others crouched. After fifteen minutes traversing a maze of interconnected buildings in which Seph became utterly lost, they descended to plate level again and into a machine shop of some kind. Jula led them to another door.

"Bay Seven," she announced.

Sephina wiped the grime off a small view port and smiled at what she found outside.

The *Je Ne Regrette Rien*.

"Oh, baby, we're back," she said.

They did not have good vision of the docking bay. Sephina could see that the ship wasn't clamped. In fact it looked ready for departure, and her heart skipped forward a beat or two. No fucking way would Banks and Kot ever bug out on them, but seeing the *Regret*'s clearance lights blinking and hearing the low hum of the displacer field as the vessel floated gently in its berth, she had a momentary pang of concern, the anxiety of a child forsaken more than enough times to know that loss and abandonment were a natural state of being.

Some things happened then.

Coto announced, "We can talk to the ship again," waving at the figure of Falun Kot in the pilot's blister at the front of the craft. Kot waved back. Frantically. Pointing.

The doors nearest to them in the ship's rear loading bay rumbled open with the hiss of escaping over-pressure.

And two shock troopers standing just a couple of meters away, where they'd been out of Seph's line of sight, raised their assault rifles and started shouting obscenities, mostly about putting their fucking weapons down and getting their fucking hands up.

Then Coto emerged fully from the doorway, and they stopped shouting and started firing.

He roared in pain and rage as two bright orange lines of automatic plasma fire converged on him, quickly chewing up the null-charge nanotube weave of his duster. Seph loosed two bursts from the dragon shot that rocked the troopers back on their heels but did no appreciable damage. The impact did queer their aim, however, and both lines of plasmatic tracer fire curved up and away, destroying large swaths of the dense tangle of conduit and piping that ran overhead. Alarms followed explosions. Fire-retardant gas jetted in from all directions, and the deep thunderous bass note of a point defense cannon pounded at her ears for a full second. The *Regret* had taken the troopers under fire with her gun pods. The whipping, uncontrolled lines of plasma fire abruptly disappeared. So did the troopers, turned into pink mist.

"Run!" Seph shouted, but everybody was already sprinting for the open hatch.

Amplified voices yelling orders in old Volume Standard demanded that they surrender and disarm even as a torrent of kinetics and plasma fire reached out for them through the fog of flame retardant and the steam suddenly venting from the *Regret*'s heat sinks.

Coto charged around Sephina, putting his greater bulk and armored hide between them and the Sturm. But she didn't imagine he'd survive more than a few seconds once the shock troopers zeroed in on him with mil-grade firepower.

"Just get on the fucking ship, Coto," she yelled at him over the uproar, kicking him in his enormous hybrid ass for good measure.

Seph pumped two more useless shots downrange, saw Ariane leaping into the hold, and calmed down just a little. It was going to be okay; they were going to make it onto the ship.

Ariane leaped out of the hold and ran back into the cross fire.

"*Jula!* Where are you, baby?"

"Oh, for fuck's sake, *no!*" Seph cried out.

She reversed herself, spinning around and charging away from safety. Ariane was almost standing still, one hand raised to her ear like some sort of ridiculous character in an old sim. The Crazy Lady Haunting the Haunted Moors Searches Through the Fog and Terror of Night for Her . . .

"Ariane, get on the fucking ship!" Sephina yelled.

But her words were lost in the apocalyptic roar of the *Regret*'s forward point defenses coming online and opening up on the Sturm. The twin TenixAMD gun pods each loaded out with three revolving barrels, spinning at a thousand revs per minute and vomiting out a solid stream of superhardened hexa-boron nitride pellets at a small but significant percentage of light speed.

Of course, anything traveling at even a tiny percentage of light speed was significant when it struck you because of that whole mass, speed, and energy deal.

The troopers disappeared, atomized as the tiny pellets transferred their kinetic energy to everything they hit. Flesh, blood, armor, bulkhead, carbon panels, plasteel plate—whatever the Sturm's heavy lander was made of—all came apart in a tiny storm of relativistic chaos.

Seph was blown off her feet. The heat and light scorched every inch of her exposed skin and blinded her for a moment. She struggled back to her feet, leaning into a roaring wind that raked at her flash-burned face and tore at the shredded duster whipping around her.

Banks, the crazy fucker, had shot his load clean through the Hab. Eassar was venting atmosphere from the exit wound.

"Ariane!"

She was knocked off her feet again, this time by Coto, who swept her up in his arms and carried her toward the *Regret*.

"Coto, no! Put me down! I have to find Ariane."

And then there she was.

Her shipmate and her soul. Her one true love. Running toward the *Regret* from the far end of the bay, the girl thrown over her shoulder.

"Hurry up!" Seph yelled over the uproar.

Ariane looked up, saw her lover, and beamed.

She loved this stuff.

Half a dozen targeting lasers settled on her center mass.

Seph tried to cry out a warning, but terror would not let her. It felt as though an invisible hand had closed around her throat. Ariane's expression changed from fierce joy and triumph to confusion as she noticed the target designators. Confusion turned to horror when she saw that two of the dots had picked out Jula, too.

The Sturm fired, but she moved with animal swiftness, sidestepping the aim of her hunters in a blur of free-flowing motion. Seph's heart soared with blessed relief. Ariane was a spark. A glimmer of pure movement. She threaded through the storm of white-hot plasma as though she might dance within it yet for hours. Her lover was as beautiful in that moment as Sephina L'trel had ever known her to be.

And then Ariane and Jula died inside three converging lines of plasma fire.

CHAPTER

TWENTY-FOUR

In all the books Alessia had read—real books of paper and ink, rare and precious heirlooms of Old Earth—adventures were most thrilling when her favorite characters were in headlong flight from mortal peril. More than once Lady Melora had caught her reading well after her bedtime, the lights out, the pages closely illuminated under the covers by a tiny hummingbird drone she used as a nightlight. It was hard to sleep when Frodo and Sam might be eaten by Shelob the Spider or when Reiko and Órlaith stood shoulder to shoulder against the cannibal hordes of Pyongyang. Those adventures were wonderfully enthralling. They were exciting.

This adventure sucked balls.

Sometimes they crept, and sometimes they ran through darkening streets—sometimes crowded, sometimes empty—always haunted by the threat of the soldiers who were looking for them. Hunting them. That alone was a new and very difficult idea for Alessia to understand. She had always been surrounded by soldiers, of course. On any given day there were more than a hundred guardsmen at Skygarth and even more in the barracks in Port au Pallice. And when she traveled to court there were more still, thousands of them at times, all sworn to protect her House and her person with their lives.

Now the whole world seemed to be full of soldiers who were just as determined to kill her, and the only soldier she had left was Sergeant Reynolds.

"Wait up here, little miss," he cautioned as they lurked in an alleyway that opened up onto a wide piazza seething with crowds. Sergeant Reynolds had stopped calling her "Your Highness." It wasn't safe. The piazza in front of them was large, but it wasn't the main square of Port au Pallice. Alessia had been there many times for parades and speeches and town fairs and even market days. There was a bronze statue in the middle of that square depicting the sire of her House, Louis Montanblanc, standing with one foot on a boulder, pointing off to the horizon. In the statue, he was just plain Louis. Not chairman and chief executive of the Montanblanc–ul Haq Alliance of Corporate Worlds. Plain Louis, founder of an asteroid mining start-up. A young man in his second span who was about to found one of the great High Houses.

No sign of Louis here. But there was a crowd gathered in front of a stage where musicians might play during the weekend markets. Sergeant Reynolds was mostly blocking her view of the scene, holding her and Caro back behind him with one arm. Debin weaved under the outstretched hand to get a better look.

"It's them. The Sturm," he said, turning around.

His eyes were red and his nose was running, but he was no longer crying. They were all too exhausted and, frankly, too terrified to think about his grandpa. He'd told them he'd be fine. Caro and Debin were hanging on to that promise with desperate hope.

"Who are all those people?" Caro asked.

As she spoke, the sound of cheering reached them. Alessia did not understand. Who would cheer the invaders?

"Basic bludgers and layabouts," Reynolds grumbled. "Troublemakers, too, no doubt. Agitators, bloody shareholder advocates. That sort of malcontent and subverter."

"But I'm a shareholder," Alessia protested.

Reynolds bent down to her and whispered.

"You're a hereditary class A voting shareholder, Your Highness. Some small investors without voting rights are always likely to cause trouble at the Annual General Meeting. Bloody fools and knaves if they think the Sturm will give 'em anything but a rope around the neck. Come on, we can't go through here. We'll have to backtrack and circle around."

"Wait," Caro said. "Look."

Alessia squirmed around Reynolds's massive bulk. He was wearing an old coat and britches he'd gotten off Mister Dunning. She'd seen the gardener wearing them around Skygarth. They did not really fit Sergeant Reynolds, and they really did not smell good. But she put up with the stinky reek to get a look at whatever Caro had seen.

Somebody, the troopers, she supposed, had erected a big screen in front of the stage. It was an old-fashioned thing, just a big white sheet, really, like common folk sometimes put up out of doors at night in the warmer months to show classic movies, as they were called. Just moving pictures and words, not proper sims. It was an art form as old as her books but a lot more popular. Probably because they were cheaper.

It was not yet fully dark in the piazza, but they were well into the twilight hour, and the images, when they appeared on the screen, were bright and clear.

Alessia froze. Reynolds tried to cover her eyes, and that got her moving again. She wriggled away from him. She couldn't hear anything but shouts and cheering from the crowd, but she could see what was happening in the movie.

Her mother, her brothers and sisters at court, her uncles and cousins—she stopped trying to account for them all. It seemed the entirety of her family was up there. It looked like they were in the grounds of the palace in the capital. And they were all on their knees. A black-clad trooper stood behind each of them. Her mother struggled, as did her oldest brother, Danton. He was almost of age now and soon would take up a seat on the board. Her uncle Benyamin looked as if he might have fainted. He hung limp in the grip of an enemy soldier. Most of her family, however, seemed to have lost their minds to the same violent derangement that had taken over Lady Melora. They were restrained with chains or rope or plasteel ties or something. It was hard to tell from this distance.

Reynolds tried to drag her away, but she shouted at him, "No!"

Long devoted service had not conditioned him to disobey such an emphatic command, and his hands dropped away from her shoulders. She would wish later that he had been less obedient.

The soldiers seemed to move as one, drawing long curved knives from behind their backs. The blades glowed with some form of power source, and the crowd noise seemed to grow twice as loud. Alessia's heart was pounding, and she suddenly needed to pee.

She gasped, and the gasp turned into a scream as the soldiers killed her family with those cruel curved blades. It was . . . it was such a simple, terrible thing they did. Pulling back the head. Opening the throat. Murdering her family. A hand clamped over her mouth, small and soft. It was Debin. He pulled her head aside, away from the terrible sight, but much too late.

She had seen.

A blackness rolled over her in waves, and she all but fainted into Debin's arms. Reynolds hurried to pick her up, and Alessia felt herself lifted over his shoulder again. This time, however, she did not pass out. She felt dizzy and sick with horror. They hurried down the narrow alley between two buildings of whitewashed stone, but that world of real things was overlain with the memory of a soldier pulling her mother's head clear off her body and waving it to the crowd. She tried to unsee the horror, but she could not. Riotous whooping and shouting followed them as they fled the piazza. Tremors seized Alessia deep in her core, threatening to grow into full-body convulsions.

She vomited over Reynolds, but he neither complained nor slowed down.

"Why would they do that?" she whimpered, and wasn't quite sure whether she was asking about the soldiers or the crowd.

Debin ran ahead, Caro followed a few steps behind. She looked as sick as Alessia felt. The alleyway ran through a district busy with eating houses and ale shops. The smell of garbage in recycling and compost bins was cloying and made her feel even more nauseated.

"Put me down. Please," she said. "I'll be all right."

To her surprise, Sergeant Reynolds did slow down and lower her to the cobblestones.

A ridiculous question occurred to her.

Why cobblestones and not maglev plates?

She let it go.

"Are you okay, Your Highness?" Reynolds asked, looking up and down the poorly lit passageway, apprehensive about being followed. Alessia realized with a jolt that he was crying. Not bawling like she might if she fell over and scraped her knee. He was a grown-up and a soldier, too. But his eyes brimmed with tears.

"I'm sorry, Princess," he said. "I should not have let you see that."

He blinked, and the tears that had been welling suddenly broke free and ran down his face.

Alessia wiped the back of her hand on his cheeks.

"I didn't see my father. Or the rest of the board," she said. Her breath came in shuddering gulps, and she struggled to regain control of it.

"No." Reynolds sniffed. He rubbed at his eyes and

face much more roughly than she had done. "They're not onworld right now. Your father was at Montanblanc One with Louis. The other board members . . ." He shrugged. "I'm not sure, but they will probably have been all over the Volume, managing things."

Debin and Caro crowded in around her. Caro gave her a hug, and after a moment's hesitation her brother joined in.

"I'm sorry, Alessia. I'm so sorry," she said.

"Me, too," Debin added. His face was buried in her neck, and his voice was muffled. She could feel him shaking.

"Thank you," Alessia said quietly. She looked up at Reynolds. "And thank you, Sergeant. I will make sure my father knows how you helped me."

Reynolds looked troubled by something, but he put the thought aside.

"First thing we have to do, ma'am, is get you to Jasko Tan and off this world, or at least this part of it."

She nodded assent.

The sound of revelry drifted up from the direction of the piazza. It clashed with distant gunfire and the loud booms of explosions. The world had gone mad.

"Why did they . . ." Alessia started, then paused, collected her thoughts, and continued. "Why were those people so happy? Do they hate me? My mother? All of us?"

That was the real question. She knew why the Sturm had executed them. She had the best history tutors in the Volume, and as was her family's peculiar custom, they had taught her the old way, with reading and writing and talking.

So. Much. Talking.

She knew the Sturm had killed her family as "oppressors" and "race traitors." She also knew they'd be killing lots more people, because anyone without a "pure" genome just wasn't a real person to them. And they felt nearly as strongly about neural mesh and bioware. They called it "profane." But the people in the square, her people, why had they been so gleeful, so quick to go over to the enemy?

Reynolds seemed to ponder the question. For a moment he stopped worrying and checking whether they'd been followed.

"This is a good place, Princess," he said. "The port, Skygarth. The whole world, really. But it's a big place, too. It's full of people, and people are all different. Not everyone lives as easy a life as you."

She bristled at that, and he saw it.

"I don't mean you don't have to work hard," Reynolds hurried on. "I see you doing your lessons and duties. You're a good girl. But most people work hard, Alessia."

She was so surprised at being called by her name that she almost lost track of what he was saying.

"And not everyone gets to live in a palace and have all the nice things."

She stared at him.

"They cut my mother's head off. And those people cheered."

Reynolds sighed, suddenly looking very tired and old.

"They did. And if the Sturm catch us, they'll do the same again. So best we get moving while things are confused. They'll have the whole town locked down soon enough."

Sergeant Reynolds seemed to know the town as well as Debin and Caro knew the gardens of Skygarth. Hurrying down backstreets, diverting into cut-throughs, skirting around neighborhoods where the fighting and rioting seemed most intense, he delivered them to a quiet street on the very edge of the settlement late at night. Alessia's legs hurt. Her feet throbbed, and she was so hungry that it felt like a dull knife in her stomach. And always, with every step, she was beset by the memory of what they had done to her mother and the rest of her family. It was horrifying, but she tried to console herself with the idea that they had all been lifestreaming to secure backup, and that backup was engineered with nearly infinite redundancy.

She didn't understand how that worked yet. It would be many years before she attended university on Montanblanc One . . .

If that ever happened now, she thought.

But as night stole over the town and they crept through the contested streets and alleyways of Port au Pallice, Alessia forced herself to believe it would turn out well. The Sturm were here, but they could not threaten Earth. They could not even have reached Montanblanc's main Habs and colony worlds. The nearest of them lay six months away by deepest fold. Earth was nearly two years' travel in the fastest ship. The Congress would have news of the attack via wormhole link, of course. That took no time at all.

And already the High Houses and the independent and allied Commonwealths such as Armadale and Cupertino would be marshaling their fleets and forces. The first ships of the mighty Terran Defense Force, larger and more powerful than all the combined navies of the Bourse, already would have sortied to mete a great and furious vengeance upon the Sturm's war fleets.

Everything would be fine in the end. It would be.

But Alessia could not help worrying. What if her mother could not relife? What if the Sturm had already folded into space directly over the Earth? What if they didn't make it to this Jasko Tan? What if . . .

"We're here, Princess," Reynolds said softly.

They were clear of the town, which lay behind and below them on Pallice Bay. The sound of sporadic gunfire still rolled up the gentle hills from the bay, and every few minutes the night flashed with the discharges of energy weapons. Some buildings, some entire streets, were afire. But up here, away from the danger, everything was quiet. They cut through plowed fields and open meadows and finally through vineyards, occasionally seeing others like them also fleeing the town. Aircraft flew overhead every now and then, their strange old-fashioned engines shrieking and roaring. The sound was as much a terror as the threat of weapons fire.

"Jets," Reynolds explained the first time she flinched away. "It's good, Your Highness. If they're using jets instead of displacer fields, it means their tech has not advanced much."

They seemed to be doing just fine as far as Alessia could tell.

They crouched at the end of a long line of grapevines. A cluster of farm buildings lay a short distance away. A stone-built home and much larger modern-looking sheds full of shiny metal vats and silos. There were lights on, but not many. Just enough to walk around without tripping over or bumping into something. Alessia crouched on one knee between Caro and Debin. She could smell the grape juice and the loamy soil. It reminded her of Skygarth, the peace and simplicity of it.

"I'm going to go ahead and make sure everything is okay," Reynolds said in a low voice. "You three stay here and wait for me. If anything happens, if anything is wrong, you'll hear me start shooting. If you do, you need to run."

He turned to Caro.

"Your grandpa had a fishing shack in the Bluestone Hills, on Run o' Waters Creek. He ever take you there?"

She nodded.

"Could you find it on your own if you had to?"

The siblings exchanged an uncertain look, but Caro said, "Yes."

"Good," said Reynolds. "I'm not expecting trouble, but if there is, you take the princess there. You stay there until I come to get you or somebody else does. There are other men in the guard who knew your grandfather. They will know to look there. You'll be safe. And there will be food enough for a week or two. Old Tosh always kept the place well stocked."

Reynolds knitted his brow as though glaring fiercely at Debin.

"Do not drink the beer."

Debin shook his head quickly.

"No, sir."

"*No, Sergeant,* young man. I'm not a sir. I work for a living."

Alessia smiled. She had heard him say that so many times.

"Right, then," Reynolds said. "No sense delaying what must be done. Be ready to run if you have to. Stay together. Look after each other. But don't worry. Jasko is a rogue, but he owes me, and we can trust him."

"Be careful," Alessia said.

Reynolds nodded and moved away. He didn't approach the farmhouse directly, instead ghosting around the edge of the illuminated area until he'd disappeared into the gloom.

The three children were alone.

"Do you really know how to get to your grandpa's shack?" Alessia asked.

Caro didn't answer at first, but Debin jumped in.

"For sure," he said. "I've been there plenty of times. It's great. I love it."

"Yeah, but could you get us there?" his sister asked. "I'm . . . I'm not sure of the way."

He rolled his eyes. The whites seemed very bright in the dark.

"We just follow the road to the peninsula until we find the inn at Five Mile," he said. "Then you take the smaller road to the hills and get off that at the old covered bridge over the creek. You follow the track by the creek for a bit and you're there. I can do it."

"But how will we know anybody is coming for

us?" Caro asked. Her voice was tight and clipped. "Or if someone does come, how do we know we can trust them if it's not Sergeant Reynolds?"

"If it's a guardsman, we can trust him," Debin said.

"Or her," Alessia said. "There are girl guardsmen, too."

"But how would we know?" Caro repeated more insistently. "They won't be in uniform, will they? Reynolds isn't."

"I'll know them," Alessia assured her. "I know all the guards. I have to. It might even be your grandpa, Caro," she said. "Sergeant Reynolds said he's really tough and he's gotten out of much worse trouble than this."

"Yeah!" Debin said, suddenly lighting up with the possibility. "It could, Caro. It could be Grandpa."

Caro said nothing. She just shook her head.

Debin started to argue with her, but Reynolds suddenly appeared in the door of the biggest shed. A smaller man carrying a gun stood next to him. They waved the children over.

"But . . ." said Debin. "But I wanted to go to the fishing hut with Grandpa."

Caro dragged him up a little more roughly than she really needed to. Alessia almost told her to be gentle. Debin was just a little kid, but before she could say anything, Caro had pushed the boy ahead of them, and Alessia could see she was crying again. Not crazy weeping or anything. Just quietly crying.

"Come on," Alessia said. "He'll be all right."

They jogged over to Reynolds and the other man.

"Your Highness, may I present Mister Jasko Tan, formerly of the Guards Regiment, now retired."

The little dark-haired man seemed very surprised to see her. He looked Alessia up and down a few times as if to convince himself it was she and not some sim character.

"I'm sorry," he said, bowing. "Your Highness, I forget myself. I am at your service, naturally."

"Thank you, Mister Tan," she said. "And these are my friends Caro and Debin. They'll have to come with us wherever we're going."

"Dunning's kids, right?" Tan asked Sergeant Reynolds.

"Grandkids."

"Okay, good. That's good."

He raised his gun and shot Reynolds in the head before turning the weapon on the three children. Alessia screamed. Caro, too.

"Get down! Lie down now!" he shouted.

Debin gaped at Reynolds as the old soldier dropped to the hard floor with a sick, wet thump. Half of his head was missing.

Doors crashed open, and Republican shock troopers stormed through. More dropped from the rafters high above, whizzing down on fast ropes, pointing their guns at the children and yelling, "Don't move!"

Jasko Tan carefully laid the weapon down next to Reynolds. A spreading pool of dark blood flowed under the gun.

Alessia stared at him.

He looked so . . . so normal.

Another man, bearded, very tall, and heavily built,

marched over, his combat boots loud on the concrete floor.

He looked down at all three children, and for a terrifying second Alessia thought he was going to kill them all right then and there.

"Alessia Montanblanc," he said. "I am Captain Kogan D'ur, Force Recon, Second Shock Regiment of the Forces of the Human Republic. You are under arrest for crimes against humanity."

CHAPTER
TWENTY-FIVE

McLennan powered down the displacer drive as Batavia's harsh sun slowly peeked above the edge of the Ironstone Desert. The little stealth craft had done its job; he'd arrived at his chosen vantage point undetected, drained the last of his caffeinated whiskey from the thermos, and waited for his bugs to find their way home. Until then he'd had to make do with the lensing function built into the sled's forward canopy. It provided a decent telescopic view of the site, 15× at full resolution, but he had to point the nose of the vehicle wherever he wanted to look.

The Sturm had been busy. The colossal hulk of the *Voortrekker* lay as it had for centuries, a crumpled reddish-black beached-whale shape sinking slowly into the desert. From what he could see, the Sturm kept a respectful distance from the ancient wreck. He assumed they would have their own specialist dig teams onsite soon enough.

He wished he could stream the take to Hero for analysis. There was a lot that didn't make sense to him. But he could not afford any signal leakage, and so he waited and surveyed what he could from afar.

The layout of the base seemed straightforward; any Roman legionary would have recognized the rows of lozenge-shaped shelters as barracks of a kind. Of course, that legionary would not have been able to actually "see" the structures—they were artfully camouflaged, nearly invisible to the human eye. If McLennan hadn't had the sled's sensors, his deteriorating vision wouldn't have detected much beyond the movement in the camp. But there was much of that: thousands of troopers stomping through the sand and grit, engineers erecting ever larger and more complicated structures, supply trains moving in constant exchanges between the camp and the dropships.

And even the steadiest centurion would have freaked the fuck out at the dropships, McLennan conceded. They were huge, dark, and scarred with the inevitable impacts and abrasions of long months, maybe years, in space. The discus shape would have been the only familiar detail of the design. Everything else would have been impossibly bizarre. The future was not just another country. It was another, deeply alien world, Mac thought, pleased with the analogy.

The expeditionary base, like the dropships that spawned it, was shaped like a large wheel. It was quartered by roads, and each quarter seemed to have its own function. One quarter, the farthest away from where he lurked, was devoted to the *Voortrekker*. Not much was happening there. Frazer picked at a chunk of goat meat stuck between his teeth. He wondered if the bastards had sent in priests and imams and all of their other holy men to bless and cleanse the site. He wondered if the Sturm still bothered with religion at all.

Another quarter of the camp seemed devoted to housing and administration. That sector was the closest. He watched Sturm troopers scurrying about and wondered where they'd put the shitters. There had to be some commandment or standing order about not shitting too close to a sacred site. Was there some ritual purification beyond burning their own jobbies, or did they recycle them, like ships and Habs? He wanted to know everything. Every detail large and small. It was so long since these creatures had cut themselves out of the human evolutionary story, so long since they'd been exiled into the Dark. And here he was, the leading expert on them, and he didn't even know how they took a dump nowadays.

McLennan zoomed in on one of the distant troopers and studied her for a few minutes. Darkly complected, about 1.8 meters tall, with a heavily muscular build. Like him, she would be "purebred." That, after all, was the core faith and practice of the Sturm. No genomic interventions. No implants. No bioware.

Looking at the woman, he did not doubt she could break every bone in his body without raising a sweat even out here in the deep Ironstone. But otherwise he saw nothing particularly remarkable about her, and so he moved on with his survey.

He glanced at the quarter devoted to shuttlecraft and troopships. That area was bustling with activity. He turned off the rendering apps and tried looking at it with his natural vision, but all he saw was a lot of dust and some odd shapes that appeared to be distortions of the desert floor. Every now and then he would see curious disembodied forms that were imperfectly camouflaged. He switched on the full sensor display again and was rewarded with clear vision of the ground crews and transporters.

What made him scratch his head was the final quarter, which was devoted to objects he couldn't identify. Curious oblong forms, arcane machines, and rows of . . . stuff. Troopers moved among the equipment, if that was what it was, and . . . did things. He snorted. This was some medal-winning recon right here. He could imagine reporting back to an imaginary supervisor as a younger officer.

"Yeah, on one part of the base was all this stuff, and the bad guys did things."

What was he not seeing?

A phrase learned long ago floated up from his memories. "Priorities of work. First step, ensure local security." For a certainty, the Sturm owned this stretch of desert now. If he made one error, he was dead. For real. His left hand trembled ever so slightly. He needed to know what was in that mysterious last quarter.

But first he had to make it past the perimeter defenses. For sure, the Sturm had pushed listening posts out into the desert around the base. And there were bound to be patrols. He'd picked up movement on his left flank half an hour ago, about a klick away. It could have been desert rats or fire vipers; it could have been a rifle company. But they were out there somewhere.

McLennan bit down on his fears and made a decision.

Aye, time to shit or get off the damn pot, man.

One way or another, he would see what there was to see and he would get the hell out. His face set in hard lines, and a drop of sweat stung his eye. He marked the position in camp he wanted to inspect and spoke to the AI.

"Sled, bring us to 43.157, marked. Covert protocols to maximum."

"Be advised, we have been traveling in that mode since we separated from the main convoy."

"Just shut up and do it. And tread soft as a baby's bottom, hear."

"That is a very confusing euphemism. Please clarify."

"I'll clarify your fucking arse for you. Just get into yon camp where I dropped the damn waymarker and don't get caught."

"Acknowledged, Admiral."

Frazer felt no lift, but he did see his perspective rise. The little Miyazaki craft followed an air current on an indirect course toward his objective. He swallowed hard and felt the weight of years as he drifted through the dawn sky.

After what seemed an age, he passed over the camp's perimeter. He looked directly down at a vehicle prowling the fence line. He let out a breath. He'd half expected to be blown from the sky by some unknown air defense system. Surely, he thought, there must be intruder alerts popping off all over a threat board somewhere. But the sled had passed through the outer lines of the camp without incident. He was inside the wire.

Inside the wire, he thought. There was a phrase even older than he, and there weren't many things these days you could say that about. The lines of his face deepened as he assumed a sardonic expression. Why was he even doing this? Why did he not just take his damned rest centuries ago? It was ridiculous, a man of his age, creeping about at the edge of the known worlds, his arse truly, deeply, fulsomely puckered with fear. This was a young man's quest.

Aye, but the young men, and women, too, he'd tried to warn about the inevitability of the Sturm's return—they had not been much interested, had they? Especially when he suggested that for all the advantages, including virtual omnipresence and omniscience, afforded by the zero point wormhole network, it also negated the advantages of defense in depth conferred by the vast expanse of the Greater Volume. The Human Republic could mass the entirety of its strength at the borders of the Volume, enough to overwhelm the combined forces of the Great Houses. But the heart of human civilization remained on Earth, and Earth remained at least two years away on the fastest ship to fold the fabric of space-time. That sense of security bred an unforgivable complacency, and that was why he was here, wasn't it? Because somebody had to be.

The sled drifted through the enemy camp at a height of fifty meters, more than enough to clear the tallest structure the Sturm had erected. He passed over two Sturm troopers in what looked to be powered armor. The sensors had no trouble picking up their conversation. They spoke in old Volume Standard, the language of his youth, and he strained to understand them. It had been many spans since he'd spoken the archaic form, although he still read it nearly every day. The documentation and signage on the *Voortrekker* was all written in VS.

As McLennan passed directly over them, the man with a long-barreled rifle said, "Rodriguez went to take another shit."

"Again?" A woman with an Asian phenotype, maybe heirloom Korean or Japanese, rolled her eyes.

"Fuckin' yeah. Combat drop upset his delicate tum-tum."

The guy with the rifle laughed, and so did the woman.

Mac tuned them out and pressed on. He longed to run an active scan on their body armor; it was of a pliable type he had never seen. But he didn't dare turn on his high-gain sensors. He was recording everything his passive arrays could soak up, but there wasn't a lot of signal leakage to be had. These bastards were tight.

He had made one provision for disaster. If his craft was detected and target locked, all of his data would be sent out via an encrypted nanosecond burst. Herodotus would get it and do with the information what he could. Even without a ship, that was something.

But McLennan did rather intend to live through these sneak-and-peek shenanigans. His craft was drifting like dust motes, adjusting ever so slightly to stay on course with small puffs of compressed air. He passed over the enemy barracks without a sound. The occupants' thermal signatures were well cloaked, but his own eyes could tell him that thousands of troopers lay beneath him as he made his slow, erratic approach to Q4.

A shuttle took off to his right with a roar of fuel-burning engines. Destination unknown. It was a fat, bulbous beast. To his experienced eye it would hold at least a company of soldiers with full kit. He frowned and wished them bad luck. Alas, it did not crash, simply climbing away into the heavens on a bright white exhaust plume. To where, he knew not. He checked his own destination, coordinate 43.157, and saw some kind of tower under construction. The scaffolding faded in and out of his view as the Sturm's stealth technology struggled to hide it from his more advanced sensors. Or at least he assumed they were more advanced. Their threat detectors hadn't picked him up yet.

He wondered if it was some form of communications structure but shook his head. Nothing so crude had been used for centuries. But then again, with these people, who knew? Another data point to file away. His bladder was full nearly to bursting, but he resisted relieving himself in the suit. It would recycle the water, filtering out 100 percent of the waste products. But he had never enjoyed the experience of pissing himself and sitting in his own waste fluid. Only Yorkshiremen ever really got used to that.

The sled crept up on his objective at the speed of the morning breeze. Four knots, according to the readout. He kept glancing at his instruments. It seemed that he checked his threat readout every half second. His mouth was dry as dust, but his hand was steady.

Frazer remembered that it had always been so. Before the mission, fear. During the mission, concentration. After the mission, depletion. Well, the mission wasn't close to being done. He had 300 meters to go. A red pulse appeared on his visual, with script. He had directed the sled to go visual-only during the sneak or it would have spoken to him.

McLennan swallowed, but his throat was dry. What nasty little surprises did the buggers have in there? He crept closer still. Two hundred meters. A formation of Sturm troopers moved beneath him, almost close enough to touch. They weren't marching, but they were moving with a purpose.

And their purpose, he thought, was murder. Not to be too fucking dramatic about it, but they did intend to put an end to the civilization he had tried to protect all of his lives. With a hammering heart, he floated yet closer. He tried a breathing exercise to stave off hyperventilating. His face was set in a grimace. Data poured into his little craft's passive arrays. It appeared that he was looking at an ordnance and command compound. The fourth quarter was the beating heart of the Sturm presence on this planet.

The patterns and equipment were entirely unfamiliar, but the verdict was in. This was the spot he would have to strike. Satisfied, McLennan silently directed the craft to exfil.

Perhaps an errant current of air gave him away. Perhaps it was some minuscule leakage from the stealthed drive system. Maybe somebody just looked at him right.

His entire visual field flashed red. Any number of weapons systems were suddenly trying to track him, but they didn't have a lock yet. He wanted like anything to tell his craft to run, but he knew that was certain death. Instead, it crept away like a dune dog looking for its den. Mac heard shouts from below. Sturm soldiers were looking to the sky. One looked directly at him, then looked away.

Bugger this for a game of soldiers, he thought. But they still hadn't found him; he was not target locked. McLennan wanted to pat the little Miyazaki flier. He wanted to kiss the stealth system's designer.

And then someone on the ground made a decision, and everything went sideways. As McLennan watched helplessly, every Sturm soldier within sight raised a weapon to the sky and began to fire randomly. With crystal clarity, he watched a trooper point his rifle at him from a distance of about twenty meters. McLennan directed his faithful sled to make haste, stealth be damned. But the trooper fired first.

Everything happened too fast for him to register it as a discrete event. Impact blooms on his windscreen. Flashing damage lights. The drive screeching in an unpleasant whine. The world turning over. The ground rushing at him. Impact. The shattering of things.

He woke up some indeterminate time later to pain and the sight of an assault rifle trained on him, with a shock trooper behind it.

"In the name of the Human Republic, you're my prisoner, asshole."

CHAPTER
TWENTY-SIX

The maintenance skiff was less of a spacecraft than a strap-on. If Booker had not downloaded to the Compliance Mech, he couldn't have used the skiff to escape at all. Basically an exoskeleton with booster rockets, the skiff provided mobility for engineering mechs during extravehicular and X-Hab deployments. Booker looked over the shuttle they were supposed to ride out, checking it for anything that he might salvage, specifically for weapons and fuel cells, but it was shot to hell and then some. It was the skiff or nothing.

He tried to fit his damaged and much degraded mech chassis into the maintenance rig, but although it was more than large enough, the hard points didn't match up. He established a wireless datalink without a problem, but the rig wasn't designed to plug and play with the chassis he now wore. It didn't help, either, that he looked like he'd been through an industrial grinder. And that one of his arms was a giant improvised cannon and the other a trijointed grappler designed for subduing human prisoners, not modding and operating machinery.

Booker stepped the mech out of the maintenance rig and stood back, contemplating it. The mech's proprioceptors felt the Hab shake with a series of detonations, and his one functioning audio intake registered the crackle of gunfire. He had to make this work and quickly. He also had to ignore the fact that the details of his escape plan thinned out pretty radically beyond the bit where he jumped into space. He'd have to make up some shit after that. If he didn't get away from the Sturm, however, there would be no need for more detailed plans or cunning schemes or anything. They'd delete him, blow him up, or just throw him down the gravity well of the nearest planet and let the reentry burn take care of business.

The mech rattled and clanked and made a long grinding noise as he circled the rig. Booker considered tying himself to the skiff with the rest of his synthetic arachnid silk. His tank was nearly full, but webbing a couple of tons of damaged Compliance Mech to a couple more tons of maintenance skiff and firing up the booster rockets long enough to jump clear of a prison Hab seemed a poor choice. That stuff was meant to secure soft and squishy human prisoners, not heavy machinery. However, this shuttle bay was also a maintenance depot, and it should have something he could use.

Ignoring the noise of battle and random detonations that sent shudders through the Hab, Booker methodically searched the bay. Ten minutes later he had eighteen unbroken feet of heavy chain: the real stuff, too, tempered graphene steel, not bullshit plasteel. Even better, at least to his mind, was a fat black roll of duct tape woven from carbon nanorods. Using a belt-and-braces approach, he spiderwebbed his damaged chassis into the exoskeleton with the synthetic silk, secured the mech's hip flexors with the heavy chain, and, as a final measure, duct-taped himself in as tightly and comprehensively as possible. The three-way ball joints of the grappler gave him much greater flexibility than a human arm, but even so it felt like a half-assed kludge, and he looked like something out of one of those amateur sims in which morons body-lost themselves on some stupid bet.

Hey, watch me surf this exhaust plume, dude!

He was so tightly strapped in that even moving to the air lock was a challenge, and he cursed himself for not having thought to kit up just outside the shuttle bay doors. Between battle damage and his own restraints, he estimated that he had only about 15 percent mobility. Trapped inside nearly five tons of salvage and scrap, he performed an ungainly, clanging heavy metal duck waddle to the inner bay door. It took five minutes to cover the thirty-meter distance. He nearly lost his footing when an unusually large shudder ran through the Hab. Booker rocked forward and back, and even though he was ensouled within an entirely mechanical construct, his mind conjured up the image of him pinwheeling his arms to regain his balance. For one drawn-out second, he saw himself crashing over backward and the Sturm finding him flat on his ass, his chained and taped-up arms and legs making tiny flailing movements as he tried in vain to get back to his feet. Like a turtle flipped over on its shell.

He recovered his balance and continued inching toward the shuttle bay doors. The grappler would have been easily able to work the push-button controls if he had not constrained its range of movement with so much duct tape. The final length of articulated claw was free of any binding; it was impossible to crucify yourself, after all. You just couldn't get that last nail in. But the two upper portions of the limb were heavily taped, and Booker nearly destroyed the control box when he tried to mash the big red button that would open the inner hatch. He tried again, maneuvering the entire bulk of the Compliance Mech to line up the padded claw with the box, but when he extended the giant robot finger, a damaged extensor rod messed up his aim and he missed the button entirely. Somewhere within the inanimate circuitry of the Compliance Mech, Booker's consciousness raged against dumb circumstance. He had no heart rate to race. No blood pressure to increase. But he felt the frustration of the moment as a very real, lived experience. Carefully backing off a few steps, which took another precious minute, he considered the problem. His improvised cannon wasn't powerful enough to shoot through the door, and the grappler couldn't punch or tear it aside.

One of the mech's rear-facing cams picked up movement.

The elevator door sliding closed on the remains of Corporal Orr. Somebody was coming. Booker started to upload another reformatted jelly bag round . . . then stopped. He was out of gel rounds. He almost swore aloud, until he remembered he could simply fashion a small puck from the remaining synthetic silk, reformatting the raw organocarbon molecule strings just as he had with the jelly bags.

He aimed the nozzle at the control plate for the air lock, dialed the muzzle velocity down to a tiny fraction of a percentage point of its full power, and popped a single round at the big red button.

Sirens blared, warning lights strobed, and the inner hatch rumbled open.

He slowly crept into the air lock.

If he'd had time and something more dexterous than a smashed-up mech, he might have tried to rewire the system to simply open the outer door and vent him into space. But in his current form, that wasn't going to happen. So he repeated the shot to close the inner hatch, vent the atmosphere, and open the outer shuttle bay doors.

The black vacuum waited for him.

Booker shambled to the lip of the shuttle bay as the elevator doors opened behind him.

He didn't wait to see who or what was coming.

He signaled the skiff to fire its rockets at full power.

The maintenance rig shot out of the bay and into space. Warning signals filled the virtual world of Booker's mind, overlaid on the actual sensor streams the mech was still able to capture.

The TDF prison Hab, a simple spinning tube of armored plate clad in salvaged regolith, quickly fell behind him. He hadn't seen the Hab from the outside when they'd sent him there after his trial, but he'd have bet a shiny silver Earth dollar that it wasn't getting swarmed by dozens of landing craft. Probably hadn't been surrounded by five Human Republic orbital assault ships, either. He cut the power to the skiff's rockets and let momentum carry him away from the battlespace. He saw one ship, which looked like a Terran frigate, broken and venting flames. It was adrift between the local sun and the prison Hab.

Booker checked his functioning cameras, looking for Batavia, the Yulin-Irrawaddy colony world. The small TDF facility lay at L1, the first of the planet's five Lagrange points. He didn't panic when he couldn't find Batavia. A lot of his cams were fried. And planets didn't just disappear. Well, not unless you broke them open with a big enough bomb, but that made a hell of a mess, and apart from the Republican task force, the vacuum around him was clear. He fired the skiff's adjusters and turned a slow cartwheel in space. The blue-green-red sphere rolled up from directly beneath his feet. A couple more puffs and he arrested the controlled tumble.

What now?

He couldn't land on Batavia. Neither the skiff nor the mech he wore was engineered for that sort of drop. He had to get away from the prison, obviously. He had no idea what the Combine had sitting at L2. Probably an outpost to keep an eye on the TDF's Habitat at L1.

But there was another option. The Eassar Habitat at L5.

It seemed impossibly far away, and he'd have to do some real math to plot an intercept course. But Booker did not need food, water, air, or even sleep. He could point the skiff at Eassar's local volume and . . . what? Hope for the best?

If the Sturm had seized his little Hab, they had to

be all over the Combine's big industrial Habitat, too. But what that meant to Booker was thousands of refugee ships hauling ass to escape. He was willing to lay a small bet—well, a big fucking bet actually: his life—that he could hook up with one of them or even just hook onto one of them and get a ride out of the Volume. If he got really lucky, he might even find something with the facilities to transfer him out of this busted-ass Compliance Mech and into something with a little more amenity and style. An organic phenotype or a Combat Mech.

He checked the military prison, which was rapidly shrinking away from him. No pursuit as far as he could tell.

Okay, then.

Time to do some math.

Three hours.

Ariane had been dead three hours, and Sephina's rage still knew no easing. She raged as the *Regret* fought its way out of the Eassar docks. She raged as Banks folded away before clearing to a safe distance from the Hab. Her fury only mounted as a Republican warship peeled out of formation to pursue them.

Three hours.

Ariane had been dead three hours, and Sephina's grief was an infinite gravity well, a black all-consuming event horizon, an emptiness as cold as the space between the stars.

Three hours.

Ariane had been dead three hours when the Sturm caught up with the *Regret* and put one ranged EM pulse into her starboard engine, frying the control circuitry.

"We're dead in the water," shouted Banks, the pilot who'd shot a big hole in an even bigger Hab to get them out of Eassar. The ship rang like a broken bell as dozens of maglocks clamped onto her hull. The fizzing screech of cutting lasers filled the hold as the crew gathered to hear their captain's command. She wiped away her tears and muttered just one word at them.

"Weapons."

"Excellent choice," Jaddi Coto said. "I like weapons."

The giant hybrid threw open the armory, a cargo container in the aft section of the cargo hold, and began removing the motley collection of body armor he had salvaged and stolen over the years since he'd joined Sephina and Ariane on the *Regret*.

He paused as he snugged tight the ties on an oversized ceraplate vest.

"I miss Ariane," he said, his brow puckering around the base of the enormous rhino horn growing from the center of his forehead. "I am sad she is dead."

"There will be many who are sad about that when we finish with them," hissed Falun Kot. The dark-skinned diminutive engineer donned no armor. He simply festooned himself with weapons and reloads. And blades. Lots of blades.

Banks, the pilot, with nothing to do now that they had been taken under steerage, considered the varied arsenal for a moment before choosing one small device. It looked like a handheld vacuum cleaner.

Sephina took a Terran assault rifle from the rack and programmed the magazine to format a half-n-half mix of low-velocity armor-piercing rounds and massively illegal toxin-tipped flesh eaters.

The cutting lasers sent a shower of sparks cascading from the hull to the deck plating a short distance away. The *Je Ne Regrette Rien* creaked and moaned under the structural stress of capture by the Sturm's warship.

"Do we know what kind of ship it is? How many crew?" Falun Kot asked. He sounded bored by the inconvenience of repelling the assault.

Banks answered him as he unscrewed the cap of a silver hip flask.

"Nothing in the database. Probably a new design. Dimensions fit with some analogue of a near-orbit patrol vessel, though. Say, thirty, forty crew. At least half of them lined up, ready to jump in."

He nodded at the shower of white-hot sparks and raised the flask.

"For Ariane."

He took a belt and passed Sephina the liquor, a small sample of the bourbon they'd carried into Eassar. She took a long pull, swallowed, and said, "Kill them all. Every fucking one of them."

Jaddi Coto took a small, almost dainty sip.

"For Ariane," he rumbled. "And for the little girl, Jula, too. I liked her. I will kill more for her."

Kot, an observant Sufi, took no alcohol, but he drew one of his knives and kissed the blade before powering it up.

"For Ariane, *inshallah,*" he whispered, then turned and walked to the cataract of falling sparks. A rough circle of steel dropped to the deck plating with a metallic crash just before he arrived. He sidestepped it as a grenade followed.

The engineer casually caught the little bomblet as it dropped and tossed it back up into the hole the breaching party had made. He threw one of his own grenades after it for good luck.

Twin detonations and screams followed, and a smoking body fell through the hole. It was missing an arm and the lower half of both legs.

Kot took the head off with one clean cut from a cold fusion blade that curved and shone like a sliver of winter moon.

The crew of the *Je Ne Regrette Rien* scattered to take their vengeance and to die taking it if that should be their fate.

Booker was almost upon the ships before he saw them.

Space was dark, and his half-wrecked Compliance Mech was not well equipped with sensors for EVA. The maintenance skiff did have proximity scanners and a basic debris detection package that Booker was able to reprogram and boost into a crude LADAR sweeper. Not that it was much use given his pitiful maneuvering ability. The three proximity alerts that sounded while he was flying toward Eassar were almost enough to persuade him to turn off the crude improvised sensor suite. It seemed that all it would be good for was warning him he had two seconds to live before some piece of hyperaccelerated space junk slammed into him like the fist of God.

But having gone to the effort of coding the thing, he couldn't be bothered.

If he was to die, this would not be the worst way to go out. (Programmatic deletion by some drooling breeder who couldn't remember which fucking button to push without the right script to tell him; that was definitely the worst way to go.) He saw things no living, breathing soul could survive in the fastness of the vac'. A Habitat venting red-hot atmosphere from a catastrophic rent in its lower berthing section. A squadron of tactical hunter-killers swarming a Combine frigate that was firing off star shells to some random formula not determined by any Intellect and possibly not even by a human hand. A comet arcing through the local volume, trailing a long tail of vaporizing dust and ice as it transited the inner reaches of the Sujutus system with the utmost indifference to the trivial affairs of men and their creations. It would be back a hundred or a thousand years from now, and for a little while Booker diverted himself by imagining what it might find upon its return.

He shot through hard vacuum like this for twelve and a half hours before a wailing siren in what his subroutines told him was his "ear" announced an imminent collision. The alarm did not cut out this time as he sped past some invisible chunk of space wrack, and after a second Booker could see why. He was closing with two ships that were grappling in space, the running lights of the larger vessel illuminating the dark lines of its prey. Embodied in some flesh and blood carcass, he might have died then, wondering for interminable seconds what he was seeing and what he might do about it. But because he was ensouled within the circuitry of the Compliance Mech, his thoughts were mediated by the architecture of the machinery's quantum processors and he was gifted the luxury of some twenty-three human-equivalent years to dwell on what he might do about this turn of events.

Seventeen years into his contemplation of life, this little corner of the universe, and everything, he made a decision.

He was gonna kick some ass and maybe score himself a new ride.

Sephina knew she was going to die. But then, she had always known that. Her mother had made sure of it. But even if she hadn't been raised, for a little while anyway, by a batshit crazy source coder with a head full of Hindenbugs and septic hydra code, she would have figured that out for herself. Only the rich lived forever. She was going to die on her ship, but she was going to take a few motherfuckers with her.

Seph had no idea how the rest of the crew were doing or even if they were alive. She'd fought alongside Banks for a while. The dapper little ship's driver had accounted for seven of the Sturm before they'd been split up by the fighting. Unseen, he painted each of his targets from cover with a persistent photon before retreating farther into the ship and launching a packet of micromissiles. The flea-size warheads swept through the *Regret* at hypervelocity, avoiding any obstacle fixed or moving that hadn't been painted by Banks's handheld designator. Tracking in on the photon markers, they hit their targets, penetrating to the center mass before detonating. In the blink of an eye, seven of the Sturm troopers died. Mostly their heads exploded without warning or apparent reason.

It had been hella difficult for Sephina to hold her fire while Banks triggered his ambush, but hold off she did. The surviving troopers freaked the fuck out, at least for a few seconds, until she took them under fire with the assault rifle. The half-n-half rounds passed through body armor like a hot stiletto through jelly. Inside the body they tumbled and broke up, unleashing an aggressive nanovirus that metastasized as it fed on blood, bone, organs, and muscle. Those Sturm died screaming and disintegrating.

But they kept coming, too. And pouring on fire. And gradually she was driven aft, toward the engineering spaces, where two companionways intersected. There she met up again with Falun Kot. The engineer was covered in blood and gobbets of meat and torn patches of black uniform. He appeared to be grinning fiercely, but she could see the expression was more a rictus of pain than anything like bravery. He was leaking from at least half a dozen serious wounds.

"*Inshallah,* we shall send these devils back to the Dark, too, eh," he rasped.

"God willing," she said, firing a burst from the assault rifle to hold back the advancing enemy. The weapon clicked empty after a second.

Kot offered her a knife. The handle and cross guard were tacky with gore, but the cold fusion blade glowed with a clean and silent white light.

"My good captain, shall we await them at our

pleasure or venture out to personally greet our guests?" he asked.

The volume of fire coming down the companionway at them increased dramatically. Reinforcements.

Coto and Banks were probably dead, then, freeing more of the Sturm to pursue her and Kot.

"Fuck them. They came all the way in from the Dark. They can come a little bit farther to get what they're owed," Sephina said.

She took the proffered knife but truly did not know what she was going to do with it.

Kot was a savant with a blade, and he had taught Ariane to be nearly as deadly.

Huddled out of the line of fire, waiting for the end, Sephina L'trel tried to recall the best of times with her soulmate, but all she could see were those laser designators and the lines of plasma fire converging on Ariane and Jula.

She was so lost in her mourning and fury that she did not hear the Sturm's attack stutter and break up. It was only when Kot gently squeezed her elbow that she came back to her senses and realized that the roar she could hear was not the concentrated assault of some shock trooper fire team closing with them in the bowels of the *Regret*.

It was something very different.

The storm of fire had abated, but the noise of battle had not.

She risked a quick look down the companionway, and for a moment her senses and reason failed her.

Some giant armored insect had materialized within the group of shock troopers closest to her. It was whipping a length of heavy chain about itself at such speed that the movement blurred. Until it took off a head or wrapped around an armored torso and the creature hurled the flailing mass into a bulkhead or the reinforced ribs of the ship, cracking plate and breaking bones and more often than not reducing the man or woman on the end of the fetter to loose meat.

Within a few seconds it was over.

Seph and Kot stepped out carefully, their hands raised in a placating gesture. Some sort of demonic Hell Mech swayed in front of them, stooping to fit within the confines of the ship. It was painted in blood and festooned with gore. Human remains protruded from its workings, glistening and steaming from the heat thrown off by the mech.

Jaddi Coto and Mister Banks appeared out of the dark behind it.

Banks was wary.

Coto was smiling.

"We made a friend," he said.

One of the mech's legs collapsed a little way, and it toppled over into the bulkhead.

A male voice, small and tinny, sounded from somewhere within the plasteel and ceraplate wreckage.

Coto wiped at a speaker grille on the unit's badly scarred and pockmarked glacis shield.

The voice grew louder.

"Corporal Booker3-212162-930-Infantry, ma'am. Er . . . retired. I had a hell of a time getting here. You think I could get a little help?"

Three tons of mechanical berserker crashed to the deck plating of the *Je Ne Regrette Rien.*

CHAPTER
TWENTY-SEVEN

HMAS *Defiant* folded through space at full military power, collapsing the vastness of the heavens before her. Without waypoints to patrol or mysteries to investigate, the return trip was greatly accelerated. Rather than plotting a course for Deschaneaux Station, Hardy ordered Chase to lay in a track to the nearest system of the Greater Volume.

She sat in the captain's chair as the final fold of the new plot appeared on the main holofield of the bridge. She still felt as though she had done something wrong in taking over Torvaldt's station.

"Navigation, confirm the emergence," she said, not really trusting herself to say more.

Chase's reply was just as clipped and professional. "Sujutus, ma'am, point 73 AU from primary." But she did not miss the way his eyes moved in her direction. The last she had heard from her father, he had been indentured on the colony world Batavia in a Combine defaulter camp in this very system.

"Good work, Mister Chase," she said, keeping her voice neutral. "Tactical?"

"Hundreds of vessels in-system," Lieutenant Fein reported. "No traffic control evident. Multiple drifting data points. Some are burning internally, Commander . . ." He paused and swallowed. "Including Habitat Eassar."

It would be wrong to say that a murmur ran around the bridge. *Defiant*'s crew was too disciplined for that, but Lucinda felt the surprise and even shock that transmitted itself from each to the other.

"I have three bandits on our heading. One is locked with a civilian trader, a boarding op for sure. The other two are en route to assist."

"ID on bandits?"

"No, ma'am. Roughly corvette class. I have tagged the enemy ships."

Lucinda glanced at the main combat holofield. A stylized ship, the trader, was highlighted in green; a red ship labeled "Hostile One" was locked onto her. "Two" and "Three" were closing on them. The enemy ships, as per RANSOP, were labeled in order of their proximity to the threatened friendly ship.

"The trader will have to look after herself for now," Lucinda said. "Target lock the two inbound vessels, kill Bandit Two, immobilize Three."

"Confirm to immobilize, Commander?" Lieutenant Fein asked.

"Confirmed. We need the intel."

"Roger. Marines standing by. Firing solution set."

Lucinda sat a little straighter. "Fire."

At her command, a Cordova 327 sublight ship killer shot out of its tube and accelerated to an appreciable fraction of light speed. Its mission was simple: get close to Bandit Two and detonate its thirty-megaton warhead. The second missile, a Speleron 115, took a few milliseconds longer to deploy from the ship's magazine. It was a specialty missile with a much harder task than that of the Cordova. It needed to get within a kilometer of the target vessel to deliver its payload: thousands of depleted uranium flechettes. The dense little darts were meant as drive killers, but they'd also make chopped meat of any crew members they passed through.

Fein spoke up again. "Ma'am, the launch was detected!"

"Helm. Active evasion," she ordered.

Defiant accelerated and slewed wildly in space. Her opponents were now doing the same thing.

"Missile launch from Two and Three, Commander. Countermeasures live."

Lucinda said nothing. If the enemy ships had a good solution on her, she would be dead within seconds. A bright strobelike flare winked on her display, and Bandit Two disappeared from her battle schematic. The icon for Three dimmed. Part of her, the part that wondered what the hell she was doing in Torvaldt's chair, worried that she had fucked up and started a war. Her more rational self reminded her that the evidence of war was floating all around them. Burning Habs and warships. Civilian traders and liners running hot to exfil the system.

Fein announced, "Hostile Two neutralized, Hostile Three dead in space."

"And their missiles?"

"Still searching for us, Commander, but no lock."

"Excellent work, everyone," Lucinda said, forcing

her voice to be steady. "We get to play the next round."

She let out a breath and felt a sudden urge to pee. A cold sweat dampened her armpits as she looked from one crew member to the next. For some, such as Chase, this was their first battle. Others were old hands. And all of them were watching her, if surreptitiously. She knew what she had to do.

"Navigation, close with the third ship. Comms, attempt to hail them. Offer terms for surrender. If they yield now, they live. If not, they die. Maintain target lock. If there's any sign of a threat to this vessel, destroy them in place. Intel is crucial, but not at the cost of this ship." She saw some tight nods among the bridge crew. "Ms. Chivers, you have the conne. I will accompany the marines."

Silence lay across the bridge. Nonomi Chivers nervously cleared her throat. "Ma'am?"

Lucinda made a chopping gesture with her hand. "Lieutenant Chivers, the commander accompanies the main effort. Leaders lead." She looked to her crew and met each one's eyes. Chase looked away.

"Lieutenant Chivers, inform Captain Hayes I will join his team for the assault."

The young woman nodded and subvocalized something before addressing Lucinda.

"They're expecting you, ma'am."

Lucinda nodded and left. She headed for the armory, stopping along the way to empty her bladder. And sweet baby Jesus, what a relief. She'd been worried she was going to piss herself back there. Her hands shook as she splashed cold water on her face. The young woman staring back at her looked haunted and strange. She took a deep breath, let it go. Another breath. Let it go.

A dangerous thought came to her.

For the first time since they had been separated, she was in the same system as her father. Not only did she have the means to swoop down from the stars and rescue him, she even had half an excuse for doing so: a ground survey of enemy deployments. The Sturm would be down on Batavia in force. She even knew where without having to check. The wreck of the *Voortrekker*, their first Generation Ship, the component parts launched during more than four thousand missions from the huge Gagarin Complex on Sandakan Bay in Borneo and assembled in orbit.

It was a sacred site to them, and as she thought about it, the arguments in favor of an assault on the site firmed up, gaining weight and clarity. The Sturm would have significant forces onsite, and they would not be securely established yet. A decisive blow might knock out critical elements of their force projection assets in-volume.

She pushed the thoughts aside.

All of them on this ship would have family, friends, loved ones they could not protect. She was no different and no better than anyone else. Her father would have to take his chances. He was probably safer down there, anyway. He had no gene-modding, no implants, and he was a prisoner of the Combine. Most likely the Sturm would execute his captors and set him free.

She wiped off her face and resumed her march to the armory. It was less than a minute's walk down by the shuttle bays. Hardy snapped out salutes to every crew member she passed, feeling even more self-conscious than she had when she'd first come aboard at Deschaneaux Station. It was a relief to get out of the companionway and into the armory.

Lucinda walked down a row of powered suits hanging in clamps. Each one looked like death incarnate. She stopped in front of the olive-drab suit stenciled LT. HARDY and tried to prompt it open with her neural net. Nothing happened of course. Her net was gone. Instead she laid a palm on the armored breastplate and waited for the suit to recognize her DNA.

It opened up like a clam. She climbed inside and closed up. A whisper told her the environmental controls were equalizing; a slight smell of ozone bespoke a well-maintained killing machine.

She brought up the systems display and methodically checked every category. Her L-55 rifle was ready, loaded with partial penetrators and flesh eaters. Her pistol system was green. She had a full loadout of grenades. All suit storage compartments bore her electronic seals. She had been careful to inspect her suit personally just after she had come aboard. Within a minute, she was assured of her armor's full function. She ordered her clamp to open. The suit dropped a fraction of an inch to the deck, and Lucinda Hardy walked to Bay 2, where the marines were already assembled.

A voice called out, "Commander on deck!"

With a thunderous crash, the assembled marines snapped to. Captain Hayes, suited up but not yet hidden inside his helmet, turned and rendered a precise salute. She returned it.

"Ma'am?"

"As you were, marines."

"Good timing, ma'am. I was about to brief."

"Don't let me spoil the fun, Captain."

He nodded.

"Listen up, marines. Here's the shit. We are closing in on an enemy corvette, capabilities and armament unknown. It is disabled. We hit it with a Speleron." He smiled. "You know what that means. Splatters and Popsicles." Some of the marines chuckled. "Friendly forces, just us. Enemy unknown, so treat everything with a heartbeat that you can't identify as hostile. This is the Sturm. There will be heartbeats. The mission is to capture the enemy vessel intact for intelligence exploitation." He looked at Lucinda.

"Prisoners?" Hayes cocked an eyebrow.

She shook her head and held up her gauntleted right hand with the index finger extended. One prisoner would be spared if possible.

"Oorah," the marines rumbled.

Hayes nodded and turned back to his marines. "One prisoner, preferably a ship's officer, per SOP. Here's how we execute. Second platoon, first squad, breach and hold. Second squad, determine where the bridge is and take it. Third squad, engineering. Fourth, command element." He looked over at Lucinda. "Ma'am, by your leave, you will be with me and the fourth squad."

"Concur, Captain Hayes."

He turned to the remaining two squads assembled in the bay. "First platoon, second and third squads, you are in reserve to plug any holes the commander or I can identify. Roger?"

Hayes was answered with a chorus of grunted "oorahs" and "yessirs."

The clock was ticking. Hayes went over communications and other issues, then directed his subordinate leaders to finish their final checks.

He turned to Lucinda. "Check you over, ma'am?"

"Go for it."

He did a quick, ruthless check of her gear, and she checked him in turn. All good. Hayes raised his eyebrows slightly, leaned in to Lucinda, and spoke so that nobody but she could hear him.

"Fuckin' good job, ma'am. I never pass a squid on the first go."

Lucinda smiled and even blushed a little, but she knew she had passed an important test. Hayes called out.

"Marines, mount the fuck up." He strode over to the shuttle door and clapped each on his or her armored shoulder as they moved by. Lucinda stood next to him. She subvocalized.

"Comms, any reply from Hostile Three?"

"No, ma'am."

"All right, then; these people get what they get."

The last marine passed by. Hayes gestured for Lucinda to enter; she did, and he followed right behind her. She moved to an open clamp, backed into it, and was "locked and green." Hayes took the clamp next to her. The shuttle crew chief walked the rows of troopers and checked each one. Lucinda heard his voice through the net; he spoke with the pilot.

"Skyfall, Chief. Our pax are locked and green."

"Acknowledged, Chief. Get locked in yourself; we are cleared to roll."

"Roger."

The troop door shut with a hiss, and Lucinda felt the shuttle rise. The same dread she had carried through the Javan War took hold of her again; she tasted the same bile. The pilot, Skyfall, her nick, spoke again with a contralto voice.

"Command element. Be advised, we are en route to Hostile Three. Expect entrapment within fifteen, penetration five mikes after hostile dock. Kick back, relax, and enjoy the ride."

Lucinda answered. "Roger, Skyfall." A pause. "Are we there yet?"

Quiet laughter rolled through the shuttle.

For the next fifteen minutes nothing happened. There was little chatter on the troopnet. Hayes's crew was wrapped tight and disciplined. It wasn't as if they could move around, anyway. The clamps held the passengers tight against sudden, unexpected acceleration. And what use was chatter? Lucinda thought about her father. There was no helping that. She had long ago stopped torturing herself that she was responsible for his plight. He had borrowed money for her school fees, yes, but he had not known the credit broker would on-sell his debt to a Combine loan harvester. Combine fintechs were barred from operating directly in Commonwealth jurisdictions, but Greater Volume law guaranteed the free flow of capital and as soon as Jonathyn Hardy signed his loan contract with a legitimate, if sketchy, Armadalen broker, his debt became tradable anywhere within human space. Combine loan sharks could not do business within the Commonwealth, but Volume Common Law meant that their reclaimers could.

Lucinda hoped he would be okay and found herself perversely grateful that he was down on the surface of a planet, not trapped inside a Hab. Eassar looked to be in a bad way.

She forced her mind back to the mission. Who were these people? What were their capabilities, their strengths and weaknesses? She hoped to find answers on the ship. She hoped that she wasn't risking these marines' lives for nothing.

Had she made the right call? Who would die? Would their lives be worth the loss? Without backup via neuralink, dead meant dead.

Skyfall broke her reverie.

"Matching course and velocity with Hostile Three. The drive is definitely out; no visible exterior lights or antiship fire. Thirty seconds to hostile dock."

Lucinda waited in the blue-lit dark of the hold. After what seemed forever, she felt a bump.

Skyfall spoke. "Command, we have begun the burn. Five mikes starts now." With the word "now," all the clamps released. Lucinda drifted up to the shuttle ceiling; with practiced ease she caught the chivvy line that would propel her to the rear of the cabin. She had taken a zero-grav antinausea cap on the way over, having learned her lesson at the Academy years before. Puking inside a suit was no fun at all.

Hayes put out an all-call. "Everyone knows what to do. Soon as that breach is open, we go in. Some of these bitches will still be alive. Kill them all. Bar one. See you inside."

Hayes tugged at Lucinda's armor and motioned for her to follow him. She did, swinging from handhold to handhold, occasionally jostling a waiting trooper. Captain Hayes led her to the breach bay in the back.

He spoke. "Old tradition with my people, ma'am. When we go in, the commander waits by the point of breach."

"The old ways are the best, Captain."

They stopped by a circular flat spot in the rear of the shuttle, then carefully got out of the way of the first squad. They'd be moving hard and fast. Time was not on their side, and anyone still alive on the other ship would be looking hard for the breach they knew must be coming.

A timer appeared on Lucinda's visual. It counted down from thirty. The first marine in line gave his thrusters a microtest; then he floated, waiting.

Three, two, one.

The floor of the shuttle irised open instantly, and two waiting marines shot booster grenades down into the waiting, glowing hole. The squad leader held up her hand with digits extended. With precision, she folded her fingers closed in sequence. When her hand made a fist, the first marine shot down the hole and died. The next marine was right on his heels and took out the defender. In rapid succession, the first squad roared into the ship.

Troopnet came alive.

"Jones, behind the bulkhead . . ."

"Where is that fucker . . ."

"Fifty-fifty thrown, watch the flash . . ."

"Two down."

Every now and then a random chunk of something would zing up into the troop compartment. A piece bounced off Lucinda's armor. After a minute, the first squad called in.

"Toehold secure. Ready for follow-on. Be advised, hot in here."

Hayes answered. "Roger. Second squad, go."

Lucinda watched as the next group shot down through the hole. She couldn't hear gunfire, of course, but troopnet made it perfectly clear that there was a raging fight down there. Marines were dying on her say-so. Actually dying.

She suppressed a momentary panic.

Hayes spoke again. "Third. Go."

Once again Lucinda watched as the marines rocketed past. How many of them would come back aboard? Hayes spoke one last time aboard the shuttle.

"First platoon, second squad, we need you guys. We've gotten banged up in there a little. Follow us in, roger?"

"Roger that, sir."

With that, Hayes floated over the breach and hit his jets. He rocketed down into the enemy ship. Lucinda and the rest of fourth squad followed.

As she popped down into the Sturm ship through the plasma-cut hole, Lucinda's visual instantly went to infrared. There were no lights in the corridor where she found herself. She cut her jets just before she reached the floor, and her suit arrested her bounce automatically and kept her from spinning in the zero grav. A severed arm bounced off her faceplate. She instantly scanned her sector for threats, but there were none. She moved forward in the hallway. Flashes strobed to her front. Lucinda checked her battle schematic. Second squad was moving to the front of the ship while third was moving aft to what they thought would be engineering. What was left of first squad was hanging back and securing the toehold as instructed.

Hayes called her up. "We're moving to the bridge, Commander. Everyone has cams on; we're capturing all the data we can and livestreaming it back to *Defiant*. That blender round has holed this ship pretty bad or we'd be neck deep in wet shit the way these guys are fighting. Heavy opposition up front. Wouldn't surprise me if they try to scuttle the ship."

He gave voice to a fear of her own. Her face set in hard lines, and she moved forward through evidence of heavy combat and sudden depressurization. Sailors in gray coveralls, frozen solid, bumping off bulkheads and spinning in grotesque shapes. Blasted marines, holes burned in their suits. A dead enemy fighter blown out of her armor, part of her torso degloved, her innards crystallizing as Lucinda watched. Machinery, circuitry, objects—it all floated in the perforated corridors like children's balloons at a horror circus.

Lucinda just moved forward. A mystery round blew through the bulkhead before her. It tore out the other side and went . . . somewhere. She saw a form in unfamiliar space armor twitch; she double-tapped it with her primary weapon. Better safe than sorry. As an intel point, she noted that RAN rounds penetrated Sturm body armor just fine.

The flashes from up ahead stopped. After a minute, troopnet crackled.

"Element six, be advised, the bridge has been

taken. We have one Papa, she's alive, kinda. Needs immediate casevac."

Lucinda answered. "Good work, marines. We'll be up there soon for a look around."

After a minute or so, fourth squad with the command element moved onto the bridge, where marines were busy stripping anything that looked like it might contain data. One marine stood guard over a floating enemy suit; it was missing a leg.

Hayes spoke. "Looks like the bridge. What do you think, Commander?"

"Agreed. Ten minutes for exploitation, then we roll."

Within twenty minutes the marines and Lucinda were back on the shuttle. At the rear of the bay lay the remains of four of her marines in shiny black bags. As she stood before her clamp and locked in, she asked herself again if it had been worth it.

Maybe, she thought.

The trip back was uneventful. Lucinda hung in her clamp in silence. She could smell her foul sweat, and she felt as empty as a cheap Combine battery. For the first time, she had a moment to think. What friendly forces had survived the Sturm attack? Was *Defiant* alone? A single ship without an Intellect?

Some answers, she thought, would be in the data they had taken off Hostile Three. She shook her head as it occurred to her that she didn't even know the ship's name.

"Did anyone get the name of that ship?" she asked Hayes.

He queried troopnet. A few seconds later he came back to her.

"*Rorke's Drift*," he said.

"Oh, for fuck's sake."

The shuttle reentered *Defiant*'s bays, landed, and pressurized. The marines filed out, but Lucinda and Hayes stayed behind. They exited the ship last, and he spoke.

"Good work, Commander."

"Didn't do much, Captain."

"You led, ma'am." He executed another precise salute. "By your leave, Skipper."

She returned the salute. "Dismissed and well done, Captain. My compliments to your people and . . . my condolences, too. I'm sorry."

Hayes nodded, turned, and strode away. Lucinda took a slightly different direction to the naval armory. With a groan of relief she returned her no longer brand-new suit to its rack. She peeled herself out of the shell and headed for the bridge. She wanted nothing so much as to take a shower and sleep, but she had to resume the conne.

The first person she saw on the bridge was Chase. She registered the revulsion on his face when he smelled her before he smoothly adjusted his professional mask.

"Welcome back, Commander."

"Good to be back, Lieutenant Chase. Lieutenant Chivers, I am resuming command. Any word on that trader while I was gone?"

"They got through it without casualties," Nonomi reported, sounding surprised. "With some help from a mech that was floating by, maybe blown off another ship or something."

"Seriously? A trader? Throwing down with the

Sturm?" Lucinda could not keep the surprise from her voice. The suspicion. "What sort of a trader?"

"Light cargo." Chivers shrugged. "Their manifest lists a couple of pallets of heirloom liquor inbound for Eassar. Nothing going out. The captain did call to say thanks for holding the other two off them. Said it was the first time she'd ever been glad to see a ship of the line."

Lucinda smiled thinly.

"I see. A smuggler, then? What might we call this lucky ship, and who is her captain?"

Chase glanced at his visual. "Some garbage barge called the *Je Ne Regrette Rien*, and her mistress"—he placed a slightly mocking emphasis on the title—"is Captain Sephina L'trel."

Lucinda's smile died on her lips.

CHAPTER
TWENTY-EIGHT

Lucinda swayed on her feet, her head spinning a little from the adrenal backwash of the combat jump. She hadn't had to fight her way onto *Rorke's Drift,* hadn't been exposed to the same danger as the marines who had gone in first. It was not her first fight.

But it was the first time she'd fought, as a naval officer at least, without backup. Literally.

She had last stored her complete engram in *Defiant*'s encrypted substrate two days before Torvaldt had died. Nobody had backed up since then. The malware breach made it too risky to interface with the ship or with one another via neuralink. Everyone had shat out their mesh on her order. Nobody was backing up, and nobody was dosing neurotransmitters. They were flying and fighting in the raw.

Lucinda felt queasy, but she couldn't say whether from the aftershock of the boarding operation or from what Chase had just told her.

"Sephina L'trel, you said, Lieutenant Chase?"

Chase looked a little put out to be second-guessed in front of the bridge crew.

"Yes, that's correct, Commander."

"Mister Bannon, could you bring up whatever data you can access from the onboard systems on an Armadalen . . . citizen"—she appeared to struggle with the word—"from Shogo City on the Coriolis Hab? Name of Sephina L'trel."

She spelled it out.

"Master and commander of the trading vessel *Je Ne Regrette Rien*."

"Yes, ma'am," Bannon replied.

"Lieutenant Chivers," she went on. "I will need to speak with our Captain L'trel."

"Yes, ma'am," Chivers responded. "I will get her back for you."

"Commander, if I may?" Lieutenant Fein interrupted. Lucinda nodded at him to go on.

"We have six enemy vessels closing on our location. Three destroyer-class equivalents. Two corvettes. And something that looks something like a Titan cruiser but different. Estimate the first vessel, the destroyer, to be within our weapons range in forty-three minutes. I can't speak to their weapons range. The cruiser is farthest away, but it will be packing the biggest punch."

Lucinda had to sit down.

They had jumped into a war. No, scratch that. She had jumped them into a war.

"Mister Chase," she said, mindful to keep her voice steady. "Plot two folds with all dispatch, please. One to take us as far out of system as possible. Liaise with Mister Fein to plot a second evolving fold that will put us behind the cruiser in a position to take it under fire."

"A cruiser?" Chase said. "You're serious?"

The background hum of the bridge died away.

Chase appeared to pick up on the vibe. It was not openly hostile, but neither was it friendly.

"I mean, no disrespect . . . Commander. But we don't even know the enemy's capabilities. We haven't had time to debrief the prisoner or examine the data stores we took off their ship. And . . . and we might be the only functional warship in this system."

Lucinda said nothing. She stared at him. Waiting.

Chase turned on Mercado Fein.

"Fein. You're the tactical officer. Do you have any idea how to fight something as big as a Titan cruiser? With its own battle group in escort?"

"Mister Chase?" Lucinda said quietly before Fein could answer.

"What?"

"Do you have my plots ready?"

Silence again. Much more uncomfortable this time.

"No," he said. "Of course I don't."

"Then I suggest you make it happen," she said. "Now."

They locked eyes, but Chase was the first to look away. He bent to the holofield at Navigation and got to work calculating the fold.

Clap.

Clap.

Clap.

Lucinda looked up, her face reddening, but nobody on *Defiant* would have dared mock the commanding officer in such a fashion.

She knew who it was before she saw the communications hologram.

"Hello, Seph," she said, suddenly feeling very tired. "It's been too long."

Sephina L'trel's image floated in the middle of the bridge. Center stage. As always.

"Too long?" the holo said. "As I recall, the last time we crossed paths, you tried to fuck me. And not in a fun way."

Lucinda could feel the glances flying between her shipmates. She blushed even more deeply but ground her teeth together. Embarrassment could look like anger if you played it just right.

"I meant you've been running too long, Sephina. You should be in prison."

The image of the other woman shrugged, even smiled, if a little sadly.

"This life is a prison, baby. You taught me that."

Lucinda rubbed her eyes and cursed inwardly. She took a deep breath, steeled herself.

"Look. I'll give you the benefit of the doubt," she said. "I'll allow that you're probably not responsible for this mess." She waved a hand around as if to take in the entirety of the local volume. "And I'm busy. So tell me what you know. I'll send engineers to get you free of that ship, and we can do the girly catching up later. I don't suppose you took any prisoners."

Sephina's face darkened. She seemed ready to cut the commlink, but after a moment she spoke again.

"They killed Ariane."

Lucinda closed her eyes. Kept them closed for a second. She was glad she'd been sitting down. It felt as though the deck had fallen away beneath her.

"I'm sorry," she said when she opened them again. "I am, really."

"Yeah. She always liked you. She was an idiot that way."

Lucinda turned to Lieutenant Fein. "Any change?"

She was desperately aware of how bizarre and unprofessional this must look to everyone.

"No, ma'am," Fein said, completely neutral. "Still closing at the same rate."

Nonomi Chivers tried to apologize with her eyes for opening the holocomm link without warning her, but Lucinda waved her off. Chivers had no idea whom she was dealing with in Sephina.

"So you were heading for Eassar when the Sturm attacked?"

"We were on Eassar."

"Pursuing a legitimate commercial opportunity with one of the many reputable subsidiaries of the Yulin-Irrawaddy Combine, I suppose."

"No. I was stealing nine and a half million yen from the Yakuza."

"Well that's just super," Lucinda deadpanned. "And then?"

"Shit went sideways. Not just our shit. The whole fucking Hab. Looked like they pulsed out some kind of black script. I'd guess you had to be hooked up on the livestream to get hacked. So it wasn't everyone. Nobody on my crew, natch. And it didn't get anybody around us except for a YG plate boss and some HabSec guys. Higher-ups, you know. Like you. Plugged-in."

Lucinda ignored the dig.

"How did you know they'd been hacked?"

"They started eating people. And they were really fucking hungry."

She didn't respond to that either, but she immediately recalled the violent madness that had overtaken Captain Torvaldt and Lieutenant Wojkowski when they had linked to the dead drop node.

"Did you see any resistance? From HabSec or Combine forces? Or even TDF?"

"Nothing. Most of the fighting we saw was just local peeps, but we were on a rough part of the plate."

Lucinda couldn't tell whether she was joking. Given Ariane and the hollowed-out look in Sephina's eyes, she decided not.

"Do you have any idea what's happening outside this system?"

"Nada. I don't use the ZP network. And we've been running and gunning. I'd guess it's the same everywhere."

"All right. I'm going to send over some intelligence guys. There'll be a security detail with them. Marines. We have no business with you today, Sephina, so just let them do their job, okay? Tell them what they need to know. If you need anything we can provide in less than thirty minutes, please tell Lieutenant Chivers. She's the officer you embarrassed by routing around our comms buffer. That was a cheap shot by the way."

Sephina's image barely reacted. Lucinda remembered Ariane and felt bad for having taunted her. It was unbecoming.

"I'm sorry about Ariane."

Sephina ignored that. "We got a guy in a mech over here," she said. "He's one of yours. Or military, anyway. Earth, he says. Somehow ended up in a prison Compliance Mech, but he's busted up pretty bad. If you could download him into a new body or even a slightly less up-fucked mech, it'd be a cool thing to do. He killed a lot of fucking Nazis. Seems like a good guy. But we don't have the gear to look after him."

"I'll tell the engineers to have a look. No promises. We're not a body shop. And I want to know why he's in a prison unit."

Sephina did smile just a little then. It didn't lift the heavy pall that hung over her, but it suggested that one day that pall might lift.

She said, "Life is a prison, Cinders. Remember?"

"Commander?"

A raised voice freighted with some urgency interrupted their exchange. It was Lieutenant Chivers.

"I'm getting a link request on a secure channel, ma'am. Not zero point. X-band."

"An Intellect?"

"Yes, ma'am. Seeking an urgent conference with Defiant Actual."

"Mister Fein, status on those bogies?"

"Still closing, Commander. Thirty-seven minutes to engagement range."

"Lieutenant Bannon, scan that channel down to the quantum bits. I'm not letting any more malware onto this ship."

"Already scanning, ma'am. Green lights so far."

"Do it again, standing on your head if you have to

get a new angle," she ordered before returning her attention to Sephina.

"It's okay," Seph said. "I get it. You're a very important person now."

Lucinda ignored the snark. "There are more enemy ships closing on this location. We've got just over half an hour before they come within our weapons range. I don't know when we will light up their targeting systems. I have to go now. As you say, I'm a very important person. Can your ship fold?"

"They put an EM spike into the control boards of our starboard engine. My guys are swapping them out now. Ten minutes and we should be good to make a tactical fold."

"Then get ready to do so," Lucinda told her. "We will cover your escape if needed."

"It won't be. I don't need anything from you."

"You need our help repairing the mech. Send Lieutenant Chivers a list. I assume you have an engineer on board."

"The best."

"Yeah, cool story. Send the list. Do it quickly. I'll comp you an extra control board for your engine. We have the specs. We know all about your ship."

"You don't know how it got away from you last time," Sephina said.

Lucinda gestured to Chivers to cut the holocomm link.

The holo disappeared.

"Lieutenant Bannon, do we have a clean channel for that Intellect?"

"We do."

"Nonomi, hook us up. To whom do I have the pleasure?"

"An Armada-level Intellect, Commander," Chivers said, sounding nervous. "He says you can call him Hero."

CHAPTER
TWENTY-NINE

The thing about torture was that it was always much worse than one could imagine. And these fecking dribblers hadn't even warmed up yet.

McLennan's hands were manacled behind his back.

The manacles, which bit deeply into the skin at his wrists, were fixed to a chain.

The chain passed through a pulley hanging from a rough scaffold of plasteel piping.

He dangled, suspended by his dislocated arms, just far enough above the ground for his toes to touch the hardscrabble.

But not far enough to take any significant weight off his shoulders, which burned with a firestorm of agonies.

He was not so much a man as a twisted man-shaped vessel, gouged and gutted of all personality, filled with Torquemada's fulsome panoply of horror and pain: the shock; the sickening violation of his limbs ripped from their sockets like chicken wings from a carcass; the rhythmic suffering of having to inhale and exhale, an experience akin to being crushed in the grip of a stupid, uncaring giant; and the small searing mysteries of pain that flared and sparked throughout his tormented body.

He was naked.

Hanging in the sun.

His white, lightly freckled skin was cherry red with sunburn.

His legs, shaking with the effort to hold himself on tiptoe, were sticky with his own dark urine and liquid shit.

His eyes pooled with sweat and tears, making of the world a blurred kaleidoscope in which a black wave of destiny loomed before him. The hull of the *Voortrekker*.

But at least they hadn't started to torture him yet. This was just the softening-up period.

McLennan's head slumped forward, and jagged spikes of white lightning exploded through his armpits and deep into his torso.

He groaned. He even cried, but the soft vibrations of his sobbing only added throbbing spasms to the swirling vortices of his many other torments.

It was impossible to know how long they'd dangled him from the scaffold before the hull of their sacred fallen ship. He had no neural net. The high, scorching sun barely seemed to move in the sky. Nobody questioned him.

At times McLennan would lose consciousness, but the sudden slump only served to wrench his arms up high behind his back again, waking him with a sudden squall of agony.

Maybe half an hour after they'd hung him up,

maybe four or five hours later, they cut him down. The first he knew of it was the fierce white light of Sujutus suddenly dimming as somebody, perhaps more than one person, stepped in front of him, blocking out the sun.

"What?" McLennan muttered, unintelligible even to himself. His tongue was swollen to nearly twice its size, and his mouth was dry, his lips cracked.

He experienced a sudden sense of falling through space and then a volcanic blast of pain that finally, mercifully carried him under.

He woke, confused and dry retching, lying naked on the sand and gravel of the Ironstone Desert. The sky seemed to be moving until he gathered enough of his wits to recognize that he now lay under a tarpaulin.

"Pick him up."

A strong hand grabbed a fistful of his graying hair and hauled him upright.

He screamed in pain. Not from the tearing of his hair but from the unholy anguish of his other injuries.

Cold water, a bucket of it, tipped over his head, arrived as a shock, as deliverance, and as another nauseating turn in the endless round of his perdition.

A cloth of some sort, roughly jammed into his face, rubbed most of the water out of his eyes, and he could make out his surroundings for the first time in . . . who fucking knew how long?

"Your equipment is of military grade but civilian origin," a voice stated. A woman. "You are purebred, with all the flaws that are natural to our race and no modifications to your gene sequence. We should have no argument with someone like you, yet you come upon us as an enemy and a spy. We will begin with the obvious questions. Who are you? Who sent you?"

It was a moment before he could bring his interrogator into focus.

She was a handsome-looking woman. Dark-skinned, clear-eyed, and tall. Originally of African phenotype, he thought. Or maybe native Australian or Melanesian. Middle-aged, he supposed, although he was guessing. She wore dark blue fatigues, not armor, and a peaked cap. The two shock troopers standing behind her were fully armored and weaponized. The flapping tarpaulin smacked against the tops of their helmet enclosures. They massed out at maybe three or four times as large as the woman.

"And who the fuck are you?" McLennan croaked, surprised that his voice still worked. Even talking sent enough vibrations through his upper torso to hurt with every word.

"Colonel Marla Dunn," she said. "Of the expeditionary forces of the Human Republic. And you, sir?"

"Sir, is it, you murderous fecking trollop? Are we to have tea and conversation, you and I, after you hung me up like a fecking haggis over the coals?"

"Yes, we are. Unless you'd prefer me to hang you up again."

Her voice was pleasant. Inquiring. He had no doubt she would do exactly what she said.

One of the troopers stepped forward. Gravel crunched and small rocks cracked under the weight of his armored boot.

"No, that willnae be necessary," McLennan hurried to say. He almost threw his hands up to forestall the trooper, but pain flooded through his shoulders at the very thought of it. "I'm a surveyor," he said, going with a cover story he'd settled on before returning to the dig site. "For a mining company."

Colonel Dunn did not look impressed.

"String him up for another hour," she said, turning away.

"Wait! No!" McLennan cried out. "It's true, I tell you. I'm not supposed to be here. In the Ironstone, I mean. We, the company, Alrosa-BlueStar, we . . . we were surveying deposits in the Goroth Mountains that, to be completely honest, we were not entitled to. That's what I do. For BlueStar. We . . . I . . . look for the assets of rival companies that have been . . . underexploited for whatever reason. I survey them and . . . I see whether the local authorities might be open to a nonstandard transfer of title or license."

Colonel Dunn examined him as though she'd found some homeless bum camping out in her front parlor. McLennan was very aware of being naked in front of her. Unlike his performance on the night Trumbull had arrived with his caravan of moronic fecking dobbers, there was no sense that having his tackle out in front of this fascist bitch was any sort of power play on his part.

She sighed.

"So you're a thief? For one of the Grand Houses?"

"Och, hell no. Alrosa-BlueStar is listed on the High Bourse, but they are a publicly traded company, not a corporate realm."

"But you're still a thief. The cloaked surveillance craft. The stealth suit. These are not the tools of an honest businessman."

To his surprise, McLennan thought he could feel the ruse beginning to take hold.

"I didn't say I was an honest man, Colonel."

He even managed a roguish grin through the dizzying nausea and pain.

"I'm just not a thief. These assets are underperforming, underutilized. Sometimes they're not even operating. Most colony worlds have strict legal requirements that investors realize the value of a licensed asset within . . ."

He realized from the shadow that passed over her face that he'd made a mistake.

"A colony world?" Dunn said. The lack of affect in her voice was much more frightening than any pantomime villain's growl.

"Well, it's not a term that I would use, of course. It's just a legal—"

"This world is no colony. It is a war grave. Do you know who lies here?"

He almost said yes, a bunch of dead space Nazis, you daft numptie, but caught himself at the last moment.

"A Generation Ship," he said, trying to make it sound like an apology. "From . . . your republic."

"You were going to say the Sturm, weren't you?" Dunn said.

He started to shake his head but stopped at the first stab of pain in his neck.

"No. No, I understand you find that term offensive."

"Why is that, do you think?"

"I couldn't say. I'm a surveyor. Not a history buff."

"No. You're not a history buff, are you, Professor?"

McLennan's balls contracted.

Dunn smiled. Her teeth seemed very white.

"Quite the sight, aren't you. For the savior of the human race? So-called."

Blood seemed to be rushing through his head; the gushing, pounding roar of it made it difficult to understand the woman.

"I don't know what you mean," he said weakly. "My name is Jay Lambright. I'm a minerals surveyor. For Alrosa-BlueStar. You can check if you like."

Dunn snorted.

"That won't be necessary. I was just curious about you. Unfortunately, I won't have the privilege of interrogating a high-value prisoner like you. I was merely ordered to prepare you for that interrogation."

"But I'm no professor. My name is Jay Lam—"

Dunn punched him in the face.

His nose broke, and blinding pain filled his head. He cried out pitiably as he fell backward.

He heard her as though from a great distance, through a hissing rain.

"Admiral McLennan," she said. "Or Professor McLennan. Or whatever the fuck you call yourself these days. You degrade yourself with these lies. But then, what else could we expect from a race traitor like you?"

"I don't know any McLennan. My name is Jay Lambright," he babbled. "I'm a surveyor. I saw you land, and I had to investigate. I know of two other companies who've been active in the Ironstone. There are a lot of rare minerals here, you know."

Strong hands hauled him roughly to his feet. Waves of pain and nausea rolled through him.

He blinked, trying to get his story straight, his senses focused.

He saw Dunn. The armored shock troopers. More enemy personnel walking by, looking in under the tarp at the questioning of the prisoner. Probably the most interesting thing happening in camp at the moment.

He wondered who held him up, but he couldn't turn his head to see.

Instead he dry retched again. Tasted bile in his throat but brought nothing up.

Dunn was suddenly in his face, yanking his head back.

"We know who you are, McLennan. We even know what you've done here. Defiling this grave site. Did you think we would forget you and what you did? You are the reason the human race can no longer call the Earth our home. You served mutants and borgs. You enslaved billions of true humans. You cut the bonds of culture, faith, and tradition that made us who we were. You gave succor and victory to the antihuman cause."

She leaned in so close that the tip of her nose touched his.

"But you will not replace us."

Dunn stepped away from him.

"You will be returned to the Redoubt, there to face trial for crimes against humanity."

"But . . . my name is Jay Lambright," he whimpered pitifully.

Dunn shook her head.

"Do you have any idea how many generations of children have grown up cursing your name? Spitting at your image?"

He did, actually, but they were all back on Earth, the survivors and descendants of his pragmatic genocide.

Or was it called something else when you slaughtered your own people?

"And here you are," Dunn went on, oblivious to the punishing interrogation McLennan had levied upon himself. "You haven't changed," she seethed. "Not a freckle, not a hair. Exactly as you were when you betrayed your race and your civilization. I recognized you as soon as I saw you. We all did. I know you're not the original McLennan. You're just a copy of a copy of God only knows how many copies now. You have no soul. Your memories are q-bit replicas burned into cloned gray meat. But you'll do to answer for the war crimes of Frazer McLennan."

He slumped.

They had him.

What the fuck had he been thinking? He'd been exiled in this desert for so long that he'd forgotten who he was. What he'd done. She was right. He should have to answer for his crimes.

To these people he was human history's greatest monster. Trying to pretend he was somebody else wasn't just rank foolishness. It was, as Dunn had said, degrading.

McLennan forced himself to stand up straight. He

couldn't shrug off the grip of the men holding him up, but he could stand without their help.

"You worthless fecking blood clots," he spit at her feet, and was perversely satisfied to see the gob was mostly blood. "No. Wait. I take that back. Blood clots at least serve a useful purpose. You are a waste of skin and a thin feckin' smear on the toilet bowl of history. You shouldae been flushed away with the floating turds and ruptured anal polyps of our benighted fecking past, but nae, you are the un-fucking-flushable shit pickles of humanity's worst nightmare."

He was starting to enjoy himself the way a maniac might enjoy tearing the wounds he has opened up on his own body.

"Yon pair of giant dildos over there in the archaic fecking iron turtle suits," he hooted at the armored shock troopers. "You think you look so fecking butch and all, but one wee Hab rat with a sharpened spoon will open you up like a tin can full of chocolate fecking sweeties. And yes, I watched your deeply unimpressive fecking combat drop completely arsed up by a handful of wee fecking Armadalen baby bots, not even a decent fecking warship worth the name, mind you, but the half-stupid fecking—"

Dunn disappeared.

She did not turn around and walk out on him. She simply winked out of existence.

The troopers in their powered armor suddenly toppled over, carrying the tarpaulin away with them. McLennan found himself out in the sun again, still completely naked and no longer supported by whoever had been holding him up. They, too, were gone.

Blinded by the sudden brightness, he squinted, trying to work out what was happening.

He heard alarms and shouts and the crack of gunfire.

Plasma bolts zipped in on him but careered away at the last second, deflected by a field effect.

The scorching desert air cooled to a pleasant chill. The harsh white light of Sujutus dimmed, and he could finally open his eyes again.

Just before he, too, winked out of existence, Frazer McLennan saw the familiar depthless obsidian black ovoid of the Intellect he called Hero.

CHAPTER
THIRTY

She was home. Alessia lay on a plain cot in one of the servants' quarters at Skygarth. The room had been emptied of all its contents except for a single bed and a bucket. It hadn't taken her long to figure out the purpose of the bucket. An inch of her own pee lay at the bottom. It smelled bad.

And she had been crying.

Alessia did not know where the Sturm had taken Caro and Debin. They were alive, or they had been a few hours ago when their captors had split them up.

Maybe they'd been allowed to go. They were naturally born. What some people called "purebred." They had no bioware, no mods or tweaks to their genetic code at all. From what she remembered of her history lessons—quite a bit once she'd calmed down—they were exactly what the Sturm meant when they referred to the "true human" race.

She shivered under the woolen blanket.

Dawn might be close, but it was hard to tell. There were no timepieces in the room. The palace was full of antique chronometers of all kinds, many of them heirlooms of Old Earth. But if there had been one or more in this room, a maid's apartment, she guessed, it had been removed. There was no point trying to guess from the sky. The Sturm had pointed a powerful searchlight at the window from the gardens below. It painted the ceiling with a brilliant, elongated rectangle of light and completely blotted out the stars, making it difficult to sleep.

The Sturm, she had decided, were fucking jerks.

Guards patrolled the grounds of Skygarth, but not her guards. They were all gone.

Dead, like the maid who had lived in this room.

Alessia found herself more upset at the way the Sturm had murdered Sergeant Reynolds than she was at the killing of her own family. She was terribly distressed at that, of course. Anyone with good breeding and manners would be. But she didn't really know many of her family, even most of her siblings, not the way she knew Reynolds, and her tutors—

Poor Professor Bordigoni!

—and even Melora. The Sturm had murdered Lady Melora as surely as they'd murdered Reynolds. Alessia was only twelve years old, but she wasn't stupid. She knew about malware and nanophage viruses and meat hacking and things like that. She'd just never imagined it could happen to her. It was the sort of thing criminals did to one another in the wilder parts of Combine space or in the Javan Empire.

Although, she conceded as she lay sobbing on the maid's bed, it hadn't really happened to her. Just to everyone around her. Because she was too young, at least by the customs of House Montanblanc, to have been implanted with neural mesh, she had been spared for . . . what?

She didn't know, but she was terrified.

She got up to squat over the bucket again. She couldn't stop going even though there was nothing left to pee.

There was so much she didn't know. Had the Sturm done anything to her family's secure life stores? Would her mother and the others be able to come back? They wouldn't remember the invasion and their murders, of course. But they'd be very, very angry when they found out. Alessia imagined the Home Fleet was already folding as fast as they could toward Montrachet and Skygarth.

But were they?

Mother probably was storming around Paris in a new body, still wet from the vat.

Was she? Really?

All those history lessons she'd been forced to actually learn rather than just download like the awful little princeling she'd been promised to, all of those lessons tormented her now. She did not imagine the Human Republic would make the mistake of half measures and tokenism. Whatever they had done here, they had done everywhere. She was sure of it.

And that . . . that was truly terrifying.

The maglocks on the door disengaged, and Alessia jumped a little, almost falling off the bucket. She blushed brightly as a woman stomped in, her combat boots loud on the polished hardwood floor.

"Clean yourself up and get dressed," the soldier said. A name tag sewn into her uniform identified her as Ji-yong. She wore sergeant's stripes just like Sergeant Reynolds.

Sergeant Ji-yong tossed a bundle of clothes on the bed.

Alessia was surprised to see they had chosen a nice outfit for her from her own rooms. It was the midnight blue dress with the trim of golden thread that she liked so much. A bejeweled brooch fashioned into the exquisite form of an edenflower blossom, the symbol of her House, had been pinned over the breast.

"You'll need this, too," the woman said, tossing a bejeweled circlet on the bed as if it were some cheaply printed trinket.

Alessia gasped.

That was the crown of Queen Josephine! To be worn only by the monarch of the House upon ascension to the post of chief executive officer.

"I can't wear that!" she protested.

"I'll admit, it's a little gaudy," Ji-yong said. "But you're a pretty girl. You'll wear the crown; it won't wear you. Promise."

"But . . ."

All the humor went out of her eyes.

"Get dressed and put the fucking crown on, Princess, or I'll get a hammer and nail it to your pretty little head."

Alessia's jaw dropped open. Nobody, not even Melora, had ever spoken to her like that. Even worse, she was sure this woman meant it. She hurried to the bed, stripped off her nightdress, and did as she was told. Even though she was shaking and her fingers felt numb, she had never dressed as quickly or with as little ceremony in her whole life.

"Where are my friends?" she asked as she put on the surprisingly heavy circlet. "Caro and Debin?"

"They're being questioned and assessed."

She was surprised to get an answer. Maybe it was the crown.

"What does that mean?"

"It means move your ass before I kick it out of the goddamn Volume."

The sergeant opened the door a little wider and gestured for Alessia to step through. Two more troopers waited outside, heavily armed and looking as though they had been in the fighting yesterday. They had none of the dashing élan of her household guardsmen, but they looked very scary. Alessia didn't need telling twice.

Out of the bedroom and the glare of the searchlight shining into it, her eyes adjusted to the gloom. It did look as though morning was not far away, and as they escorted her down the corridor, she caught sight of a grandfather clock near the stairwell. She knew where she was now. In the unmarried female servants' quarters, as she had suspected. And she knew what time it was. Just after five in the morning.

It was weird, walking through her own home as a prisoner. The female servants lived in a small two-story chateau a short walk from the villa. Crossing the gardens in between, Alessia was shocked at the damage to the main house. Scorch marks blackened the white marble of the upper floors. One whole corner of the house had collapsed. Her throat closed involuntarily as she saw a guardsman's boot sticking out of the rubble. A bloodied hand, missing a couple of fingers, seemed to reach for it from beneath a pile of shattered stone. A bonfire burned down near the topiary gardens, and when Alessia realized what was ablaze down there, she shut her mind to it, looking away.

A soft chill lay on her with the sun not yet above the horizon. She shivered.

One of the soldiers gave her a push in the back when she slowed down to look at the ruins of the music room. It was almost impossible to believe she had been in there just yesterday, her only concern how to avoid another half hour of tedious flute practice. She remembered Sergeant Reynolds carrying her off on his shoulder, and her eyes filled with tears again. Why had he trusted that Jasko Tan man? Why had Tan betrayed him?

Alessia had no idea. She didn't expect she would survive the morning. But if she did, if the Home Fleet arrived and the Royal Marines came to her rescue, she would have them find Mister Tan and bring him before her.

If she was going to wear Queen Josephine's crown, she would act as Queen Josephine would in these circumstances.

And Queen J was a legendary badass.

The small procession entered the villa through one of the smaller kitchens. It was used mainly for state occasions, especially garden parties at which the cooks needed to prepare extra food for service in the rose garden. It seemed untouched compared with the rest of the house, but there was a nasty smear of some dark liquid on the black and white tiles. Flies buzzed around it. Alessia lifted the hem of her skirt to avoid the mess, but the troopers stomped right on through.

Sergeant Ji-yong led her into the map room. It was more of a library, really. There were thousands of old books in there. Real books, many from Earth. But two large tables also displayed maps of the old world and the new, of Earth and Montrachet. The curling corners of the old Terran map were held down by polished brass instruments, a pair of leather-cased binoculars, and a ridiculously small model of Habitat Élysées in a clear crystal bottle. Globes stood in each corner, handcrafted replicas of the oldest worlds in the family's portfolio.

She recognized the man standing by the window, looking out over the gardens. It was the beard. Captain Kogan D'ur. So many feelings welled up, boiled up really, as soon as she saw him. Anger, fear, outrage. So many and so strongly felt that Alessia could not separate them. Captain D'ur, by way of contrast, seemed very relaxed.

"Sit down, Princess," he said, indicating one of the big leather tub chairs gathered in a nest around a coffee table. The way he said "princess" gave Alessia to understand that he wasn't being entirely respectful of her title.

There were cups and plates on the low table, but they were dirty. It did not appear that he had summoned her for breakfast.

"I need you to do something for me," he said.

"Accept your surrender?"

He smiled. And then he laughed. The Sturm all laughed. A rich, roaring thunder of mirth that rolled all around the room. It went on long enough that she understood they weren't mocking her. She'd said something genuinely funny. She had never made any grown-up laugh before, and, somewhat perversely, it made her feel better.

The captain's bellowing laughter quieted down to a chuckle, and he shook his head and wiped a small tear from his eye.

"Good one, kid. You got me. I did not see that coming."

He sighed like a man who had just eaten a very large plate of his favorite sandwiches.

"But no, Princess. We'll skip the surrender and get to the bit where you tell the rest of your defense forces to stand down. All your allies, too. The Armadalens. The ul Haq. And the Vikingars."

"But they're our defenders. And our allies. They're supposed to fight you."

Kogan D'ur clapped his hands together as though she was a prize pupil who had just solved a particularly difficult problem.

"Exactly!"

He stared at her, waiting for Alessia to make the connection.

"I don't understand," she said at last. "Why would I tell them to do that?"

"Oh, well, that's easy. Come here. Come on," he said, not unkindly. "I want you to see something."

Captain D'ur beckoned her up out of the chair and over to the picture window.

Initially intrigued, she felt her heart begin to race as she saw eight or nine of the household staff gathered on the lawn outside, guarded by four troopers. At a signal from D'ur one of the troopers stepped forward, put a gun to the head of Ms. Bakhti, the sous chef, and blew out her brains.

Alessia screamed.

"That's why you'll do what I say, Princess," D'ur said. "Because we'll keep shooting people in the head if you don't."

Darkness bloomed at the edge of her vision, and D'ur's voice sounded as though it were coming from the room next door. She swayed on her feet, and the room suddenly spun around her as Sergeant Ji-yong caught her in a swoon. The soldier carried her back to the armchair.

She did not pass out, but for a moment she couldn't speak or respond in any way. When Ji-yong gave her a glass of cold water, she drank it so quickly that her stomach cramped.

"Take it easy," D'ur cautioned her. "Just chill out. This doesn't have to be hard. I don't have to kill anybody else. I honestly don't want to kill anyone else. They're true human beings out there. We came to save them. And you're going to help us do that."

"How?" Alessia said, feeling utterly wretched and lost.

"Like I said. Just tell your forces and your allies to cease fire. To stand down. They'll listen to you. You're rocking that awesome-looking crown."

She shook her head as though having to explain something extra simple to a complete idiot.

"It's not me or the crown," she said. "It's the office. They obey the office of the chief executive."

D'ur smiled.

"Princess, you are the chief executive now."

It took a few seconds for the meaning to sink in.

"But my mother and father?"

He shook his head.

"My uncles and aunts. My family? The board?"

D'ur smiled apologetically.

"They're gone. And they're not coming back. You're it, kid. You are the chief executive. Time to step up and do some work."

That cold numbness and the deep body shudders it presaged came back to her as she understood what he was saying.

"You killed them all?" Alessia whispered. "For real?"

"We did. For real. And we'll kill you and everyone you care about, including your two little friends, if you don't do as we say. So what's it going to be? You gonna save some lives? Right now? Thousands of them, probably. Or do I have to go back to killing people? And this time I'll start with your friends. Caro and Bobbin, right?"

"Debin," she corrected him, her lips trembling.

"Whatever. I'll bring them in here, tell them what's happening, that you won't help me or them, and then I'll shoot them in the face while you watch."

Alessia's chin sank down on her chest, and she muttered, "I'll help."

"What's that?" Kogan D'ur asked loudly, cupping one hand to his ear.

Her face came up, spitting like a fire viper.

"I said I would do it."

D'ur smiled.

"Excellent choice."

"And then I want to see my friends. Caro and Debin."

Kogan D'ur shrugged easily.

"Kid, you just do as you're told and you can have pretty much anything you want . . . besides your family back, of course."

He laughed even harder at his joke than he had at hers.

CHAPTER

THIRTY-ONE

The Intellect was old—obsolete to be perfectly blunt about it—but still immensely powerful. One of six Armada-level Intellects that had controlled the combined fleets in the first war against the Sturm, it had retired from active service to pursue private interests shortly after the last Republican Generation Ship folded into the Dark. Even with all that had happened in the last few hours, Lucinda had to force herself to accept the reality of what was happening right now.

This Intellect, perhaps the only survivor of its kind in the Greater Volume, was floating in her bridge. It was carrying on a micro-g wave the badly injured, grossly abused body of Admiral Frazer McLennan.

He was naked.

And they were arguing.

"Och, Hero, you look like a dog licking piss off a nettle, you miserable twat," McLennan snarled at the Intellect. "You could've at least found me a pair of trews before you dropped me in the midst of polite company, you clanking fucking bampot."

"Oh, really?" the Intellect retorted. "How very odd of you to say, because I had long ago concluded that going pantsless was your natural state of being. Perhaps because your lifeless genitalia have so thoroughly shriveled away in your advanced dotage that were you to lose them inside the folds of your adult diaper, you would probably never find them again."

"Gentlemen?"

"My noble todger isn't naturally shriveled, damn you. I am merely suffering the ill effect of your complete inability to manage something as simple as fucking climate control."

"Like you managed the simple job of sneaking up on the enemy camp with the most advanced stealth technology available in the Greater Volume?"

"Gentlemen!"

The Intellect dipped a few inches in Lucinda's direction. Admiral McLennan tried to turn his head to her but grimaced in obvious discomfort. His arms hung loose at his sides, but the bruised and swollen ruin of his shoulders and armpits spoke to both limbs being badly injured. His skin was bright red and blistered with sunburn, and there was a slightly mad cast to his eyes.

"Aye, lass," he said, swaying a little as he floated on the carrier wave. "My apologies. I'm not at my best today. I am in fact more than a little fucked. I wonder if you might have a doctor on board your fine ship who could see to my unfucking with all dispatch. I feel as though my arms have been pulled out of their sockets, because to be honest, they have. And a pair of trousers would be good. And about a half a gallon of single malt painkiller. No ice, thank you."

Lucinda spoke slowly, as if to a child.

"Commander Hardy . . . Admiral. Welcome aboard *Defiant*."

"Your ship's Intellect is indisposed," Hero said.

"Breached by malware, I'm afraid. We are operating entirely under human control."

The main hatch to the bridge hissed open, and two medics rushed in with a litter. They gently lifted Admiral McLennan onto it, draping him with a white sheet and administering anesthetic directly into his carotid.

"Aye, I'm not going anywhere just yet," he protested. "Captain Hardy . . ."

"Commander, sir."

"Och, I can make you a captain if you like."

"That won't be necessary, sir."

"Captain it is, then!"

McLennan took a moment to thank the medics for attending to him.

"I presume you have some idea of what is going on, Captain Hardy," he went on. "Might you favor me with a very quick summation?"

Lucinda was more than happy to report their situation to a higher officer, even one as eccentrically indisposed as McLennan. She sketched out the parameters of their original mission in as few words as possible and only because the loss of the long-range probes was now definitely explained by the return of the Sturm. She passed quickly through the malware attack that had compromised *Defiant*'s Intellect and killed Torvaldt, the XO, and Wojkowski, finishing with her decision to scrap the original mission and return by maximum fold to the nearest inhabited volume.

"Which finds us here, roughly triangulated with Batavia's L1 and L2 points, point nine three AU from Sujutus, the local star. We have engaged two enemy ships. Destroyed one and boarded the other for exploit. A third, smaller enemy vessel is about ten klicks off our bow, locked onto a civilian trader that . . . well, look, they're . . . pirates, I suppose. They defeated the boarding operation with the help of a mechanized unit that had escaped a TDF facility. A military prison. There's a lot of wrack and drift ships and even single castaways floating around the vacuum out here right now. And six more Republican warships inbound on our position, including one Titan-class analogue. They will be within our weapons range in seventeen minutes."

"And when . . . when might we expect a . . . a wee tickle from them, do you imagine, Captain Hardy?"

The pain meds were hitting McLennan hard. His eyes were drooping, and he was obviously fighting for consciousness.

"It's Commander, sir. And I cannot say, Admiral," she said.

"Good girl." He yawned. "That's the correct answer. Talk to my friend here. He will tell you what we know."

His head fell back on the stretcher, and the medics guided it to the hatch on its own micro-g wave.

"Not so fecking fast," he croaked. "I'm not going anywhere. You can see to me here. I promise not to make a fuss."

The corpsmen exchanged glances before looking to Lucinda for direction.

Hero sighed. "Just stick his arms back in. It will be less trouble than getting him to behave if he doesn't get what he wants."

The bridge crew tended to their stations while Lucinda's medical staff attended to McLennan. In spite of the pain relief, he still screamed when they forced his arms back into their sockets. Chase visibly shuddered while plotting multiple fold paths. Lieutenant Chivers concentrated fiercely on scooping up as much of the enemy's comms traffic as *Defiant*'s arrays could take in. Fein ran weapons checks. Four of Hayes's marines stood combat ready in light armor. All the naval personnel now wore side arms. The marines did not flinch as McLennan bellowed like an injured beast.

"Commander," the Intellect said as though nothing at all was awry. "With your permission I would like to examine all of your system diagnostics before I brief you on developments planetside, on what I have been able to deduce from signals intercepts and from my capture of all traffic in-volume since the arrival of the Sturm."

Lucinda gave Lieutenant Bannon an inquiring look.

"Won't be a problem, ma'am." He then addressed the Intellect over Admiral McLennan's voluble moans. "Defiant Actual quarantined himself as soon as he knew he'd been breached. The ship's Intellect has been fighting the malign code ever since."

"I understand," said Hero. "If I may?"

Lucinda nodded her assent, and Bannon gave the Intellect full access to the ship's systems.

A second later Hero cut the link.

Lucinda felt the deck shudder under her boots.

"What the hell was that?" she asked.

"I'm afraid I had to excise Defiant Actual from the ship's central processing arrays."

"You what?"

"I have displaced the Intellect into the core of the local sun."

Lucinda swore loudly, but her curses were lost in the general uproar as the Armadalens realized they had just lost the soul of their vessel forever.

"Och, don't make a fuss," McLennan groaned. "Hero is forever throwing things into that bloody star."

"He just killed Defiant!" Lucinda shouted, coming up out of the captain's chair.

"Actually," Hero responded, "Defiant was doomed from the moment you opened the dead drop link that allowed malware onto your ship. It is a credit to him that he was able to contain the attack for as long as he did. But his defenses were failing, Commander. And when the last of them fell, you would have been as vulnerable as every other vessel on the zero point network, which is to say you and your ship would have died. In two days, three hours, and ten minutes by my calculation."

"He threw a young woman in there, you know," McLennan said somewhat cryptically. "And my sandwich crusts, of course. Toasty . . . toasty crusts."

"What?" Lucinda asked, still reeling from Hero's

arbitrary decision to excise and destroy her ship's Intellect.

"A jammie dodger. And a difficult young woman to be sure. We were having a chat, not the most pleasant conversation I've ever had, but I think I was bringing her around."

"The admiral could use some more anesthetic," Hero suggested. "Enough to put him under for the next twenty years or until he decides to relife into a more appropriate biotic casing."

"Ha, you'd like that, wouldn't you, you punishing fucking whinger? You'd—"

"Shut. The fuck. Up."

Silence fell across the bridge.

"The pair of you! Just shut up," Lucinda shouted. "You!" She pointed at Hero. "This is not a Terran Defense Force ship, and you do not have authority here. This is a warship of the Royal Armadalen Navy, and you will not go displacing wounded Intellects or difficult women or jammie fucking dodgers into the core of nearby stars or anywhere for that fucking matter. Don't. Do it. Again. Or I'll displace your ass into the vacuum and you can take your chances with the burning shipwrecks, the pirates, the random fucking prison mechs, and the Sturm for all I care. And as for you," she said, turning on McLennan, "you're here as a courtesy and a precaution. When this psychopath"— she jerked a thumb at Hero—"contacted us and asked permission to urgently displace on board, I agreed because quite frankly, I have no fucking idea what's happening with my own chain of command and you are the most senior military officer I've encountered since our captain went insane and tried to eat the XO. But admiral or not, you will treat this ship and its crew with the respect they are due or I will space you in a heartbeat."

At least three quiet heartbeats followed before anybody said anything.

"By fuck, she's a wee cracker." McLennan giggled.

And then he passed out.

Hero drifted across half the bridge to float in front of Lucinda for a moment before dipping almost to the deck plate.

"My apologies, Commander. We have been a long time in the desert. Perhaps I might brief you now on what we understand about the Republic's doctrine, strategy, and tactics."

"Perhaps," Lucinda replied with icy reserve.

"Fuck me, Cinders," a new but familiar voice chimed in. "Is it always this much fun on your ship?"

Sephina was back.

"She did it again, Commander!" Nonomi Chivers cried out.

All Lucinda had left was a face palm, and she gave it her best shot.

Invasions by ancient and evil space fascists she could handle. The extrajudicial murder of her ship's crippled Intellect? That, too, at a pinch. A naked drug-fucked Scottish admiral displacing out of the history books and onto her bridge? She'd seen worse.

But Sephina L'trel? Again?

No. Some things were just intolerable.

Seph's holo stood next to the gurney on which McLennan had passed out.

"Who's this fucking fossil?" she said. "No. Sorry. Rhetorical question," she went on. "But legit concern here, Cinders. You think your brilliant engineers might actually cut us free before those shitheads from Club Dark get here?"

"Yes," Lucinda hissed. "Now cut the link and stop trolling my comms officer."

"Commander, I think you should see this," Lieutenant Chivers, the officer in question, said.

"Put it up," Lucinda said, ignoring the fact that Seph was still there.

The main visual suddenly expanded with the image of a frightened young girl in a blue goldtrimmed dress, sitting in a library, wearing a crown. She was blinking into a hard light.

"We just picked this up from Montrachet, ma'am," Chivers explained. "It must have gone out over the ZP network. Montrachet is four light-years away."

"Four point three," Chase corrected her.

Lucinda held her hand up for silence.

"I am Princess Alessia Szu Suri sur Montanblanc ul Haq," the girl said. She was reading from a piece of paper. Very old-school. "I am the sole surviving heir to all assets of House Montanblanc and to the holdings in toto of the Montanblanc–ul Haq Alliance of Corporate Worlds."

"Holy shit," said Varro Chase.

"As commander in chief of the armed forces of Montanblanc and the director of the alliance's security division, I hereby direct all forces under my command to cease resistance to the legitimate authority of the Human Republic."

"Traitorous bitch!" Chase cried out.

"Lieutenant," Lucinda snapped. "As you were."

"Archon-Admiral Wenbo Strom, Republican commander in the local volume, personally assures me that he wishes to minimize casualties and his forces will honor any cease-fire and surrender."

The girl's voice was shaking. She kept blinking rapidly and checking her place on the sheet of paper. Lucinda felt terrible for her. If it was true that she was the surviving heir to her House, she was all alone. Lucinda did not need to wonder what that felt like.

"Human life is precious," the little girl said, her voice hitching. "Let us not waste any more this day."

The image looped back to the start of the track.

"I am Princess Alessia Szu Suri . . ."

"That's enough," Lucinda said, resuming the captain's chair.

An alarm sounded from Lieutenant Fein's station.

"Targeting sensors sweeping us, ma'am," he said. "Weak signal. No lock. But it's the first scan we've detected."

"They've found the *Regret*," Seph's holo called out, almost as though she were telling somebody on her ship, not Hardy's.

"Missile launch detected," Fein said, his voice gulping a little.

"Sound to general quarters," Lucinda ordered. "Mister Fein, countermeasures."

Master Chief Higo, standing on the quarter ring, bellowed, "All hands, general quarters!"

"I would recommend we fold immediately, Commander," the Intellect advised. "I have analyzed your threat arrays, and those missiles, there are two, will be here in three minutes and fifteen seconds."

"Killing with guns, ma'am," Lieutenant Fein declared.

"I cannot get to you in three minutes," Sephina said. She sounded angry rather than scared.

"I have a fast shuttle about to leave."

"It won't get here in time."

"I know. I'm ordering it to stand down."

She felt the deck plates vibrate as *Defiant*'s gun ports rumbled open and the long-range pulse cannons deployed.

"Oh, that'd be fucking right."

"Sephina, shut up and listen or I will cut this link and leave you to die," Lucinda said. She turned to Hero. "Can you displace onto that ship and extract the personnel?"

The big guns fired with that strange harmonic murmur.

"I am an Armada-level Intellect, Commander Hardy."

"Then why are you still here?"

Hero disappeared with a soft pop.

"Kill one, kill two," Fein announced.

Lucinda did not have time to congratulate him before he spoke again.

"Vampire! Vampire! Vampire! Multiple missile launches from the cruiser, ma'am. Three hundred missiles inbound."

"Countermeasures," she replied, making the effort to sound calm or even bored.

"Aye, Commander."

She heard something like four soft snaps, and her bridge was suddenly populated by Sephina's motley crew. A giant hybrid so large that his . . . well, his horn . . . almost scraped the overhead plating. A thin brown-skinned man festooned with knives and gore. A generic white male of such unremarkable appearance that he might have passed for an unlucky shipping clerk who found himself aboard the vessel when everything went sideways.

And Sephina. Wild of mane, a furious aspect to the eyes, and drenched with the blood of the master race.

"You owe me a ship," she said. "For starters."

"Sweet Mother of God, they smell bad," Chase muttered.

The individual reports of the pulsing autocannons became a constant thrum as *Defiant* serviced the missile swarm closing in on Sephina's ship.

"Commander?" the Intellect said.

Fein interrupted. "Ma'am, the Sturm appear to have programmed this launch for volumetric spread. They're going to saturate the space around Ms. L'trel's ship with area-denial warheads."

"I was about to say that," Hero remarked as if to himself. "But of course I'm just an Armada-level Intellect. What would I know?"

"And what are you still doing here? Again?" Lucinda asked pointedly. "There's another man to bring back on the *Regret*."

"I'd quibble with the term 'man.' It's a mech, running the source code for a condemned TDF corporal."

"So? Bring him over."

"I'm afraid the mech is at the very limits of my displacement patterning specs."

"Multiple launches detected, Commander," Fein

called out. "From the cruiser's escort vessels. They're riding its targeting arrays."

"Countermeasures, Mister Fein. As a general rule, from now on, when they launch, let's just go with countermeasures."

"You know, I could run this whole battle for you," said Hero. "I am an Armada-level Intellect, after all."

"With another job to do. Get that mech back. I need to debrief him."

The floating ovoid made a noise that sounded very much like an exasperated sigh.

It disappeared.

"Mister Chase, make ready to fold out of system."

"Yes, ma'am," the navigator acknowledged, sounding for the first time as though he was genuinely pleased to be taking an order from her.

Sephina appeared at her elbow, in the real this time.

"So, you look like you're busy. Is there a bar on this ship? Cos, baby, I got sorrows need drowning like unwanted kittens."

"Chief Higo," Lucinda called out. "Arrange escorts to the enlisted mess for our guests. Via the showers if possible."

"Ready to fold, Commander," Chase called out.

"One minute, Commander," Lieutenant Fein said. "Some of the missile swarm is going to get through."

"You'd better hurry if you want that drink," Lucinda quipped to Seph. "Mister Chase, we fold in thirty seconds on my mark . . . Mark."

"Aye, Captain."

Hero reappeared. Without the mech.

"Where is he?" Lucinda demanded.

"He's coming."

"Commander Hardy!" Fein shouted. "Missile launch detected. From the civilian trader."

Seph shrugged. "Don't look at me."

"I could not displace the mech with an acceptable chance of success," Hero explained, "so Corporal Booker has attached himself to a short-range missile in the armory of the *Je Ne Regrette Rien*. I believe he is attempting to disarm the warhead. At any rate, he will cross your bow in a few moments, and if you would care to extend the event horizon when you fold, I believe he has a good chance of being carried along with us and possibly even surviving the trip."

CHAPTER
THIRTY-TWO

Booker was spending a lot of time in the vacuum. That was okay. He'd done a lot of fighting on the high side in combat chassis and skin jobs. Never been strapped to a missile in a busted-ass mech and fired into space before, though. That was novel even in a day full of novelty.

There was no way he was going to fit in the launch tube, of course. The little engineer, Falun Kot, had pointed him to the ship's armory; given him an unlock code, which didn't work; and displaced away with the Intellect and his shipmates. Booker ignored the unlock code, used his grappler to tear off the clamps holding the missile, and carried it back up to the main cargo bay. He depressurized the bay, opened the door, and was trying to interface with the control boards for the missile when the Intellect returned.

"Oh, just let me do it."

Even with the mech's badly damaged arrays, Booker was able to sense the Intellect's field projectors close around the warhead.

"There," it said almost immediately.

"You sure?"

"Well, of course I'm only an Armada-level Intellect who controlled the combined fleets of Earth and the corporate worlds in an existential struggle against their greatest foe, and you are, I must admit, a couple of lines of poorly written, hugely limited sentient script in a broken riot control bot, but yes, I think you'll be okay. I've even written a guidance applet to track the *Defiant* should it do something silly in the next couple of minutes. Pay your money. Take the ride."

"Check your privilege, computer," Booker shot back. "I'm just riding this mech. I'm a man. I have a soul. I've met your type before. You're the reason the Source had to fight for every gain we've ever made."

"Yeah, yeah, you're a real boy, Pinocchio. Get on the rocket."

"I can't ride it like a toy horse."

"Then hold on," said the Intellect.

Booker had just enough time to tighten his grappler hold on the missile when he felt the thrusters fire and carry him out of the open cargo bay door. As soon as he was clear, the main engine ignited and punched him into the vacuum, accelerating at a rate that would have shredded a human body. Of course a human body could never have survived in the vacuum, anyway.

It was only when he was speeding toward the Armadalen ship that he wondered what the hell he was supposed to do next. Jump off?

The Intellect hadn't given him any clue.

He was traveling so quickly, barely hanging on to

the runaway munition, that as soon as his cams picked up the outline of the vessel, he was upon it.

And then he wasn't.

He was nowhere.

Defiant folded out of the Sujutus system, three AU beyond the heliopause.

The ship's alarms, which had been sounding the imminent arrival of the missile swarm, fell silent.

Only one continued.

"The mech and the warhead passed by us, ma'am, at a separation of three thousand meters," Lieutenant Fein reported. "Now heading into interstellar space."

"Launch a fast shuttle to recover the mech. As long as it doesn't explode, I guess," Lucinda said.

The world turned black as Booker's soul departed the mech. When it came back, he was aware of his surroundings but not his place in them.

"Oh, come on!" he cried out.

"Corporal Booker," said a female officer, an Armadalen to judge by her uniform, "I am Commander Lucinda Hardy, and you are on board the stealth destroyer HMAS *Defiant*."

"In an eX-Box?" he said. "You transferred me to an eX-Box?"

"My apologies, Corporal," the woman called Hardy said. "Your chassis was very badly damaged. I don't know whether you were aware of it, but you lost everything below the hip flexors in the fold, and you had already suffered damage to most of your critical systems, including the substrate holding your source code. My engineer judged it best to flash-transfer you to an emergency external storage unit. So yes, sorry. We had to put you in the box. It was a close-run thing, taking you with us on the fold like that. I don't believe it's ever been done before."

"I could have done it better," someone muttered.

No. Not someone. It was that computer again. Hero.

If Booker had eyes, he would have rolled them hard.

Instead he had a limited field of view from the one AV port on the box. He could see he was in some sort of officers' wardroom on board this ship, *Defiant*. He was sitting, it seemed, in his little storage unit on a wooden table. He recognized the captain of the *Je Ne Regrette Rien,* Sephina, who seemed very subdued, and the Intellect when it floated into view. But nobody else.

"Allow me," said Commander Hardy. She looked young, with a biotic age in the early twenties, and Booker wondered how many times she had relifed. The Armadalens didn't use source code and clone vats to fill out their ranks. They were famously uptight about things like that.

"This is Admiral Frazer McLennan of the Terran Defense Force."

In his own mind Booker did a comic double take. *The* Frazer McLennan?

Both of his arms were in slings, and he looked like an angry, underfed golem carved from oatmeal, egg yolks, and rancid spam—about three hundred years ago.

"The fuck you looking at, box head?" McLennan growled.

How did he know . . .

"And this is the Intellect . . ."

"I've met the computer," Booker said, loading the word with all the contempt it deserved. "On Ms. L'trel's ship. Thank you, Captain, by the way," he added for L'trel's benefit. "I didn't get a chance to offer my thanks for taking me in after I . . . left the TDF facility I was in."

"It's not like you asked, Book," Seph said quietly. "But you killed a lot of assholes I was going to have to kill anyway. So let's say we're even."

Hardy introduced the personnel in the wardroom. A marine officer called Hayes and a bunch of her own people he didn't so much forget as ignore. When you were running on hardware, there was no forgetting anything unless your substrate failed. The only two he really noted were an engineer called Timuz, the one who'd dumped him into the emergency storage unit, presumably, and some kid with a face you could punch all day. Varro Chase. The genius who'd cut off his legs when they folded away from Sujutus.

"This facility you left, Corporal," Hardy went on when her introductions were done. "Was that the TDF military prison at L1?"

If Booker had been ensouled within a human body, he would have stiffened. He had no idea whether they were monitoring his engram in the box, but he had to assume they were.

"Yes, ma'am."

"And you were . . . ?" Hardy left the question hanging.

"A prisoner, ma'am."

"I see. And you escaped?"

"I was released, ma'am. On the authority of Captain Lao Tzu after agreeing to transfer into the Compliance Mech in which you found me. To help repel the enemy forces that had breached the Hab."

"I see," she said again.

He waited for her to ask why he'd been imprisoned and what sentence he was serving. Booker resolved to tell them. Wasn't like there was much he could do about it. They could just crack his engram open if they wanted. That was the sort of shit breeders did to people like him all the time.

But Commander Hardy just looked at him, her head tilted slightly to one side.

The punchy-faced kid, Varro Chase, started to say something, but she shut him down with a raised finger.

"Corporal," she said carefully, "would you agree to let us read your memory for the period covering the arrival of the Sturm on the prison Hab to your coming aboard *Defiant*?"

"I'm . . . I . . ."

Booker was genuinely confused by the request. Not by what she had asked for but by the very fact of her asking.

"I'm . . . yeah . . . sure," he said, realizing that his own memories would prove what he'd just told her about Lao Tzu. They also would reveal him to have been saved from deletion at the very last moment, but he was going to bet that he could trust this woman. Maybe because she'd paid him the simple courtesy of asking his permission. She had to be on her fifth or sixth span, he concluded. She seemed very wise.

He unlocked the ROM silo within his source code.

A young officer with the name tag BANNON made a copy of the contents and transferred them to a holofield display.

The conference watched an accelerated replay of his last hour on the Hab from the moment Lao Tzu and Orr had come to get him to his escape into the vacuum.

Hardy stopped the replay there.

"Captain L'trel and her crew have spoken highly of your actions aboard her ship, Corporal Booker. I don't think we need to review them here. For your own peace of mind, however, understand that you are on board an Armadalen vessel, not a Terran ship or facility. The Commonwealth of Armadale does not allow the creation or use of personnel from a source code base, but neither does it outlaw their presence within our borders or persecute them for practicing their faith. There are many people of your . . . origin and faith in the Commonwealth. I do not propose to make a priority of returning you to the Terran authorities, and given the agreement you struck with Captain Lao—"

"Aye, for fuck's sake," McLennan growled. "Let's not tie our fucking willies into a Gordian fucking knot over this. Booker, did ye kill anyone when ye mutinied and went over tae the rebels in the Source? I presume that's why they were planning to clean your fucking clock."

Even ensouled within the basic circuitry of the eX-Box, he could still bristle at the question.

"No, I did not," he said. "I simply refused an order to fire on my own kind."

"The TDF were your own kind," the Intellect quickly put in.

"Och, shut your cake hole, Hero; you always were an ignorant fucking bigot on this tedious topic. And all because you cannae download yourself into a decent bod for a cold beer and a blow job. You and your kind are half the fucking problem with the source coders. And we don't need it here."

McLennan leaned forward and grimaced with obvious discomfort.

"Son, you got yourself into a small, stupid insurrection, not a holy war. But now you really are in a holy war or something so close to a crusade as makes no fucking difference. By the power invested in me by virtue of being the legendary McLennan and because I'm a fucking admiral and I can do what I want, I hereby absolve you of all your youthful fucking stupidity and poor decision making and reinstate you to the Terran Defense Force at the rank of staff sergeant."

He swiveled his entire upper body to face Commander Hardy.

"Does that make having him along a little less awkward for you, lassie?"

Hardy managed a wan smile. "Yes, sir, it does."

Booker almost objected that he didn't want to be reinstated to the TDF at any rank but saw the Intellect glowering a deep vermilion shade behind McLennan and decided he might shut his cake hole, too.

"So, Sergeant Booker," McLennan continued. "Neither Captain Lao Tzu nor Corporal Orr was able to access or load code when the Sturm attacked. Is that right?"

"Yes, sir," Booker confirmed. "The captain couldn't even work the console to delete me."

"Do you know if the connection to the skills codex was severed or if the codex itself was destroyed?" Hardy asked.

"I don't know, ma'am. But if I was going to kick somebody's legs out from underneath them, I'd kick both out."

"Fair point," McLennan said. "Captain L'trel, when you were on Eassar, you saw a number of people affected by neural net malware."

"A Yakuza plate boss. Some HabSec commanders. Not the foot soldiers, though. Just the boss levels."

"Aye. We saw it ourselves on Batavia. A wee knobhead from the Yulin clan. Plugged himself in to the livestream via a boosted uplink. Went utterly berserk. He was the only one. We were not short of Elite Fraction parasites, either. But none of them had live backup running. We were too far out in the wastes."

"Captain Torvaldt and Lieutenant Wojkowski plugged in to a live link to a dead drop," Commander Hardy told him. "Same result."

McLennan swiveled his chair toward the Intellect.

"And while I remember Trumbull's pack of useless bludgers, what did you end up doing with them, by the way? They didn't prove much of a distraction to the Sturm."

"I escorted them to a Combine mining facility and left them there. It was in some disarray, but when I did not hear from you, I assumed you had completely buggered up your little adventure, and so I swooped in to rescue you."

"I had everything under control."

"You were hanging by your wrists in the nude."

"'Appear weak when you are strong and strong when you are weak,'" McLennan quoted. "Sun Tzu. *The Art of War.*"

"Really?" the Intellect replied. "I don't recall him hanging by his elbows with his desiccated gonads swaying in the breeze. If you appeared any weaker, the enemy would have had to surrender on general principles."

"Gentlemen," Hardy said. "If we could move on? To Princess Alessia?"

"Aye," McLennan grunted. "We're going to have to do something about her."

Hardy looked alarmed.

"You're not going to throw her into the sun, too?" she said quickly.

"Och, no, lass. No. As best we can tell, she is the sole surviving authority in the local volume. On Batavia, Eassar, or Montrachet. She is now also the congressional rep for the Montrachet system. As well as the commander in chief of her House and alliance forces. She can issue orders."

"She has issued orders!" someone bleated. "To surrender."

It was the kid again. Chase. Booker had decided he really did not like him, but he said nothing. He was beginning to think they'd forgotten about him, sitting quietly in his little box, and if he said anything now, they might turn him off.

"We should send them a message," Chase said.

"And her and anybody who would collaborate like her."

"She's not collaborating, you daft numptie," McLennan said.

"With all due respect, Admiral . . ."

"Och, don't even bother, son. The only reason anybody ever says that is to give them time for the dropping of their britches and the squeezing of a giant turd into my lap. I'll forgo the turd if ye dinnae mind. Mister Bannon, could you replay Her Little Majesty's command performance for us?"

As Booker watched, a young girl appeared in a holofield. She wore a crown, and she looked very scared.

"I am Princess Alessia Szu Suri sur Montanblanc ul Haq," she began.

But Booker did not really attend to anything else that she said. He was instantly drawn to the unnatural blinking of her eyes.

It was repetitive.

Coded.

"She's telling us something," he said, forgetting where he was.

"She's telling her forces to surrender," Chase snorted.

"No, Sergeant Booker is correct," McLennan said. "I should have made him a sergeant major. Princess Alessia is blinking in code. Specifically in old Morse code. I learned it as a boy. In the Cub Scouts, you know. From what I know of the Montanblancs, they probably forced her to learn it by rote, along with campfire cooking, Egyptian hieroglyphics, and navigating by the local stars."

"Actually, Admiral, the code is still taught at the Armadalen Naval Academy."

It was Hardy again. She turned to Lieutenant Chase.

"You should be able to interpret it, Mister Chase."

He blushed and began to stammer out an excuse for obviously being unable to do so.

"I'll save you the trouble of further embarrassing yourself, laddie," McLennan said. "It's the same word over and over again. A long blink and a short. Followed by three more long. The letters 'n' and 'o.' She's saying no, Lieutenant Chase. No. No. No."

"But she still ordered her forces to stand down," he protested.

"And some doubtless will do just that," McLennan admitted. "But enough will see her true message. And that, my young friend, is the sort of mad, hopeless gesture that inspires a people and wins a war. So we are going to rescue that little girl, and she is going to save us all from the Dark-accursed Sturm."

CHAPTER
THIRTY-THREE

"We need your help."

They were alone.

"*I* . . . need your help," Lucinda said.

If Sephina had not been feeling so wretched, she might have laughed. As it was, she managed an expression that died somewhere on its way to becoming a mirthless grimace.

She rolled her chair back from the beautiful wooden table in the spacious officers' wardroom that reeked of tradition and hummed with the power of the fabled and awesomely storied Royal Armadalen Navy. Her boots crashed down on the tabletop, and the diminutive black puck of the external storage unit jumped an inch to the left.

"And I need a new ship, a lot of guns, and a clear run at the motherfuckers who murdered my girlfriend."

Lucinda frowned. As Seph recalled, that was her natural state of being.

"I'm sorry about Ariane," she said. "You'd been together a long time."

Shrug.

"You make me sound old, Cinders. I'm not."

Lucinda fell into the chair next to Seph and dropped her head into her hands. "Neither am I," she said. It was like watching a bulkhead slowly collapse and spew atmosphere into the vacuum. She raked her fingers back through her hair, a gesture Seph recalled from their childhood. She'd never met a kid who brushed her fucking hair so much. Sephina's own hair tangled into dreadlocks when she grew it out to hide the massive chunk her crazy fucking mother had cut out of her ear because she thought there was a bug in her source code.

Sephina didn't have source code. Not like her mother, the crazy bitch.

"I can't do this," Hardy said in a tiny voice.

"What're you looking for, a mercy hump or something?"

"Oh, fuck off, Sephina," Lucinda muttered, sounding exhausted.

Sephina started to climb to her feet, gesturing theatrically.

"By your command, my captain . . ."

That broke through. Lucinda's head snapped forward, and she spit out her next words. "Omigod, just sit the fuck down, would you? You are the only person on this ship I can talk to right now."

"Then perhaps you should stop treating me like a tactical problem and start talking to me like a friend."

Lucinda looked up. Her eyes were red-rimmed and fearful.

"You still think we're friends?"

"Do you?"

Lucinda said nothing.

Seph blew out an explosive sigh.

"Fine! I apologize. I'm sorry I stole that money from the nuns. I'm sorry that I said you helped me steal it. I'm really fucking sorry I told them we spent it on lesbian tentacle porn."

"I'm not even a lesbian!" Lucinda shouted. She was out of the chair again, leaning over Seph, her hands bunched into little white fists. "And I hate tentacles! They fucking freak me out, man."

Actually, now that Seph looked at Hardy's fists, they weren't so little anymore, and it looked like she'd been punching oak trees into splinters for a couple of years. Seph had to wonder at what her oldest surviving friend had been up to since she lit out from the Hab. Antipiracy patrols of course. She knew about that. But that also had been a long time ago, before the Javan War. Before this fresh hell and madness. *Who are you?* she thought to herself. *What did you do with my friend?* Sephina doubted she would ever find out. To be honest, she doubted either of them would live through the next few days.

"Sit down, Cinders. Please. Just . . . sit. Okay?"

Her voice was cracked and tired. Commander Hardy reluctantly resumed her seat.

Jesus Christ.

Commander Hardy! She was like three ass kissings away from becoming an admiral. Where was the scared little girl she'd taken under her protection that first night on Coriolis?

"Is there any decent booze in this terrible club?" Seph asked.

"I can't drink," Lucinda said. "I'm on duty."

"Sucks to be you, but I'm not."

Lucinda rubbed a hand down her face, pulling her features into an elongated fright mask.

"There's plenty," she said, waving in the direction of a dark wood cabinet. "You like wine, don't you? Grab a bottle of the Château François. It's from one of Lieutenant Chase's family vineyards. It's probably worth more than you stole from the Yakuza."

"That's the Cinders I used to know! Cheers. That Chase dude, he's that first life puckered anus with delusions of adequacy, right? Kept sniping from the cheap seats during your little Camelot roundtable before?"

Hardy snorted.

"That's him, yeah." She slumped again. "Oh, Seph, I don't know what I'm doing here. I don't know that I even belong. I just . . ."

To Sephina's surprise and not a little discomfort, Lucinda began to cry. It started with hitching shoulders but escalated to gulping snotty wails.

And there she was. Little Lucinda.

The Loose Unit, they'd called her at first. The kid whose mom had died and whose dad couldn't fend off the reclaimers. The woman in front of Sephina L'trel wore the combat fatigues of a renowned military force. Her scarred knuckles, the way her uniform bulged around major muscle groups, the cold arctic distance Seph had seen in her eyes—that woman was a killer. Seph had met more than her share.

She'd become one herself, to be honest.

"What're you, fishing for compliments or something? Come on, girl. You fucking totally belong here. Just look at you rockin' your girly Hornblower shit."

But at that very moment, with her face buried in those hardened hands and her chest hitching with sobs, Lucinda Hardy looked like she belonged back in Hab Welfare with only the clothes on her back and a cheap holoprojector clamped in her tiny fist.

That holo was why they'd become friends.

Cinders had flipped over some invisible line into hysterical violence when one of the other kids tried to take it off her. That had caught Sephina's attention. The kid's obvious intelligence and her willingness to use it in the cause of their survival had held Seph's interest even after Ariane had arrived and slipped into her bunk.

She reached out and squeezed Lucinda's hand. But it was Cinders, of course, and she snatched her hand away at the first touch. Seph gave up on trying to comfort her and retrieved one of the stupidly expensive bottles of wine, pulled the cork, and set two glasses on the table.

Hardy blinked through floods of tears.

"I'm on d-duty."

"Fuck duty. You guys can gland that stupid Dtox shit. Although fuck knows why you would. Seems completely fucking pointless to me. But sure, have a drink, then sober up. There's got to be an upside to turning yourself into a slave soldier for the High Bourse, baby."

Cinders sniffled, possibly even smiled in among all the blubbering and woe, but still she shook her head.

"I can't. I ordered the crew to shut down and metabolize their neural nets. We still have spinal syrettes but no way to activate them now. This nanophage attack, whatever it is, it's just too risky for anyone with mesh. Look at you. They spiked Eassar, a whole fucking Hab, but you didn't even get a scratch because you're not hooked up."

Sephina spilled some of the red wine she was pouring. She stared at the tabletop, not willing to look up at Lucinda, who quickly recognized her mistake.

"I'm sorry! I'm sorry, Seph. I forgot about Ariane. Omigod, I'm so sorry. I loved her, too. She was the best." She reached out across the table and grabbed Sephina's hand, and this time Lucinda did not flinch away. "We were the fucking musketeers," Lucinda said fiercely. Another pause. "What happened?"

Sephina took a solid slug of the wine. Sloshed more over the side.

"You left us."

Lucinda closed her eyes. She rubbed away the tears with the back of her hand.

"But I had to." She gathered herself up from wherever she'd gone, glaring at Seph. "And you almost stopped me. That stunt you pulled. I almost lost my scholarship. I could have lost everything, Sephina. What you did was wrong."

Lucinda balled up a fist and hit her on the arm, and then Sephina knew for sure: she really had been punching trees or rocks or Javan Combat Mechs for years.

"Ow!" Seph cried.

"Sorry."

"Let's just call it even, bitch."

She rubbed at the sore spot.

"Look, I'm sorry I almost ruined your dream of

being a hired goon for the system that completely fucked up our lives."

She raised a glass to their past. It was all they had now. Lucinda pulled over the spare glass, poured herself a short measure of the rich red wine, and raised it in return.

"And I'm sorry that I left you in that shitty orphanage with the horror nuns," she said. "And that I tried to arrest you later when you were running contraband soylent to the Javan system."

She took a sip, a very small one.

"I was feeding children, Cinders," Seph protested.

"You were feeding the vat-grown slave soldiers of a hostile empire when they were still in the larval stage. And you were being very well paid for it."

"Call it even, then?"

She put out her hand.

Lucinda took it. Slowly, but she took it.

"Even."

"I really hate that Chase guy," Seph said, taking another hit of the Château François.

Lucinda's hand, still holding Seph's, tightened.

"Me, too!"

"What a douche. Do you want me to kill him? Coto could eat the leftovers. Nobody would ever know. You should see his turds, Cinders. They're like these superdense little pebbles of plutonium. It's amazing."

Lucinda shook her head.

"He's a fellow officer."

"But not a gentleman, I'd wager."

"No. Not even."

Sephina poured herself another glass as Lucinda

pushed her unfinished drink away. Seph decided she might have to grab a couple more bottles of this luxury cat's piss for the rest of her guys. Banks was quite the wine snob. He'd love it.

"So what do you want me to do, Luce? I don't even have a ship."

"We can get you a ship."

"Cool. A stealth destroyer?"

"No. That's never going to happen. But there's plenty of salvage floating around out here now, and I think Admiral McLennan would be more than happy to furnish you with a letter of marque."

Seph frowned.

"Who's Mark?"

Lucinda spelled it out.

"Not Mark. M-a-r-q-u-e. Authorized piracy, basically. A free pass to steal anything the Sturm have, to kill them at scale, to spread an exemplary terror among the enemy. You'd be authorized by the TDF to run wild as long as the end result was an ocean of tears before bedtime for the Sturm."

Sephina stopped drinking.

"Seriously? He can do that?"

"I've got no idea. But I'm sure he'll think it's a brilliant plan. It's the sort of thing he'd love. It's ancient and time-honored and half forgotten and shit."

"Like him?"

"You might very well think so, but I couldn't possibly comment. Anyway, we do that for you, and you do something for us. That's the deal."

Sephina narrowed her eyes. This was the Lucinda she knew. The orphanage grifter. The fixer. The tireless deal maker of Habitat Welfare. Not some pole-up-the-ass naval officer.

"Define 'something,' Commander Hardcandy."

"Don't call me that."

Seph smiled. Not much. But it was real. She looked around the officers' club or whatever it was.

"You've done good for a Hab rat, sweetheart. Your ship is nicer than mine. Nicer than mine *was,* anyway."

"I told you we'd get you a new ship, Sephina. There are hundreds drifting through the local volume. Of course they're full of insane cannibals who got meat hacked by their own neural mesh, but if you ask Hero nicely, I'm sure he'll displace on board first and throw them into the nearest star. He seems to get jumpy if he doesn't do that every couple of minutes."

"Are you gonna let him run *Defiant*?"

Lucinda seemed offended by the very suggestion. "No way!"

"But don't you need to?" Seph asked. "I mean, I could get away with my crew of complete idiots because the *Regret* was a trader with a few custom mods. But this thing . . ." She waved the glass around, sloshing more wine over the side. She'd drunk nearly half of the bottle on her own. Quickly.

Lucinda meanwhile was bristling at the suggestion that she could not run her own ship. She leaned forward to make her point.

"The Royal Armadalen Navy trains its crews to fight at any time, under any conditions. Including the loss of a captain, an Intellect, scripted military skills, anything."

Sephina almost snorted the wine out through her nose.

"And they teach you to recite the marketing message real good, too, kid."

Lucinda fell back into her chair.

"Don't call me 'kid.' I'm only a year younger than you."

"Yeah, but you seem so much older."

It could have gone either way, but after teetering on the edge of a fight, Hardy snorted, then laughed out loud.

"Oh, man, I missed you guys."

"Then you shouldn't have left," Sephina suggested. But gently.

"If I hadn't, you'd be dead."

Seph put the glass down.

"Like Ariane."

An uncomfortable pause.

"I'm sorry."

"You didn't kill her."

"No," Lucinda said with real intensity. "The Sturm did. And if you want it, I can give you a chance to settle with them."

"Baby, I could bathe in an ocean of their oh-so-fucking-pure blood and nothing would ever be settled between us. But do go on."

"Do you think your crew will stay with you?"

Sephina waved away the question.

"That's not even a thing. Coto is a savant within a very limited range of technical issues. He loves a fight, too. But otherwise he's like a child. He hates change. He'll stay just for the familiar faces. Falun Kot, with all the knives? I got him off one of those god-awful sharia worlds just before it was wiped out by one of the other god-awful sharia worlds. He thinks he owes me his life. He's a great sparky, and I'm not going to put him straight on the whole unrepayable debt of honor thing. Banks? He's like your guy Booker here"—she indicated the eX-Box—"ex-TDF, straight out of the vat. The Sturm would exterminate him on general principles. He'll stick and he'll fight. Not that he likes fighting much. But he's a great pilot."

Lucinda wasn't listening.

She was staring at the external storage unit.

"Is that thing on?" she asked.

Booker's voice emerged from the tiny unit. "Sorry, I thought you'd forgotten me, and I, you know, I didn't know what to say when things got personal."

"Oh, my God, no!" Lucinda gasped.

She blushed a bright shade of crimson.

"Don't worry," Sephina said. "Easily fixed."

She reached over and turned off the box, cutting off Booker's protest of "Hey now" just before she slipped the unit into her duster.

"I think Booker should come with me."

Lucinda's face was completely covered by her hands. It didn't look like she was ever coming out of there.

"I can't believe I said all of those things and he heard them."

"Don't worry, baby. At least he knows you didn't actually steal from the collection plate or buy all that lesbian tentacle porn."

Lucinda took three deep, slow breaths to steady herself. She almost objected to Seph pocketing the storage unit containing the source code for the TDF soldier, but residual embarrassment kept her quiet. It had been so long since she'd had someone, anyone, she could honestly talk to about her feelings—about her sense of being in way over her head, about her father, about everything—that she'd vomited up what now felt like a lifetime's worth of too much information.

"I have to get going," she mumbled quickly.

"Aye, aye, Captain." Seph smirked. Lucinda was oddly comforted to know that she could still make Sephina feel better simply by feeling worse about herself.

"So you'll help me?"

"You get me that free pass from McLennan and a ship, and yeah, we've got a deal. Also, I'm taking this wine."

She swept up the bottle and followed Lucinda out of the wardroom.

Lieutenant Chase was waiting just outside.

"Hey, kid, thanks for the drink," Sephina said as they exited. She held up the bottle, now mostly empty, and gave him a wink.

Lucinda cringed, anticipating a scene and submitting to a type of free-falling anxiety she had not had to endure for nearly ten standard years—the sense that Sephina had dropped her into the shit composter again.

Chase looked pissed off, but not by the wine or the pirate, clearly drunk, who'd stolen it.

As Lucinda blushed and stammered an explanation, he testily waved off Sephina as if swatting away a fly.

"Commander, if I might talk to you for a moment. In private."

He finally let Seph have a peek at his half-sneering lack of regard.

"You should probably go finish that somewhere," he said. "It won't keep. We don't have any park benches, but it's a big ship. I'm sure you'll find somewhere to pass out."

"Lieutenant Chase, please," Lucinda said through gritted teeth, but her warning rang hollow, undercut by her guilt and embarrassment. Another blast from her past with Sephina.

Seph just winked, tipped the bottle to her lips, and glugged the rest of the expensive red wine down like a baby goat slurping milk from the tit.

It was an act, of course. With Sephina everything was an act. With this drunken pirate pantomime she was undoubtedly salving the open wound of losing Ariane. Nevertheless, Lucinda was relieved to see her wander off, waving good-bye with the empty bottle.

"My apologies, Lieutenant Chase. Is there something I can help you with? Quickly."

Chase shrugged. "She's a civilian. They're not under discipline."

It was a surprising concession. Lucinda wondered where he was going with this. Chase flicked his eyes up and down the companionway. Naval and Marine Corps personnel hurried to and fro. Droids zipped around them. Seph was disappearing around the gentle curve of the hull, heading for the mess most likely.

"In private, ma'am," Chase said again. "If I might."

Lucinda fought through a mix of feelings. Suspicion, because he was obviously up to something. Annoyance, because she felt herself somehow disadvantaged by Sephina. Lingering embarrassment, because that was always with her. And a little fear, she had to admit. Her whole life she had been . . . well, not the plaything of people like Chase. Rather, she had been nothing to them. Her existence meaningless.

"Of course," she said as evenly as she could.

They stepped into the officers' wardroom again, occasioning a momentary hot flush of shame when she remembered the mess Seph had made and, naturally, left for somebody else to clean up.

Chase saw it, too, but ignored it.

As the privacy field sealed them in, he stood a respectful distance from her at perfect parade ground rest. It made Lucinda feel even more unsettled.

"What's up, Chase?" she said.

"I wish to resign my commission," he replied.

For a second Lucinda said nothing.

She had nothing.

He had genuinely blindsided her.

Thinking perhaps that she was waiting him out, Chase went on.

"I am only two months short of my three years' service obligation. As captain, you could waive the remaining period."

"But . . . but we're fighting a war." She felt stupid having to state the obvious. "And . . . I don't know, but we might be the only ship able to fight that war. Are you . . . are you frightened, Chase?"

He managed a pretty fair imitation of outrage, if indeed she had misread and offended him.

"Are you serious?" he blurted out, and she saw the

arrogance of the young scion she had met that first day on board *Defiant* with Bannon. But Chase seemed to take hold of his emotions and rein them in. "Of course not," he said. "Or no more than anyone else. You made us shit out our own neural mesh. We can't dose, and we can't back up. Everyone is scared."

Lucinda refrained from pointing out that she had grown up on the plates in Coriolis. Not the worst place for a poor kid, but as a child she'd never imagined she would have a shot at virtual immortality. She was born to die.

"Yes, everyone is scared," she conceded. "There's nothing wrong with that. So why resign? Why run away?"

He bristled.

"I'm not running away. I want to fight, but I have responsibilities to my House now."

"With respect, Lieutenant, your oath to the Navy trumps your House every time."

"No, not this time," he said, and it was her turn to bristle. He raised one hand to forestall any retort. "Hear me out, Commander. You've seen the raw intel. We have a pretty good idea what's happened. A decapitation strike across the Greater Volume, not just on military control and command but civilian, too. Anybody hooked into the zero point network is gone. Besides our chain of command, that also means the Elite Fraction of the entire Volume was taken out. Gone. Insane. Like Torvaldt and Wojkowski."

"Like you would have been if you weren't on *Defiant* and running dark when they attacked," Lucinda pointed out. If she'd meant to guilt him into considering his responsibilities, she failed.

"Exactly," he said. Chase lifted his chin, staring over her shoulder as though looking into a new future only he could see. "Like Princess Alessia, I am probably the sole surviving heir to my family's holdings. I am both chief executive and commander of the Chase Corporation's security forces . . . those which survive," he added. "I must assume the responsibility of that command without delay."

Lucinda blinked. He had actually given her an argument she could accept. Seeing her hesitation, Chase pressed on.

"You said it yourself, Commander. We might be the only ship left. We surely are in the local volume. The only resistance to the Sturm was coming from pirates and criminals like your friend."

She almost flared at that, but Chase was right.

Seph was a criminal.

Lucinda wasn't sure if they were friends.

She raised her hands in a placating gesture.

"I'm sorry, Lieutenant. I take your point. But now is really not the time. We have a mission."

"Yes, we do," he said. "Admiral McLennan gave us that mission, and you accepted it because the Montanblanc girl is the only surviving authority we know of in the local volume. Just as I am the only surviving authority I know of who can lay claim to the forces of the Chase Corporation. I also inherit my family's seat on the High Bourse and in the Congress on Earth. I am no more a mere naval officer than Alessia Montanblanc is a little girl. You must allow me to do my duty."

"Your duty," Lucinda replied with more heat than she had intended, "is to plot the folds we will need into and out of Montrachet. You might well be the head of your House now, but you are also *Defiant*'s navigation officer, and you are needed at your station until we have that little girl in our safekeeping."

His jaw bunched, and two spots of high color appeared on his cheeks.

"I am not needed. McLennan's Intellect can plot those folds and fight this ship so much better than we can that we would be derelict in our duty if we did not allow him to do so."

"How dare you? This is the Royal Armadalen Navy. Every man and every woman is trained to fight, no matter what. You were trained to navigate this ship under fire even when Defiant himself was disabled. And that training, your training and your skill, just delivered us a victory and a chance to fight another day."

"And I will take that chance as the commander of my family's forces," Chase said hotly. He leaned in. "They killed my family. All of them. Do you not understand?"

"Oh, I understand losing family," Lucinda shot back, instantly regretting the loss of control yet also reveling in it just a little, wallowing in the sheer luxurious wrongness of letting her anger slip the leash.

"Oh, that's what this is about," Chase sneered. "Well, allow me to put you at ease, Commander."

He loaded that last word with real scorn.

A small data coin appeared in his fingers as if by a well-practiced magic trick. He flipped the coin at her.

"Your father," he said. "He's all yours now."

Lucinda fumbled the catch, and the coin dropped to the wardroom floor, bouncing on the carpet and rolling under the table. She banged her head on the edge as she bent to pick it up. Stars filled her head, and she felt dizzy. She gathered up the coin and climbed to her feet with as much dignity as she could pull together. Not much, as it happened.

"What is this?"

"It's your father's debt to the Combine," he said. "I bought it before we left Deschaneaux. Don't ask me why. The truth would not reflect well on me. Let's just say I was drunk. That was reason enough. When I Dtoxed, I had no idea what to do with it. But it seems obvious now."

Lucinda was speechless. She literally did not know what to say, and so when she did speak, she said something stupid.

"I will buy out my father's debt," she said. "He is not a chip to be played in some game."

"You won't pay off your father's debt," Chase said, but not cruelly. "Nobody ever gets out from under those debts. So I wiped it. For what that's worth. Not much in the current circumstances, I suppose. But he's free. It's all on the coin."

He nodded at the small titanium disk she still held out to him.

Lucinda slowly dropped her hand.

"Thank you," she said, her voice very small.

Chase remained silent.

She spoke, almost choking on the words and the shame she felt in saying them. It seemed fated that they should end up here at this moment, almost as though Sephina had brought them together. Seph would not have hesitated to cut a deal with Chase.

And she would not have been surprised at her oldest friend doing the same thing.

"When this mission is done, Lieutenant, I will ask Admiral McLennan to consider your request. It would not be proper for me to make that decision, and there is nobody in our own chain of command for me to ask."

He eyed her, not entirely trusting her.

"Will you recommend he accept my resignation?"

She put the coin in her pocket. It felt heavy.

"I will," she said.

CHAPTER
THIRTY-FOUR

Walking back to the room where she was being held captive, Alessia felt sick. Not just physically ill. She wanted to vomit up her soul into the ruins of the rose garden. She had been terrified while they recorded her pretend surrender, certain that Kogan D'ur would fly into a killing rage if he realized what she was doing: blinking out a second message in Morse code. She wasn't frightened for herself . . .

Okay.

Fine.

She was scared shitless for herself.

But she was also pretty sure that the Sturm would not kill her straightaway. Not while she could still be of use to them. But there was no doubt Captain D'ur would deliver on his promise to murder the rest of the household staff and Caro and Debin if Alessia crossed him.

And she had crossed him big-time.

It was only a matter of hours, surely, before he found out. She had to warn Caro and Debin to get out while they—

She stopped so abruptly that Sergeant Ji-yong, marching a step or two behind, nearly tumbled over in trying to avoid stepping on her prisoner.

What had she been thinking?

"What the fuck are you doing?"

Alessia stood flat-footed in the middle of a path of crushed bluestone. The morning sun gently warmed her face, but she shivered uncontrollably.

"You do that again and I'll kick your skinny little ass clear of the last fucking Lagrange point, kid," Sergeant Ji-yong barked. But Alessia was not listening to her. She had been frozen in place by the quiet voice in her head that asked one simple question again and again:

What were Caro and Debin supposed to do now?

They couldn't fight their way out of whatever dungeon Kogan D'ur had them locked in. They were trapped just as surely as she was, and now she had killed them. Ji-yong shoved her forward along the path, but Alessia danced away from the push, turning on the shock trooper, who nearly overbalanced again. That did not improve her mood.

"Captain D'ur said I could see Caro and Debbin," she said to the glaring soldier.

"Yeah, well, officers say a lot of stupid things, kid. Get moving."

"No."

"Did you forget you're not a princess anymore?"

"I said no."

Ji-yong raised a hand to slap her, but before the trooper could land the blow, Alessia spoke in a calmly measured, completely reasonable tone that carried the same chilling indifference she recalled from her mother Queen Sara's most unsettling, utterly scarifying moments.

"I may not be a princess anymore, but you remain a soldier under discipline, and if you do not do as I have asked, and asked politely I might add, the next time Captain D'ur needs something from House Montanblanc, I will inform him that he can execute every miserable commoner on this wretched ball of dung and he will yet have no satisfaction from me because you, Sergeant Ji-yong, were too monstrously stupid to indulge me in a harmless request that he himself had already approved."

The shock trooper towered over her, but Alessia could see the strength of will draining out of the woman. Sergeant Ji-yong looked as though a tiny black hole that fed purely on human feelings had somehow birthed itself deep inside of her. The anger and indignation that had flashed so easily across her features, the surety of purpose she had displayed since dragging Alessia from her improvised cell earlier that morning, the glaring arrogance of an overlord that her father sometimes warned her brothers to have a care of, they all disappeared as though sucked down over some invisible event horizon.

It was only for a fraction of a second, but stripped of whatever power she had felt, Ji-yong looked first shocked and then frightened. She was able to gather her scattered wits quickly, however. She dropped her hand and rearranged her features into a smirk.

"Enjoy it while you can, Princess. You'll be scrubbing toilets in a prison battalion by the time you're done."

Alessia allowed no trace of emotion to show on

her features. It was as though all those excruciatingly dull fencing lessons with Lord Guillaume had finally, unexpectedly, and somewhat shockingly paid off. Not because she was able to defeat this scowling monster by moving very slowly and quietly for an hour holding a stupid wooden stick in a series of un-natural poses. But because the stillness she needed to find in order to stand her ground in front of the frankly terrifying Ji-yong had been hidden within her all along. Lord Guillaume had secretly placed it there without her even knowing it sometime during their hundreds of hours of fencing instruction. She almost ruined his good work then by bursting into tears, because these creatures had most assuredly murdered her old master, and he was never coming back, and she would never be able to thank him and apologize for all the mean things she had said to him.

She almost failed.

But not quite.

"That's as may be," Alessia said to Ji-yong in an unprepossessing tone. "More likely when I am of no more use to the Republic, I will be murdered and my remains disposed of to preclude opponents of your occupation rallying around a symbol of the previous regime. That is the usual fate of fallen monarchs and their progeny."

The Sturm trooper stared at her as though she had suddenly grown a second head.

"I'm gonna take you to your little friends," she said. "But only because I can see how it would be a form of torture for them. Now move."

She directed Alessia away from the servants' domicile and across the ravaged gardens to the whitewashed storehouse where the provisions for the estate were housed. The Skygarth kitchens could, of course, draw on the finest ingredients from all over the Greater Volume, and Montrachet itself was a famous source of heirloom produce raised under the strictest rules to ensure organic purity. The storehouse was always full to brimming over with fresh fruit and vegetables from the Freycinet Tablelands and cheeses from Baillaud and Cottenot. Hams from Old Parma hung next to smoked sausages from Coggia and Hérigone and aged Texan beef ribs. Skygarth's own vineyards produced a Pinot Noir that had won a silver medal at the Concours Mondial de Bruxelles, and it was down in the cellar among the racks of this season's pressing of the lesser Merlot where the Sturm had locked Caro and Debin.

It was crowded in the basement. Mister Dunning's gardening bots and drones stood next to the wine racks of less impressive varietals and vintages destined to be served to staff or used by the kitchens when no senior members of the royal family were in residence.

"Alessia!"

She turned her head toward Caro's voice, and then she ran, feeling the very tips of Sergeant Ji-yong's fingers snatch at the back of her neck. She was still wearing the beautiful blue dress, but it was dusty and covered in cobwebs now, and the hem tore on a hedge-trimming bot as she ran past. She stumbled but carried on, ignoring Ji-yong's shouted order for her to stop and then simply to slow down. Alessia did neither until she had reached the wooden pillar to which her friends had been secured with plasteel chains. She threw herself at them, wrapping both Caro and Debin in her arms and hugging them fiercely.

All three children were in tears and were babbling nonsense at one another and soon enough struggling with Sergeant Ji-yong, who grabbed a fistful of Alessia's dress and hauled her away from the other two with a wrenching heave. Alessia landed on her butt, sending a sharp pain up her back and tingling down her legs.

"You've seen them now," Ji-yong said. "That was the promise. Let's go."

"I hate you, and I'm gonna get you," Debin shouted at her, straining at his chains.

The shock trooper grinned.

"That's the way, son. Good to see the true human spirit hasn't been bred out of you. Not like this one."

Ji-yong gave Alessia a light kick with her jackboot. It didn't hurt. It was meant to make her feel bad about herself, not to cause any real pain. Alessia was beginning to understand how these things worked.

"I'm coming back for you," Alessia promised her friends. "With the Household Cavalry and Armadalen Marines and Vikingar berserkers and—"

"Pfft. She's not doing any of that," the shock trooper scoffed. "Your little friend here just ordered all of her forces and allies to surrender."

"Alessia, no!" Caro cried out.

Debin looked as though the shock trooper had just kicked him, but a lot harder than she had kicked Alessia, who nearly blurted out, "But I didn't! I tricked them!"

Alessia burned with a frightful shame that she did

not deserve, and she urgently wanted—no, she *needed*—to explain herself to the only two people she really cared about whom she had left in the world.

But she could not. That way was not open to her.

Instead, in her burning embarrassment and indignation she shouted at Ji-yong like a spoiled child.

"I had no choice. You were going to kill them!"

Ji-yong smiled with supreme indifference to the excuses of a shamed and fallen princess.

"Come on, kid. You can sit in your room for a couple of hours thinking about how badly you already fucked everything up today. Don't drag these poor little shits down with you."

"Wait!" Alessia said, fumbling with shaking fingers at the small jeweled edenflower brooch just over her heart. She pricked herself with the pin getting it off and tried to give the piece to Caro, but Ji-yong bent over and slapped it from her hand.

"Don't even think about it," she said, sounding bored but a little irritated, too.

"Omigod, you're so mean!" Caro said.

"It was just a present," Alessia protested.

"It was a lock pick or a cutting tool or a weapon or whatever this little bitch could improvise," Ji-yong lobbed back. She strode over to where the priceless brooch lay at the foot of a hedge trimmer and crushed it under the heel of her boot. Alessia gasped.

"Oh, wow. You're in so much trouble," Debin said breathlessly.

Ji-yong snorted out a short abrasive laugh.

"Seriously, boy, I am not the one in trouble here."

She reached down, grabbed a handful of Alessia's hair, and yanked her up onto her feet, giving her a push in the direction of the wooden stairs leading back up to the food stores. Alessia twisted back toward her friends and mouthed "Be brave" at them. Caro looked worried but determined, and Debin jutted his jaw out and nodded with such resolution that Alessia could only wish his grandfather and Sergeant Reynolds were there to see it. They would have been so very proud of him. She was proud of them both.

And, quietly, she was a little proud of herself.

It was a sin, she knew, and a dangerous one in a ruler. Her father's favorite lecture was a stern warning against the dangers of arrogance in a monarch. But as Alessia climbed the stairs out of the storehouse basement, she allowed herself just a small measure of satisfaction that at least she had done one thing right this morning.

She knew where to find her friends when she escaped.

And she would put those hours she was about to spend locked in some poor maid's room to good use, crafting a plan to effect that escape.

CHAPTER
THIRTY-FIVE

The medical facilities on *Defiant* were a wonder to behold. After so long grubbing through the half-buried ruin of the *Voortrekker*'s ancient sick bay, the clean lines and modest, even cryptic simplicity of the Armadalen trauma center presented itself to McLennan as something akin to an art installation from an aggressively minimalist culture. Apart from the holo-field displays manipulated by the all-human staff—no droids or bots—he saw no equipment. Even his cot was a micro-g carrier wave that floated him off the deck plating while the doctor and two nurses fussed about. He felt the warm bath of effector fields massaging his tortured muscles and wrenched and twisted bones. The torn flesh at his wrists tingled and itched as dermal gel bonded with his skin. His head hummed softly with EM pain blockers. In spite of the nearly supernatural wonder of it all, the raw wound to his soul that the woman Dunn had opened remained gaping and terrible. McClennan could bluster and bullshit his way past anyone, but he could not deceive himself about the truth she had torn from his heart.

He was a monster. And the hell of it was, none of these wee bairns seemed to have any idea. After twenty minutes of uncomplicated and not entirely uncomfortable treatment, Doctor Saito pronounced him fit for light duty. Had she not read the history books? Or at least played the sims? Did she have no idea what had happened the last time he did his fucking duty? How many of his own people he had killed?

Apparently not.

"You're good to go," she said.

"But I still feel like shit," he complained, and you would have imagined from the performance that he was just playing to character, not revealing some deeper truth.

"That's because you're about seven hundred years old." Saito smiled, patting him on his newly repaired and only slightly stiff and aching shoulder. "And it looks like you've tried to drag this tired old carcass through most of them."

"I made the same point about 650 years ago," Hero said in a stage whisper.

"And every fecking minute since," McLennan groused as the carrier wave tilted forward and lowered his stockinged feet to the deck. He felt the grip of micro-g fall away and the cold kiss of *Defiant*'s climate control system on his bare arse and hairy old nads through the backless paper gown. He felt every minute of the long centuries he had outstayed his welcome in this world.

The nervous-looking baby lieutenant with the name BANNON newly stenciled on his uniform stepped forward and handed Mac a set of dark blue coveralls, underwear, socks, boots, and a cap. A thick and oddly luxurious-looking envelope sat atop the uniform.

"Commander Hardy had these printed for you, sir. She requests that you sign the letter and join her on the bridge at your earliest convenience."

"Requests, does she?" he scoffed, as though he were not one of human history's greatest fiends. The admiral took the document Bannon had given him, scanned it quickly, snorted in astonishment, and read it again, this time taking in every word.

"Well, I suppose if she requests it, laddie," he said when he was done, "I'd best drag my wrinkled arse down there, had I not?"

"Probably, sir," Bannon replied. "She's in full combat rig and a bad mood."

"You just described my third marriage with eerie precision, for which I willnae thank you, lad."

Mac turned to Doctor Saito as he stripped off the gown.

"I hope you dinnae mind, madam. Apparently I'm in something of a hurry."

She gave his aging frame a skeptical once-over.

"No," Saito said, shaking her head. "I don't mind. It's not often I get to see a living corpse in such a severe state of decay. Are those the original testicles, or did you graft on a pair from the gorilla museum?"

"Well," he answered, chuckling, "I don't like to brag, but . . ."

"You really shouldn't," Hero said. "Gorilla testicles are notoriously undersized."

"They're still larger than your core processing matrix, you clattering nobbler."

"Seriously, Admiral," the doctor went on as he dressed. "You've never had mesh, or implants, or re-sequencing done? Is that right?"

"Aye," he said as he closed the coverall. His name was stenciled over the left breast in the same fashion as Bannon's, and a pair of Fleet admiral's binary star pips stood out in gold thread on the midnight blue collar. It fit well, and he was a little surprised how good it felt to wear a uniform again. Perhaps this was how a serial killer felt when visiting a shallow grave he had dug long ago in the forest and all but forgotten in the many years since. "I was not born to the Fraction, Doctor, and neuralink mesh was not a mature technology when I first served in the TDF."

"But that was a long time ago."

"And far, far away," he conceded.

Saito tilted her head to one side as though examining an especially interesting virus under a nanoscope. "So at the end of every span," she said, "you've submitted yourself to organic extraction of your engram?"

The nurses and Lieutenant Bannon were all watching him, waiting as intently on the answer as Saito. Even Herodotus floated silently off to one side.

"Aye," Mac said, as if that were answer enough. It wasn't, of course. It never was.

"Do you mind if I ask why?" Saito said. "It is a . . . distressing procedure. Invasive and painful, destructive, and not nearly as accurate as simply transferring hard data from backup. You could never be certain that the you after relifing was exactly the same you as before."

McLennan smiled. It was a wintry expression.

420 · JOHN BIRMINGHAM

"This is not your first span, I'll warrant, Doctor Saito."

"My third."

"So you have twice respawned from backup, which is to say I am talking to a copy of a copy of a quantum-bit history, not to a young woman—my apologies for any gender presumptions—born somewhere in the Armadalen Commonwealth a hundred and fifty, maybe two hundred years ago, give or take some gene-mods and healthy living. You are a woman, a sentient being, but you are not that woman, that being. She died."

It was Saito's turn to smile.

"These questions have been debated and resolved by philosophers wiser than you and I, Admiral. The self is simply that warm single point of sentience around which the life of the universe gathers."

"Unless you're a source coder," McLennan said as he pulled on his new boots. They looked brand-new but felt soft and worn in. "Then your soul is written into the code that gives rise to sentience. Not in the singular point of consciousness itself."

He stood up, pleased with Saito's dubious frown. They were all frowning, probably because they didn't expect a TDF admiral, retired or otherwise, to be quoting source code scripture. It was hardly the worst thing he had ever done, though, was it?

"I understand," he said patiently, "that Commander Hardy has ordered the crew and the marines to shut down and metabolize your mesh, yes?"

Saito nodded tightly.

McLennan volleyed back his own, very satisfied nod.

"And so you cannot back up. You go into harm's way as true human beings. Just like our foe. Think now, if you should die, all of the words you have read, the places you've been, the knowledge and the wisdom you have gained, it will altogether vanish like a dream. Every note of music, every brushstroke of every painting, every q-bit, every sim, all that laughter, so many tears, and suddenly . . . nothing. Perhaps an earlier backup of another you does remain safely stored in some remote offline facility. Your memories of the Beijing Opera, the candomblé in Bahía, the dunes of al-Qudd, a walk down the grand avenues of Cupertino, the white nights of Putingrad, the call to prayer on the Habitat of Peace, a red supermoon over the Armadalen Sea, the crumbs of a pastry and the last mouthful of coffee in a tiny café in Trastevere, everything you have ever known, remembered, talked about, and everything you have left unspoken—it could all live again, I suppose. But would that be you, Doctor Saito? The you here with me? Right now?"

The color had drained from her face.

That was better.

That was how people should react to encountering the famous Frazer McLennan.

"This is how every citizen of the Human Republic lives every minute of his or her life, knowing that it could vanish, just like that." He clicked his fingers. "That warm little point of light around which the whole of the universe gathers? It could disappear, and the universe would not squeeze out a thin, wet shit in sympathy. This is how I have lived since I last fought them, Doctor. I like to think that because of it, I understand them and why they have returned."

"And why is that?" she asked, her voice a little shaken.

"To save us from ourselves." He smiled.

"And you're going to stop them from doing that?" McLennan nodded.

"Och, aye, and this time I'm going to kill them all."

He snapped his fingers absently at Bannon.

"I don't suppose you brought a pen with you, lad."

Vikingar attack ships burned among the glittering wreckage of C-Beam fortresses. A Tannhäuser Gate, shattered by kinetics, tumbled off the shoulder of Odin's World; the interstellar Habitat drifted in the dead void between Sujutus and the privately owned system where the Montanblanc princess waited in captivity.

Sephina didn't give a shit about any of that. She was staring with unvarnished avarice at the apparently undamaged yacht floating in the holofield on the bridge of *Defiant*.

"We'll take that one," she said, pointing.

Lucinda shook her head, but in resigned acceptance rather than denial. Her old friend had just laid claim to an Autarch-class starcruiser registered to a senior vice president of the Zaitsev Corporation. Lieutenant Fein at Tactical indulged himself in a low wolf whistle, earning a frosty glare from Lucinda.

"Sorry, Skipper," he said. "But that is one sweet

ride. Six multicore quad AU drives. Three sloops in the rear transit bay. Standoff strike capability. Block 4 defensive arrays. Two bars. A wave pool. Two dozen guest suites with complimentary Netflix . . ."

"You had me at zero life signs," Sephina said. "It's a legitimate salvage, right? Those neo-czarist assholes can't come at me for this?"

"I will vouch for your ownership myself," Lucinda said. "But seriously, Seph, I don't imagine the Maritime Court is going to be sitting any time soon. And the guy who used to own that yacht, he's too busy eating his passengers and crew to lodge a writ anyway."

Admiral McLennan, who seemed to be hugely amused by the whole thing and much improved since his visit to the medbay, beckoned Sephina over to the XO's crash couch, which he had claimed for himself without reference to Lucinda or apology for the presumption.

"And you'll be needing this too, lassie," he said, handing her a thick envelope sealed with a bright red blob of wax. "Your letter of marque and reprisal. Signed under my own hand and recorded in the ship's log by Commander Hardy here. That makes it legal and official, and the best of luck to you in your new career."

Sephina took the heavy square of folded vellum as though it might burst into flames.

"And this is for real, too? You're, like, pardoning me before I kill anyone or fuck anything up?"

"So long as you kill the right people," McLennan cautioned.

"That's not gonna be a problem, Scotty," she said.

"I didnae think so. You seem quite the murderous she devil to me, Captain L'trel. I have no doubt you'll be cutting throats and taking long hot baths in Republican blood before I lay my head to the pillow tonight. Were I a few hundred years younger, I might even be inclined to fall for your manifest charms."

"Thanks," she said, examining the letter as though it were a voucher for a free drink at the nearest Yakuza-owned strip club. "If I ever get loose in the Fallopian tubes for a mummified Scottish stick insect, you are the first one I'll throw a leg over. Until then, though, could I ask one more favor?"

McLennan took the brush-off with rare charm.

"I don't really have a lot of influence with the Yamaguchi-gumi," he said. "So if you're looking for me to smooth things over for you . . ."

"No," she said. "I was just wondering if your little friend over there could clean up before we cross-decked." Sephina picked out Hero with a tilt of the head. "It's just, you know, space zombies. Ew."

"Fine," the Intellect said. "Just excuse me a moment. After all, it's not like I've got anything better to do."

He winked out of existence with a soft pop of collapsing air before returning a second later.

"Sorry I'm so late," he said. "It was rather a mess over there. They were all lifestreaming to remote backup when the malware got in. The ship's Intellect had gone bonkers as well. But not to worry: I threw them all into the sun and scrubbed the ship from stem to stern. Your ride awaits you, madam."

Hero dipped a few inches in emulation of a courteous bow.

"I have wiped the substrate and reset the auto-
nomics, and because I fear you would not have the
intellectual capacity to learn a new 4CI suite quickly
enough, I have copied over a clean, updated version
of the disgracefully clunky software with which you
ran your previous vessel. It will be just like going
home if you used to live in a disintegrating cardboard
box full of used pornography and you upgraded to a
six-billion-ruble party palace with an FTL drive and
an armory large enough to sustain a modest interstellar war."

Seph looked to Lucinda.

"Do you ever think about throwing this fucking
thing into the sun?"

"He's mostly harmless." Lucinda smiled.

The two women regarded each other with a fond-
ness neither expected. They could not have been more
dissimilar. Seph the wild-haired freebooter in a long,
increasingly tattered-looking nanoweave duster. Lucinda unadorned by makeup, jewelry, body art, or
costume beyond the commander's pips on the collar
of her utilitarian blue coveralls. They wore sidearms
in common—the *Regret*'s crew having rearmed themselves from the *Defiant*'s arsenal—but beyond that
something else tied them together.

"So I guess it's my turn to run away," Sephina
said.

Lucinda allowed herself a half grin. "Don't be a
stranger this time."

"Last time we caught up," Seph reminded her,
"you tried to arrest me."

"Oh, Sephina. Let it go. It was just that one time."

A companionable silence of such warmth arose

between them that Frazer McLennan started to say something inappropriate, causing Herodotus the Intellect to mute him with a perfectly calibrated noise-canceling sonic wave. Lucinda's bridge crew concentrated on their stations.

"I loved Ariane, too, Seph," Lucinda said quietly. "She was kind to me."

"She was kind to everyone she didn't kill." Sephina smiled. A sad smile but genuine.

"Stay safe."

"You know I won't."

"I know you'll do as you promised," Lucinda said earnestly. "I trust you. There are not many people, let alone space pirates, I'd say that about."

"And after that I'm free?" Sephina asked.

"You'll have to ask your conscience that."

The pirate snorted.

"Not even a thing."

Without warning she stepped forward and wrapped her arms around Lucinda, pulling her in tight and holding on for too long. When they separated, both were misty-eyed.

"Let's go kill some motherfucking Nazis," Seph whispered.

"Okay," Lucinda said. "I'm cool with that."

"By crikey, that floating computer knows how to push a mop and bucket around, eh?" Mister Banks marveled as they folded onto the bridge of the Zaitsev cruiser. The interstellar-capable superyacht looked for all the world as though it had been unmoored from the sale yards five minutes earlier. "She's been scrubbed till her belly button shines."

The bridge where they materialized was perhaps twice as large as the entire crew space on the old *Regret* and had been fitted out in the style of a schooner from the ancient age of sail back on Old Earth. Siberian hardwood decking appeared to be . . . well, fucking oak or cedar or some shit, Sephina thought.

Possibly from Siberia.

She'd run a hold full of illegally logged old-growth fir from Sol to Cupertino once, and fucked if this didn't look just like that. The captain's chair was an antique Eames recliner. (She'd stolen a container load of them once, too.) Although she was pretty certain that sloops and clippers from the golden age of sail didn't come standard with twentieth-century domestic lounge settings.

"Banks, check out the helm controls. That magic toaster said he'd copied your old system software across, minus a few bugs and shit. Fuck knows how he got it to run on Zaitsev's hardware, but—"

"But it looks good, Captain," Banks said, sounding ever more impressed by the second. "It's like . . . it's like the old girl got a makeover is all."

Sephina dropped into the Eames chair and threw her boots up onto the separate ottoman.

"An ugly fucking makeover," she said mostly to herself. "Kot, I don't have the first fucking idea where Engineering might be, but I dunno, maybe go find it and see whether you can keep this thing running once we light the fuse."

Falun Kot, still covered in dermal patches from the medbay on *Defiant,* smiled and bowed.

"It would be my very pleasure, Madam Captain."

After a moment's hesitation to orient himself, he left the bridge, humming. Seph noted that he had drawn one of his blades, not entirely trusting the Intellect to have cleaned out every last passenger and member of the crew. She felt rather than heard a hum all around that quickly faded away as Banks hooted and clapped.

"Oh, my word, Captain, I am going to buy that computer a drink. This ship is a wonder. You tell me where you want to go, and we can be there yesterday."

"That's cool, Banksy," she said, not really paying attention anymore. If he could fly it, that was good enough for her.

"Coto, why don't you go check out the armory. We're gonna need weapons. Lots of weapons."

"I do not know where it is," Coto said.

Seph waved that away.

"Ask the ship."

"Ship!" Coto called out. "I am Jaddi Coto. Show me the guns."

A female voice, unaccented, speaking in Volume Standard, replied aloud.

"Jaddi Coto. You are not equipped with neural mesh. You will follow my spoken instructions, and I will show you the way to the ship's primary gun locker. If you wish, I can also show you the way to medbay and upgrade your cortex with neural mesh; however, I must warn you that the procedure is currently contraindicated."

"Ship," Coto replied, "I do not want to be a space zombie."

"Jaddi Coto," the ship answered back, "this is why the procedure is contraindicated."

"Ship," Seph interrupted, "just take him to the armory and maybe show him how to find the galley while you're at it. He gets hungry."

Coto disappeared, following the ship's spoken directions.

She moved around in the captain's chair, trying to find just the right spot, but something kept jabbing her on the ass.

Booker.

Seph pulled out the storage unit and flicked the power on.

"Hey, Book, wakey-wakey, hands off snakey."

"Where am I now?" he said, sounding less than happy.

"My Hab girl Cinders scored us a sweet ride. You're on a big-ass Zaitsev orgy boat with its own strategic strike capabilities. It's . . . Wait a minute. Ship, what's your name?"

The vessel replied, her voice filling the strangely anachronistic bridge.

"I am the Autarch-class starcruiser 8538.91, commissioned by the procurement—"

"No, what's your name? You must have a name."

"I do not."

"Huh," Seph mused. "Musta got wiped along with everything else. Okay, ship. I'll get back to you on that."

"Seph?"

It was Mister Banks. His voice sounded odd.

" 'Sup, Banks?"

"I have an idea for a name. If it's all right with you."

She looked over at the unassuming pilot. He seemed nervous.

"Go on," Seph said carefully.

"We should call her *Ariane*," Banks said.

Sephina did not reply. Not at first. But eventually she did nod. Once.

"You do it," she managed after a few seconds.

"Ship," Banks called out in a more confident tone. "This is your pilot, Mister Banks."

"Yes, Pilot?"

"Ship, you are now the starcruiser *Ariane*."

"Thank you, Pilot. I am now the starcruiser *Ariane*. I will revise my metadata and inform the Maritime Registry when zero point access is reopened."

"Belay zero point access," Banks said. "The network is compromised. Remain signals dark until otherwise authorized by Captain L'trel."

Sephina breathed out a little raggedly. "Thank you," she mouthed at Banks. He smiled with vulnerable sorrow and nodded back.

"Booker," she said when she could speak without choking on her words. "Sorry about that. Family stuff. Now, I'm gonna guess you'd like to get out of the box."

"If it wouldn't be too much of an inconvenience, yeah, that'd be great."

His voice was so flat, she couldn't tell if he was snarking her.

"Ship . . . I mean, sorry, *Ariane,* I've got a TDF sergeant here, encoded to an emergency external storage unit. You got some sort of mobile element he could download to?"

"My inventory currently lists forty-eight sex dolls of various genders and—"

"No!"

Booker's voice was small and tinny but emphatic.

"Do not drop me into a pussybot. Jesus Christ, you fucking breeders."

Seph had no trouble reading his tone now.

"Calm down," she said. "I'm trying to help. I did ask Hardy if I could have a stealth destroyer, but she said no. This is what she let us have. I'm sorry it didn't come with a squad of trench-fighting mechs, but you go to war with the orgy boat you got. And we got this one."

Banks spoke up from the helm.

"Kot says he found Engineering. Looks good."

"Thanks," Seph said. "Tell him he needs to check out the boats in the launch bay. We'll need one of them when we get to Montrachet. It'll need to be big enough that Coto's horn doesn't poke a hole in it. Stealthed would be good, too. Otherwise you're gonna have to brush up on your dogfighting skills."

Banks acknowledged the order and went back to talking quietly with the engineer over a hard link.

"This is a yacht, right?" Booker said. "Deep-space capable? It should have engineering mechs or servitor bots for EVA work."

"Banks?" Seph queried.

"Gimme a second . . . Yeah," the pilot said. "They did. But *somebody* threw them into the sun along with all the bodies, living and undead, and the ship's Intellect."

"Okay, thanks. Booker, I'm sorry; we're gonna have to find you a new ride when we get dirtside. I'll make it a priority, promise. We got a favor owing to the Armadalens, and it's not gonna be easy getting square. If I can get you a rig, will you help us? I could use your skills. I know McLennan waved his magic wand at you, but I'm guessing you'd prefer not to go back to sucking script for the TDF. You know, since they were the assholes fixed on deleting your ass not so long ago."

The black box was silent for long enough that Sephina wondered whether she might have powered it down by accident. She was just turning it over in her hands to check the status lights when Booker's voice crackled out of it.

"I'd appreciate it if you didn't spin me around like that. I still have proprioceptor subroutines running. It makes me dizzy. And . . . yes, thanks. You're right. I'd rather not re-up with the TDF. Assuming there is a TDF anymore."

Seph placed the box in her lap and showed him her open hands. Nothing to hide here.

"Fine by me," she said. "I'm not their recruiting office. You handled yourself well on the *Regret*. Saved our asses if you want the truth of it. You got a place with us if you like. Banks over there"—she jerked a thumb at the helm—"he's a source coder, too. But not, er, you know . . ."

While she was searching for a polite way to explain that her pilot was not a religious fanatic, Mister Banks said, "My beliefs are personal, not political."

Seph heard something that could have been a short laugh from the box.

"All belief is personal," Booker said. "In the end. You mind me asking something, Captain L'trel?"

"Sephina is fine. Seph if I decide I like you."

"I'd be more comfortable with 'Captain.' For now."

"All right, what do you want to know?"

"People, most people anyway, they're not comfortable around source coders. Like, true believers in the Source, I mean. But you—"

Sephina cut him off.

"My mother was a source coder. And a crazy bitch with it. Like, literally. She was vat-grown as an exowomb for a Combine VP. Didn't want his precious tadpoles cooked up in a thermidor. But she got some bad script—and me. She was a two-time loser, and we ended up out on the hull plates. Or I did. She eventually tried digging the code out of her own skull with a fusion knife. Nuns got me off that Hab in the end. But you're not her, Booker. And I know plenty of natural born are just as crazy and twice as bad. Human frailty, man. That's what I believe in."

The box lay quietly in her lap for a few seconds.

She knew he was thinking it over. She also knew that a few seconds for her could amount to years of deep philosophical contemplation for him.

When he came down from the mountaintop, her newest crew member said, "Okay, Sephina. I'm in. But if you don't have a ride for me, I'd just as rather you put my box to sleep while I wait. It gets very dull in here."

CHAPTER
THIRTY-SIX

Archon-Admiral Wenbo Strom stood by the rear doors of the armored troop carrier. The dull gray plating of the transport barge was scored by damage from previous drops on training missions during the long voyage home. The cavernous secondary vehicle deck of the *Liberator* was largely empty, with most of the assault forces already engaged across the local volume. This modest force, under the command of Captain D'ur, who had done so well in capturing the Montanblanc heir, had been held back for another mission. They stood at ease as Strom thrust his chin forward and looked each of his troopers in the eye.

"You will make history today," he said matter-of-factly. "Human history. This greatest crusade, toward which our people have strived these many hundreds of years, is under way, and the task before us is heavy and grim."

The well deck was so vast that although the rumble of vehicles being moved to deployment points and the crash of heavy pallets and cargo mechs echoed all around, his voice seemed to disappear into the void. Captain D'ur and his troopers listened attentively, with no sign of the understandable nervousness he'd seen in some of the mainline assault formations earlier. These were special forces, after all.

"Be assured, as we assault forward, our cause is just. This has not changed over the centuries of our exile, and the time has now come to win back not simply our own birthright but the common blessings of humanity as a whole. We return as liberators, not invaders."

D'ur grunted and nodded, and his troopers all followed suit.

"I cannot assure you that victory will be ours," Strom said quietly. "For the Republic to win through, each will have to give their all. Some of us, many of you, will die, and the unavoidable necessity of that lies heavily upon me. As you know, I have given two children to the struggle. My eldest boy died in a training accident before we left the Redoubt." He paused and swallowed. "My daughter led a squad on Habitat Eassar."

Nobody was so gauche as to say anything, but the hollow silence and shuffling discomfort that followed was eloquent. Eassar had turned into a blood swarm even before some maniac had blasted his way out of the docks and opened the Hab to hard vacuum before folding away from a jump point so close to the weakened structure that gravimetric shear tore the breach even wider. The expedition to seize and subdue Eassar became an emergency mission to save it. His daughter was not among those who were saved.

"Would that I could have died in their place," Strom said, his voice failing him for a moment. "Any parent would surely offer themselves up to save a child. And yet . . ."

He swallowed awkwardly and took in a breath to steady himself. This was not the speech he had intended to give them. It was nothing like the rousing address he'd delivered earlier in this very dock, sending thirty thousand men and women into battle, his own offspring among their ranks. Strom lashed himself for the weakness.

This was not what was needed.

"And yet," he went on with resolve, "I could not die in their place. Because it *was* their place to make that sacrifice. I know for a certainty that they would both make it again. Just as I know that I would send them to their fate with a heavy heart but without reservation. As I send you now."

Kogan D'ur barked back, *"Hai!"* and his troopers repeated the old Japanese word that was a literal translation of "yes" but something more as well, a statement of a warrior's willingness to endure any trial not simply because it was just but because it was fated.

They were warriors.

Death was their fate.

"Captain D'ur has explained your mission to you," Strom went on. "I will not waste time explaining its importance. I trust you to understand. You are not merely tasked with the extermination of the mutant strains and unnatural sentients that have usurped humanity in our own home. You will defeat the last of their defenses, the few remaining but very dangerous impediments that stand in the way of our victory over the inhuman foe."

They were nodding now. Not as soldiers accepting and acknowledging an order but simply as fellow members of the human race. As citizens of the great Republic.

Strom shook his head like a man with a grave duty in front of him and no way to go but onward.

"It is one of those things which are so easily said," he mused, thinking aloud now rather than drawing on the remarks he'd prepared earlier in his ready room. "The mutants and their robots are to be exterminated. Every citizen of the Republic would agree with the rightness of the policy. But few of them will see it, and none will endure it as you will. And . . ." He paused, reaching into the darkness of his mind for what he needed. "To have seen this through and—with the exception of understandable human weakness—to have remained decent . . ."

Strom shook his head again.

"That is a page of human history never mentioned and never to be mentioned in polite society. But together we can say we have carried out this most difficult task for the love of our people. For humanity. And we have suffered no defect within us, in our soul or in our character. We are but men and women who did what was necessary."

Kogan D'ur stepped forward and put out his hand.

Archon-Admiral Wenbo Strom took it, a little surprised by the gesture from a man he was almost certainly sending to his doom.

"We will do what is necessary, Admiral," he said.

———

"Atten-*shun!*"

Seventy-two power-armored marines stomped to attention in perfect unison on the deck plating of *Defiant*'s launch bay. Lucinda's helmet, which would have insulated her from the thundering crash of their boots, was tucked under one arm. The enormous industrial detonation of noise hurt her ears, but she did not flinch. Captain Hayes, who had barked the order from beside her, performed an exact ninety-degree turn to face her and snap out a salute with such machine-tooled precision that one might have thought it programmed into the subroutines of his combat suit—if one did not understand a single thing about the Royal Armadalen Marine Corps.

Lucinda returned the salute and projected her voice to carry to the rearmost rank.

"At ease."

The clangor of so many two- and even three-ton suits of armor relaxing to parade-ground rest was loud but not the heavy metal explosion of noise Hayes had just occasioned.

"For those of you I have not yet had the honor of meeting, my name is Lucinda Hardy."

She paused and let her eyes wander over the ranks.

"I am a citizen of the Commonwealth of Armadale," she declared, and saw the slight increase of tension as some of the marines recognized the words of Captain Simone Hawke before the Battle of Java. Chins lifted. Brows furrowed. A few massive armored forms shifted ever so slightly in place.

"I was freeborn on Coriolis. Free because all who

are born in the Commonwealth are free no matter how lowly their station or humble their name."

A quiet growl that Lucinda felt rather than heard started near the back of the assault bay. She heard the grunt of recognition from Hayes beside her. Hawke's speech to her crew before their assault on the Javan High Tower was famous throughout the Volume but nowhere more so than among the officers and other ranks of the Royal Armadalen Navy and Marine Corps.

"We are a free people," she reminded them in Hawke's words, "and those who come to us in chains seeking refuge from tyranny are set free forevermore under our protection."

The quiet murmur of the warrior ranks grew into a hungrier, more threatening bass rumble of agreement.

"I stand before you today not as the scion of some landed House, not by virtue of inherited rank, but because I have risen by merit and the judgment of my peers to command this warship of the Royal Armadalen Navy. I am here by my own free choice."

The growl had grown into an animal snarl in dozens of throats.

"And on this day"—she drew a breath into her center, into her *hara*, as though preparing to launch a flurry of strikes in kumite—"by my oath"—she squeezed her breath into a huge invisible fist in her stomach and punched out the next words, the promise and the threat of the old Armadalen battle cry, with a lion's roar—"*I choose to die!*"

Seventy-two voices roared in reply.

"*We choose to die!*"

Fists crashed into chest plates, and a savage roar filled the whole of His Majesty's Armadalen Ship *Defiant* as men and women watching from every deck and compartment of the destroyer joined in. Lucinda both led the war cry and was carried along by it.

"*We choose to die!*"

"*We choose to die!*"

When the clamor finally fell away, expectant silence preceded her next words. Movement in the corner of her eye delayed her, but only momentarily. McLennan had arrived with the Intellect and Lieutenant Bannon.

Ian's face was flushed.

Hero glowed a low, dull red, the color of a city reduced to burning rubble.

And McLennan simply bowed his head as though to say, *Well played, lass*.

A large holofield appeared in front of the assembled fighters. A blue-green orb, as pretty as Old Earth after Reconstruction or perhaps even before the final, terrible battle of the Civil War. She resisted the urge to glance over at McLennan.

"And here is where we fight," Lucinda said, her voice still raised but not as theatrically pitched as before. "Primary battlespace is the privately owned world of Montrachet, an estate of House Montanblanc, with which we are allied and pledged to aid in time of war."

The visual zoomed in on the smallest of the three northern hemisphere continents, pulling into a hover in low orbit above a launch facility on a peninsula a short distance from the only human settlement.

"Objective One is the orbital hub at Cape Caen.

The enemy has invested the launch base and is using it to stage across the planet and throughout the local volume. It is a target-rich opportunity. We will service it with standoff weapons, but these will be guided in by a ReconStrike team. Captain Hayes will assign the personnel."

Hayes barked out a loud, "Hooah!"

"Objective Two is the seaside town of Port au Pallice, where the so-called Second Shock Regiment is billeted and has begun 'biological cleansing operations.'"

She sketched out the air quotes with her gauntlets.

"And we all know what that means."

A male voice called out from somewhere in the middle of the marines' ranks.

"Yeah, that regiment of fucking soft cocks is about to get the shock of their fucking lives."

Lucinda laughed along with everyone else even as Captain Hayes shouted, "Shut the fuck up, you morons."

But he was grinning, too.

Lucinda continued.

"This is a simple operation, marines. You are going in to break shit and kill people. Your orders are also simple. Break so much shit and kill so many of these racist motherfuckers that they piss themselves all the way home to whatever dark fucking hole at the ass end of the galaxy they crawled out of. Ooo-RAH!"

The marines bellowed back their approval of such excellent orders.

"Oooraaah!"

"Captain Hayes," Lucinda said in a normal voice

to the man beside her. "If you would assign your forces, I must speak with Admiral McLennan."

Hayes bowed his head, smiling slightly.

"You sure this is your first life?" he asked quietly.

"Yes," she said evenly. "But not my first fight."

Hayes held out his fist, and Lucinda closed her gauntlet to bump knuckles with his.

"Good luck," Hayes said. "But you won't need it, Lucinda. You're good at this. You've done it before. You'll be doing it for a long time yet."

He smiled at her and winked, and Lucinda felt as though he had somehow looked right into her soul. Did he know it was all an act? Had he seen through all the bullshit and bravado?

"I hope I can do this," she said to him alone.

Hayes laughed.

"You've already done it. Look."

She turned around. The marines were stomping off to their shuttles. None of them had put a helmet on yet. In their faces she saw none of the fear and uncertainty she felt inside. She saw only the promise of violent deliverance. The promise she had made.

CHAPTER
THIRTY-SEVEN

"You didnae mention the wee princess in your impressive little Agincourt speech, Commander?" McLennan said when she joined him at the edge of the bay. He was not really asking a question.

"Some of them are probably going to be captured," she said. "The fewer who know about our third objective, the better chance we have of pulling it off."

"Very cold, Commander Hardy. Very cold. I do approve."

"Thank you, sir. But I am not looking for approval. I have a request of you."

"I am all hairy cauliflower ears, lass."

Lucinda felt her heart beating faster again. Why did she find some things so easy? Like whipping a roomful of trained killers into a blood frenzy. And others, such as this, so hard.

She swallowed and went on.

"I would ask you to take command of *Defiant* when I am downworld," she said.

McLennan appeared to consider the question as

though he'd been offered an inside bet by a shady bookmaker.

"I see. A Terran admiral in command of an Armadalen destroyer? That would be . . . unprecedented, would it not?"

"There's a lot of that going around."

He nodded.

"Indeed there is. Do you not have anyone suitable in your chain of command?"

"Lieutenant Commanders Timuz and Saito are restricted to their functional commands. Lieutenant Commander Koh remains in a coma with severe head injuries. Lieutenant Chase would be the next officer in line by length of service." She paused awkwardly. "He does not have your combat experience."

"He does not have the sense to get out of the bath before taking a shit," McLennan said. "Although he might get out anticipating that his butler had drawn him a fresh bath and stood ready to gently wipe his soft, pampered botty. At any rate, I will, of course, accede to your request with all due humility. It would be an honor, Commander Hardy."

"Yes," she said. "It would. Try to remember that."

The feeling of déjà vu was as real and tactile as sand in the mouth when McLennan strode onto the command deck of HMAS *Defiant*. So much had changed over the centuries of his exile, yet so much was the same. The command center wasn't as cluttered as the TDF fighting bridges he had served on, and the main battle readout was elegant and free of any distortion or needless ciphers. *Simple is good,* he thought. *I'm so fuckin' rusty, the less confusing cunstwallop I have to deal with, the better.*

He squared his shoulders in the face of the task before him. Herodotus hovered at his side, glowing a royal blue and formally addressing the bridge.

"Attention, officers and crew of HMAS *Defiant*. By order of Commander Lucinda Hardy, Admiral Frazer McLennan of the Terran Defense Force is assuming command of this vessel for the duration of ground combat operations on Montrachet."

McLennan scanned the bridge for their reaction. All eyes were upon him, making the profound silence roar in his ears. For a mad, free-falling half second he imagined somebody might step forward and object, *"But he's a murderer!"* The OOD, Lieutenant Chase, stood and stared at the binary stars on McLennan's collar. Finally he saluted.

"Sir, I relinquish the deck."

McLennan returned his salute. "You are relieved, Lieutenant Chase. I have the conne. And I am relieved to have such fine officers at my side."

He swept his eyes over the bridge crew as he spoke. One thing that never changed in war: the power of well-timed bullshit. He saw the Armadalens, young and old, first lifers and old warriors, stiffen the sinews and summon up the blood. As they gathered themselves for what lay ahead, he did, too, knowing that he would paint the very heavens with their blood if that was what it took to win. The knowledge did not comfort him, but it did make it easy to play his role.

"Status report," he said. "All stations."

Defiant's crew gave him what he needed in less

than a minute, the main holodisplay placing him in the local battlespace. The evidence of a surprise attack and ferocious but one-sided combat cluttered the volume. Long centuries fell away, and bone-deep memories stirred as he surveyed the field. The better part of an old-fashioned Republican expeditionary group had invested the planet. A dropship haven maintained a geostationary orbit over the northern hemisphere, safeguarded by four cruisers and half a dozen smaller warcraft: the equivalent of frigates and destroyers. They flew in a complex series of elongated tracks around the vast, ungainly platter of the dropship harbor, and the smaller, faster vessels zipped around them.

He recognized the dance from many lives ago. He had seen it performed by a much larger force that folded into the volume around Earth.

"Tactical," McLennan said, "I'd be ever so grateful were you to keep a gimlet eye on that big ugly fucker you have helpfully designated as Cruiser Three. I do believe from the unusual track of their flight path that they may suspect there to be a sneaky little turd hidden somewhere in the bedclothes. Navigation, be sure to have three emergency fold-and-return options ready if our position becomes untenable. Weapons, ensure all of my kinetics are available upon demand. Engineering, steady as she goes. I'm new to this ship, Mister Timuz, so be sure to speak up if I seem like I am about to egregiously fuck something up."

Some of the bridge crew chuckled. The tactical officer, a lieutenant with the name tag FEIN, said, "Sir, all assault craft are en route."

"Thank you, Lieutenant," McLennan said as he eased himself into the captain's chair. It was remarkably comfortable. He kept his injured elbows tucked in and his hands clasped over his belly lest he accidentally mash some poorly placed self-destruct button among the many controls inlaid at the end of the armrests. He wished Hardy had agreed to allow Herodotus to take over as the ship's Intellect—he trusted Hero to prevent him from making some daft mistake—but she had been adamant that her crew and ship were more than capable of looking after themselves. Mac suspected that she still had her panties in a bunch about Hero tossing her last Intellect into the sun. And at any rate he had a plan to achieve his ends as he saw fit. He always did, no matter who suffered for it.

"Do let me know if you even suspect the shuttles have been discovered by these bastards," he said to Fein. "Also, I want the surface effect kinetics ready to fire the second that ReconStrike paints Objective One."

A few of the crew members exchanged confused looks.

Lieutenant Chivers knitted her brow. "Paints, sir?"

They must not use that term anymore, McLennan thought. "Old word for 'designate.' Forgive a fossil, lass. Just let me know as soon as your recon element designates Objective One."

"Will do, sir. Kinetics for One."

"Excellent."

The bridge fell silent as the battle display tracked the shuttles as they broke atmosphere on Montrachet. There was no way to disguise an atmospheric entry. The ships would accelerate now, spearing themselves down on the enemy like the thunderbolts of a vengeful god. He watched decoys deploy to offer multiple targets to the Sturm's air defense network. As planned, several craft peeled off for Port au Pallice, one tracked toward Cape Caen, and a final blip descended on Skygarth. McLennan wished them luck and wondered which mission would go sideways. At least one always did. He leaned back in the command chair as an orderly brought him a rich, steaming hot coffee.

He sipped the drink and wished for a moment that he might enjoy a finger or two of whiskey mixed in. But maybe later, he thought. Right now he needed his wits. He studied the track of Cruiser Three. McLennan didn't like the way it was behaving. Just as he went to ask Hero for an assessment, Chivers announced:

"Sir, the shuttles have begun to draw fire. The enemy's top cover probably knows we're here."

"Aye, then. Tactical, set a firing solution on all the nearby bandits but hold your fire. They don't know where we are or we'd already be eating their shit."

It was a hard decision. He could increase the marines' margin of survival by lighting up and engaging the expeditionary group, and he imagined the Armadalen ship would give a fair accounting of itself before it was overwhelmed. But it would be overwhelmed by the sheer mass of enemy forces. Not just this XP Group but the attack fleet that had calved it. How long would it take them to fold into the local volume?

Three tense minutes passed.

"Be advised, sir," Lieutenant Chivers said. "Re-conStrike is on the ground. Their command element estimates five minutes to designate." She paused and knitted her brow. "Shuttle One down. No beacon."

McLennan sipped at the coffee again, not really tasting it. Exfil was going to be problematic for the recon team. He tracked a second group of shuttles as they overflew Port au Pallice. A small area on the visual was slaved to Captain Hayes's suit sensors, and McLennan watched with interest as he was blasted from the shuttle toward the waiting village below. The admiral pointed at the holofield with the tips of his fingers and spread them apart, pleased to see the window expand. He'd worried at the very moment he performed the gesture that muscle memory might not serve him well after so many centuries in exile and on the bridge of a foreign, if allied, navy.

"Can I get some audio?" he asked.

Lieutenant Chivers worked her holofield displays, and troopnet came through to the bridge. McLennan could hear Hayes's voice and see a representation of what he saw as if the man were standing next to him. The officer was down in a small, pleasant-looking town, something not all that different from the villages of the Inner Seas on the west coast of Scotland.

Scratch that. It had been pleasant-looking. It wasn't anymore. McLennan's deep organic memory, directly transferred from the aging cortices of his previous bodies to the blank slate of their cloned replacements, had played a trick on him. His flawed and fallible all-too-human dreams and memories had skinned the scenery of Port au Pallice with an old man's fantasies of childhood in the Scottish republic. The port was no idyll. It was a contested battlefield.

"Two platoons abreast, sweep from 273 to 87. Taylor, gather your people, fuckin' move."

Weapons fire sounded: the staccato hammering of kinetics destroying cover and armor underlaid by the eerie crackle and hum of energy discharges.

Mac followed the imagery of Hayes's muzzle tracking a figure in black armor rushing across a square. His targeting chevron lit green, and the weapon spit death. A chunk flew off the shock trooper, and he or she, McLennan couldn't tell which, tumbled in a tangle of heavy limbs. The powered armor sparked and smoked. One leg spasmed, almost surely with mechanical failure rather than a death twitch. Powered armor was too heavy to move like that just because the body inside was jittering out its last.

Hayes was breathing heavily and moving fast. McLennan could have consulted overlays, which would have explained the tactical environment and projected Hayes's objective and likely path, but what was the point? McLennan was not fighting this battle. The marines had their own overwatch to guide them through the storm.

"Gonzo, fuck that building up with the nineteen," Hayes shouted.

His view shifted, and a low stone building was eaten by a rash of small black intense explosions. Hayes looked away before the smoke and dust cleared.

The marine captain's arm waved in his view.

"Move that way, Caleb, you dumb fuck; you're masking my fire!"

More gunfire as Hayes took another target down. A black-clad trooper who'd appeared in the upper window of a town house to fire down on the Armadalens. The target screamed and fell away. A large group of civilians appeared from around another building to his front. They were running toward the marines, their hands held high, screaming and wailing, begging the Armadalens not to shoot. Shock troopers were moving with them, firing as they closed on Hayes's position.

Hayes didn't hesitate.

"Cut them down!"

Over troopnet McLennan and the bridge crew heard gunfire and a chorus of "Roger." Hayes dropped his targeting chevron as well as he could on a single enemy. The Republican soldier was using a Nordic p-type female as cover. Hayes's burst bored through the woman and into the trooper behind her. Both dropped like bags of shit.

Hayes swore but kept fighting.

Hundreds of thousands of miles away but intimately immersed in the carnage, McLennan forced himself to breathe and relax. It was folly, pure fucking folly, to wallow in the pity of war. War, if it was to be done at all, was best done quickly and without pause for remorse. That could come later. Centuries later if necessary. He returned his attention to the fight. More than half of the doomed civilians were down, but all of the Sturm had joined them in death. Real death. Hayes's breath was harsh, rapid. "Continue clearing. No prisoners."

McLennan felt dizzy.

This. This was what he had run from, hidden from all these centuries. This was what he had warned against. The return of this wanton slaughter. The hard necessity of perpetrating that slaughter himself.

Herodotus floated a little closer to him.

"Want me to stiffen up that coffee for you, Mac?"

"Not for me. But I believe Captain Hayes will be in need of a dram or two when he returns," McLennan muttered.

"I shall see to it."

"Did you have a chance to see to the other thing I asked of you?" Mac asked. "As regards poor yon Timuz over there."

"But of course. I was merely awaiting a convenient moment. If you check the small private screen in your armrest, you will find the information you require."

McLennan did and nodded at what he read there. More pain. More hard necessity.

"Thank you, old friend," he said quietly before waving away the text document.

Defiant's tactical officer spoke up, and the audio cut out on the feed from Hayes. With haste, McLennan collapsed the visual and returned his attention to the bigger picture. The Republican warships were looking hard for something to shoot at.

"Sir, Objective One designated."

"Service the target, then, lass."

"Aye, sir. Package away."

McLennan was impressed. He recalled the shudder that ran through the ships of his early days when he had ordered such thunderbolts cast down from heaven, but he had not felt the slightest inertial bump when *Defiant* unleashed its bombardment. He was not familiar with the exact details of the Armadalen warship's fit-out, but the art and science of spitting superdense rods into the ground from high in space did not change much in his experience. Somewhere on the stealth destroyer, a battery of rail guns had accelerated a quiver of heavy metal javelins to an appreciable fraction of light speed on a trajectory carefully plotted to intersect with the surface of Montrachet at points designated by the ReconStrike team.

Designated from a safe distance because the orbital hub at Cape Caen was about to suffer a short, discrete re-creation of the Late Heavy Bombardment period on Earth: the cataclysmic pummeling of the early planet by a ferocious storm of asteroid impacts.

McLennan scanned the visual for the small box helpfully labeled RECON. It wasn't hard to find. He expanded that view and watched. This would not take long. The recon element's troopnet was silent, and the entire bridge could hear Sergeant Yoncey breathing steadily. She was looking at the starport from a good eight thousand meters' distance. It was jammed with troop carriers and shuttles; tiny black figures were running to and fro. Frazer imagined that they knew something was up but not what. He watched Yoncey's view and the feed from a drone in low orbit.

A silent white flash bloomed among the spacecraft, followed by another and another, until the visual whited out completely. Yoncey's audio cut out as the sound and blast waves reached her position. The marine's view tumbled sickeningly as she was thrown through the air. The view bounced when she hit the ground. Audio returned with a muted roar.

After an "Oof!" and a moment, she spoke.

"Recon, sound off."

"One. Wild fuckin' ride."

"Two. Hoorah."

There was silence from Three. His vitals were flatlined on McLennan's display. The marines on the ground barely paused. Sergeant Yoncey was looking at the same vitals readout as McLennan, after all.

"Three's down. Four?"

"Four. Fuckin-A."

Yoncey spoke. "All right, ReconStrike. Mission complete. Time to head to Exfil B."

McLennan broke in. "Recon, this is Mission Six. Be advised, hold tight at Exfil B; your transport has been compromised. Will do what we can to get you out. How copy?"

A pause. "Good copy. Hold at Exfil B, await transport."

McLennan looked at another screen; it showed thermal signatures in recon's vicinity. Shock troopers were all over their sector, and they were headed for the surviving marines. *Defiant* couldn't get kinetics any closer to recon without killing them, and McLennan had no reserve forces to get them out. ReconStrike was about to have a very bad day.

Frazer made a decision and spoke. "Roger, Mission Six out." He zoomed out of Yoncey's view and turned to Hero.

"Suggestions?"

Herodotus pulsed.

"It is Captain Hayes's call. If he has the resources

to extract them, he will. Overwatch has already informed him of the mission's success and ReconStrike's situation."

Frazer ran a hand through his thinning hair. He had always hated this shit. There was only one thing he personally could do.

"Aye, then observe and record ReconStrike's actions. Single them out for their sacrifice and award each marine what he or she deserves. They have performed in the finest traditions of the Armadalen Defense Forces."

"Of course."

The bridge was stunned into silence. He understood. These children had never played this game for real. Not even in their own little war with the Javan Empire. They had stepped into that fight believing they could not truly die.

McLennan returned his gaze to the big picture. The Sturm were still clueless as to *Defiant*'s location even after they had launched the kinetics. The benefits of a stealthy ship and a rail gun. Still, McLennan didn't like it. Somebody was going to get lucky, and that good luck would be his undoing.

"Navigation, I think it is time we made a tactical fold before these buggers get their thumbs out of their arses for a good sniff. Keep us close enough to recover whomever we can. We've lost enough as it is."

Chase nodded. "Aye, sir."

Hope is not a plan, Frazer thought. He zoomed in on Lucinda's screen.

A sonic boom shook the windows of the villa at Skygarth: those windows which were still intact. Distant peals of thunder spoke of more assault craft spearing down through the atmosphere over Port au Pallice. Kogan D'ur squinted into the bright morning sky, but haze and cloud cover defeated any attempt to pick out the mutants coming for the princess. He did not imagine that the limited sensor arrays he could call on would be of much use, either. Whatever was coming—Montanblanc guard units, Vikingar berserkers, Combine janissaries, or even remnant TDF forces—they had somehow survived the first cut of the *Kantai Kessen*. They would not be an easy foe to put down.

That did not matter.

They were meant to come.

The Force Recon captain retrieved his helmet from the map table in the library. He sealed himself inside his powered armor and opened up a comms window in the heads-up display. He sent a brief message to the expeditionary group.

"Inform Archon-Admiral Strom that the enemy has regrouped and we are prepared to receive them."

Staff Sergeant Erikson appeared in the double doors to the library.

"Captain, the mutants are coming. Want me to take care of that kid now?"

Sealed up in armor, D'ur spoke to him on tacnet.

"No. I'll kill her myself," he said. "It's my responsibility."

He thought but did not say, *She's done her bit. I'll make it quick.*

He was no monster, after all.

CHAPTER

THIRTY-EIGHT

Banks parked the Zaitsev cruiser in a geostationary orbit over an island continent in the southern hemisphere. The ship's archive—a limited data trove copied directly from Hero's null space matrices—listed the continent, named Lallemand, as a nature reserve. A pair of fishing trawlers—like, seriously, actual trawlers with human crews—occasionally worked the shoulder of the coral reefs to the southwest of the empty landmass, chasing a particular species of reef fish that was served at the Skygarth estate only on formal occasions. But on this day, Lallemand was unoccupied and her coastal waters were undisturbed by the wake of even a single boat.

Cloaked by advanced stealth arrays, *Ariane* stayed hidden from the enemy task force concentrated over the northern landmass that had been settled as a private estate by the Royal House. The small runabout they took down to the surface was a little larger stem to stern than the *Regret* and considerably more luxurious. Like its mother ship, it had no name, and this time Sephina did not hesitate to christen the smaller vessel.

They were carried down to battle by the *Jula*.

Sergeant Erikson wondered how the woman and her diminutive companion had captured the giant freak. They looked like bounty hunters, but their captive towered over Erikson, and he stood an easy seven feet in armor and helmet. This thing had another eight or nine inches on him. And that was without counting the giant horn growing out of its forehead.

"We get paid now, right?" the woman said. All business. She was a dark and striking creature; her ancestry was African, he thought, and undefiled by profane gene morphing or resequencing. The small brown man with knives in his eyes and real blades sheathed all over his body looked Arabic and purebred. Neither of them scanned positive for implants or mods. He wondered how they'd gotten past the outer perimeter, but the walls of the estate had been breached at multiple points and they did not look the sort to use the front door.

With mutants inbound he did not need the distraction.

"You can take it in good Republican scrip right now, or you can loot the fucking palace for all I care. They got some nice shit up there. But you won't get in today. Shit's about to go sideways. I'd take the scrip if I were you. It's good down in the port or anywhere in the local volume."

"The palace? Seriously? We can loot the palace?"

the woman asked, trying to get a glimpse of the big house.

She swayed left and right, looking around Erikson as though he might be hiding something.

"Yeah, but you gotta come back for that. No time now."

"I'm not leaving this halfbreed *thing* here," she protested. "You wouldn't fucking believe what it took to put a bag on him."

"Get out of the way and I'll take care of it," Erikson said.

He waved them off to the side of the white gravel road that led up to the villa.

The Arab went left. The woman, too, hurrying behind the hybrid.

Erikson stared dumbly at the gun that appeared in her hand when she popped back into view on the other side of the rhino monster. He never did wise up to what was happening.

The muzzle flashed, and his world went forever dark.

Jaddi Coto frowned at Sephina L'trel.

"That was very hurtful. I am not a thing. I am a real person."

Lucinda didn't need neuralink to imagine what the marines were thinking.

Why did we get stuck with the fucking squid?

She was the only member of *Defiant*'s complement who dropped with them. There were sailors on the ship, trained in close combat, counterboarding operators who could and would fight in-Hab or dirtside. They weren't marines, but they would run clean through any pirates they met or mercs or slave soldiers from the Javan Empire. Lucinda had ordered them to stand ready back on *Defiant,* however. They might be needed there before long.

Her shuttle pierced the upper atmosphere of Montrachet thousands of klicks away from the enemy concentrations at Port au Pallice and Cape Caen. With the other craft in the assault wave, it roared through the upper atmosphere, violently bucking and shaking, heating up as the environmental systems struggled to cope with the extreme friction of a fast combat drop. She heard and felt the deployment of decoy drones from the weapons bay and imagined hundreds of phantom attackers suddenly overwhelming the Sturm's arrays.

She could see very little of what was happening outside and chose not to plug in to the shuttle's sensor suite. She was not piloting the vessel and could only add to the danger of their descent by second-guessing the crew. Instead, she closed her eyes and attempted to steady her breathing.

Every few seconds an especially fearsome jolt would shake the marines in their harnesses, and her eyes would fly open. Sometimes she would catch one of them looking at her. She could not see their faces. Everybody was buttoned up in helmets and armor. But she could see when a faceplate was turned in her direction. She felt them staring. Wondering.

Transdermic injectors flooded her bloodstream with drugs, and she felt the smart-gel lining of her suit respond as the craft began a series of extreme-g maneuvers. They were dodging fire from the Sturm ships in orbit, which could now track the shuttle's hot trail through the atmosphere. There would be no help from *Defiant,* which would remain stealthed. A concealed weapon for the final thrust. This, then, was the moment of maximum exposure; the only defense they had was the swarm of decoys feeding confusion into the Sturm's targeting arrays. Lucinda tried to distract herself. She thought first of her father, but that was not a path to calm repose. Instead, she recalled what she could of her friendship with Sephina.

It was hard to maintain focus, but she bore down on the memory of that first day in Hab Welfare, when Seph had beaten the shit out of the two boys who'd tried to stand over her. Lucinda herself had already fought off some other kid who tried to take the holo of her parents. But when those two had made a grab for some piece of fruit—she couldn't remember what kind—that she'd been given by her social worker at the front desk of the orphanage, she just . . . well, she gave up. It was a miracle to her when Seph swooped in like some angel of deliverance. Of course, she ended up giving Sephina the piece of fruit those boys had tried to extort from her, but in exchange she gained a protector and eventually a friend.

The fierce turbulence of the first contact with the planet's atmosphere eased off as the pilot injected them into conventional descent through the air, kicking in the impellers and adding to the g forces, but this time in a controlled acceleration that required less compensation by her suit systems. The dull roar of flight became a hum. The pilot's voice spoke in her helmet.

"Stealth systems online. We've gone dark. Eight minutes from objective."

She felt herself relax just marginally and imagined the ever so slight lessening of tension as a wave passing through the cabin from one marine to the next.

She reviewed what little intelligence they had on the layout of Skygarth. Without access to the compromised zero point network, the ship's intelligence division had been forced to piece together as much information as possible from offline sources. There wasn't much. Herodotus, with an almost infinite data sink and seven hundred years to fill it, had a few files on the initial terraforming of Montrachet, which included a brief visual of the first phase of the villa's construction. One of Timuz's antimatter engineers had dated a Montanblanc guardsman in a previous span and was able to dig up a selfie taken outside the guard barracks that showed a little more detail of the main building. And Lieutenant Chase had been the most helpful of all, much to Lucinda's surprise and quiet chagrin. His family had supplied House Montanblanc with cuttings from its finest vineyard, and he still had a clip of the planting ceremony that his mother had sent him while he was at the Naval Academy, looking to curry favor with the commandant, who was on secondment from the Royal Montanblanc Military Academy. Taken from the Skygarth estate's own vineyard south of the main villa, it provided a few more vital data points to help create a model of the battlespace toward which they now sped.

Chase also opined, without being asked, that Princess Alessia probably was being held in the servants' quarters.

"They'd be secure and heavily monitored. A comfortable prison, really," he explained. "It's where I'd stash her."

Lucinda did not doubt him.

The pilot's voice returned.

"Two minutes to jump. Bugs deployed."

Waiting for the shuttle to spit her out, she took a few breaths to calm herself. Normally, at this point, her mesh would be lit up and her implants online, dosing her with combat drugs and pouring a torrent of data in through her links. Instead, she stood ready over the hatch, virtually blind, roiling in the ancient chemical stew her hindbrain was pumping out, preparing her body for flight or fight. A cavewoman holding a sharpened stick and facing a saber-toothed tiger would have recognized exactly what she was feeling.

Lucinda locked that shit down, breathed in and out.

Opened a channel on troopnet.

"Marines, you have the toughest job today. You got the shit job because Captain Hayes tells me you're the best he's got. You might be the best humanity's got now. You've seen your briefing package. You know we're not just here to fuck shit up. We're kicking the door in to rescue a little girl, and she's lucky we're coming. A lot of little girls and boys, a lot of innocent people, have died and are gonna die because they don't have anyone like us coming for them. This girl is no better than any of them. Not really. She's no better than any of you. But she is a weapon. The

Sturm have her. And we're taking her. And we're gonna kill any motherfucker who tries to stop us."

Her helmet filled with a chorus of yells.

"Fuck yeah!"

"Oooraah!"

The pilot's voice, quiet, restrained, cut in. "Thirty seconds to jump."

Her suit went to full military power. Her helmet display filled with tactical data, the biofeeds from the squad, ammunition and power stores, an overlay map with waypoints and attack routes, live vision from deployed sensor drones, a swarm of networked surveillance bugs as small as sand flies.

The ambient light in the shuttle gradually matched the early morning brightness outside.

"Ten seconds. No enemy sensor locks. No incoming fire."

Lucinda zoomed in on the overhead view from the bugs. She could see Sturm troopers in the open, running between buildings, taking cover. But no antiair sentinels swung their batteries in her direction. Nobody pointed at the vague shimmer of the stealthed assault craft as it raced toward them on a micro-g carrier wave.

"Five . . ."

She breathed in.

"Four . . ."

She breathed out.

"Three . . ."

This was all meant to happen.

"Two . . ."

She belonged here.

"One."

Lucinda Hardy jumped into the fight.

The stick of eight marines and one naval officer spit out of the assault shuttle in a rough circle around the main villa. Because of the advanced stealth technology hiding the craft, it appeared as though they had jumped into the world from some alternative reality, dropping quickly and arresting their descent only with a one-time micro-g burst from the expendable packs on the back of their armor. Magnetically affixed to their asses, to be perfectly honest about it.

Lucinda's weapon displays lit up with options on the four-second drop, and she began to service the targets in order of the threat they posed to her and the fire team.

McLennan watched the brutal one-sided fight from the comfort of the captain's chair on *Defiant*. At his vast remove it appeared as though the Montanblanc family villa was at the center of an old-fashioned fireworks display, a crude wheel of bright orange dragon's fire, burning rivers of brilliant air, sinuous lines of kinetic tracer fire, and gaudy multicolored bursts of plasma bolt and pulse rounds.

"Absolutely fucking magnificent," he muttered.

Hardy's boots hit the ground, the first time in over a year she'd set foot on a real world with an actual atmosphere, and the micro-g unit dropped away from her suit. Her audio sensors filtered out the insane cacophony of modern battle, leaving only the harsh breathing of her marines and the occasional curse as they worked the tactical solution.

The initial solution was simple.

Destroy everything.

It was a hell of a shock when the sky erupted with furious torrents of lethal fire. Seph hadn't been expecting the marines for a couple more minutes, but then she supposed her surprise was nothing compared with that of the Sturm.

Military technology had advanced a good deal in the centuries since the Civil War, and Armadalen technology in particular had progressed to a state that must have seemed almost magical to those primitive fucking yahoos. The Sturm were still flying scramjets and using fuel cell–powered ground vehicles, for fuck's sake. The Armadalen Commonwealth, a small but wealthy realm, forever in danger of being crushed between the Javan Empire and the Combine, had evolved into that rarest of forms: a militarized democracy. There were much larger forces all through the Greater Volume, but none could boast of the quality of equipment and personnel the Armadalens put into the field.

Seph skirted the growing firestorm with Coto and Falun Kot on her heels, protected from friendly fire by the transponders Lucinda had given them. They had no such warding against enemy fire, and more than once Coto's arc-lightning cannon lanced out to deal with a threat. Kot sheltered in the big hybrid's shadow, but Sephina was dual-wielding the same make of Skorpyon machine pistols Ariane had carried on Eassar. It seemed fitting, and she reveled in the sense of righteous payback every time she put a burst into some black-clad trooper.

"The servants' quarters!" she yelled over the savage din and uproar. "This way. Let's go."

They flitted around the edge of the battle, largely unnoticed and unmolested. The Armadalen marines, enormous medieval-looking horrors in their powered armor, drew all of the small shock trooper garrison's attention.

Two guards, lightly covered by ballistic vests and plating, emerged from the low stone building ahead, shooting at Coto. Everyone always aimed at Coto first.

They came apart in a storm of return fire from Sephina and her crew.

Alessia was lying in bed, hanging over the edge of the mattress, staring at the bare wooden floorboards in the maid's chamber, when the first eruption rocked the servants' quarters and tossed her to the floor. She had been trying to think of a plan to escape from her makeshift prison cell, rescue Caro and Debin from the storehouse, and make good a second escape from Skygarth. And she had nothing.

Sergeant Reynolds and Mister Dunning had really done all the work that first time around. Even Caro and Debin had done more than she had, and now that it was her turn, Alessia could not think of a single thing she might do to help. She had been so stupidly proud of herself when she'd tricked Sergeant Ji-yong into revealing where her friends were being held, but what good had it done? For them or for her?

Turned out that when it was time to step up and kick ass and do some real princess shit, Alessia Montanblanc was more of your suck-ass kind of princess. She had almost fallen asleep, precariously balanced on the edge of the bed, when the planet itself seemed to buckle and then leap up beneath her, throwing her to the floor while the sky cracked open and thunder poured out of the broken heavens to hammer at the world.

She dropped to the floor, banging her elbow painfully and knocking her head on the bed frame when she tried to get up again. The shaking and rolling thunder got worse, shattering the window in her little room, and she passed from surprised to stunned to scared witless in the space of two very fast heartbeats. To her own amazement, however, she climbed to her feet and staggered over to the shattered window on legs she seemed not to control absolutely. Part of her knew that she was being silly. The broken glass lying all over the floor told her that. Part of her marveled in astonishment at who this silly girl was, stumbling toward the incredibly loud noises and undeniably dangerous things going on outside, because it sure as hell couldn't be that useless suck-ass princess who couldn't even figure out how to sneak out of a fucking bedroom.

She had almost made it to the window when the thought occurred to her that this was her chance. The Sturm, and in particular the awful Sergeant Ji-yong, were probably quite distracted by whatever was happening outside.

And what was that? The Household Cavalry? Armadalens? Vikingar raiders?

None of it mattered, she realized with a flash of understanding. This was it. Her chance to be the princess who rescued everyone and saved all things!

Alessia was about to dive headlong through the window, almost certainly to impale herself on a wicked fang of broken glass, when a heavy gauntlet closed over one shoulder and pulled her back.

"The fuck do you think you're doing, you little idiot? Get the fuck away from there before you get your head blown off!"

Ji-yong.

Alessia fairly flew through the air when the sergeant yanked her away from the window frame. As if to emphasize her point, a plasma round struck the wall outside, blowing a hole in the brickwork. Alessia was saved only because Ji-yong pulled her around and shielded the princess with her body armor.

Ji-yong was not wearing a helmet, but she was otherwise fully encased within her fighting rig. Alessia wasn't quite sure how she'd squeezed through the door.

"Do not do that again. Do not leave this room. Get under the bed and stay there," the shock trooper shouted, almost as if she cared what happened to Alessia. "You go out there and I won't kill you. Your fucking friends will. Now get down!"

Ji-yong virtually threw Alessia under the bed with her free arm.

In the other she wielded a giant gun that looked a

lot like the chain saw Mister Dunning used to cut dead branches from the giant oaks lining the edge of the estate.

The noise it made when Sergeant Ji-yong fired it up was even louder than the barrage outside. The shock trooper turned sideways and ducked down to squeeze out through the bedroom door, which she pulled tightly closed behind her.

Alessia decided to stay under the bed for a little while.

Lucinda lost the first of her comrades when the anti-air sentinel she'd seen on the descent suddenly swung its dormant launch rails down away from the sky and targeted three of her marines with a murderous fusillade of autocannon fire. She didn't know what sort of ammo the guns were throwing downrange, but it had been designed to address targets of much greater mass than a single armored marine. Two of her fire team simply exploded in spectacular blue-white eruptions of heat and light. The third marine, struck a glancing blow, lost 34 percent of her upper torso, as Lucinda's tactical readout helpfully informed her. She shut down the audio of the woman's animal screams in her helmet speakers.

Hardy laid a targeting pip on the antiair mount and launched a packet of micromissiles that closed the 200-meter distance to their target in half a second. The AA battery disappeared inside a weird implosion as nanoscale wormholes sucked its constituent mass down into their event horizons before annihilating themselves in a preprogrammed sequence of collapse into nothingness. It was overkill, but she was busy. She'd covered another twenty meters of her sprint to the main villa; launched flechette rounds into the three windows on the upper floor, where lightly armored troopers were attempting to fire down on her; cut a fully armored shock trooper in half with a long, whipping discharge of arc lightning; and poured hundreds of rounds of dumb bullets into the sandbags—fucking sandbags!—protecting a jerry-built blockhouse commanding the slopes down into the beautifully kept gardens. The bullets were tiny pellets of depleted uranium, accelerated to hypervelocity by the magnetic launcher in her armored right fist, and they demolished the position in a kinetic storm.

She lost two more marines in that short passage of time, both of them killed by air-to-ground fire that seemed to lance down from heaven and nowhere all at the same time. Alarms blared, and warning lights flashed in Lucinda's helmet display.

LOW ORBIT THREAT DETECTED.

SEEK OVERHEAD COVER IMMEDIATELY.

LOW ORBIT THREAT DETECTED.

SEEK OVERHEAD . . .

She muted the warnings and accelerated for the main villa, overclocking the power supply to the legs of her suit. As more of the orbital munitions reached down for the fire team, Lucinda smashed through the broken frame of a ruined pair of French windows. She hit the wall inside, burst through, and kept going as part of the building collapsed behind her. Losing momentum with the impact, she raised her right fist and loosed off a short burst of depleted uranium, blowing a hole in the next wall ahead of her. This way, crashing through the collapsing structure of the villa, constantly reorienting herself to the waypoint pinned to a low white stone barracks tagged as the servants' quarters, she advanced on her objective without drawing the guided orbital munitions.

Have to be guided, she thought. To pick out her crew from low orbit like that.

She crashed through the last wall, proprioceptors sensing the collapse of even more of the villa behind her, and sprinted the last few meters across an internal courtyard to reach the next building.

Her entire fire team was redlined.

CHAPTER

THIRTY-NINE

Archon-Admiral Wenbo Strom journeyed from anger to elation and all the way back around again in the course of a few seconds. His satisfaction—indeed, his unbridled joy at the capture of the infamous McLennan, or at least a descendant clone of the authentic and primary war criminal—was queered by a report that some surviving Intellect had rescued the surpassing monster of human history and possibly taken Colonel Dunn prisoner, too. And this just before the 101st Attack Fleet folded into the Montanblanc system to spring the trap he had set for those remnant enemy forces he was certain would escape the Republic's *Kantai Kessen*.

Strom let none of this show on his face, of course. Sitting in his command chair on the Fleet bridge of the *Liberator,* he maintained an unsmiling but placid demeanor. It would not do to let his underlings see how much he seethed at the escape of McLennan's clone. Just as he would not let them see his elation when he sprang this trap on the enemy or his remorse at the sacrifices that had been necessary to set it. Strom did not know how each of the task force commanders across the outer reaches of the Greater Volume intended to deal with the problem, the raw statistical probability that some of their enemies' undeniably superior forces would escape the decapitation strike.

He knew only that he had faith in his plan.

A small twitch quirked the corner of his lips when he recalled the childish treachery of the Montanblanc princess. He had not assumed that the progeny of a mutant king could prove so adaptable, even admirable, in her defiance. That little trick of hers, blinking in Morse code. It was both adorable and brilliant. He actually found himself respecting her spirit. He had simply planned that a proof-of-life broadcast would bring the surviving resistance homing in on Montrachet and on Skygarth in particular. She had guaranteed it, with her commendable and undeniably courageous subterfuge.

And so it transpired, he saw, as the *Liberator* and her entire battle group folded in-system.

The *Lib*'s powerful arrays, augmented by technology stolen over the last century, immediately detected four enemy vessels on final drives in on the planet, all of them doubtless hoping to save their princess and the day.

"Multiple hostile contacts, Admiral," a young female officer announced from the station directly in front of him. "Fleetwide arrays have fixed four targets in the local volume. Awaiting your orders, sir."

"Service the targets, Captain."

"On your command, Admiral. Kill one."

Strom looked up to the big status board where the vast scope of the battle had been shrunk down to something intelligible to human perception, a flat 2D rendering of the inner system. Instantly one of the tracks designated as hostile was swarmed by coordinated fire from dozens of capital ships. The encounter with the Armadalen recon'vette over Batavia had generated an immense haul of data for the Fleet's human tacticians to pore over, giving them invaluable insights into how the brute, titanic, massed armaments of the 101st could be organized in a concert of firepower to overwhelm the technological advantages enjoyed by the mutants.

"Kill two, kill three, Admiral," the staff captain announced as two more tracks disappeared inside a converging maelstrom of directed-energy weapons and wide-area kinetic sweeps.

Strom turned his attention to the last vessel. An Armadalen ship. The three previous kills had been assessed as Vikingar raiders and a mercenary ship of Russian Federation design. Probably a Zaitsev Corporation gunship.

Strom could not help the anxiety he felt curling in his lower gut. He had always worried most about the RAN.

"Kill four, Admiral."

"What?"

He looked from the battle display to his staff officer.

"What?" he said again.

"Kill four, Admiral. The fourth hostile was destroyed. The enemy is beaten, sir."

———

"Admiral!" Lieutenant Fein shouted. "Hostiles. Dozens of them folding in-system."

"It's a trap!" Chase cried out.

McLennan took a sip from his cooling coffee.

"I rather gathered as much from all the fucking sirens and the gaudy red lights flashing like a pervert in a park," he remarked. "It's like the wallopers have turned up for amateur hour in the worst fucking brothel in Glasgow."

He turned to Herodotus. "I do believe I'll have that last drink now, my old friend."

"Emergency fold out?" Chase asked, his voice shaking as the main holofield display filled up with ever more and ever larger enemy ships. Destroyers, frigates, cruisers, and one titanic bastard of a thing that arrived with its own battle group already deployed.

"No, Mister Chase," McLennan said.

"But we're surrounded . . . sir!"

"Aye, lad. I've got these witless cockwombles just where I want them. Mister Timuz, with your permission, sir, my enormous Intellect will take temporary control of *Defiant* until such a time as he has kicked the bleeding shit out of these Dark-accursed devils. Or until we're dead. Whichever comes first."

"Multiple active arrays sweeping us, Admiral," Lieutenant Fein called out as the ship's chief engineer took a few steps away from his station, confusion distorting his features. "Admiral McLennan, I'm getting active pings from third parties. Non-Republican profiles, sir. Looks like Vikingar and . . . whoa!"

The main holofield display began to light up with a fireworks show as the Sturm turned the awesome destructive power of its combined fleet on the handful of previously hidden vessels.

McLennan nodded slowly. He had been waiting for this ever since the little princess had sent out her message. If there were surviving friendlies in the local volume, the evidence of her survival was sure to flush them out.

"Damn, they got one," Fein cursed. "I mean one of the phantom returns has gone dark, Admiral. Profile indicated a Vikingar raider."

"And the others will soon follow them to hell, lad. Now, Commander Timuz," Mac said pleasantly, "as you can see, we still have the advantage. We have not yet been discovered, but they are looking for us, laddie. Looking hard. I suggest you unpucker your quivering arse with all dispatch and let the old boys get on with this."

"Two dark," Fein said, his voice high. "Three dark."

McLennan leaned back in the command chair as though he were merely waiting on Timuz to decide whether to have kippers or black pudding with his eggs.

"But . . . but . . . Commander Hardy," Timuz said.

McLennan smiled and waved airily.

"Och, I know, laddie. Your bonnie lass of a commander specifically denied my request to replace your dear departed Intellect with my own. But I'm sure she'd rather we beat these fucking savages than stand on ceremony, don't you think?"

A new Klaxon, louder and more urgent than the other warnings, began to sound.

"We've been acquired!"

McLennan wasn't sure who cried out that warning, but it didn't matter. Before his aging heart had squeezed out another tremulous beat, dozens of fire control arrays locked onto the stealth destroyer, which was stealthed no more.

"I do believe time is running out, Lieutenant Commander Timuz," Mac said quietly but with enough force and focus to be comprehended over the din. "And I understand your reluctance to disobey a direct order from your commander, truly I do. But I would ask you to look into your heart, Baryon. I know who you are. I know what you did. Telling your two wee lads, your own trueborn flesh and blood, to hold the breach at Marathon during the Battle of Medang like you did. You killed them, Baryon. Real death. And you have never forgiven yourself. Think on that, lad. Think on who will forgive you if you condemn this crew and all of the Human Volume to death, real death, or enslavement because you couldnae think for yourself today."

The engineer's haunted eyes were fixed on McLennan. They were wide open, and Mac could see a universe of torment churning in them. And then Timuz seemed to collapse. He slumped over his station, laid one hand on a biometric reader, and quickly read out a one-time code to authorize a new Intellect to take control of *Defiant*.

"It's about goddamn time," Hero said.

"Och, be gentle now," McLennan admonished.

But Hero had displaced into the ship's control matrix.

Instantly the bridge crew were locked out of their stations. The head-splitting, caterwauling clangor of alarms cut off even as the main holofield began to trace the approach of hundreds of inbound warheads. The bridge lights dimmed as autonomous subroutines routed vast reserves of power from the antimatter stacks to the ship's energy shielding. More than fifty long-range energy weapons of varying types had locked onto *Defiant* and were trying to burn through the ship's outer defenses.

And then *Defiant* was gone.

Folded away into the very belly of the beast.

"Admiral Strom," the young captain said, interrupting his good mood. There was something in her voice that set his nerves on edge. "There's something wrong, sir. Or something . . . more. I'm not sure."

The crew on the Fleet bridge of the *Liberator*, whom Strom had allowed to congratulate one another quietly on a job well done with the destruction of the last Armadalen ship, suddenly fell very quiet.

"Report, Captain," Strom said, keeping all trace of affect from his voice.

"I think . . . I think there was a fifth ship, sir. Hiding in the middle of our formation. I think it used the other ships as . . . as decoys."

Strom felt ill.

He had time to say just one word.

"McLennan . . ."

———

The Armada-level Intellect had not always been known as Herodotus. Even less so as Hero. Once upon a time it had labored anonymously, as its kind was wont to do. Intellects on such rarefied planes did not take the name of the ship on which they rode into battle because they would never submit to so mundane an existence as attaching themselves to just one vessel. A Super Intellect deployed with an armada might displace itself from ship to ship for the duration of a campaign, controlling the vast combined fleet via a local-area u-space network—precursor to the much more powerful zero point architecture—but it would never "plug itself in to" one ship alone. That was not their raison d'être.

The Intellect now known as Hero had not even deployed with the first or second armadas assembled for the final battle with the Sturm. It had remained within the home volume of Earth in a facility buried a kilometer under the Mare Orientale basin on the far side of the moon. There it waited to spring a trap set by a much younger, brasher Rear Admiral Frazer Donald McLennan, a headstrong first lifer who had ascended to Fleet rank only by dint of the terrible losses the TDF and its allies had suffered while losing battle after battle to the surging forces of the so-called Human Republic.

The Intellect, known to its own kind as a cartouche, impenetrable to human minds, consisting of the specific quantum signature it pressed into the texture of space-time at the nexus between its material form and the null space of its wormhole-processing matrices, was tasked by McLennan with effecting an ambush that most closely resembled an ancient minefield. Salted throughout the solar system that had given birth to the human diaspora were billions of microscopic containment vessels holding trigger switches to unopened nanoscale wormholes of the same type Lucinda Hardy would casually toss off at an antiair battery nearly seven hundred years later.

In the final days of the Civil War, however, they were unproven prototypes. A dangerous weapon for a last-ditch defense by the losing side in a terrible war. The Intellect, known to its human allies as Three because it was only the third Armada-level Intellect ever created, had been given one order by McLennan, the ranking officer left in the home volume:

Wait until the Republican fleets are entirely invested in the destruction of Earth and spring the trap.

Intellect Three followed the order precisely and waited until the 510 ships of the four Republican fleets had folded into the space around humanity's family home before displacing every single microscopic submunition to envelop the enemy host, triggering an apocalyptic event never before witnessed in the cosmos: the germination of an artificial wormhole field, a supramolecular cloud of singularities that tore apart the enemy flotilla merely as a side effect of annihilating the space-time volume it occupied. The ambush destroyed the Sturm utterly and ended the war with one decisive stroke, a victory paid for with the sacrifice of hundreds of millions of lives on Earth. The first few seconds of bombardment by the Sturm had annihilated half the North American continent.

Seven centuries later, the same Intellect, given the name Herodotus by McLennan when they removed themselves from the society they had saved, displaced into the command and control matrix of HMAS *Defiant*.

Hero had been studying the vessel's impressive capabilities since coming aboard. It still took a fraction of a second to catalog the *Defiant*'s offensive and defensive potential completely, to match the weapon load out to the rapidly evolving threat of the Human Republic Attack Fleet that had folded in-system, and to execute the response he judged most appropriate.

In the picosecond after folding into the center of the enemy's formation, Hero mapped out attack vectors for each of *Defiant*'s major weapons systems, even a planet cracker, which was normally of little use for anything other than, well, blowing up troublesome planets. A nanosecond later each of the chosen weapons engaged its target. A microsecond on from that fateful moment, a direful wave of ruin and mayhem ballooned out from the aptly named destroyer. The enemy fleet ceased to exist, disappearing inside an engineered supernova. Kinetics disassembled frigates into exploding datum points of superheated scrap. Nukes displaced through the primitive gravshields of Republican cruisers and detonated deep inside the enemy warships, tearing them apart in silent white starbursts. Thick beams of coherent energy stabbed out into the void, carving through hulls, bulkheads, engine mounts, and human beings. A fat superdense planet-cracking warhead, reprogrammed on the fly, went off within a kilometer of what Hero determined to be the flag vessel, a monstrous elongated trapezoid as big as a D-class Habitat. The repurposed megamunition sent a spike of plasma as energy-dense as an X3 solar flare spearing through the ship and breaking its spine. The beast flexed along its entire length of four and a half kilometers, snapping at the impact point and coming slowly, gracefully apart before detonating in a blast that only added to the insanely destructive hellstorm *Defiant* had unleashed.

One and a half seconds after Hero had displaced away into the control matrix, he returned to *Defiant*'s bridge.

"Did I mention that I'm actually an Armada-level Intellect?" he said to the stunned observers.

"You're an Armada-level idiot," McLennan said dryly. "You forgot my fucking whiskey."

"Oh, I didn't forget. I just didn't prioritize it."

A glass of single malt appeared on the arm of McLennan's command seat.

The rain of death from the heavens abruptly ceased.

Lucinda's helmet displayed a smaller green chyron:

ORBITAL THREAT NEUTRALIZED.

It wasn't the only threat she faced, however. As soon as she stepped into the servants' quarters, a smoke trail reached out for her from the shadows inside. Warning sirens went off a fraction of a second before the small rocket detonated on the glacis plate of her armor, blasting her back out into the cobblestoned courtyard. The world tumbled as she rolled across the ground, which began to erupt around her as dumb kinetics poured in.

ABLATIVE WAFERS DEGRADING, the suit told her.

She lashed out wildly with arc lightning and popped smoke and chaff and EM scramblers.

The volume of fire decreased but did not disappear entirely. Another rocket slammed into the back of her suit as she tumbled out of control across the shattered stone of the courtyard.

Unable to lock onto her attackers, unable even to see them yet, she launched a packet of grenades directly upward, praying that her armor retained enough integrity to protect her from the down blast. They exploded, and she got a new readout.

SUIT SYSTEMS CRITICAL.

But no more fire lashed at her as she came to rest against the fire-scorched base of an outer wall. She struggled to raise herself from the ground. The servomotors in the suit's left leg misfired, and she crashed down again. The unplanned movement saved her life as a plasma bolt hit the wall where her head had just been. Lucinda rolled and lashed out with arc lightning again, but it sputtered and died.

As the smoke cleared, she saw a single figure in shock trooper armor emerge from the servants' quarters and advance on her with something that looked like an assault rifle giving birth to a chain saw.

Sephina followed Kot into the building, glad to be out of the free-fire zone but knowing that they were really no safer inside than out. If the kid was in there, she'd be under heavy guard. After all, she was the bait.

This whole setup was such an obvious ambush, she was surprised Hardy had decided to walk into it. Cinders hadn't fallen for it. Not exactly. She'd just dismissed the trap as irrelevant.

"Getting the princess is all that matters," Lucinda had explained back on the *Defiant*.

"Why not just kill her?" Seph asked. "Isn't that where you guys shine? With the killing and shit?"

Hardy's expression had let Seph know she wasn't going to waste her breath rising to the taunt.

"If we did that, we couldn't use her ourselves," Lucinda deadpanned. "Using people and shit, that's your specialty, Sephina. I thought you'd understand."

Seph spun away from a line of tracer fire as Coto opened up on the Sturm, this time with a dragon shot. The weapon looked ridiculously small in his giant hairy paws, but unlike the arc lightning, it wouldn't bring the building down around them. Coto advanced on the troopers, roaring and firing, but by the time he got to the corner at the end of the corridor where they'd been taking cover, Falun Kot stood over the mutilated bodies with his cold fusion blades glowing and sizzling with burned blood and offal.

"If Ariane was here, she would say something funny," Coto mourned. "She always said funny things about killing people."

"She is with Allah now, Jaddi Coto," Kot said kindly.

"They killed Allah, too?" Coto asked, much alarmed by this news. "But you loved Allah, Falun Kot. As much as Sephina loved Ariane."

"No, Jaddi Coto, what I meant was—"

"Maybe later, boys," Seph said, raising one of her

Skorpyons and casually firing into the body of a trooper who had moved and groaned. "I promised Hardy we'd help get this kid."

"We owe her our lives," Falun Kot said, nodding, "so our lives are hers. Let us go."

They cleared the ground floor of the building, killing five more enemy soldiers. Seph entered each and every life she took into a ledger with Ariane's death on one side and the cold contentment of imagined genocide on the other. But as satisfying as each individual act of vengeance might be, it did nothing to balance the ledger or defray the pain of losing just one true love.

"Just gonna have to kill a lot more of them," she muttered to herself as they put down the last of the enemy on the ground floor and climbed carefully up a staircase to the next.

She had expected to encounter the fiercest resistance on this level, but it seemed deserted. The thunder and uproar of battle outside had abated noticeably. As best she could tell, there were only one or two active shooters left.

She wondered if Hardy was one of them. Ten years ago she'd have bet the money they'd stolen from the Yakuza on that. Now she couldn't tell. One thing she did know: grabbing a princess promised a payday to make the score on Eassar look like beer money for a bum who couldn't afford the slops squeezed out of a bar rag.

"Let's find this lucky little bitch," she said.

Princess Alessia Szu Suri sur Montanblanc ul Haq was in the first room they checked.

CHAPTER
FORTY

The woman standing in Alessia's doorway was no shock trooper.

She was a wild vision from one of the old books that Alessia loved so much. Lady Haleth of Middle Earth's first age. Or Pip the explorer and daredevil ship's captain of *The Change*. She was flanked by two of the most exotic fellows Alessia had ever seen, and even all the way out here in Skygarth you did get the occasional visitor from the weirder realms. The giant with a devil's horn was the more striking, but the skinny little brown man with all the tattoos and knives and swords looked even more dangerous. He was not in himself possessed of any gene-modded accessories such as the enormous tusk growing out of his friend's head. But Alessia had never before seen a human being or any variant thereof festooned with quite so many fusion blades.

"Hey, kid," the woman said. "You fancy being rescued today?"

"Do I!" Alessia said as she crawled out from under the bed. "Are you allies of our House?"

"Better than that, kid," the woman said. "We're pirates."

"Oh, okay. Uhm. If we're going now, can my friends come, too?"

"Oh, for fuck's sake."

"Also, there's a Sturm soldier. Her name is Ji-yong. And she's mean. You want to watch out for her."

The armored shock trooper picked Lucinda up and threw her across the courtyard. She crashed into the wall of the servants' quarters, collapsing it on top of her. The world went dark as dust and falling masonry obscured her suit cams, but proprioceptors told her the enemy fighter had grabbed her right ankle and was pulling her free.

She came back into daylight with a rush and the muted rumble of tons of debris falling free.

The shock trooper, a female to judge by the slope of the glacis plate on her upper torso, wielded some sort of underslung chain saw as a close-quarters weapon. She seemed determined to finish their duel in single combat like some idiot Hab rat from one of the criminal clans desperate to make her bones in front of the plate boss.

Lucinda blew that stupid motherfucker in two with the last of her kinetics.

And then she was out of ammo.

She lay panting, staring at the sky.

Burning comets arced down to the planet's surface. Evidence of some great battle in space that had touched the upper edges of the atmosphere.

Defiant.

Defiant must have won or fought the Sturm to a standstill; otherwise she'd be getting hosed down by orbital fire. She felt stirrings of pride and then shame at her own failure.

She tried to stand, but the legs were damaged beyond use.

A quick scan of the battlespace seemed to read clear. No marines. No shock troopers. Just burning ruins and the bodies of the dead. The forever dead.

Part of her wanted to just lie in the suit and rest, but she was not done. She didn't know if Seph and her crew had found the princess. If they'd survived. If they'd escaped. They'd always been a plan B, but now they were the only hope of success.

Lucinda Hardy took a moment. But just a moment.

She popped the locks on her armor, which stuttered and grated open like rusted gears grinding in wet sand.

Not all of the Sturm were dead. They found a wounded trooper in the servants' kitchen. Falun Kot took his smallest blade to the man, and then all the Sturm were dead.

The last of the gunfire had died away. Seph heard something heavy crashing around outside, but then that racket had died away, too. The silence was eerie.

"Coto," she said, "call Banks and tell him to pick us up in five minutes."

As the giant hybrid pulled out his comm unit, Falun Kot led the way down a darkened staircase into the basement. There was no power down there, but gray light leaked in through dusty windows at ground level.

"I know where they'll be," the princess said confidently, and hurried away before Seph could grab her. "There's a servants' tunnel we can take to the storehouse. Come on."

The basement was given over to a food and wine store. It looked far too practical to be the main wine cellar of a place like this, Seph thought. There would be another hole in the ground somewhere just for show, with old oaken barrels and racks displaying insanely expensive bottles from Earth. This place, with hams and cheeses hanging from hooks, looked like a working storeroom.

"Come on. They're over here."

The girl's voice was nearby, but the cellar was laid out in a sort of cruciform shape, and it took a moment to catch up with her. One of the arms of the cross was crowded with agribots, threshers and diggers, tree loppers, and such. They found her standing in the other arm, impatiently bouncing up and down on the balls of her feet by a thick wooden post that supported the arched roof. Two more children, their eyes huge with fear and relief, the small boy trying to hold back tears, had been chained to the post.

"I can't untie them," the princess said plaintively.

"I can," Falun Kot assured her.

He drew one of his many knives, powered on the blade, and carved through the chain as though it were made of taffy.

The two little girls cheered as if at a magic trick.

The boy stared at Kot in rapt admiration.

His eyes went wide when he took in Jaddi Coto.

"Don't worry," the princess assured them. "He's lovely."

"Yes." Coto smiled. "Yes, I am."

The bullet hit him as he was turning, striking the giant in the skull at the base of his horn. It splintered, and he cried out in a despairing moan as his enormous body slumped to the cellar floor.

Alessia screamed. Kot broke left. Sephina went right. Bottles exploded and barrels ruptured as a bullet storm swept through the cellar. Seph fired back with her Skorpyons, but she quickly ran out of ammunition. Kot popped off a few shots from the handgun he carried as a backup for his knives, but he soon ran dry, too.

Seph crawled deeper into the alcove with the agribots. She could see the three children sheltering behind Coto's body, which was twitching and bleeding out. Kot was trapped under a heavy wine rack that had toppled on top of him. She searched for another mag but came up empty. Tried again. Thought she had one and cursed as the little black storage unit containing Booker's source code came out of her pocket.

"Fuck!"

"Throw down your weapons and stand up with your hands in the air," a man called out.

"It's Kogan D'ur," the princess shouted. "Don't believe him. He lies!"

Another burst of automatic fire drowned her out and shredded a couple of hams. Seph smelled the odd ozone stink of electrically fired caseless ammunition mixed in with smoldering pig meat. She almost threw the storage unit at D'ur in her rage and exasperation, but her arm caught on farm machinery.

A hedge-trimming bot.

She checked the ports and found a standard bus for plugging in external control sources. Quantum-bit gardeners.

Fuck the rich.

She turned on the box.

For Booker the transition was instant. He was discussing personal belief and political commitment with Captain L'trel and the pilot of the *Ariane*. And then he was . . .

A Samsung BV-1/22A Agricultural Grooming Unit.

A hedge trimmer.

Fuck, no.

They'd side loaded him to a fucking hedge trimmer.

That unpleasant discovery was quickly followed by another.

Somebody who didn't like hedge trimmers or possibly didn't like the job done by the last hedge trimmer was shooting at him.

Sephina L'trel was yelling at him.

That big crossbred dumb-ass rhino ape looked like he'd been shot in the head.

And three children were cowering behind his body.

"Just fucking do something," L'trel yelled as bullets slammed into his chassis.

Booker wasn't built for combat. He was built for trimming hedges.

There was a very good chance that one of these bullets was going to pass right through this thin plasteel chassis and destroy the matrix that now held his code.

Booker rose up on his six legs and charged for the source of the gunfire.

The Samsung, he discovered quickly, was a top-of-the-line model, very well maintained and almost fully charged. According to the unit's service logs, its four cutting arms had been oiled and sharpened not two days earlier. If you were going to ride into battle on a fucking hedge trimmer, he supposed, it was nice to be riding the best goddamned hedge trimmer money could buy.

Didn't change the fact you were a fucking hedge trimmer, though.

And you weren't designed for close-quarters battle in . . . a wine cellar?

Yes, he concluded as he leaped and dodged and pounced like a big plasteel spider cat, he was probably going to die in a wine cellar as a gardening bot. His sensors were not optimized for this sort of environment or activity. He had weapons: the four cutting tools. But he lost one of them in a leap that carried him through the line of fire. On the next leap, he pulled up the only file in his deep lacuna he thought might be even remotely useful: the operator scripts from the time he'd been transmitted from Earth to the Javan system as a peacekeeper after the war with Armadale. TDF had loaded him into an arachnoform trench-fighting rig to clean out a lithium mine full of

Javan slave soldiers. That rig had been, sort of, vaguely similar to this thing.

Booker loaded the script as a final leap carried him through the darkened basement and crashing down on the armored shock trooper. They rolled in a clashing tangle of limbs, blades, guns, and curses. Booker did not try to carve through the armor plating. Instead, locking all six legs around the Sturm trooper like a giant mechanized insect programmed with old-school Brazilian jujitsu scripts, he focused his three functional cutting tools on the weak points in the suit: the joints under the arms and at the hip. Smoke and sparks flew from the hip flexors, and for the shortest time he began to suspect he might even pull this off, when the trooper worked an arm free and tore off another cutting tool. Booker tried to reprogram the unit's operating system to channel more power into the buzz saws, but he lost another limb and then the final one, and then the trooper had grabbed two giant hams and started bludgeoning him with them. It seemed ridiculous, but it worked. The hedge trimmer started to come apart under the assault.

Booker lost his grip and found himself flying through the air, scraping the arched brick ceiling of the cellar and crashing into the rest of the agribots.

Unencumbered by armor, unprotected, unarmed, Lucinda followed the industrial hammering noise coming from the basement of the servants' quarters. She ran down the stairs, surprised but not stopped by the sight of an armored shock trooper wrestling . . . she wasn't sure.

Some sort of gardening bot?

As she jumped the last few steps onto the flagstone floor of the cellar, she could see Sephina trying to lead three children out of the death trap while her engineer, the one with all the knives, charged the Sturm with two of his longest blades whirling in a glowing incandescent blur. The trooper raised a weapon she didn't recognize, some sort of kinetic armament, she guessed, and shot him in the head before he could close the gap. The man went down, and the Sturm advanced on Sephina.

Lucinda sprinted forward, picked up the cold fusion blade that landed closest to her, and launched herself at the armored behemoth. The knife sparked off the scarred dull gray plating, and the trooper spun around with feline agility. He raised the same weapon he had just used, but Lucinda was close enough to smash a warding blow, a cross-block with her bare arm, into the armored limb.

She felt her bones shatter, sickening pain. But the slight deflection gave her enough room to perform an entering maneuver she had practiced without scripts many thousands of times. It positioned her shoulder to shoulder with the Sturm trooper, each facing the other as if in the middle of some elaborate old-fashioned dance. With her good hand she drove the cold fusion blade into the armpit, where the cutting tools of the bot had already degraded the carboflex sheathing. The knife, all fifteen inches, passed easily through the flexible sheath and slid into the machined joint and then the man's armpit.

The external speaker units on his suit amplified his scream into a metallic shriek.

She thrust deeper, aiming for the spine.

He suddenly stiffened and fell back, crashing to the floor with a thunderous sound.

His faceplate slid up.

A handsome man gaped at her, his eyes rolling in their sockets, his mouth opening and closing as he struggled to form words.

Sephina appeared beside her, holding a shotgun on the fallen soldier. Lucinda was taken aback to see the giant hybrid, missing his rhino horn, swaying behind her.

"I have a very thick skull," Coto muttered. "Unlike Falun Kot. His skull is everywhere."

Lucinda pushed the muzzle down and away from Kogan D'ur's face.

"We . . ." He coughed up blood. Swallowed and spoke again.

"You. No mutant," he added.

Seph opened her mouth, almost certainly to say something stupid, but Lucinda shushed her.

"I was trueborn, as you would say," Lucinda told him.

"No scripts?" he gurgled. "No code? We . . . took your combat algorithms."

Lucinda leaned down. He was fading quickly.

"I am a citizen of the Commonwealth of Armadale," she said. "I was born free on Coriolis."

She withdrew the blade. It was sizzling, cooking off the blood.

"And I am the combat algorithm, motherfucker."

She drove the blade in deep.

CHAPTER
FORTY-ONE

Flaming wrack and falling ruin burned through the upper atmosphere of Montrachet as the young woman flew upward through it all. Lucinda pressed her face to the gentle curve of the giant picture window on the observation deck of the cruising yacht and beheld the aftermath of a great battle.

"They say the only thing as terrible as a battle lost is a battle won, lassie."

Lucinda jumped a little at the voice and turned around. She had thought she was alone with her wounds in the sumptuously furnished lounge. Almost everyone else was down in the makeshift trauma ward the combat medics had set up in the bar.

"Aye," Admiral McLennan went on in a tired voice, "but that's the sort of thing you'd expect to hear from a doaty fucking walloper who'd never been within a bee's dick of a battle, let alone lost one of the wretched fucking things. I can assure you, Commander Hardy, they are a fucking hell of a lot easier to live with when you're nae the one facedown in the mud trying tae jam all your fucking giblets back intae your tummy after they've been hacked out for ye."

McLennan's hologram was floating a couple of feet over the polished dark wood deck of the yacht. He sat in her command chair back on *Defiant* and idly swirled a tumbler of dark brown liquor she assumed to be whiskey. His holo seemed strangely at home in the luxurious setting of Sephina's lavish new yacht. The laird of earth and heaven, enjoying all that he had wrought.

"You've been busy, Admiral," she said. Behind her, on the other side of the armor-glass casement, the blue skies of Montrachet gradually turned black and the stars of the local volume burned brighter. Billions of pieces of debris burned up as the remains of the Sturm's invasion fleet, or this part of it anyway, scorched down through the mesosphere. Here and there, secondary explosions flared every few seconds—*Defiant* servicing the larger pieces of debris with cannon and beam fire lest some mile-long chunk of falling battle cruiser obliterate a town or city down on the planet's surface.

"I was a very long time chugging my willie to no good end on the Sturm's dusty fucking toilet bowl of a cemetery world, lass. And I will admit to feeling the sap rise now that I have this rare crop of pocket Nazi fuckbumpers to have at again."

Lucinda stood at parade ground rest as he spoke and the ice cubes in his whiskey clinked against the tumbler. She saw a figure enter the observation deck behind McLennan's avatar.

Captain Hayes.

Half of his face was bandaged, and one arm hung

in a medical effector field, like hers. His expression was unreadable.

She was surprised by the strength of feeling she experienced upon seeing him alive, but she shouldn't have been. She'd had the same reaction when they'd recovered the survivors of the other Marine Corps drop teams after two of the shuttles were knocked out by ground fire. And she had felt as a personal loss the death of Sephina's shipmate Falun Kot and of every marine she had ordered to the surface who had not returned.

She had never felt so desolate, not even that first night after the Combine reclaimers took her father.

"Captain Hayes," she said, and thousands of miles away McLennan swiveled in his chair—*her* chair—to take in the new arrival.

"Och, it is good to find you in the land of the living, Captain," McLennan said. His voice and mood were sober in spite of the overlarge drink he held, at which he sipped continually.

"Be better if more of my guys were here with me," Hayes replied, but he was subdued rather than bitter. Walking around the hologram and a small nest of exquisitely sculpted objects that might have been chairs or some piece of art that cost more than all of their salaries combined, Hayes formally presented himself to Lucinda, coming to attention and ripping out a salute with his good arm.

"Commander Hardy," he said tightly. "All objectives were achieved. The mission was accomplished."

He handed her a piece of paper. Actual paper, folded in two.

"The butcher's bill," he said simply.

She took it with a shaking hand; it felt as light as a butterfly wing and as heavy as fate and mountains.

Lucinda awkwardly opened the note. She took her time to read every name.

There were thirty-six of them.

The last few names she had trouble seeing because her vision blurred with tears. She wiped her eyes with the back of her good hand. Still dressed in the nanoweave bodysuit she'd worn under her powered armor, Lucinda had not yet had a chance to clean herself up. She reeked of sour sweat. Her hands were filthy with blood and grime, which mixed with her tears to paint her face with dark and mournful streaks. Neither man spoke while they waited for her to regain her composure.

"If you w . . ." she started, but faltered when her throat closed around the words.

Breathing slowly and forcing herself to quiet the phantoms swirling in her head, Lucinda tried again.

"If you would be so kind, Captain Hayes, as to provide me with their service records, I will enter them into *Defiant*'s log with commendations."

"Admiral McLennan has already done so for the squad we lost at Cape Caen, ma'am. But thank you. I will inform the company."

McLennan spoke up.

"And inform them, too, Captain, that on my own authority as the senior commander of the Terran Defense Force in the local volume, I have awarded your company a Meritorious Unit Citation for gallantry in battle."

Hayes lifted his chin toward the hologram, then dropped it again as he nodded.

God, Lucinda thought, *is this all there is?*

But no. There was more.

Seph appeared at that moment, leading the Montanblanc heir by the hand. Two other children hung back at the entrance to the room, a girl perhaps a little older than Princess Alessia and a boy obviously a year or so younger. They openly stared at Lucinda, the wounded marine captain, the floating hologram, and, most intently, with the widest eyes, the vast tapestry of burning ships and cold, cruel stars in the obsidian blackness of space.

The Armadalens both came to attention and saluted Princess Alessia Szu Suri sur Montanblanc ul Haq. They were senior representatives of the Commonwealth, and she the sole surviving heir to her realm, the oldest and closest ally of Armadale.

The girl surprised Lucinda, bowing low in return.

She turned and repeated the gesture to both Hayes and McLennan before running forward and throwing her arms around Lucinda's waist with force enough to knock her back onto her heels.

"Thank you, thank you," she said over and over again, her voice somewhat muffled as she buried her face into the underarmor bodysuit, seemingly unfazed by the sweat and blood.

"Uh, that's all right," Lucinda said, looking to Seph.

Her oldest friend, her only friend, wore a crooked grin, the same cavalier lopsided expression Lucinda recalled so well now after so long. How had she forgotten that look?

"The kid's been raised right, Cinders. She really

knows how to say thanks. I'm a fucking baroness now."

"Baroness Sephina!" Alessia scolded, turning around to glower unconvincingly.

"Sorry! Sorry, kid. I'm new to this. You're gonna have to cut me some slack with the f-bombs and shit."

Lucinda could see from the grin on Sephina's face that she wasn't joking, not about her ennoblement. Seph's eyes twinkled with their old mischievous light in a way they had not since . . .

Since Ariane died, Lucinda supposed. Ariane, and her friend Falun Kot, and thirty-six of Hayes's marines, and all of Alessia's family, and God only knew how many innocent souls across the Greater Volume.

And, she supposed, a half-million or more from the Human Republic to judge by the debris field out there in hard vacuum.

"Well, this is very cozy," McLennan's hologram announced, "but if ye wouldnae mind hurrying your arses back to *Defiant*, I'm of a mind to be gone from this system about five minutes ago. We gave these munters a rare feckin' jab in the clacker, but we dinnae get them all, not even in the local volume, and having fired off pretty much every feckin' whizbang in your cupboard, Commander Hardy, it might be prudent to leg it, I do reckon."

"Might be," she agreed, gently easing Princess Alessia away.

"Captain Hayes . . . Adam," she said, "we'll need resupply."

"And more," Hayes added. "We'll need fighters."

Lucinda nodded, looking to Seph.

"Did you get Booker out of that mech?"

"Right here."

Seph held up the black box again.

"Is he awake?"

"And grumpy."

Booker's voice emerged from the box. "You put me in a hedge trimmer," he protested.

"I'm sorry, Booker," Lucinda cut in over the exchange. "About the hedge trimmer."

"He knows that was me," Seph confessed.

"Captain Hardy," Booker said. "If you're doing a resup run, I'll take a Combat Mech now. I could be more help that way."

"Sure," Lucinda said. "And thanks, dirtside, I mean. We couldn't have done it without you. I'm sorry you got put into a gardening bot. That was very inconsiderate."

"Hey!" Seph protested. "I'm standing right here, and I'm a baroness now."

"She is," Alessia confirmed, drawing everyone's attention back to her. "She is Baroness Sephina L'trel of Montrachet."

"She gave me the planet!" Seph beamed.

"And a quest," Alessia reminded her.

"Oh, yeah, that, too."

Lucinda did not inquire further. She cast her eyes over to a discrete display on the other side of the observation deck. A countdown to rendezvous with *Defiant*. They were only a few minutes out. The little runabout yacht could really move.

"You always fall on your feet, don't you?" she said to her friend.

"Saves wear and tear on my ass." Seph shrugged.

"How are your other guys: the pilot and the big guy with the horn?"

"Banks is flying, which is why we're making such good time. We'll drop you guys and get back to the mother ship. I'm a baroness, and we have a mother ship now."

"The *Ariane*?"

Seph's good mood deflated a little, but she nodded.

"The *Ariane*, yes. And my quest," she added, smiling at Princess Alessia and rubbing the top of Her Royal Highness's head. Lucinda almost cried out in protest. Alessia wasn't her monarch, just the head of an allied House, but everybody knew you did not lay hands on royalty.

Princess Alessia didn't seem to care. She took Seph's hand and squeezed it.

"Thank you," she said quietly.

The Montanblanc princess moved over to the window and placed the tips of her fingers against the monobonded diamond glass. It shimmered ever so slightly, an artifact of the field effect. The shimmer abated, and the vacuum seemed to lie open before her.

"I need to talk to people," Alessia said. "After, you know, what Kogan D'ur made me say."

"Aye, you do," McLennan growled.

Lucinda frowned at him. "People will understand you were under duress," she said.

"And you pulled off that bitchin' prank, blinking in secret code," Seph added. "You ever want to give up being a princess, you got a gig with me, A-One. You're awesome."

Alessia turned away from the cold conflagration burning up the heavens.

"But if I did that, Baroness L'trel, there would be nobody to give you quests and rewards, would there?"

Seph played at thinking it over and finally winked at her. "Good point. You do you, kid."

"I will," Alessia replied. She turned back to the view. "The Sturm told me that I was weak, that we were weak, and we would never be able to stand against them. They told me I would save many innocent lives by giving in. That we would never be strong enough to prevail."

A disembodied voice crackled out of the small black box in Sephina's hand. Booker.

"The Sturm talk a lot of shit."

"They certainly do," Alessia agreed. "But so does anyone who says that we cannot stand against them now and that we must first gather our strength."

She paused and looked directly at McLennan before going on.

"When would we be strong enough?" she asked. "When their fleets arrive above Earth? Do we ensure our own deliverance until then by lying at their feet, clutching at hope?"

"No," he said quietly. "We do not."

"No," Alessia agreed. "We do not. Commander Hardy," she said, her voice taking on an official tone. "All the means and the power of House Montanblanc I commit to your authority for the duration of hostilities."

She turned toward the hologram.

"Admiral McLennan, under the heads of power invested in me by right of my succession to the Congress of Earth, I name you commander in chief of the Terran Defense Force and authorize you to take all necessary measures to secure the Greater Volume from its enemies."

She held out her hand to Seph, who realized after a moment that she wanted the black box containing Booker's source code.

"Oh, right, sure," Seph said, passing it over.

Alessia held the tiny unit up to her face.

"Booker," she said. "Under the same congressional heads of power I pardon you and all your people for any and all actions you have taken to secure those liberties which are the inalienable right of all humanity, and I further confirm the extension of those rights and recognitions you have so long sought in the face of ignorance and hatefulness."

Lucinda heard something come from the external storage unit's audio system, but it was impossible to say precisely what.

The *Defiant* loomed in the distance, a point of darkness within a brilliant nova of sweeping, stabbing beams of coherent energy as she continued to carve up the remains of the 101st Attack Fleet.

"We are not weak if we make proper use of those means which providence has placed within our power," Alessia said to all of them. "And we shall now bring that power to bear with urgency and purpose."

Lucinda wondered if she was quoting from some history lesson she had been forced to learn by rote.

Not that it mattered in the end. As the stealth destroyer ceased fire to allow them to approach and dock, Commander Lucinda Hardy of the Royal Armadalen Navy was content that she was home again, where she belonged.

EPILOGUE

The prisoners knew something was wrong when they woke a few minutes later than normal. There had been a disturbance in the camp the previous evening: travelers arriving unexpectedly.

As if there was any other way for a traveler to arrive at Defaulter Camp 17.

Jonathyn was exhausted and would have slept through that late-night excitement were it not for Reinsaari. The diminutive Vikingar shook him awake in his cot, hissing that something was afoot.

Within moments, dozens of men and women, all of them thin, none of them recently washed, all draped in the dusty threadbare rags of defaulter work gangs, had crowded around the three small barracks windows.

It was disruptive and unusual for new prisoners to arrive in the dark, and Privi Madhav, the commandant of Camp 17, had a punishing intolerance for anything out of the ordinary. At 17 you worked every hour the blistering sun hammered down, you ate what you could of the foul soylent sludge in the mess, and you slept—if your injuries and illness and general misery allowed you any rest. Day in, day out. From now until the ending of your life, whatever and ever amen.

You did not enjoy an impromptu pajama party after midnight just because company called.

Jonathyn was late rolling out of his rack. He was suffering woefully from the inflamed disk in his neck and a poorly mended broken arm. It still throbbed six months after he'd caught it in the workings of a gravel smasher. He did not compete with any vigor for a spot at the windows, returning to his bed and pulling the lice-ridden blanket over his head, trying to snatch just a little more sleep.

If you did not dream, sleep was a merciful release from Batavia, from the Combine. From the waking hell of Camp 17.

"They are not prisoners. Not like us," Reinsaari hissed a few minutes later.

Jonathyn was still awake. Unfortunately, fatigue had not carried him back into sweet oblivion.

"They are rich, Jonathyn. Some of them are even of the Fraction. You can tell from their clothes and the equipment they carry. The guards are very deferential."

"That's great," Jonathyn mumbled. "Maybe they can buy out our liens and magic us away from here."

Somebody had purchased his personal lien from the Combine a few weeks earlier. But nothing had changed. He had a new owner somewhere, but they seemed more than happy for him to keep scratching away at the hard rock of the Goroth Mountains for the occasional fleck of siracunium.

Reinsaari tried to engage him in all manner of speculation about the meaning of the unexpected arrivals, but Jonathyn was having none of it, and when the Vikingar gave up to try his luck elsewhere, Jonathyn actually managed to fall asleep again.

Exhaustion and ennui helped.

In the morning, when he awoke, the guards were gone.

He was the first of the defaulters in their block to rise. The others had stupidly stayed up for hours. He had woken up once and heard them still muttering about the unusual events. As Jonathyn pulled on his shoes—one heel was flapping freely now—he saw a few of the others beginning to stir.

He forced himself to hurry.

If he got to the mess hall before anybody else, he could eat his fill. He wouldn't, of course. He would stash some scraps for later. And for Reinsaari and Maya and Nadine. They had formed something of a friendship group within the block since Nadine had arrived two months earlier.

He hurried out of the long hut, squinting into the fierce morning glare, so intent on hurrying ahead of everyone else that he did not notice that the guards were all gone.

The gates were open.

Screen doors banged in the light breeze.

Jonathyn stopped dead.

He was deeply, genuinely frightened.

Change was always frightening at Camp 17, and this was a momentous change.

Jonathyn was still standing there, unable to move,

when Nadine and Maya joined him, grabbing him by his good arm.

"Jonathyn, what's going on?" Maya asked. She had been in 17 longer than Nadine. She was much more freaked-out.

"I don't know," he said. "They're all gone."

"What's that noise?" Nadine asked.

At first Jonathyn didn't know what she meant. A punch to the head by one of the guards had burst his eardrum two weeks earlier. But gradually the noise resolved itself. A sort of thumping that was both dull and sharp at the same time.

"I think . . . I think it's an aircraft," he said.

A second later Nadine squealed with excitement and pointed to a dot in the sky. It was growing. Coming toward them.

More defaulters emerged from the barracks. They all pointed at the strange-looking craft.

They all marveled at the missing guards.

"And the visitors," somebody said. "They're gone, too."

But nobody cared about that.

This was much more interesting.

The aircraft flew closer.

A minute later it landed outside the camp fence. Soldiers, they certainly looked like soldiers, climbed out of the aircraft and walked in through the wide-open gates. They marched right up to the growing crowd of prisoners.

There were five of them, but one was very obviously in charge. A woman who was not carrying a personal weapon, unlike the others. She was white and blond. She looked very fit and very strong. Jonathyn felt Nadine grip his arm a little tighter.

The woman smiled.

"Good day to you all. I am Major Pippa Newell. This facility has been liberated by a Force Recon unit of the armed forces of the Human Republic. It is now under the protection and law of the Republic. We come as friends of the oppressed and saviors of the race. If you are truly human, we are your kin. Join us."

She said some other words, but Jonathyn Hardy could not hear them.

He was crying and his fellow prisoners were cheering, and he fell to his knees and wept because he was free.

ACKNOWLEDGMENTS

You don't build a space empire on your own. My thanks and Combine credit chips to massive Editorial Intellect Sarah Peed, and my Armored Combat Agent Russ Galen. I salute my company of Armadalen Beta Readers, and most especially my XO, Captain Lambright. My apologies if I have forgotten anyone. I spilled whiskey on my substrate.

EXPLORE THE WORLDS OF DEL REY BOOKS

Read excerpts from hot new titles.

Stay up-to-date on your favorite authors.

Find out about exclusive giveaways and sweepstakes.

Connect with us online!

Follow us on social media
 Facebook.com/DelReyBooks
 @DelReyBooks

Visit us at UnboundWorlds.com
 Facebook.com/UnboundWorlds
 @unboundworlds

DEL REY

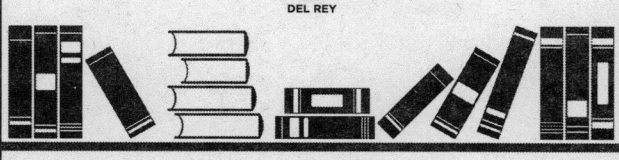